From Randy Johnson to Dallas Braden

No-hitters Beyond the Box Score
Volume II

Written by
Kevin Hurd

Edited by
Bruce Hurd

From Randy Johnson to Dallas Braden
No-hitters Beyond the Box Score
Volume II

Copyright © 2024 Kevin Hurd

All rights reserved. No part of this publication may be reproduced, distributed, or transmitted in any form or by any means, including photocopying, recording, or other electronic or mechanical methods, without the prior written permission of the publisher, except in the case of brief quotations embodied in critical reviews and certain other noncommercial uses permitted by copyright law. For permission requests, write to the author at the address below.

ISBN: 979-8-9902594-3-0 (E-book)
ISBN: 979-8-9902594-4-7 (Paperback)
ISBN: 979-8-9902594-5-4 (Hardcover)

Library of Congress Control Number: 2024918733

Cover design by Cherie Fox at www.cheriefox.com

Printed in the United States of America

Kevin Hurd
P.O.Box 1272
Aledo, TX 76008

For more information on this book, the author, and book-related programs and events, please contact me at kevinhurd@sbcglobal.net

To my parents, Ann and Walt Hurd,
who were always there when I needed them

And to my lovely wife Doris, and my two beautiful daughters
Christine and Catherine, who have supported me throughout my life

Table of Contents

Acknowledgements ix
Introduction xi
Chapter 13: Bo Belinsky: A Star is Born in Hollywood 1
    Table 13-1. Fastest Expansion Teams to a Winning Season 5
    Table 13-2. Angels Highest Game Scores 7
    Table 13-3. 1961 Little Rock Travelers Career MLB Pitching Statistics ... 12
    Table 13-4. Retired No-hit Pitchers with Lowest JAWS Scores 14
    Buck Rodgers Interview 17
Chapter 14: Tom Seaver: The Long Wait is Over 21
    Table 14-1. No-hit pitchers who lost three or more no-hitters in the ninth . 22
    Table 14-2. Mets Highest Game Scores 24
    Table 14-3. Highest JAWS differential between no-hit pitcher and catcher 28
    Don Werner Interview 31
Chapter 15: Mike Warren: David vs. Goliath 35
    Table 15-1. Largest Negative Team Record Disparity in a No-Hitter 39
    Table 15-2. Largest Positive Team Record Disparity in a No-Hitter 43
    Table 15-3. Best teams to be no-hit 45
    Table 15-4. Athletics Highest Game Scores 46
    Table 15-5. Athletics Highest Game Scores of 10 innings or less 50
    Table 15-6. Lowest Number of Career Starts by a No-Hit Pitcher 55
    Mike Heath Interview 57
Chapter 16: Joe Cowley: Effectively Wild 61
    Table 16-1. White Sox Highest Game Scores 66
    Table 16-2. White Sox Highest Game Scores of ten innings or less ... 68
    Table 16-3. No-hit Pitcher Draft Round and JAWS Level Breakdown 74
    Table 16-4. Drafted No-hit Pitcher Career Success Analysis 75
    Ron Karkovice Interview 77

Chapter 17: Eric Milton: Facing the "B" Team 82
    Table 17-1. September No-hitters with four or more substitutes. 84
    Table 17-2. Senators and Twins Highest Game Scores 88
    Table 17-3. Senators and Twins Highest Game Scores of
        10 Innings or Less 92
    Table 17-4. Best Pitchers Born in Venezuela 96
    Terry Steinbach Interview 99
Chapter 18: Jonathan Sanchez: Journeymen Battery No-Hitter 103
    Table 18-1. Lowest Pitcher-Catcher Career JAWS Totals 107
    Table 18-2. Relief Pitchers who Threw No-hitters 109
    Table 18-3. No-hit pitchers with lowest complete game percentage 112
    Table 18-4. Best Pitchers Born in Puerto Rico 115
    Eli Whiteside Interview 119
Chapter 19: Edwin Jackson: One Hell of a Long Night 123
    Table 19-1. Highest Pitch Count in a Nine-Inning No-hitter 127
    Table 19-2. Most Walks Allowed in a No-hitter 128
    Table 19-3. Lowest Game Score of any No-hitters 130
    Table 19-4. No-hit Pitchers who Played for the Most Teams 133
    Table 19-5. Diamondbacks Highest Game Scores. 138
    Miguel Montero Interview 142
Chapter 20: Henderson Alvarez III: Walk-off No-hitter. 146
    Table 20-1. Walk-off No-hit Games 149
    Table 20-2. Highest WPA for Wild Pitch Walk-off Wins. 152
    Table 20-3. No-hitters on Last Day of the Season. 154
    Table 20-4. Marlins Highest Game Scores 155
    Koyie Hill Interview. 159
Chapter 21: Gaylord Perry: Clash of the Titans. 163
    Table 21-1. No-hitters Featuring Opposing Hall of Fame Starters 165
    Table 21-2. Highest Starting Pitchers JAWS in a No-hit Game. 166
    Table 21-3. Best Pitchers of the 1970s 168
    Table 21-4. Career Hit By Pitch Leaders 170
    Table 21-5. Hit By Pitch Highest Rate 172
    Table 21-6. Shortest Time Between Two No-hit Games 173
    Table 21-7. No-hit Pitchers Who Excelled After Turning 30. 176

Chapter 22: Bob Gibson: Hall of Fame Combination 180
    Table 22-1. Pitcher-catcher Highest Combined JAWS 183
    Table 22-2. Cardinals Highest Game Scores of 10 innings or Less 185
    Table 22-3. Cardinals Highest Game Scores 189
    Table 22-4. Pitchers who won and lost no-hitters 191
    Table 22-5. Best Starting Pitchers of the 1960s 193
Chapter 23: Joe Musgrove: The Padres Have a No-Hitter 196
    Table 23-1. Time from Expansion Team Start to First No-Hitter 198
    Table 23-2. Franchises With Only One Single-pitcher No-hitter 201
    Table 23-3. Padres Highest Game Scores 202
    Table 23-4. Interleague No-hitters 206
Chapter 24: The Remarkable 2022 and 2023 Seasons 210
    Table 24-1. No-hitters Thrown in 2022-2023 210
    Table 24-2. Postseason No-hitters 213
    Table 24-3. Multi-pitcher No-hitters 214
    Table 24-4. Tigers Highest Game Scores 218
    Table 24-5. Tigers Highest Game Scores of 10 innings or less 220
    Table 24-6. Phillies Highest Game Scores 224
    Table 24-7. Phillies Highest Game Scores of 10 innings or less 226
    Table 24-8. Longest Time Between No-hitters 228
    Table 24-9. Recent No-Hitter Attempts Broken Up with
        Two Outs in Ninth Inning 231
    Table 24-10. Catchers Who Have Caught the Most No-Hitters 232
Chapter 25: Best Games and Best Pitchers 235
    Table 25-1. Highest Braves Game Scores 235
    Table 25-2. Highest Braves Game Scores of 10 innings or less 239
    Table 25-3. Highest Browns and Orioles Game Scores 243
    Table 25-4. Highest Browns and Orioles Game Scores of
        10 innings or less 246
    Table 25-5. Highest Cubs Game Scores 251
    Table 25-6. Highest Cubs Game Scores of 10 innings or less 254
    Table 25-7. Highest Indians Game Scores 258
    Table 25-8. Highest Indians Game Scores of 10 innings or less 262
    Table 25-9. Highest Rays Game Scores 267
    Table 25-10. Highest Red Sox Game Scores 270

Table 25-11. Highest Red Sox Game Scores of 10 innings or less 273
Table 25-12. Highest Rockies Game Scores 277
Table 25-13. Highest Royals Game Scores 280
Table 25-14. Best Pitchers of the 1900s (1900-1909) 284
Table 25-15. Best Pitchers of the 1910s 286
Table 25-16. Best Pitchers of the 1920s 288
Table 25-17. Best Pitchers of the 1930s 289
Table 25-18. Best Pitchers of the 1940s 291

Conclusion 295
Appendix II: Career Ranking of All No-hit Catchers. 299
About the Author 313

Acknowledgements

This two-volume set of books is the result of an entire team of dedicated people who put in countless hours helping me compile information, research, and write this book. Specifically, the three who helped me the most were:

My brother (fellow Air Force aviator and coach for first-time authors) Bruce Hurd, who provided detailed content editing and publishing expertise so my book would be informative, insightful, and entertaining.

My friend and teammate on the KKUP Klones recreational league softball team Kevin McCaffrey, who conducted in-depth interviews of Hall of Famer Randy Johnson, multi-season All-Star Dave Stieb, rookie sensation Bud Smith, and renowned Milwaukee Brewers broadcaster – and no-hit catcher – Bill Schroeder.

My friend from grade school and junior high school Rob Adams, who inspired me to write this book and conducted an in-depth interview of perfect-game pitcher and highly talented Oakland A's broadcaster Dallas Braden. Rob came up with the idea for me to write about no-hit games. Without his initial push, this book wouldn't have happened.

With eternal gratitude to all the pitchers and catchers who graciously provided their time and permission to be interviewed for this book. I cannot thank you enough (listed in order of appearance): Jim Maloney, Johnny Edwards, Juan Nieves, Bill Schroeder, Dave Stieb, Pat Borders, Randy Johnson, Robby Hammock, Ed Halicki, Andy Hawkins, Bud Smith, Dallas Braden, Buck Rodgers, Don Werner, Mike Heath, Ron Karkovice, Terry Steinbach, Eli Whiteside, Miguel Montero, and Koyie Hill.

I would also like to extend my sincere gratitude to numerous organizations and websites that provided detailed and authoritative information on these players, teams, and games referenced and analyzed in this book: baseball-reference.com, stathead.com, the Society for Advanced Baseball Research (SABR), nonohitters.com, and the Baseball Almanac. This book would not have been possible without your generous contributions.

INTRODUCTION

I am proud to present Volume II of *From Randy Johnson to Dallas Braden,* a celebration of baseball's ultimate pitching achievement: the no-hitter. As you will discover, Volume II is a continuation of the extensive work done in Volume I, with all new material and even more interviews and analysis. Welcome back to more fun!

Volume II has many of the same features included in Volume I, such as rankings of the best pitched games in every team's history, the best pitchers of each decade, and – in this volume – the best pitchers born in Venezuela and Puerto Rico. Volume II features eight fascinating interviews with eight unsung heroes of no-hit games: the catchers.

While Volume I addressed the question of which game was the best-pitched no-hitter of all-time, this volume looks at a different question: what was the most unlikely no-hitter ever thrown?

Was it 22-year-old rookie Mike Warren's September 1983 no-hitter against the 99-win Chicago White Sox, champions of the American League West Division by 20 games? Warren had been unceremoniously sent down earlier in the season after a disastrous start to his major-league career and was out of the majors within two years with a career WAR of negative 0.9 and an ERA north of 5.00.

Was it the two no-hit games thrown by St. Louis Browns pitchers Ernie Koob and Bob Groom on consecutive days against one of baseball's best teams ever: the 1917 Chicago White Sox – featuring Shoeless Joe Jackson, Eddie Collins, and Buck Weaver – who finished that season with 100 wins and beat the New York Giants in the World Series?

Was it Bullet Joe Bush's 1916 no-hitter for the Philadelphia Athletics against Hall of Famer Tris Speaker and the Cleveland Indians? While Bush was an accomplished pitcher with 196 wins over a 17-year career, his 36-117 Athletics had the worst record of any team in the Twentieth Century. Bush led all of baseball with 24 losses that season.

Was it Don Black's no-hitter for the Cleveland Indians against Connie Mack's Philadelphia Athletics in 1947? With a career winning percentage of .382, Black had a JAWS of negative 1.9 – the lowest of any pitcher who ever threw a no-hitter.

Was it career reliever Jose Jimenez's 1999 no-hitter against Hall of Famer Randy Johnson and the 100-win Arizona Diamondbacks? Jimenez was in the starting rotation only in 1999, and even then, he had a dismal 5-14 record with a 5.85 ERA. Traded to Colorado prior to the 2000 season, Jimenez had much greater success as a closer with the Rockies over the following five years, but he never started another game.

There are many other games that stand out as contenders for the "unlikeliest no-hitter" award, but the ones I listed above seem to me to have the strongest cases. Between the two volumes, I'll be touching on all of them, and I'll provide my final thoughts on the subject in this book's conclusion.

Other topics I'll be discussing are the no-hitters from the 2022 and 2023 seasons. As I began this study, I decided I needed to have a cutoff date for the data I would be analyzing, as I wanted all the chapters to be consistent. Because I decided that we would only analyze no-hitters and associated statistics from the beginning of the modern era in 1900 through the 2021 season, quite a bit has happened in the two years since the end of 2021. During 2022-2023, eight no-hitters were recorded, including four multi-pitcher no-hitters and one in the postseason. Chapter 24 near the end of this volume revolves around telling the stories of those no-hitters.

This volume continues in the same vein as Volume I, as it tells in-depth stories and analysis of 11 different no-hitters. It also has a wrap-up chapter at the end that focuses on the top Game Scores of the teams who were not included in previous chapters, along with a compilation of the best pitchers from each decade from 1900-1949.

While Volume II covers material different from Volume I, it is meant to be a continuation of the work I began in Volume I. This volume, and each chapter within the volume, is a stand-alone story that can be enjoyed without reference to what has been written in Volume I or anything included in previous chapters.

So, dig in wherever you want. I hope you enjoy reading Volume II as much as I enjoyed putting it together.

Chapter 13

Bo Belinsky:
A Star is Born in Hollywood

May 5, 1962
Rookie Bo Belinsky bursts into the headlines with a no-hitter
for the surprising Los Angeles Angels

"This crowd about to explode. Ball one, strike one the count. Can he do it? ... There's two men away ... Belinsky now looks out toward center field ... turns, walks back on the hill ... and the 1-1 pitch ... is swung on, it's popped up into shallow left field ... into foul territory goes Torres ... it's going to be a no-hitter ... IT'S A NO-HITTER FOR BELINSKY! Belinsky a no-hitter! How about that one? Belinsky, in his fourth Major League start, has startled 15,000 fans here tonight. His teammates mob him."

Angels broadcaster Buddy Blattner describing the last out in Bo Belinsky's no-hitter (as described by Chuck Richter, "Top-50 Greatest Moments in Angels Baseball," *The Sports Daily*, March 9, 2017).

"I started thinking about (the no-hitter) in the sixth inning but I didn't get cautious, in fact, I started throwing harder. I wanted to get to the ninth inning as fast as I could because I knew that's what the fans wanted...."

Bo Belinsky (as told to Ross Newhan, *Independent-Press Telegram (Long Beach, CA)*, May 6, 1962).

"He could challenge anybody with that fastball. He got the screwball over early, but the fastball set up everything. When Bo was on, he had that electric kind of stuff."

Angels catcher Buck Rodgers (Linda Dougherty, "Trenton's Belinsky Dead At 64: 'Bo' knew both starlets and baseball glory," *The Trentonian*, November 25, 2001)

"He could be the best pitcher on our club. His improvement just between his first and second starts for us was amazing. There is no telling how far he can go. It's up to him."

Angels pitching coach Marv Grissom (as told to sportswriter Braven Dyer following Belinsky's no-hitter, "Belinsky, Ex-Pool Shark, Pockets Wins for Angels," *The Sporting News*, May 9, 1962).

"Bo had a great, live fastball that night. Having said that, I wasn't confident he would get a no-hitter until the last Oriole got out in the ninth inning."

Angels' catcher Buck Rodgers (Interview with the author, May 24, 2021).

"My only regret is that I can't sit in the stands and watch myself pitch."

Bo Belinsky (as told to sportswriter Pat Jordan, "Once He Was an Angel," *Sports Illustrated*, March 28, 1972).

O f all the no-hit pitchers in this book, none got more mileage out of his accomplishment than 25-year-old Bo Belinsky. By his own admission, "I got more ink for doing less than any pitcher who ever lived." Countless articles have been written about Bo Belinsky. There have even been books dedicated to his story. The 1973 book, *Bo: Pitching and Wooing* by prolific sportswriter Maury Allen is the most prominent example, however, Bo Belinsky's story intrigues writers even to this day. For example, in 2021, the latest Bo Belinsky book *From the Hill to The Hall: The Legacy of Bo Belinsky A Baseball Playboy* by Shelby Luse was published.

All these books and articles have several things in common when describing Bo Belinsky:

1) Bo was a very talented pitcher who got off to a blazing start in the major leagues.
2) Bo was a carousing, undisciplined, womanizing playboy who stayed out all night and didn't play by the rules.
3) And Bo is shown as Exhibit A of what happens if a player, or anyone else living in a world of fame and glamor, lets his desire for the spotlight and the pleasures it brings run his life.

The story of Bo Belinsky is always presented as a cautionary, made-for-Hollywood tale full of beautiful starlets, wild parties, and the ultimate downfall the unbridled pursuit of those things brought him. Describing the entirety of Bo Belinsky's journey through life and his playing career is beyond the very short summary just presented and is far beyond the scope of this book.

Like the other chapters in this book, the focus here will be on the events in the game, along with the important takeaways from this no-hitter for the players and teams who were involved. I'll also show how Bo Belinsky was an accomplished pitcher, even by major league standards. Along with that, I'll describe how the Angels were one of the most accomplished expansion teams ever, achieving a winning record and putting together a highly competitive team in only their second year of existence. Bo Belinsky was a big part of the team's success in 1962.

The no-hit game itself was exciting, and Bo Belinsky pitched masterfully. The Baltimore Orioles fielded a very good lineup that night, with Hall of Fame third baseman Brooks Robinson, and All-Stars Jim Gentile at first, Jackie Brandt in center, and catcher Gus Triandos in the heart of the order. Those four dangerous hitters, combined, went 0-for-11 against Belinsky, although they did draw four walks. Gentile also reached base when he was hit by a pitch to lead off the second inning, and Triandos got to first on an error by Los Angeles third baseman Felix Torres in the fourth. Those six baserunners represented the entirety of the Baltimore offense that evening. Nobody else reached base. Overall, Belinsky struck out nine Orioles. He also induced nine groundouts, seven flyouts, one lineout, and one popout that ended the game.

The Angels backed up Belinsky with two early runs. In the first inning, Los Angeles second baseman Billy Moran scored on a Steve Barber wild pitch to cleanup hitter Steve Bilko (more on him later). Moran had gotten to third on a bloop double from slugger Leon "Daddy Wags" Wagner. In the second inning, the Angels struck again when Earl Averill scored from third on a fielder's choice when second baseman Johnny Temple threw to third to get Wagner, rather than throwing home. That would be all the scoring for the Angels, as they tallied a total of six hits and one walk en route to a 2-0 win.

In the midst of Belinsky throwing the first-ever no-hitter at Dodger Stadium, there were some tense moments for the home team. In the top of the fourth, after Brooks Robinson struck out to lead off, Belinsky loaded the bases on walks to Gentile and Brandt, and the error by Torres on a Gus Triandos groundball. With the 2-0 lead on the line, Belinsky proceeded to strike out Baltimore's Dave Nicholson for the second out. The next batter, light-hitting shortstop Ron Hansen, hit a deep fly to center field, which was snagged by speedy Albie Pearson to end the inning.

Perhaps the closest the Orioles were to breaking up Belinsky's no-hitter came in the sixth inning. By that point, people were starting to think a no-no might be a possibility. After Jim Gentile grounded out to Steve Bilko at first, #5 hitter Jackie Brandt came to the plate. Brandt got ahold of one and sent it sailing into the night. As it arced towards the bleachers, Albie Pearson ran over and caught the fly on the warning track in front of the center field wall. That made it two outs in the sixth and there never was another serious threat for the Orioles to score a run or even get a hit. The next batter after Brandt flew out in the sixth was Gus Triandos, who walked. After Triandos, no other Oriole even reached base, as Belinsky struck out three as he retired the next 10 batters in a row.

Los Angeles catcher Buck Rodgers summed up Belinsky's performance in a 2001 interview when he said "(Bo) could challenge anybody with that fastball. He got the screwball over early, but the fastball set up everything. Even on the last out, it was a 3-1 fastball to Dave Nicholson right down Broadway. He fouled out to third. When Bo was on, he had that electric kind of stuff."

The Angels themselves were having their own electric season, and Bo was right in the middle of it. A second-year expansion team with low expectations before the season started, Los Angeles vaulted themselves into contention for the American League pennant right from the start. Finishing third out of 10 teams, the Angels established themselves as a league powerhouse, even placing ahead of established contenders like the Chicago White Sox and Detroit Tigers. By comparison, the other American League expansion team, the Washington Senators, finished dead last with a record of 60-101.

Taking this a step further, the Angels can arguably be called one of the most successful expansion teams ever, at least in the early years of their existence. The chart below shows the top five quickest starts from among all 14 expansion teams from both leagues. Note the Angels and the Diamondbacks both achieved a winning season during the second year of their existence. Arguably, Arizona's achievement is more impressive due to their winning 100 games that year, as they eventually became World Series champions in their fourth season. The Florida Marlins aren't far behind, achieving their first winning season in their fifth year (1997), the same season they won their first World Series.

Table 13-1. Fastest Expansion Teams to a Winning Season

Rank	Team	Year Established	First Winning Season	Won-Loss Record	Seasons in Existence
1 (tie)	Los Angeles Angels	1961	1962	86-76	2
1 (tie)	Arizona Diamondbacks	1998	1999	100-62	2
3 (tie)	Kansas City Royals	1969	1971	85-76	3
3 (tie)	Colorado Rockies	1993	1995	77-67	3
5	Florida Marlins	1993	1997	92-70	5

METHODOLOGY: Expansion teams are ranked based on the shortest amount of time it took them to achieve a winning record. For example, both the Angels and the Diamondbacks registered winning records in their second year of existence as a franchise. Expansion teams are defined as teams that came into existence in 1961 (Los Angeles Angels and Washington Senators), 1962 (Houston Colt .45s and New York Mets), 1969 (Kansas City Royals, Montreal Expos, San Diego Padres, and Seattle Pilots), 1977 (Seattle Mariners and Toronto Blue Jays), 1993 (Colorado Rockies and Florida Marlins), or 1998 (Arizona Diamondbacks and Tampa Bay Devil Rays).

LEGEND: Team names are presented as they were during the team's original expansion season. First Winning Season is the season in which the team registered more wins than losses. Win-Loss Record is the team's win-loss record at the end of its first winning season.

NOTE 1: Since their initial seasons, many teams have changed locations and/or names.

- The Houston Colt .45s were renamed the Astros in 1965.
- The Seattle Pilots moved to Milwaukee and became the Brewers in 1970.
- The Washington Senators moved to Arlington and became the Texas Rangers in 1972.
- The Montreal Expos moved to Washington and became the Nationals in 2005.
- The Tampa Bay Devil Rays shortened their name to the Tampa Bay Rays in 2008.
- The Florida Marlins were renamed the Miami Marlins in 2012.
- Meanwhile the Los Angeles Angels changed their location name several times, finally settling in as ... the Los Angeles Angels.

NOTE 2: The Arizona Diamondbacks were the quickest expansion team to win the World Series, beating the New York Yankees in 2001 in only their fourth year of existence. The Marlins were close behind Arizona in that regard, winning the 1997 World Series in their fifth year of existence.

NOTE 3: On the other end of the spectrum, the Seattle Mariners didn't log a winning season until their 15th year (1991), the longest record of futility achieved by a modern expansion team. The runners-up in this category were the Houston Colt .45s/Astros (12th year), Montreal Expos (11th year), and Tampa Bay (Devil) Rays (11th year).

NOTE 4: The Washington Senators/Texas Rangers have the dubious distinction of having the longest drought of any expansion team without a World Series championship. They currently stand at 61 seasons and counting. And, yes, we all know how they came within one strike of winning it all in 2011. This isn't the longest drought without a title in the majors, though. The Cleveland Indians/Guardians last won a championship 73 seasons ago in 1948. (Postscript: just before this book was published, the Texas Rangers broke their championship drought and won the 2023 World Series in their 63rd season. That leaves the Milwaukee Brewers and

San Diego Padres with the longest expansion team championship drought of 55 seasons and counting. The Seattle Mariners are the only expansion team to not have played in the World Series).

Bo Belinsky recorded the first no-hitter for the brand-new Angels franchise. Since his extraordinary game in 1962, the team has registered numerous outstanding pitching performances. The table below shows the highest Games Scores of any Angel pitcher since the team began play in 1961.

Table 13-2. Angels Highest Game Scores

Rank	Pitcher (Team Home)	Date Score	Opponent	GSc	IP, Hits, Runs, ERs, Walks, Strikeouts
1	Dean Chance (Los Angeles)	6/6/1964 NY 2-0 (15 inn)	NY Yankees	116	14.0 IP, 3 Hits, 0 Runs, 0 ERs, 2 BBs, 12 Ks
2	Frank Tanana (California)	9/22/1975 Cal 3-0 (16 inn)	Chicago W. Sox	105	13.0 IP, 6 Hits, 0 Runs, 0 ERs, 3 BBs, 13 Ks
3	Frank Tanana (California)	8/27/1976 NY 5-0 (15 inn)	NY Yankees	104	13.0 IP, 7 Hits, 0 Runs, 0 ERs, 2 BBs, 13 Ks
4	Rudy May (California)	7/9/1971 Oak 1-0 (20 inn)	Oakland Athletics	103	12.0 IP, 3 Hits, 0 Runs, 0 ERs, 6 BBs, 13 Ks
5 (tie)	Nolan Ryan (California)	7/9/1972 Cal 3-0	Boston Red Sox	100	9.0 IP, 1 Hit, 0 Runs, 0 ERs, 1 BB, 16 Ks
5 (tie)	Nolan Ryan (California)	7/15/1973 Cal 6-0	Detroit Tigers	100	9.0 IP, 0 Hits, 0 Runs, 0 ERs, 4 BBs, 17 Ks
7	Nolan Ryan (California)	8/20/1974 Det 1-0 (11 inn)	Detroit Tigers	99	11.0 IP, 4 Hits, 1 Run, 1 ER, 5 BBs, 19 Ks
8 (tie)	Bill Singer (California)	8/3/1973 Oak 2-1 (11 inn)	Oakland Athletics	97	11.0 IP, 3 Hits, 2 Runs, 1 ER, 1 BB, 13 Ks
8 (tie)	Mike Witt (California)	9/30/1984 Cal 1-0	Texas Rangers	97	9.0 IP, 0 Hits, 0 Runs, 0 ERs, 0 BBs, 10 Ks
10 (tie)	Nolan Ryan (California)	5/15/1973 Cal 3-0	KC Royals	96	9.0 IP, 0 Hits, 0 Runs, 0 ERs, 3 BBs, 12 Ks
10 (tie)	Frank Tanana (California)	10/1/1976 Cal 2-0 (12 inn)	Oakland Athletics	96	11.0 IP, 5 Hits, 0 Runs, 0 ERs, 5 BBs, 14 Ks
10 (tie)	Chuck Finley (California)	5/23/1995 Cal 10-0	NY Yankees	96	9.0 IP, 2 Hits 0 Runs, 0 ERs, 2 BBs, 15 Ks

Rank	Pitcher (Team Home)	Date Score	Opponent	GSc	IP, Hits, Runs, ERs, Walks, Strikeouts
13 (tie)	Jered Weaver (LA of Anaheim)	5/2/2012 LA 9-0	Min Twins	95	9.0 IP, 0 Hits, 0 Runs, 0 ERs, 1 BB, 9 Ks
16 (tie)	Nolan Ryan (California)	9/28/1974 Cal 4-0	Min Twins	94	9.0 IP, 0 Hits, 0 Runs, 0 ERs, 8 BBs, 15 Ks
16 (tie)	Ervin Santana (LA of Anaheim)	7/27/2011 LA 3-1	Cle Indians	94	9.0 IP, 0 Hits, 1 Run, 0 ERs, 1 BB, 10 Ks
23 (tie)	Bo Belinsky (Los Angeles)	5/5/1962 LA 2-0	Bal Orioles	92	9.0 IP, 0 Hits, 0 Runs, 0 ERs, 4 BBs, 9 Ks
23 (tie)	Nolan Ryan (California)	6/1/1975 Cal 1-0	Bal Orioles	92	9.0 IP, 0 Hits, 0 Runs, 0 ERs, 4 BBs, 9 Ks
141 (tie)	Clyde Wright (California)	7/3/1970 Cal 4-0	Oakland Athletics	85	9.0 IP, 0 Hits, 0 Runs, 0 ERs, 3 BBs, 1 K
677 (tie)	Mark Langston +1 (California)	4/11/1990 Cal 1-0	Seattle Mariners	76	7.0 IP, 0 Hits, 0 Runs, 0 ERs, 4 BBs, 3 Ks

METHODOLOGY: This table includes the highest Game Scores thrown by an Angels pitcher from 1961-2021. Games are ranked by Game Score (GSc) and consider all franchise regular season and postseason games. For comparison purposes, all 11 franchise no-hitters are included in this table. Game Score (GSc) measures a pitcher's performance in any given game started. Introduced by baseball writer/statistician Bill James in the 1980s, Game Score is presented as a figure between 0-100 — except for extreme outliers — and usually falls between 40-70.

LEGEND: Dates are shown as month/day/year (for example, June 12, 2018, is shown as 6/12/2018). While the Angels have almost exclusively played in Anaheim since joining the American League as an expansion franchise in 1961, they have changed the team name multiple times. From 1961-1964 the Angels played in Los Angeles and were known as the Los Angeles Angels. Starting in 1965, the team was called the California Angels, as they began playing ball in their new Anaheim stadium in 1966. The name California Angels lasted through 1996. From 1997 through 2004 the team took a more locally focused approach and was known as the Anaheim Angels. In 2005, they wanted to be associated with the larger metropolitan area and began calling themselves the Los Angeles Angels of Anaheim because of a contract clause that required them to have Anaheim in their name. And in 2016, the team reverted to simply calling themselves the Los Angeles Angels when the contract clause went away. "Team Home" refers to the name the Angels were known by when the game was thrown. IP = innings pitched. One-third of an inning pitched has 0.1 added and two-thirds of an inning pitched has 0.2 added (for example, 9 1/3 innings pitched is displayed as 9.1). BB(s) = base(s) on balls; K(s) = strikeout(s); ER(s) = earned run(s); inn = innings (associated with the length of extra-inning games); and (1) or (2) = first or second game of a doubleheader. *Mike Witt's 1984 perfect game against the Texas Rangers is italicized. It is the first and only perfect game in franchise history.*

    NOTE 1: While not included in the table above, the highest postseason Game Score ever achieved by an Angel pitcher was a score of 78 by John Lackey in Game 4 of the 2002 ALCS against Minnesota. Lackey threw seven shutout innings, allowing only three hits and striking out seven in a 7-1 win over the Twins. This game put Anaheim ahead three games to one, and they eventually won the ALCS in five games. They later took the seven-game World Series against the Giants for the team's only championship in the franchise's 60+ year history.

    NOTE 2: On April 11, 1990, the Angels threw a multi-pitcher no-hitter against Seattle in a 1-0 win. Mark Langston started the game with 7.0 innings of no-hit ball, earning a Game Score of 76 as shown in the table. Mike Witt relieved Langston in the top of the eighth after the Angels scored their only run of the game on a bases-loaded walk in the bottom of the seventh. The free pass came on a 3-2 count after an intentional walk had been issued to the previous hitter. Witt threw 2.0 innings to close out the game with a save. The combined statistics of Langston and Witt would have yielded a Game Score of 88 if the game had been thrown by a single pitcher.

    NOTE 3: Nolan Ryan also figures prominently in this table of the highest Angel Game Scores of 10 innings or less, achieving a team high score of 100 in two separate games. The first one was a one-hitter against the Red Sox in 1972, a game in which he allowed one hit (a single by Hall of Famer Carl Yastrzemski) and one walk to leadoff hitter Tommy Harper. Those both occurred in the top of the first inning before there were even two outs. After those two baserunners got on board, Ryan retired the next 26 batters in a row, striking out 15 of them. 1972 was Ryan's first year with the Angels, with California trading shortstop Jim Fregosi to the Mets for Ryan and three other players. That year was also Ryan's first of eight All-Star appearances, four of which were with the Angels. His second score of 100 came in 1973, when he threw a no-hitter against Jim Perry and the Detroit Tigers. This was one of two no-hitters he would throw that year, with the second being a May game against their division rival Kansas City Royals.

NOTE 4: Dean Chance's 14-inning effort was extraordinary. Allowing only three hits and two walks to a powerful Yankees lineup featuring Tom Tresh, Roger Maris, Elston Howard, and Joe Pepitone, Chance achieved a Game Score of 116, which remains the highest in Angels' history by a wide margin. The first hit Chance allowed was a single to Maris in the top of the seventh with one out. The next Yankee hit was a single by Tony Kubek to lead off the 12th inning. Johnny Blanchard hit a single with one out in the 13th inning and that was it – no other hits were allowed by Chance, although he did have to prevent New York baserunners who reached base on walks and errors from scoring in a 0-0 game.

It looked like Los Angeles might have a chance to finally score a run in the bottom of the 14th when the leadoff hitter reached first base by being hit by a pitch. Chance, the next batter, was lifted for pinch-hitter Jimmy Piersall. Piersall did move the runner to second, but the team failed to bring him home. In the top of the 15th, Elston Howard hit a two-run, two-out double off reliever Dan Osinski to provide the game's only scores in the 2-0 Yankee win.

NOTE 5: Frank Tanana, a three-time All-Star and workhorse for California in the 1970s, pitched two outstanding 13-inning efforts that resulted in the second and third best Game Scores for the Angels. His first game on this list – 13 innings of shutout ball in 1975 – was the foundation for a 16-inning, 3-0 victory over the White Sox. His second 13-inning effort also resulted in zero runs allowed – this time against a very good Yankees team in 1976. Unfortunately for the Angels, New York scored five runs in the top of the 15th, winning the game 5-0.

NOTE 6: Rudy May's 12 innings of shutout work came in his 1971 game against the up-and-coming Athletics. This contest set the record for the longest game in Angels' history, a marathon 1-0 loss that ended in a walk-off single by Oakland in the bottom of the 20th. Since then, there has been one other 20-inning game for the Angels, a 4-3 win against the Mariners in 1982.

NOTE 7: In Jared Weaver's no-hitter in 2012, he allowed only two baserunners. One was a seventh-inning walk to Josh Willingham on a 3-2 count. The other was on a swinging strikeout by Chris Parmelee where the ball got away from Angel catcher Mike Napoli for a passed ball.

NOTE 8: Ervin Santana threw a no-hitter where he allowed only one walk but allowed a run. In that game, the leadoff hitter for the Indians (Ezequiel Carrera) reached first on an error by third baseman Maicer Izturis in the bottom of the first inning. Carrera would come around to score on a stolen base, fielder's choice, and wild pitch. Santana allowed his one walk of the game with one out in the eighth inning on a full-count pitch to Lonnie Chisenhall.

There have been many outstanding pitchers for the Angels throughout the years, including Dean Chance, Chuck Finley, Jared Weaver, Mike Witt, John Lackey, Frank Tanana, and, most recently, Shohei Ohtani, among others. However, no one dominated the mound more than Nolan Ryan. The pitcher with the most strikeouts in baseball history, Ryan holds the Angel record for most strikeouts in a game, as he has struck out 19 batters on four separate occasions with the team. His highest Game Score in those four contests was 99, occurring in an 11-inning, 1-0 loss to the Detroit Tigers in 1974. Ironically, this was the only game he lost out of those four.

Ironically, it was the only game he lost out of the top 47 regular season Game Scores he registered during his career. Nineteen strikeouts in a game is the highest Ryan would ever achieve with any team, which places him in a 10-way tie for seventh place (where he occupies four of the 10 spots) all-time in the major leagues. In total, there have been only 16 times where a pitcher has struck out 19 or more batters. Ryan is the only pitcher with four entries among those 16 pitching performances. Randy Johnson has three games at 19+ strikeouts, and Roger Clemens has two.

Tom Cheney of the Washington Senators holds the single-game record, when he struck out 21 batters in a 16-inning game against the Baltimore Orioles in 1962. After that, there are five other 20-strikeout performances tied for second place. For the Angels, Nolan Ryan also appears four times among the top 12 Game Scores in the team's history. Frank Tanana is the only other pitcher to appear more than once, and he shows up three times – all in extra-inning games — among the top 12.

Tied for the team's 23rd-best Game Score, Belinsky's first-ever Angel no-hitter holds up very well. With a score of 92, Belinsky's game set the Angel record for Game Score when he threw it. The only Angels pitcher besides Belinsky to throw a nine-inning game with a score of 92 or higher throughout the 1960s was team ace and 1964 Cy Young Award Winner Dean Chance.

Despite his very impressive no-hit achievement, Bo Belinsky has often been seen as a disappointment because of the perception that he "could have been so much more." While that's almost certainly true, the feeling that he could have achieved more doesn't diminish what he did accomplish.

Bo Belinsky was a major league pitcher. It is extraordinarily difficult to even get to the major leagues, much less be a star or even a regular player. Ninety percent of minor leaguers don't make it to the majors. Of the 10% who see the majors, approximately 75% of starting pitchers who make it to the big leagues end their careers as what I've categorized as Level 5 pitchers based on their career JAWS score.

In this regard Belinsky, as a Level 5 pitcher, is in a big group. Even within the big group, though, Belinsky did a lot better than most pitchers who made it to the majors. For example, Belinsky was on the AA Little Rock Travelers in 1961. This was his last minor league season before he moved up to MLB in 1962. On that team there were 11 pitchers. Five of them saw the big leagues. Their career statistics are reflected in the table below:

Table 13-3. 1961 Little Rock Travelers Career MLB Pitching Statistics

Pitcher	Major League Team(s)	Years Played	Innings Pitched	Career Win-Loss	Career ERA
Bo Belinsky	Los Angeles Angels Philadelphia Phillies Pittsburgh Pirates Cincinnati Reds Houston Astros	1962-1964 1965-1966 1967 1969 1970	665.1	28-51	4.10
Jim Lehew	Baltimore Orioles	1961-1962	11.2	0-0	1.54
Chuck Daniel	Detroit Tigers	1957	2.1	0-0	7.71
Don Bradey	Houston Astros	1964	2.1	0-2	19.29
John Papa	Baltimore Orioles	1961-1962	2.0	0-0	22.50

METHODOLOGY: This table includes those pitchers on the 1961 Little Rock Travelers who pitched in the Major Leagues. Pitchers are ranked in order of career innings pitched. In a tie situation (such as the two pitchers having thrown 2.1 innings pitched), the top listing goes to the pitcher with the lower ERA.

LEGEND: MLB Years Played represents the years played with the team listed in the second column. ERA = Earned Run Average, or the number of earned runs allowed per nine innings pitched. IP = innings pitched. One-third of an inning pitched has 0.1 added and two-thirds of an inning pitched has 0.2 added (for example, 11 2/3 innings pitched is displayed as 11.2).

NOTE 1: The Little Rock Travelers were the Baltimore Orioles AA affiliate. The team played in the Southern Association and finished in third place with an 80-73 record in 1961. Besides Bo Belinsky, other notable Major Leaguers who played on the Travelers that year included third baseman Fred Hatfield, outfielder Dave Nicholson, utility man Bob Saverine, third baseman Pete Ward, and catcher Cal Ripken, Senior – Hall of Famer Cal Ripken Junior's father.

NOTE 2: Pat Gillick, David Justus, Roger Kudron, Charles Ready, George Stepanovich, Arne Thorsland, and Robert Walz were also on the Little Rock pitching staff in 1961. None of those seven pitchers ever appeared in the major leagues. However, Pat Gillick is a member of the Baseball Hall of Fame Class of 2011. He earned admittance to the Hall for his outstanding work as a championship-level general manager for Toronto, Baltimore, Seattle, and Philadelphia.

For the other four pitchers besides Belinsky in the table, their combined career totals are anemic: 0-2 won-loss record, 18.1 innings pitched, and a 7.00 ERA. There are a lot of major league pitchers in the Brady/Daniel/Lehew/Papa category. They made it to the big leagues for a short period and pitched a few innings.

The big takeaway is that Belinsky had a big-league career that spanned nine seasons. He even had a couple of good seasons (1962 and 1964, in particular). The vast majority of professional pitchers either don't make it to the majors or only stay for a brief period. The ones who appeared in the majors can be divided into five categories, or levels, based on their level of achievement as measured by JAWS. Bo Belinsky falls into Level 5 with a JAWS of 1.4. Digging deeper, though, it becomes apparent he was one of the better Level 5 pitchers among that group.

To break this down further, the total number of Level 1 through 5 pitchers is 3,598. Of that number, there were 919 pitchers total in Levels 1 through 4 and 2,679 in Level 5. Using JAWS as a metric, Belinsky was ranked #2,020 (out of 3,598), meaning that he was in the 56% percentile of all pitchers who ever pitched in the major leagues. Considering only Level 5 pitchers, he was #1,101 out of 2,679, which means he was in the top 41% of Level 5 pitchers. Another way to put it is that he had a higher JAWS score than 59% of the Level 5 pitchers.

Apart from being in a very select group of no-hit pitchers, Bo Belinsky can be seen as having a successful major league career. This is apart from whatever potential he may have had that was left unfulfilled. At the peak of his young career, he was a star if only for a brief period. Bo Belinsky threw this no-hitter in just his fourth career start. Only five other pitchers in baseball history have thrown them earlier in their careers – these five are listed in Table 15-6 in this volume. Further, Belinsky had won each of those first three games he threw before he no-hit the Orioles. There are many thousands of pitchers in the majors and the minors who rightfully envy Bo Belinsky's achievements.

It's also interesting to note that Belinsky did have one of the lowest JAWS scores of all pitchers who threw a no-hitter. Of course, the list of pitchers who have had the skill to throw a no-hitter is very select to begin with. The 10 pitchers listed below are all retired. Active pitchers who have thrown a no-hitter aren't included because they are expected to increase their JAWS as they continue their career.

Table 13-4. Retired No-hit Pitchers with Lowest JAWS Scores

Rank	Pitcher (Team/No-hitter Year)	JAWS	Career W-L	ERA	IP	Strike-outs	Year Retired
1	Don Black (Cleveland Indians/1947)	-1.9	34-55	4.35	797	293	1948
2	Iron Davis (Boston Braves/1914)	-1.7	7-10	4.48	191	77	1915
3	Mal Eason (Brooklyn Superbas/1906)	-1.5	38-73	3.42	951	274	1906
4	Mike Warren (Oakland Athletics/1983)	-0.9	9-13	5.06	204	139	1986
5	Bud Smith (St. Louis Cardinals/2001)	-0.3	7-8	4.95	132	81	2005
6	Bobo Holloman (St. Louis Browns/1953)	0.0	3-7	5.23	65	25	1954
7 (tie)	Rex Barney (Brooklyn Dodgers/1948)	0.8	35-31	4.31	597	336	1952
7 (tie)	Chris Heston (SF Giants/2015)	0.8	13-13	4.55	194	151	2018
9	Bo Belinsky (LA Angels/1962)	1.4	28-51	4.10	665	476	1970

Rank	Pitcher (Team/No-hitter Year)	JAWS	Career W-L	ERA	IP	Strike-outs	Year Retired
10	Philip Humber (Chi White Sox/2012)	1.7	16-23	5.31	371	272	2014

METHODOLOGY: The 10 retired no-hit pitchers with the lowest career JAWS are ranked in ascending order by their score. Pitchers had to have retired between 1900-2021.

LEGEND: JAWS = Jaffe Wins Above Replacement Score. JAWS is a sabermetric baseball statistic developed to evaluate the strength of a player's career and merit for induction into the Baseball Hall of Fame. It is created by averaging a player's career Wins Above Replacement (WAR) with their 7-year peak WAR (WAR-7). WAR measures a player's value in all facets of the game by deciphering how many more wins he's worth than a replacement-level player at his same position. ERA = Earned Run Average, or the number of earned runs allowed per nine innings pitched. W-L = win-loss record. IP = Innings pitched. JAWS, Win-Loss, ERA, Innings Pitched, and Strikeouts represent career averages or totals.

NOTE: Some of the teams listed in the table moved or changed names over the years. As the turn of the century arrived in 1900, the National League's Brooklyn team was called the Superbas. The team was known as the Dodgers from 1911-1912 before changing back to the Superbas in 1913. In 1914, the team became the Robins and stayed that way until they settled on the Dodgers for good in 1932. In 1958, the team moved from Brooklyn to Los Angeles. The National League's Boston team was known simply as Boston at the turn of the century in 1900. With the advent of the American League in 1901, the team became known as the Boston Nationals. They changed their name to the Boston Doves in 1907, became the Boston Rustlers in 1911, and then the Boston Braves in 1912. The Braves moved to Milwaukee in 1953 and to Atlanta in 1966. The St. Louis Browns moved to Baltimore and became the Orioles in 1954, the year after Bobo Holloman threw his no-hitter in his very first start.

Bo Belinsky wasn't the only player on the Angels who was famous, either. Los Angeles first baseman Steve Bilko was so renowned he had a title character in a hit TV show named after him. Bilko played in the majors on and off from 1949 to 1962. This 1962 season was his last in the big leagues, although he played one more year of baseball in 1963 with Rochester of the AAA International League. Bilko's major league totals weren't especially eye-popping, as he hit .249 with 76 home runs in just under 2,000 plate appearances.

Where he really made an impact was in the minor leagues. During his time there, he accumulated 1,666 hits and clobbered 313 home runs, most of those coming in the Pacific Coast League. Playing for the Los Angeles Angels of the PCL in the late 1950s, he was a bona fide star, as he crushed 55 HRs in 1956 and 56 in 1957. He was so well known in the Los Angeles/Hollywood area, that comedian Phil Silvers took his name (Bilko) as the name of his title character in the Emmy Award-winning comedy "The Phil Silvers Show" (also known as "Sergeant Bilko"). Seeing a local slugger with home run talent and a big-name draw, the expansion Los Angeles Angels took no chances as they filled out their team in the 1961 expansion draft. Steve Bilko was the Angels' second pick.

In the "small world" category, Bo Belinsky's opposing pitcher on the Baltimore Orioles that day was Steve Barber. Barber was a teammate of Belinsky's in the Baltimore minor league system in 1958 (Aberdeen) and 1959 (Pensacola and Amarillo) and was a favorite nighttime "running buddy" of Belinsky's. The third member of their carousing trio on those teams was Steve Dalkowski, an incredibly fast and wild pitcher who never got into the majors. The character "Nuke LaLoosh" in the movie *Bull Durham* was loosely based on Dalkowski.

Belinsky's early life was interesting as well. Robert "Bo" Belinsky was born on December 7, 1936, into a New York City working-class family. He had three siblings and attended Trenton Central (NJ) High School but didn't play any sports while in school. Instead, he became a pool hustler and fighter. He did play baseball in semi-pro leagues around Trenton, though, and Pittsburgh signed him as a free agent in 1956. He was in the minors from 1956-61, mostly in the Baltimore system. In the minors he threw for Brunswick (GA), Aberdeen (SD), Knoxville (TN), Pensacola (FL), Stockton (CA), Amarillo (TX), Vancouver (Canada), and Little Rock (AR) before getting drafted by the Angels in the November 1961 Rule 5 Draft.

The Bo Belinsky story ended in 2001 when he died from a heart attack, complicated by advanced bladder cancer and other health problems. His later life was much calmer and far more inspiring, as he stopped drinking and taking drugs and found purpose with his church, the Trinity Life Center. He himself summed up his perspective on how he might have squandered his potential when he described it this way in 1971:

"People keep telling me I never lived up to my potential, that I wasted my talent. I don't see it that way. I figure that I used all I had. I just didn't have as much as people thought."

Belinsky's catcher the night of the no-hitter was fellow rookie Buck Rodgers, a career Level 4 (JAWS 4.3) catcher spanning nine seasons with the Angels. During the 1962 season, Rodgers finished second in the AL Rookie of the Year balloting. After his playing career ended, he worked in various baseball jobs, including coach, general manager, and 18 seasons as a manager. Thirteen of those managerial seasons were in the majors with the Brewers, Expos, and Angels. Rodgers won NL Manager of the Year in 1987 with the Montreal Expos, leading the team to an impressive 91-71 season en route to a close third-place finish in the highly competitive National League East that year. I encourage you to read my fascinating interview below conducted recently with Buck Rodgers.

Buck Rodgers Interview
Conducted by Kevin Hurd on May 24, 2021

Kevin Hurd (KH): Would you consider yourself to be the best catcher/player on your Little League, American Legion, high school, or minor league teams?

Buck Rodgers (BR): Well, for Little League, there was no Little League in the early to mid-1950s. In high school I pitched, and on the days I wasn't pitching, I caught. I caught for American Legion ball, though I mostly pitched. I pretty much was the full-time catcher in college. As far as the minors, I played from 1956-1961. I was the best catcher on each of those teams.

KH: Did you feel any different, good or bad, on the day of Bo Belinsky's no-hitter?

BR: No, it was just a regular night at Dodger Stadium.

KH: What pitches – fastball, curve, slider, or something else – were working best for Belinsky that night?

BR: Without a doubt, his four-seam fastball. He probably threw it 80-85% of the time. His second-best pitch was his screwball, but it wasn't working that night for him. It was mostly erratic. His curve wasn't working well that night, either.

KH: What was the best defensive play or the closest you and Belinsky came to losing the no-hitter?

BR: I can't remember any great defensive plays.

KH: Did Belinsky shake off your signs much during the game?

BR: Not very many – maybe a couple. That was close to the normal amount. Most of our pitchers didn't shake me off much. One pitcher <u>never</u> shook me off. I had to encourage our pitchers to shake me off once in a while, so I knew they were still thinking out there. I would tell them that they had to have an idea, too.

KH: Which pitcher did you have the hardest time hitting?

BR: I wasn't a good hitter. I had a hard time hitting them all (laughs).

KH: Do you have any memorabilia/souvenirs, such as a baseball, plaque, uniform, or something else from the game in your house?

BR: Yes, a picture of Bo, me, Fred Haney and Bill Rigney together after the game. It's somewhere in the house (laughs).

KH: In the major leagues you played for Bill Rigney and Lefty Phillips. In the minors you played for several other managers. Who did you most like playing for?

BR: Well, for the majors, it was Bill Rigney. For the minors, I played for a number of different managers but the one who helped me the most was when I played for Idaho Falls in 1958. The manager was Al Lakeman. He taught me a lot of footwork that helped me behind the plate. There are a lot of minor league coaches and managers that help players make it to the majors.

KH: Do you think the number of pitches Bo threw that day led to him getting a sore arm?

BR: Well, we didn't have official pitch counts in those days. We would have the previous day's pitcher "chart" the pitches that day, but I can't remember an official count. Bo was an ordinary pitcher who, for one night, had an untouchable fastball.

KH: Did Bo request you as his catcher that night before this game?

BR: No, I was pretty much the catcher for all games. I caught 155 of the 162 games that year. Back then, you didn't want to make a habit of missing games. You felt if you took time off, you could run into a Wally Pipp/Lou Gehrig situation and never play again.

KH: Did you stay in contact with Belinsky after the game?

BR: Yes, I did go to his memorial (in 2001). He was in Las Vegas for a long time, and he'd invite me to go golfing with him sometimes. I probably had contact with him every five or six years. I also kept contact with (former Angels pitcher) Dean Chance. Dean was friends with Bo and after Dean called Bo up, he'd call me and say that Bo said hi.

KH: Did the Angels give you or Bo a bonus for the no-hitter?

BR: Well, I don't know if the team gave Bo a bonus, but they didn't give me one (laughs).

KH: During the game, when did you think "He's got a real shot at a no-hitter?" Fifth inning, sixth inning, or later?

BR: Let me re-emphasize that Bo had a great, live fastball that night. Having said that, I wasn't confident he would get a no-hitter until the last Oriole got out in the ninth inning.

KH: I know you were a very accomplished manager. Tell us about the follow-on jobs you held in the majors, minors, college, high school, or media after your playing days were over.

BR: Yes, I was a coach from 1970-74 with a couple teams, from 1975-77 a manager in the minors, a major-league manager from 1980-94 with Milwaukee, Montreal, and California. I was also a scout from 1995-97, and a minor-league manager from 1997-98.

KH: What other kind of work did you do?

BR: Well, I retired from baseball in 1998. Since then, I have volunteered as a coach for Little League teams my grandkids played on, plus being a pitching coach at a local community college. I also spent a year managing an independent minor-league team.

KH: Do you think having caught a no-hitter helped you get the baseball jobs?

BR: No, not at all. What helped me get my first coaching job (with Minnesota in 1970) was that I knew Bill Rigney, who I had played for all nine years of my career as a catcher. Rigney had just become manager of the Twins, and he hired me to be one of his coaches.

KH: Do you have any kids or grandkids who have pursued or will pursue baseball as a career? Do you encourage them to do so?

BR: I have a son who pitched for one of the colleges in the LA area. I've had grandkids who have played Little League, also. I would encourage anybody to play a competitive sport if at all possible. You can learn a lot of lessons from competitive sports – it doesn't have to be baseball – with some of the most valuable lessons being how to handle defeat.

KH: Was the no-hitter the highlight of your career? If not, what was?

BR: No, not really. My managing career was better than my playing career, so I'd say my highlight in managing was getting Manager of the Year in 1987 while managing Montreal. Having said that, I'd say my best season as a player was when I was a rookie in 1962.

KH: Have you been to the section of the Hall of Fame that focuses on no-hitters?

BR: No, I haven't.

KH: Have you spent time signing autographs in Las Vegas, or in Florida or Arizona during spring training?

BR: Yes, I have. I also get about 10 autograph requests a week.

KH: Do you have any favorite stories regarding any of these experiences?

BR: Not really. What I would like to say as an ending is that in my 40+ years in professional baseball I had a great time. There's an old saying that if you do something you love, you'll never have to work a day in your life. I wasn't cheated. I thoroughly enjoyed it.

CHAPTER 14

TOM SEAVER: THE LONG WAIT IS OVER

June 16, 1978
Hall of Famer Tom Seaver finally gets his no-hitter
as a starter for the Cincinnati Reds

"Tom runs the show out there. I was more of a spectator."
Cincinnati Reds no-hit catcher Don Werner (St. Louis Post-Dispatch, June 17, 1978).

"(Seaver's masterpiece was) more a matter of skill over power. He didn't have overpowering stuff. His fastball wasn't much. But he had control and made it look easy."
Sportswriter Bob Hertzel (Cincinnati Enquirer, June 17, 1978).

"I got stronger at the end of the game. From the seventh inning on I began to feel the excitement of the fans."
Tom Seaver (The Sporting News, June 17, 1978).

Tom Seaver, already revered as one of the premier pitchers in baseball, still had something to prove on June 16, 1978. Bursting onto the scene as a 22-year-old rookie in 1967, he rapidly became the ace for the New York Mets, a team so horrible that in the five previous seasons of their existence, they had lost fewer than 100 games and finished above last place in the 10-team National League only once before. Even that accomplishment was less than impressive: in 1966, the team finished at 66-95, 28.5 games behind the Los Angeles Dodgers and just barely above the hapless last-place Chicago Cubs. While some may have interpreted this advancement to ninth place in the standings as at least a move in the right direction, the team reverted to form in 1967, Tom's rookie season, finishing in last place with 101 losses, a full 8.0 games behind the ninth-place Houston Astros.

Despite Seaver's outstanding All-Star, Rookie of the Year season, things were still looking down in the dumps for New York's National League team. Within two years, and led by "Tom Terrific," all of this would change dramatically. In 1969, the "Amazin' Mets" would capture America's imagination by outlasting the Chicago Cubs for the NL East championship, beating Hank Aaron's Atlanta Braves in the first-ever NLCS, and soundly defeating the heavily favored Baltimore Orioles four games to one in the World Series. Yet, in 1978 – his 12th season – at the age of 33, with three Cy Young Awards, one World Series championship, two National League pennants, and 11 All-Star appearances, including one with his new team (the Cincinnati Reds), he still had one goal he hadn't achieved: Seaver had never thrown a no-hitter.

He had come very close, throwing five one-hitters – including one 1969 game against the Chicago Cubs when light-hitting #8 hitter Jim Qualls punched a one-out single in the ninth inning to break up Seaver's perfect game. He also had two other no-hitters broken up in the ninth: Leron Lee's one-out single on Independence Day 1972 against the Padres and a late-September game in 1975 when the Cubs' Joe Wallis hit a bloop single to right field with two outs in the bottom of the ninth. That's three times he had taken his no-hitter into the ninth and been denied, all while pitching for the New York Mets.

Tom Seaver's three near no-hitters is not even the record in that regard. Both Nolan Ryan (5) and Dave Stieb (4) have had more no-hitters broken up in the ninth inning, as displayed in the table below.

Table 14-1. No-hit pitchers who lost three or more no-hitters in the ninth

Rank	Pitcher (# of no-hitters)	Team(s)	Game Dates (no-hitters lost in the ninth)	Total
1	Nolan Ryan (7)	California Angels Houston Astros Texas Rangers	8/7/1974, 7/13/1979 4/27/1988 4/23/1989, 8/10/1989	5
2	Dave Stieb (1)	Toronto Blue Jays	8/24/1985, 9/24/1988, 9/30/1988, 8/4/1989	4

Rank	Pitcher (# of no-hitters)	Team(s)	Game Dates (no-hitters lost in the ninth)	Total
3	Tom Seaver (1)	New York Mets	7/9/1969, 7/4/1972, 9/24/1975	3

METHODOLOGY: This table shows the three pitchers who had the highest number of potential no-hitters broken up in the ninth inning. The pitchers are ranked from the highest to the lowest number of games. The table includes the 61-season timespan since the start of the expansion era (1961-2021).

LEGEND: Dates of each game are shown as month/day/year (for example, June 12, 2018, is shown as 6/12/2018). "# of No-hitters" = the total number of no-hitters thrown by the pitcher during his career. Since Nolan Ryan had near no-hitters with three different teams, the dates of the games associated with each team are listed on the same line as the team. Dave Stieb's games were all with the Blue Jays and Tom Seaver's games were all with the Mets.

NOTE 1: Nolan Ryan threw his first no-hitter in 1973, before any of the games listed in this table. Dave Stieb threw his four "near-miss ninth inning" games before pitching his no-hitter in 1990, all with the Blue Jays.

NOTE 2: Eight pitchers who have thrown at least one no-hitter have also had two potential no-hitters broken up in the ninth inning:

1) Justin Verlander (three no-hitters during his career) – his first two no-hitters came before the two near-miss games
2) Ken Holtzman (2) – his two no-hitters came after his first near-miss game
3) Randy Johnson (2) – his first no-hitter came before his two-near-miss games
4) Larry Dierker (1)
5) Rick Wise (1)
6) David Cone (1)
7) Anibal Sanchez (1)
8) Tom Browning (1)

NOTE 3: Doug Drabek, Michael Wacha, and hall of Famers Pedro Martinez and Mike Mussina all pitched two near-miss no-hit games broken up in the ninth inning or later without ever throwing a no-hitter.

Throughout his legendary career in major league baseball, Tom Seaver didn't emphasize individual accomplishments — he was all about his team's achievements. After his no-hit game, he told a reporter for the *Cincinnati Enquirer* "Winning (a championship) is the feeling of achievement. A no-hitter, it's momentary. You enjoy the moment, that's all." Yet, he was well into his amazing career by 1978, and he had to know that he wouldn't have many more chances for this personal milestone, if any. As it turned out, his 1978 no-hitter was his last real chance – he would never again record a one-hitter, much less a no-hitter.

While Seaver pitched very well for the Reds, White Sox, and Red Sox during the last half of his 20-year career, his greatest accomplishments came when he was with the New York Mets from 1967-1977. In addition to winning three Cy Young Awards, 10 All-Star appearances, two National League pennants, and one World Series Championship, he figures prominently in the list of best games ever pitched by a New York Mets pitcher as shown in Table 10-2.

Table 14-2. Mets Highest Game Scores

Rank	Pitcher	Date Score	Opponent	GSc	IP, Hits, Runs, ERs, Walks, Strikeouts
1	Rob Gardner	10/2/1965 (2) 0-0 Tie (18 inn)	Philadelphia Phillies	112	15.0 IP, 5 Hits, 0 Runs, 0 ERs, 2 BBs, 7 Ks
2	Tom Seaver	5/1/1974 LA 2-1 (14 inn)	Los Angeles Dodgers	106	12.0 IP, 3 Hits 1 Run, 1 ER, 2 BBs, 16 Ks
3	David Cone	10/6/1991 NY 7-0	Philadelphia Phillies	99	9.0 IP, 3 Hits, 0 Runs, 0 ERs, 1 BB, 19 Ks
4 (tie)	Tom Seaver	8/11/1971 SD 1-0 (12 inn)	San Diego Padres	98	10.0 IP, 3 Hits, 0 Runs, 0 ERs, 2 BBs, 14 Ks
4 (tie)	Jacob deGrom	4/23/2021 NY 6-0	Washington Nationals	98	9.0 IP, 2 Hits, 0 Runs, 0 ERs, 0 BBs, 15 Ks
6 (tie)	Jerry Koosman	5/28/1969 NY 1-0 (11 inn)	San Diego Padres	97	10.0 IP, 4 Hits, 0 Runs, 0 ERs, 2 BBs, 15 Ks

FROM RANDY JOHNSON TO DALLAS BRADEN

Rank	Pitcher	Date Score	Opponent	GSc	IP, Hits, Runs, ERs, Walks, Strikeouts
6 (tie)	Tom Seaver	5/15/1970 NY 4-0	Philadelphia Phillies	97	9.0 IP, 1 Hit, 0 Runs, 0 ERs, 3 BBs, 15 Ks
6 (tie)	Matt Harvey	5/7/2013 NY 1-0 (10 inn)	Chicago White Sox	97	9.0 IP, 1 Hit, 0 Runs, 0 ERs, 0 BBs, 12 Ks
9 (tie)	Al Jackson	8/14/1962 Phi 3-1 (15 inn)	Philadelphia Phillies	96	15.0 IP, 6 Hits, 3 Runs, 2 ERs, 5 BBs, 6 Ks
9 (tie)	Dick Selma	9/12/1965 NY 1-0 (10 inn)	Milwaukee Braves	96	10.0 IP, 4 Hits, 0 Runs, 0 ERs, 1 BB, 13 Ks
9 (tie)	Tom Seaver	7/9/1969 NY 4-0	Chicago Cubs	96	9.0 IP, 1 Hit, 0 Runs, 0 ERs, 0 BBs, 11 Ks
9 (tie)	Tom Seaver	4/22/1970 NY 2-1	San Diego Padres	96	9.0 IP, 2 Hits, 1 Run, 1 ER, 2 BBs, 19 Ks
9 (tie)	Chris Capuano	8/26/2011 NY 6-0	Atlanta Braves	96	9.0 IP, 2 Hits, 0 Runs, 0 ERs, 0 BBs, 13 Ks
9 (tie)	R.A. Dickey	6/18/2012 NY 5-0	Baltimore Orioles	96	9.0 IP, 1 Hit, 0 Runs, 0 ERs, 2 BBs, 13 Ks
49 (tie)	Johann Santana	6/1/2012 NY 8-0	St. Louis Cardinals	90	9.0 IP, 0 Hits, 0 Runs, 0 ERs, 5 BBs, 8 Ks

METHODOLOGY: This table includes the highest Game Scores thrown by a Mets pitcher from 1962-2021. Games are ranked by Game Score (GSc) and consider all franchise regular season and postseason games. For comparison purposes, the lone Mets no-hitters is included in this table. Game Score (GSc) measures a pitcher's performance in any given game started. Introduced by baseball writer/statistician Bill James in the 1980s, Game Score is presented as a figure between 0-100 — except for extreme outliers — and usually falls between 40-70. For comparison purposes, the lone Mets no-hitter (through 2021) by Johann Santana is included in this table.

LEGEND: Dates are shown as month/day/year (for example, June 12, 2018, is shown as 6/12/2018). One-third of an inning pitched has 0.1 added and two-thirds of an inning pitched has 0.2 added (for example, 9 1/3 innings pitched is displayed as 9.1). BB(s) = base(s) on balls; K(s) = strikeout(s); ER(s) = earned run(s); inn = innings (associated with the length of extra-inning games); and (1) or (2) = first or second game of a doubleheader.

NOTE 1: While not included in the table above, the highest postseason Game Score ever achieved by a Met pitcher was a score of 89 by Jon Matlack in Game 2 of the 1973 NLCS against a very powerful Cincinnati team. Matlack threw nine shutout innings, allowing only two hits and striking out nine in a 5-0 victory over the 99-win Reds, a team that featured all-time hits leader Pete Rose and Hall of Famers Johnny Bench, Tony Perez, and Joe Morgan in their starting lineup that day. This pivotal game tied the series at one game each. The 82-79 NL East champion Mets would win the NLCS in five games over the heavily favored Reds. The underdog Mets later took the World Series to seven games against the 94-win Athletics, losing the finale in Oakland by the score of 5-2.

NOTE 2: Called "the best pitching performance ever by a Met" by ESPN Senior Writer David Schoenfield, 20-year-old Rob Gardner threw 15 innings of five-hit, shutout ball against a solid Philadelphia lineup that included Dick Allen, Dick Stuart, Tony Gonzalez, and Alex Johnson. The second game of a doubleheader in which the Mets failed to score a run for 27 innings, this game was called after 18 innings as a 0-0 tie. It was finished the next day as part of a doubleheader that closed out the season for both teams. The Mets would lose both of those games against Philadelphia by identical 3-1 scores. New York would finish the season at 50-112, which qualifies them as having one of the 10 worst seasons in baseball during the postwar period. Traded by the Mets to the Cubs during the 1967 season, Gardner played for six different teams over eight years, mostly being used as a relief pitcher. He finished his career with a win-loss record of 14-18 and an ERA of 4.35 over 331 innings.

NOTE 3: In Matt Harvey's 2013 one-hitter against the White Sox, the only baserunner he allowed was on an infield single by Alex Rios with two outs in the seventh inning. R.A. Dickey also only gave up one hit in his 2012 game against the Orioles. That hit came in the fifth inning on a two-out line drive to right field by Wilson Betemit.

NOTE 4: New York's singular no-hitter was thrown by two-time Cy Young Award winner (with the Twins) Johann Santana in 2012 during his final season in a 12-year major league career. While the Mets offense gave him plenty of support by scoring eight runs against the reigning World Champion Cardinals, Santana's 134-pitch effort clearly stressed his arm. After his no-hitter, Santana had a record of 3-7 to finish the season, including losing his last five starts to close out his highly accomplished career.

NOTE 5: Tom Seaver is included numerous times in the list of top pitching performances for the Mets, earning five of the 14 highest Game Scores in New York history. No other pitcher appears more than once. Seaver's highest score was 106, achieved in a 12-inning performance in May 1974 wherein he only allowed one run on a solo shot by NL MVP Steve Garvey of the Dodgers. He struck out 16 batters, while he only gave up three hits and two walks. Unfortunately, after he departed the game, Los Angeles scored a run in the bottom of the 14th when Garvey knocked in Bill Buckner with a single off reliever Harry Parker. Seaver's other games on the list are a combination of one-hitters and high strikeout events. Seaver also set the Mets record for the most strikeouts in a game when he fanned 19 Padres in a 1970 contest (Game Score of 96). In that same game, he set the Major League record with 10 consecutive strikeouts in a game. That has since been tied by Corbin Burnes of Milwaukee and Aaron Nola of the Phillies, both achieved in 2021.

NOTE 6: The 19-strikeout record was tied by David Cone during a 1991 shutout thrown against the Phillies. Cone had a Game Score of 99 – the third highest score in Mets history. Nineteen strikeouts in a game was also Cone's career high. Cone had an extraordinary 17-year career that included a Cy Young Award with the Royals, a perfect game for the Yankees, five All Star selections as a member of the Mets, Yankees, and Royals, and five World Series Championships with the Blue Jays (1992) and Yankees (1996 and 1998-2000). He also pitched for the Red Sox near the end of his career in 2001.

With a Game Score of 87, Seaver's no-hitter against the Cardinals wasn't close to being his best game ever. He only struck out three Cardinal hitters and walked just as many. The key to his success that day was getting 15 batters to ground out. Of course, this approach relied on his defense, and the Reds' infield was full of superb fielders. Hall of Famer Joe Morgan at second base and Dave Concepcion at shortstop combined for nine assists, with an additional two assists by defensive replacement third baseman Ray Knight (in place of Pete Rose) making excellent plays on the first two batters Seaver faced in the eighth inning. Cardinals' star Keith Hernandez was the biggest hitting threat that day. Joe Morgan's play on his hard-hit ball in the fourth and Dave Concepcion's heads up play as he scooped up his grounder that deflected off Seaver's glove in the seventh likely saved the no-hitter.

While the Cardinals were in a team-wide competitive slump in 1978 – they would finish the season with 93 losses – they had some outstanding individual players. Besides the always dangerous Keith Hernandez, Hall of Famers left fielder Lou

Brock and catcher Ted Simmons were in the starting lineup, along with recent NL All-Stars center fielder George Hendrick, and shortstop Garry Templeton. These were experienced professionals used to success, and Tom Seaver handled them all expertly. Cincinnati's "Big Red Machine" backed him up with four runs, led by doubles by Pete Rose and Joe Morgan, along with a home run by first baseman Dan Driessen.

In addition to being the only no-hitter of Tom Seaver's extraordinary career, there was also something else that made this a one-of-a-kind game. It had the largest pitcher/catcher differential in career player value (as defined by JAWS) of any no-hitter since 1950. In other words, between Tom Seaver's career JAWS of 84.6 and catcher Don Werner's career JAWS of minus 2.3 was an enormous 86.9-point gap. To give an idea of how extreme this difference was, here are the Top 10 JAWS differentials in no-hit batteries since 1950. Tom Seaver and Don Werner have the highest differential by 5.4 points.

Table 14-3. Highest JAWS differential between no-hit pitcher and catcher

Rank	Date	Team	Pitcher	Career JAWS	Catcher	Career JAWS	Delta
1	6/16/1978	Cincinnati Reds	Tom Seaver	84.6	Don Werner	-2.3	86.9
2	6/2/1990	Seattle Mariners	Randy Johnson	81.3	Scott Bradley	-0.2	81.5
3	5/18/2004	Arizona D-backs	Randy Johnson	81.3	Robby Hammock	0.6	80.7
4	4/28/1961	Milwaukee Braves	Warren Spahn	75.8	Charlie Lau	2.5	73.3
5	8/5/1973	Atlanta Braves	Phil Niekro	75.1	Paul Casanova	2.8	72.3
6	9/28/1974	California Angels	Nolan Ryan	62.2	Tom Egan	-2.9	65.1
7	6/11/1990	Texas Rangers	Nolan Ryan	62.2	John Russell	-2.2	64.4
8	7/15/1973	California Angels	Nolan Ryan	62.2	Art Kusnyer	-1.9	64.1

FROM RANDY JOHNSON TO DALLAS BRADEN

Rank	Date	Team	Pitcher	Career JAWS	Catcher	Career JAWS	Delta
9	5/15/1973	California Angels	Nolan Ryan	62.2	Jeff Torborg	0.4	61.8
10	9/17/1968	SF Giants	Gaylord Perry	71.2	Dick Dietz	12.7	58.5

METHODOLOGY: The players in this table are ranked in order of the highest career JAWS differential calculated by subtracting the career JAWS of the catcher who caught the no-hitter from the career JAWS of the pitcher who threw the no-hitter. For example, Tom Seaver had a career JAWS of 84.6. His catcher, Don Werner, had a career JAWS of minus 2.3. Subtracting Werner's JAWS from Seaver's JAWS creates a "delta" of 86.9, landing the duo in the top position. This analysis only considers games from 1950 and later because the era before then includes dead-ball pitchers with career JAWS that eclipse modern hurlers. In other words, pitchers such as Walter Johnson (127 JAWS), Cy Young (120.8 JAWS), and Christy Mathewson (88.4) would dominate the rankings regardless of who was their catcher. This would skew the results and undermine the purpose of the analysis: to highlight the remarkable occasions where a highly accomplished pitcher combined with an inexperienced catcher (usually a backup) to throw a no-hitter.

LEGEND: Dates are shown as month/day/year (for example, June 12, 2018, is shown as 6/12/2018). JAWS = Jaffe Wins Above Replacement Score. JAWS is a sabermetric baseball statistic developed to evaluate the strength of a player's career and merit for induction into the Baseball Hall of Fame. It is created by averaging a player's career Wins Above Replacement (WAR) with their 7-year peak WAR (WAR-7). WAR measures a player's value in all facets of the game by deciphering how many more wins he's worth than a replacement-level player at his same position. ERA = Earned Run Average, or the number of earned runs allowed per nine innings pitched. Career JAWS represents the total score over a player's entire career.

The reason Werner was even in the game is that regular catcher (and Hall of Famer) Johnny Bench was injured. Backup catcher Werner was starting his 19th consecutive game in Bench's place. To put this into perspective, though, remember that only 10% of minor league players make it to the majors. Just because the catchers listed in Table 14-3 had low JAWS scores doesn't mean they were "bad." Every one of the catchers listed above with a score under 10 was a good defensive catcher. The one possible exception in the chart was #10 Dick Dietz. He was well-known as a good-hitting catcher. This is shown in his higher JAWS score due to his excellent hitting. Because he was such a good hitter, he even made the National League All-Star team in 1970. He also led the league in passed balls during the two seasons he was the Giants' starter, and baserunners had a lot of success stealing against him with an 80% safe rate.

Tom Seaver was born on November 17, 1944, in Fresno, California. Seaver played baseball at Fresno High School, graduating in 1962. He pitched two years at Fresno City College, then was recruited by Rod Dedeaux at the University of Southern California. Seaver went 10-2 at USC his junior year, then was drafted before his senior season started. He signed with the Braves in 1966 when the season was underway. Because of this violation of the rules, his contract was nullified, and the New York Mets obtained the right to sign Seaver. That decision had enormous consequences for both franchises.

Tom Seaver was a huge part of the Mets' success when he played with them from 1967-1977. During those 10+ seasons, the Mets went 830-844 (.495) and Seaver went 189-110 (.632). That differential alone indicates Seaver had a huge, positive impact on the Mets. To show this in a different way, the Mets averaged an 80-82 season while Seaver was on the team, while Seaver himself was averaging an 18-11 season. Subtracting Seaver's record from the Mets' team record, the Mets averaged a 62-71 record (.466) in games Seaver didn't pitch. There were six seasons during his time with the Mets when the team won between 82 and 86 games and were still able to stay in the division title hunt each year. Clearly, without Seaver, New York would have had no chance. No wonder one of his nicknames was "The Franchise."

All good things must come to an end, yet it can be argued that Seaver's tenure with the Mets ended way too soon. On June 15, 1977, he was traded to Cincinnati for five players. This trade followed one year of bitter contract negotiations between Seaver and the Mets. Seaver was also the Mets union representative during this time and the bad feelings this created may have been a factor in his being traded. It also begs the question why a player so talented as Seaver never got a coaching job after his playing career ended. Seaver did, however, work for years after his retirement as a broadcaster for the Mets and Yankees.

As an aside, Cincinnati is one of the few franchises that made a very significant improvement in both winning percentage and attendance after moving into a new stadium. From 1901-1969 the Reds had 33 seasons where they won 50% or more of their games, and 36 seasons where they won less than 50% of their games. During this time, they were also in four World Series. The team moved into Riverfront Stadium on June 30, 1970. For the next decade (1970-79) the Reds had nine seasons of playing .500 ball or better and were in four World Series, winning the championship in both 1975 and 1976.

The other part of the battery on the day of Seaver's no-hitter, Cincinnati catcher Don Werner, was born in March 1953, in Appleton, Wisconsin, where he also played high-school ball. He was drafted by Cincinnati in the fifth round of the 1971 draft and he played in the minor leagues from 1971-1975 before being called up by the Reds in 1975. He was Johnny Bench's relief from 1975-1978 and in 1980. Werner also played with Texas from 1981-82. In total, he spent seven seasons in the majors, encompassing a total of 118 games played. The most games Werner played in one season was in 1978 when he appeared in 50 games. Not coincidentally, this was during one of those rare times Bench was injured – and when he caught Seaver's no-hitter. After his playing career ended, Werner spent 30 years in the minor leagues as a coach (17 years) and a manager (13 years) for the Montreal, Pittsburgh, San Diego, and Baltimore organizations.

This day, of course, belonged to Tom Seaver. After numerous close calls, he finally had his no-hitter. This achievement put an exclamation point on Seaver's truly unique and impressive career, where he received more first-ballot votes for the Hall of Fame than any other player up to that point. Yet, like all no-hitters, he didn't do it by himself. A key player in this accomplishment was his catcher, Don Werner. I had the privilege of interviewing him recently. I encourage you to read the transcript below.

Don Werner Interview
Conducted by Kevin Hurd on April 26, 2021

Kevin Hurd (KH): Would you consider yourself to be the best player on your Little League, American Legion, high school, or minor league teams?
Don Werner (DW): For Little League, they had tryouts the first day, the coaches said "run out to the position you want to play." Well, I initially started running out to short stop, but I saw that the best player on the team was already there. I looked around and saw that nobody was at the catcher's position. That's how I became a catcher. (Laughs)

For American Legion ball, I was a 14-year-old playing against 18-year-olds. I was definitely not the best guy on the team at that point in time. I did get better the older I got. At Appleton East High School in Wisconsin, my school didn't have a baseball team until I was a senior. I was the best player on that team. We wound up going to the state tournament. In the minors (1971-1981), we had many players on these teams that went to the majors, including 21 of 25 players from Indianapolis in 1975. The Reds were very good at signing good players, and had a good scouting system, good coaches, and a good GM in Bob Howsam.

KH: Did you feel any different (good or bad) on the day of your pitcher's (Tom Seaver's) no-hitter?

DW: I felt great. That game was the 19th in a row I played. Johnny Bench was out with a back injury. At that stage I was the only full-time catcher available, but Ray Knight (usually a third baseman) could play catcher in an emergency.

KH: What pitches were working best for Tom Seaver that day?

DW: His sinker and slider. His fastball and rising fastball didn't start becoming effective until the fifth inning or so.

KH: What was the best defensive play or the closest you came to losing the no-hitter?

DW: There were several good plays. Joe Morgan made a good play in the fourth inning on a grounder by Keith Hernandez. In the seventh inning, Hernandez hit a line drive off Seaver's glove, and the ball bounced to Dave Concepcion who threw him out. If the ball hadn't been deflected, Concepcion still would have made the play. The best play was in the eighth inning when third baseman Ray Knight came down with a high chopper and narrowly threw out the runner at first. It was a tough play.

KH: Did Seaver shake off your catcher signs much during the game?

DW: No, Tom didn't shake me off much. We had worked together before. I called all the pitches. Tom would shake me off sometimes just to mess with the hitters.

KH: Do you have any memorabilia/souvenirs, such as a baseball, plaque, uniform, or something else, from the game in your house?

DW: Well, I still have my glove from the game. Tom Seaver also put together some pictures in one package that showed us shaking hands after the game. It's on my wall in the living room.

KH: How many pitches did Seaver throw that day? What are your thoughts about pitch-count limitations that exist today in MLB?

DW: I don't think we were officially tracking pitch counts in those days. Somebody, usually the pitching coach or a starter who just pitched the day before, would track all the pitches, but that information was rarely made public. As far as the pitch-count limitations, I see why the organization does this — they don't want injured arms — but sometimes it goes overboard, and it starts in the minors. There is a lot of weightlifting done now. I think it contributes to injuries.

KH: Did you stay in contact with Seaver?

DW: Well, Tom died last year. The last time I saw him was 4-5 years ago. Before then, the last time I saw him was in 1980, the last year I was with the Reds.

KH: Did the Reds give you a bonus for catching the no-hitter?

DW: No, although like I mentioned before, Tom did make that picture collage for me which I still have. The team did have a special night celebrating the no-hitter on our next home stand. It was mostly congratulating Tom, and some stuff regarding the outstanding defensive plays. Near the end, Johnny Bench went to the top step of the dugout and started humorously yelling, "Hey, what about the catcher?" (Laughs).

KH: During the game, when did you think *"Tom's got a real shot at a no-hitter?"*

DW: It was the sixth inning. I was in the dugout, looked at the scoreboard and thought, *"Wow, he hasn't given up a hit yet."*

KH: Were you able to get a follow-on job in baseball after your playing days were over? In the majors, minors, college, high school, or media?

DW: Yes, absolutely. I spent 17 years as a coach and 13 years as a manager in the minors. I worked for several great organizations (Montreal, Pittsburgh, San Diego, and Baltimore) and learned from numerous major league managers such as Felipe Alou, Bruce Bochy, Jim Leyland, and Buck Showalter.

KH: Which managing job did you like the most?

DW: From 1996-2000 at Idaho Falls. The way my schedule worked back then I was a roving catching instructor from spring training through early June. In early June I went up to manage at Idaho Falls through the end of August. I was able to bring my family with me, also.

KH: Which coaching or coordinating job did you like the most?

DW: They were all good – I enjoyed them all.

KH: Did you like coaching or managing more?

DW: I definitely liked coaching, but I'd have to say I liked managing more.

KH: When you were with the Reds and Rangers, which of the managers that you played for did you like playing for the most?

DW: They were all good to play for. I will say that I liked the way that Sparky Anderson, John McNamara, and Don Zimmer made everybody feel like they were part of the team. When I was a manager, I'd like to think I borrowed techniques and styles from all of them. Another thing I'd like to say is that the Reds had a great team atmosphere. Pete Rose would come up to me and ask me how things were going, I'd say that I needed to hit better, and he would say "Don't worry about it – we need you for your defense." There were no bad teammates on the Reds.

KH: I've got to ask this: Which pitchers were the hardest for you to hit?

DW: That would be Bert Blyleven (great curve) and John "The Count" Montefusco.

KH: Do you have any kids or grandkids who have pursued or will pursue baseball as a career? Did you encourage them to do so?

DW: My son Ryan coaches high-school baseball in Florida. My grandson plays catcher in Little League baseball and my granddaughter is a pitcher on her softball team.

KH: Was the no-hitter the highlight of your career?

DW: Yes, I would say so. I was with the Reds in 1975 and 1976 and got a partial World Series share both years, but I didn't play in either World Series.

Chapter 15

Mike Warren: David vs. Goliath

September 29, 1983
22-year-old rookie Mike Warren no-hits
the AL West Champion Chicago White Sox (99-63)

"That ball would have been out if it had been a day game. But the night air is heavy in Oakland. There's so much luck involved with something like this. So much of baseball is luck."
Mike Warren, commenting on White Sox pinch-hitter Mike Squires' two-out fly ball in the eighth inning that almost cost Warren his no-hitter (Steve Lowery, *Los Angeles Times*, August 20, 1988).

"Mike had an average fastball, but with great location. He had three different breaking balls: in-zone, out-of-zone to get hitters to chase bad pitches, and a change-up curve that disrupted their timing. For the change-up he would take a little off and got the hitters off-balance which would get them out front of the ball which led to fly outs."
Oakland catcher Mike Heath (Interview with the author, May 14, 2021).

"The kid had great composure. He was all around the plate and had them swinging at everything."
Plate umpire Marty Springstead (Joe Goddard, *Chicago Sun-Times*, September 30, 1983).

"Fisk was the toughest out. When he hit that fly (with two outs in the ninth), I knew I had it."

Mike Warren on getting Carlton Fisk to fly out to Rickey Henderson for the last out of the game (Joe Goddard, *Chicago Sun-Times*, September 30, 1983).

"I'm afraid this young man doesn't belong here."

Oakland Hall of Fame broadcaster Lon Simmons during Mike Warren's second consecutive disastrous relief appearance as he started his major-league career just months before. After that game, Warren was sent down to the minors and it looked like he might never be back up again (Steve Lowery, *Los Angeles Times*, August 20, 1988).

It was the top of the eighth inning. There were two outs on a cold, wet night at the Oakland Coliseum. 22-year-old rookie Mike Warren, in the ninth start of his young career, stood on the mound. He knew he only had four more outs to go, and he would have no-hit the powerful Chicago White Sox. The paltry 9,028 fans who showed up for the game that night realized they were watching something special. If only Warren could hold on for just awhile longer, the A's would have their first single-pitcher no-hitter since the mighty Vida Blue, another rookie, threw one almost exactly 13 years earlier in September 1970. Blue's game happened just before the mighty Oakland teams of the early 1970s won five straight division titles and three World Series championships.

By this point in the 1983 season, though, the two teams playing had long ago determined the fate of their efforts. This was a David vs. Goliath matchup if there ever was one. With just four games remaining in their season, the Chicago White Sox had clinched the American League West Division championship and were leading the second place Kansas City Royals by a full 19.0 games. Yet, the motivation to win was still paramount. Even though the Sox had wrapped up the division title weeks before, they still started their star-studded lineup that day against the Athletics.

Chicago was in a race with the Baltimore Orioles, who had just edged the Detroit Tigers for the AL East Division championship. Both Chicago and Baltimore started the day at 96 wins and the all-important home-field advantage in the American League Championship Series was at stake in this pre-wild card, two-division era. Eventually, Chicago would win this race for home field with 99 wins to Baltimore's

98. Yet the White Sox would lose the ALCS to Baltimore three games to one when the Orioles' pitching staff held the Sox to only three runs for the entire series.

Meanwhile, Oakland was suffering through another losing season, and their fans knew it. Despite having young stars like future Hall of Famer Rickey Henderson and Carney Lansford in their lineup, the Athletics had won only 73 games by this point in the year and had long since been eliminated from postseason contention. While this was a slight improvement over 1982's miserable 68-win campaign, things weren't looking good for the franchise. The excellent 1981 team that had made it to the playoffs was long since dismantled. With only four games left in the season, Oakland was just playing out the string in 1983.

Looking at the Chicago pinch-hitter in the top of the eighth, the light-hitting Mike Squires, Warren knew he was facing the bottom of the White Sox lineup again. He had already gone through the meat of the Chicago order three times by this point. Chicago's best hitters on a great team – leadoff hitter Rudy Law; future Hall of Famers Carlton Fisk and Harold Baines; and sluggers Greg Luzinski, Tom Paciorek, and Ron Kittle – had all been hitless against him. Of that group, Paciorek was the only one who had even reached base, on a walk issued in the fifth inning. Warren had even gathered four strikeouts against them by the end of the eighth. At this point in the game, Oakland also had a comfortable 3-0 lead, scoring three runs in the first three innings on a Davey Lopes double and a two-run Jeff Burroughs home run. Oakland manager Steve Boros even brought in Mike Davis – an exceptional fielder – to patrol right field. Warren just had to finish what he started.

As he served up his offering to Squires, Warren may have caught a little too much of the plate. Squires, with one home run to his name in 153 at bats in 1983, clobbered the ball. Warren turned toward right field and saw Mike Davis turn his back to the infield and start running back as if the ball might be going over his head. Worse, it might even be a home run. Shortly after he started back, Davis stopped on the warning track and turned around again. He reached up and caught the ball, safely within the confines of the playing field. Warren knew if that ball had been hit during the daytime, it would have sailed out of the park. Because of the heavy night air, the ball died and simply became another out in a very well-pitched game.

Squires' fly ball was the closest a Chicago batter came to getting a hit all night. Mike Warren, who had been unceremoniously sent back down to the minors after a disastrous brief call-up just three months earlier, pitched a masterful game against baseball's best team. While Warren had just five strikeouts during the game, he was an expert at pitching around the corners of the strike zone, getting the White Sox hitters to hit five groundouts, pop out three times, and fly out an amazing 13 times. Chicago shortstop Scott Fletcher was also thrown out attempting to steal second base by Oakland catcher Mike Heath in the third inning.

There are several things that make this no-hitter stand out among all the others. First, it was one of the biggest "David vs. Goliath" no-hit games in history, meaning a no-hitter thrown by a relatively unaccomplished pitcher (based on career statistics) against an extraordinarily good team. In the ratings I've used throughout this book, Mike Warren is a Level 5 pitcher, meaning he was among the least accomplished hurlers to ever throw a no-hitter. Specifically, he was a career 9-13 pitcher, with a 5.06 ERA and a Wins Above Replacement (WAR) value of minus 0.9. After his no-hitter for Oakland, Warren struggled to a 4-10 record with the A's, as he only threw a total of 139 innings over the next two years. His last major league game was in 1985.

The Chicago White Sox, on the other hand, were a juggernaut in 1983. With 99 wins, they had the best record in baseball – one game better than the eventual AL champion Baltimore Orioles, and a full eight games better than the best the National League had to offer, the 91-win Los Angeles Dodgers. As mentioned previously, the Chicago lineup was stocked with great hitters in the prime of their careers, and the White Sox were motivated to win. They had their best players in the lineup that day.

To demonstrate this disparity in team performance between Oakland and Chicago, here are the biggest "deltas" between a no-hit pitcher's team and the team that was no-hit. Warren's performance ranks tied at #17, with a delta of -25.0, meaning the Athletics were 25 games worse than the White Sox over the course of the season. While all the pitchers in this table led underperforming teams to no-hit victory against some of the best the league had to offer, only five of the pitchers were considered Level 5 pitchers: Ernie Koob, Henderson Alvarez III, Dick Fowler, Mike Warren, and Dave Morehead. This places them squarely among the least accomplished pitchers to ever throw a no-hitter. Mike Warren's no-hitter, however, can be argued to be the least likely no-hitter ever thrown when the career accomplishments of the no-hit pitcher are combined with the strength of the opposing team.

Table 15-1. Largest Negative Team Record Disparity in a No-Hitter

Rank	Date Score	No-Hit Pitcher	Team	Record (Level)	Opponent	Record (Level)	Delta
1 (tie)	8/25/1952	Virgil Trucks	Detroit Tigers	50-104 (5)	NY Yankees	95-59 (1)	-45.0
1 (tie)	5/18/2004	Randy Johnson	Arizona D-backs	51-111 (5)	Atlanta Braves	96-66 (2)	-45.0
3 (tie)	5/5/1917	Ernie Koob	St. Louis Browns	57-97 (5)	Chicago W. Sox	100-54 (1)	-43.0
3 (tie)	5/6/1917	Bob Groom	St. Louis Browns	57-97 (5)	Chicago W. Sox	100-54 (1)	-43.0
5	8/26/1916	Bullet Joe Bush	Phi Athletics	36-117 (5)	Cle Indians	77-77 (3)	-40.5
6	5/5/2021	John Means	Bal Orioles	52-110 (5)	Seattle Mariners	90-72 (2)	-38.0
7	7/30/1973	Jim Bibby	Texas Rangers	57-105 (5)	Oakland Athletics	94-68 (2)	-37.0
8	6/24/2021	Zach Davies +3	Chicago Cubs	71-91 (5)	LA Dodgers	106-56 (1)	-35.0
9	7/25/2015	Cole Hamels	Phi Phillies	63-99 (5)	Chicago Cubs	97-65 (2)	-34.0
10 (tie)	6/25/2010	Edwin Jackson	Arizona D-backs	65-97 (5)	TB Rays	96-66 (2)	-31.0
10 (tie)	9/29/2013	Henderson Alvarez III	Miami Marlins	62-100 (5)	Detroit Tigers	93-69 (1)	-31.0
12	9/9/1945	Dick Fowler	Phi Athletics	52-98 (5)	St. Louis Browns	81-70 (3)	-28.5
13	5/15/1952	Virgil Trucks	Detroit Tigers	50-104 (5)	Was Senators	78-76 (3)	-28.0
14	8/14/2021	Tyler Gilbert	Arizona D-backs	52-110 (5)	Seattle Mariners	79-83 (3)	-27.0
15 (tie)	5/15/1960	Don Cardwell	Chicago Cubs	60-94 (5)	St. Louis Cardinals	86-68 (2)	-26.0
15 (tie)	4/23/1964	Ken Johnson	Houston Colt .45s	66-96 (5)	Cin Reds	92-70 (2)	-26.0

Rank	Date Score	No-Hit Pitcher	Team	Record (Level)	Oppo-nent	Record (Level)	Delta
17 (tie)	9/16/1965	Dave Morehead	Boston Red Sox	62-100 (5)	Cle Indians	87-75 (3)	-25.0
17 (tie)	9/29/1983	Mike Warren	Oakland Athletics	74-88 (4)	Chicago W. Sox	99-63 (1)	-25.0

METHODOLOGY: This table lists no-hitters with the greatest negative record differential from 1900-2021. Teams are ranked in ascending order based upon the largest differential between win-loss records. This is calculated by taking the opposing team's (team that was no-hit) end-of-season record and subtracting it from the no-hit pitcher's team record. For example, the 1952 Detroit Tigers and 2004 Arizona Diamondbacks both finished 45 games behind the teams they no-hit, representing the greatest negative differential between two teams involved in a no-hitter. Therefore, they are tied for the number one ranking.

LEGEND: Dates are shown as month/day/year (for example, June 12, 2018, is shown as 6/12/2018). Delta = the difference in end-of-season records between the two teams. In other words, how many games did the no-hitter team finish at the season's end behind the team that was no-hit. All pitchers on this list are Category 5 pitchers – the lowest category of career accomplishment among pitchers who threw a no-hitter. For display purposes, I also categorized both the pitcher's team and the opposing team in terms of level of accomplishment over the course of that season: this is displayed as (Level) in the table.

Level 1: 60% or higher winning percentage
Level 2: 55-60% winning percentage
Level 3: 50-55% winning percentage
Level 4: 45-50% winning percentage
Level 5: Less than 45% winning percentage

NOTE 1: Warren's performance is even more amazing given that the team he faced down is clearly one of the best among the teams on this list. Ernie Koob's no-hitter in 1917, given the enormous 43-game disparity between his lowly seventh place St. Louis Browns and Shoeless Joe Jackson's dominating, 100-win World

Champion Chicago White Sox, is arguably the most extraordinary underdog no-hit win of all time. Yet, there's a legitimate question about whether Koob belongs as a Level 5 pitcher. Specifically, he pitched for the Browns in 1915 and 1917, with a stint in 1919 after Koob had served his country in the Army Air Service in 1918 during World War I.

NOTE 2: While Koob's time as a Brown warranted a Level 5 placement based on the statistics he had accumulated in the major leagues, he was still a young man with significant potential at age 26 when he was sold to the Louisville Colonels of the American Association in 1920. Even though the Colonels were considered a minor league team, the teams in the American Association were independent entities with no formal relationships with major league teams. In other words, if an American Association team wanted to hold onto a player because he brought in fans and won games, they had every incentive to do so. The result was that Koob pitched for Louisville for nine more years from 1920-28, winning 112 games for the Colonels – he even threw another no-hitter one month after he arrived in Louisville. Because of his successful stint with the Colonels, it can easily be argued that Koob would likely have been an average or better pitcher except for extenuating circumstances that prevented him from realizing his potential as a major league player.

NOTE 3: Henderson Alvarez III – with the second biggest delta for a Level 5 pitcher – had the advantage of pitching for an awful team (the 62-100 Miami Marlins) against a division champion (the 93-69 Detroit Tigers) on the last day of the season. The Tigers had clinched several days before and were resting their players in preparation for the upcoming American League Division Series against the Oakland Athletics. Understandably, the Detroit lineup was full of backup players. Even the few stars who started the game, like Prince Fielder and Omar Infante, were quickly replaced as the contest continued on. Miami won by breaking a 0-0 tie in the bottom of the ninth when Giancarlo Stanton scored from third on a wild pitch. The bottom line is that while Alvarez threw a legitimate no-hit game, it wasn't that much of a David vs. Goliath contest because the Tiger lineup was not nearly as formidable as what they had fielded en route to their 93-win, division championship season.

NOTE 4: In September 1945, Canadian serviceman Dick Fowler was released from military service shortly after the Japanese surrendered at the end of World War II. After playing for the Philadelphia Athletics during the 1941 and 1942 seasons, Fowler rejoined the team for the last month of the 1945 season. In his first start after returning, he stunned the baseball world by leading a terrible, last-place-by-a-mile Philadelphia team to victory over a very flawed St. Louis squad.

NOTE 5: The 81-win, third place Browns had a great pitching staff, leading the eight-team American League in the least number of runs allowed per game. Yet, their hitting fell far short of league average – they were second-to-the-last in batting average and OPS. The only team worse than them was, of course, the Philadelphia Athletics. While it's true that St. Louis had a markedly better record than Philadelphia, besides eight-time All-Star shortstop Vern Stephens, the Browns' hitting was closer to the league-worst Athletics than anyone else. As a result, while Fowler's performance was outstanding, it was not a Goliath-beating effort.

NOTE 6: By September 16, 1965, the day 21-year-old Dave Morehead threw a no-hitter against Cleveland, the fifth-place Indians had already been eliminated from the American League pennant race. The Red Sox had been out of the race for much longer, finishing the season with 100 losses. In ninth place, Boston ended up just ahead of the hapless Kansas City Athletics. That day, though, Cleveland fielded a competitive lineup, with Leon Wagner, Rocky Colavito, Fred Whitfield, and Chuck Hinton in the starting nine. As a result, Dave Morehead had his work cut out for him and he certainly deserved the accolades he earned that day.

Even though the difference in won-loss records between both Dave Morehead's and Mike Warren's teams and their opponents was the same at 25.0 games, I believe Warren's win was more of an underdog victory simply because the 1983 Chicago White Sox were a much better team than the 1965 Cleveland Indians. Also, the White Sox that year had a lot more to play for (home field advantage in the playoffs) than the Indians in 1965, who had already been eliminated from title competition.

Further, I would say that Warren's no-hitter was more of a David vs. Goliath performance than any of the others in the table above because he easily had the lowest career WAR (minus 0.9) compared to the other 17 pitchers listed. Warren's WAR is actually the fourth lowest score of all pitchers who have ever thrown a no-hitter.

Of course, this begs the question of what is the largest positive disparity between two teams in a no-hitter. In other words, what is the highest "Goliath vs. David" delta? Here are the top scores since 1900, and Sandy Koufax's 1962 no-hitter against the Mets stands head and shoulders above all comers.

Table 15-2. Largest Positive Team Record Disparity in a No-Hitter

Rank	Date Score	No-Hit Pitcher	Team	Record (Level)	Opponent	Record (Level)	Delta
1	6/30/1962 LA 5-0	Sandy Koufax	LA Dodgers	102-63 (1)	NY Mets	40-120 (5)	+59.5
2	5/17/1998 NY 4-0	David Wells	NY Yankees	114-48 (1)	Min Twins	70-92 (5)	+44.0
3	4/14/1917 Chi 11-0	Eddie Cicotte	Chicago White Sox	100-54 (1)	St. Louis Browns	57-97 (5)	+43.0
4 (tie)	7/22/1905 (1) Phi 6-0	Weldon Henley	Phi Athletics	92-56 (1)	St. Louis Browns	54-99 (5)	+40.5
4 (tie)	5/11/1919 Cin 6-0	Hod Eller	Cin Reds	96-44 (1)	St. Louis Cardinals	54-83 (5)	+40.5
6 (tie)	6/1/1937 Chi 8-0	Bill Dietrich	Chicago White Sox	86-68 (2)	St. Louis Browns	46-108 (5)	+40.0
6 (tie)	9/1/2019 Hou 2-0	Justin Verlander	Houston Astros	107-55 (1)	Toronto Blue Jays	67-95 (5)	+40.0
8 (tie)	6/21/1964 (1) Phi 6-0	Jim Bunning	Phi Phillies	92-70 (2)	NY Mets	53-109 (5)	+39.0
8 (tie)	6/13/2012 SF 10-0	Matt Cain	SF Giants	94-68 (2)	Houston Astros	55-107 (5)	+39.0
8 (tie)	8/3/2019 Hou 9-0	Aaron Sanchez+	Houston Astros	107-55 (1)	Seattle Mariners	68-94 (5)	+39.0

METHODOLOGY: This table lists no-hitters with the greatest positive record differential from 1900-2021. Teams are ranked in descending order based upon the largest differential between win-loss records. This is calculated by taking the opposing team's (team that was no-hit) end-of-season record and subtracting it from the no-hit pitcher's team record. For example, the 1962 Los Angeles Dodgers were 59.5 games ahead of the New York Mets that season, representing the greatest positive differential between two teams involved in a no-hitter. Therefore, they are ranked number one.

LEGEND: Dates are shown as month/day/year (for example, June 12, 2018, is shown as 6/12/2018). Delta = the difference in end-of-season record between the two teams. In other words, how many games did the no-hitter team finish at the season's end behind the team that was no-hit. For display purposes, I categorized both the pitcher's team and the opposing team in terms of level of accomplishment over the course of that season: this is displayed as (Level) in the table.

Level 1: 60% or higher winning percentage
Level 2: 55-60% winning percentage
Level 3: 50-55% winning percentage
Level 4: 45-50% winning percentage
Level 5: Less than 45% winning percentage

The perfect games (thrown by David Wells, Jim Bunning, and Matt Cain) are shown in italics.

NOTE 1: Sandy Koufax's first no-hitter in 1962 against the hapless, first-year expansion Mets might qualify as the least-surprising no-hitter of all time. Future Hall of Famer Koufax paced the National League with a 2.54 ERA as he and Cy Young Award winner Don Drysdale led the Dodgers to a 102-win regular season, only succumbing to the pennant winning Giants after dropping two games in a three-game playoff at the end of the season. Facing the mighty Dodgers that day was the 40-120 (.250 winning percentage) Mets team. The 1962 Mets still have the worst record of any team since the 1935 Braves, as Boston finished last place in the National League that season at 38-115 (.248 winning percentage). The next closest end-of-season gap between two teams involved in a no-hitter is 44 games, achieved by a powerful World Champion Yankees team over the Twins in 1998. The gap between those teams was a full 15.5 games behind the 1962 Dodgers/Mets no-hitter. With a Game Score of 95, Koufax threw a great game versus the Mets, but it was not his best ever. He achieved a Game Score of 101 in his fourth no-hitter, a 14-strikeout perfect game against the Chicago Cubs in 1965.

NOTE 2: David Wells' 1998 perfect game was part of a streak of 38 consecutive batters he retired. This was a new American League record that stood until 2007. Wells claims to have been hung over.

NOTE 3: Justin Verlander's 2019 no-hitter was the thirteenth no-hitter in Astros history. He retired the last twenty-six batters in a row after a first inning walk. By no-hitting Toronto, Verlander became the third pitcher after Addie Joss and Tim Lincecum to no-hit the same opponent twice – he no-hit the Blue Jays in 2011, too — and the first to do so on the road. He also became the sixth pitcher in MLB history to throw three career no-hitters. The Astros scored the only runs of the game on Abraham Toro's two-run home run with two outs in the top of the ninth inning.

NOTE 4: Aaron Sanchez (6.0 innings pitched), Will Harris (1.0 IP), Joe Biagini (1.0 IP), and Chris Devenski (1.0 IP) together threw the twelfth no-hitter and the second combined no-hitter in Astros history. It was the first start by Sanchez since being acquired from the Toronto Blue Jays along with Biagini. Sanchez came into the game without a win in his last 17 starts and with a 6.07 ERA, worst among all starting pitchers. The Mariners are the first team to have two combined no-hitters against them in one season.

At the end of the day, determining the most surprising no-hitter was no contest. Mike Warren was the least likely no-hit pitcher when we take into consideration his career performance and the strength of his no-hit opponent as compared to the capability of his team. The strength of the Chicago White Sox that year is demonstrated by the fact that it was one of the ten best teams ever to be no-hit, as shown in Table 15-3:

Table 15-3. Best teams to be no-hit

Rank	Pitcher	Team	Date Score	Opponent	W-L Record	Win Pct
1	Sean Manaea	Oakland Athletics	4/21/2018 Oak 3-0	Boston Red Sox	108-54	.667
2	Tex Carleton	Brooklyn Dodgers	4/30/1940 Bro 3-0	Cincinnati Reds	100-53	.654
3 (Tie)	Ernie Koob	St. Louis Browns	5/5/1917 StL 1-0	Chicago White Sox	100-54	.649
3 (Tie)	Bob Groom	St. Louis Browns	5/6/1917 (2) StL 3-0	Chicago White Sox	100-54	.649
5	Nolan Ryan	Texas Rangers	6/11/1990 Tex 5-0	Oakland Athletics	103-59	.636
6	Kevin Millwood	Philadelphia Phillies	4/27/2003 Phi 1-0	San Francisco Giants	100-61	.621
7 (Tie)	Bob Moose	Pittsburgh Pirates	9/20/1969 Pit 4-0	New York Mets	100-62	.617
7 (Tie)	Jose Jimenez	St. Louis Cardinals	6/25/1999 StL 1-0	Arizona Diamondbacks	100-62	.617
9	Virgil Trucks	Detroit Tigers	8/25/1952 Det 1-0	New York Yankees	95-59	.617
10	Mike Warren	Oakland Athletics	9/29/1983 Oak 3-0	Chicago White Sox	99-63	.611

METHODOLOGY: This table lists the best teams to be no-hit and covers the period 1900-2021. No-hit games are ranked in descending order based upon the end-of-season winning percentage of the team that was no-hit. For example, the 2018 Boston Red Sox have the highest winning percentage of any team that was ever no-hit and, therefore, are ranked number one.

LEGEND: Dates are shown as month/day/year (for example, June 12, 2018, is shown as 6/12/2018). Won-Loss Record is the end-of-season record for the team that was no-hit. Winning Percentage is the end-of-season winning percentage of the team that was no-hit taken out to the third digit (for example, a winning percentage of 66.7% = .667). (1) or (2) = first or second game of a doubleheader.

NOTE 1: The 1999 Diamondbacks and 1969 Mets had a slightly better winning percentage (.6173) than the 1952 Yankees (.6169) when taken to the fourth decimal point.

NOTE 2: The 1917 St Louis Browns no-hit the Chicago White Sox on consecutive days – the only time that has ever happened. It was not in consecutive games, though, as Bob Groom threw his no-hitter in the second game of a doubleheader. Groom had thrown two innings of hitless relief in the first game that day.

The Athletics have an extraordinary record of excellent pitchers, including Hall of Famers Eddie Plank, Lefty Grove, Chief Bender, Catfish Hunter, and Rube Waddell. They also have had outstanding modern era pitchers like Vida Blue, Barry Zito, Mark Mulder, Tim Hudson, Dave Stewart, and others. The highest Game Scores ever achieved by an Athletics pitcher are listed below.

Table 15-4. Athletics Highest Game Scores

Rank	Pitcher (Team Home)	Date Score	Opponent	GSc	IP, Hits, Runs, ERs, Walks, Strikeouts
1	Jack Coombs (Philadelphia)	9/1/1906 Phi 4-1 (24 inn)	Boston Americans	140-142	24.0 IP, 15 Hits, 1 Run, ? ERs, 6 BBs, 18 Ks
2	Jack Coombs (Philadelphia)	8/4/1910 0-0 Tie (16 inn)	Chicago White Sox	128	16.0 IP, 3 Hits, 0 Runs, 0 ERs, 6 BBs, 18 Ks
3	Rube Waddell (Philadelphia)	7/9/1902 Phi 4-2 (17 inn)	Boston Americans	112	17.0 IP, 11 Hits, 2 Runs, 2 ERs, 1 BB, 16 Ks
4	Rube Waddell (Philadelphia)	6/12/1903 Phi 2-1 (14 inn)	Cleveland Naps	110	14.0 IP, 6 Hits, 1 Run, 0 ERs, 2 BBs, 14 Ks
5	Eddie Plank (Philadelphia)	5/14/1914 Phi 1-0 (13 inn)	Cleveland Naps	105	13.0 IP, 5 Hits, 0 Runs, 0 ERs, 1 BB, 9 Ks

Rank	Pitcher (Team Home)	Date Score	Opponent	GSc	IP, Hits, Runs, ERs, Walks, Strikeouts
6 (tie)	Rube Waddell (Philadelphia)	4/21/1904 Phi 3-2 (12 inn)	New York Highlanders	103	12.0 IP, 4 Hits, 2 Runs, 0 ERs, 3 BBs, 16 Ks
6 (tie)	Rube Waddell (Philadelphia)	8/11/1904 Phi 2-1 (13 inn)	Cleveland Naps	103	13.0 IP, 5 Hits, 1 Run, 1 ER, 4 BBs, 14 Ks
8 (tie)	Rube Waddell (Philadelphia)	8/11/1902 Phi 1-0 (13 inn)	Detroit Tigers	101	13.0 IP, 4 Hits, 0 Runs, 0 ERs, 5 BBs, 7 Ks
8 (tie)	Dick Fowler (Philadelphia)	6/5/1942 StL 1-0 (16 inn)	St. Louis Browns	101	16.0 IP, 9 Hits, 1 Run, 1 ER, 5 BBs, 6 Ks
10 (tie)	Rube Waddell (Philadelphia)	9/9/1907 0-0 Tie (13 inn)	Boston Americans	100	13.0 IP, 6 Hits, 0 Runs, 0 ERs, 0 BBs, 5 Ks
10 (tie)	Jack Coombs (Philadelphia)	5/16/1909 Phi 1-0 (13 inn)	Chicago White Sox	100	13.0 IP, 5 Hits, 0 Runs, 0 ERs, 2 BBs, 5 Ks
10 (tie)	Jesse Flores (Philadelphia)	4/27/1943 Phi 2-1 (16 inn)	Washington Senators	100	15.2 IP, 6 Hits, 1 Run, 1 ER, 6 BBs, 3 Ks
10 (tie)	Vida Blue (Oakland)	7/9/1971 Oak 1-0 (20 inn)	California Angels	100	11.0 IP, 7 Hits, 0 Runs, 0 ERs, 0 BBs, 17 Ks

METHODOLOGY: This table includes the highest Game Scores thrown by an Athletics pitcher from 1901-2021. Games are ranked by Game Score (GSc) and consider all franchise regular season and postseason games. Table 15-5 below limits the eligible games to those pitching performances that were 10 innings or less. Game Score (GSc) measures a pitcher's performance in any given game started. Introduced by baseball writer/statistician Bill James in the 1980s, Game Score is presented as a figure between 0-100 — except for extreme outliers — and usually falls between 40-70.

LEGEND: Dates are shown as month/day/year (for example, June 12, 2018, is shown as 6/12/2018). The Athletics (frequently known just as the "A's") have played in three different cities since the team's entrance into the American League in 1901. From 1901-1954 the Athletics played in Philadelphia. They moved to Kansas City in 1955 and stayed there through the 1967 season. In 1968, the Athletics went further west and became the Oakland Athletics, where they remain to this day (2021). "Team Home" indicates where the team was located during the season the particular game was thrown. IP = innings pitched. One-third of an inning pitched has 0.1 added and two-thirds of an inning pitched has 0.2 added (for example, 9 1/3 innings pitched is displayed as 9.1). BB(s) = base(s) on balls; K(s) = strikeout(s); ER(s) = earned run(s); inn = innings (associated with the length of extra-inning games); and (1) or (2) = first or second game of a doubleheader.

NOTE 1: While not included in the table above, the highest postseason Game Score ever achieved by an Athletic pitcher was a score of 93 by Ken Holtzman in Game 3 of the 1973 ALCS against Baltimore. Holtzman threw eleven innings of one-run ball, allowing only three hits and one walk while striking out seven in a 2-1, 11-inning win over the Orioles. This game put Oakland ahead two games to one, and they eventually won the ALCS in five games. They later took the seven-game World Series against the Mets to become World Champions.

NOTE 2: There are no games from the Kansas City era (1955-1967) included in this table. Losers of 100+ games four out of the 13 seasons they were in Missouri, the team never had a winning record during the years they called Kansas City home. Their best season was a 73-81 effort in 1958, good enough for seventh place in the eight-team American League. The highest Kansas City Game Score was a 97 achieved by 22-year-old (future Yankee) Ralph Terry on June 5, 1958, in a 13-inning shutout against the last-place Washington Senators. Terry gave up seven hits and three walks in the 2-0 victory.

NOTE 3: The official highest Game Score for an Athletics pitcher is 128, achieved by Jack Coombs for 16 innings of shutout ball in a 16-inning 0-0 tie against the Chicago White Sox in 1910. Unofficially, he achieved a higher Game Score in a 24-inning complete game against the Boston Americans in 1906. Facing a total of 89 batters, 23-year-old rookie Coombs held Boston to one run while striking out 18 hitters, walking six, and allowing 15 hits in what was originally scheduled to be the first game of a doubleheader, but almost ended up being stopped on account of darkness at the end of the 23rd inning. The four-hour-and-47-minute game was a 1-1 tie until the top of the 24th, when Philadelphia strung together two singles and two triples to go ahead 4-1. Coombs retired the Boston hitters in the bottom of the 24th to complete the win.

The Athletics committed two errors during this game at a time there was no differentiation between earned runs and unearned runs. Because of that, it's not clear whether two points should be subtracted from Coombs's Game Score for an unearned run or four points for an earned run allowed. That said, because Coombs allowed just one run, his Game Score can only be either 142 (for an unearned run allowed) or 140 (for an earned run allowed), which would give him the team's highest score in either case. In reviewing the game write-up, it appears the run was earned as a result of a triple and a single. With a Game Score of 140, Coombs would have achieved a tie with Brooklyn's Leon Cadore for the second-highest score in baseball history.

Coombs's 18 strikeouts in this game, along with the 18 he struck out in his 1910, 16-inning shutout in 1910 against the White Sox (Game Score 128) give him the record for the most strikeouts for an Athletics pitcher in a single game. Coombs's 16-inning effort is the highest number of innings in a complete game shutout in Athletics history. Coombs was a huge star for the Athletics in 1910, pitching 353 innings and throwing 13 shutouts en route to 31 wins and World Series championships in 1910 and 1911. His 31 wins in a season set a post-1900 Athletics' record tied by Hall of Famer Lefty Grove in 1931.

NOTE 4: Hall of Famer Rube Waddell features prominently on this list, capturing six of the top 13 Game Scores in team history, twice as many as Jack Coombs (with three), the only other pitcher listed more than once. A dominant pitcher in his prime, Waddell registered five of those scores in just three seasons from 1902-1904, while he led the American League in strikeouts each of those years. He also led the majors five years straight from 1903-1907 as well.

NOTE 5: Vida Blue's 11-inning, 17-strikeout performance against the California Angels is remarkable for a number of reasons. His 100 Game Score is the highest of any Athletics pitcher after the team left Philadelphia following the 1954 season. Blue's 17 strikeouts are also the most of any Athletics pitcher after the post-Philadelphia period. Further, he was the starting pitcher for what turned out to be the longest shutout in team history – a score that was surpassed only by the Astros (24 innings against the Mets in 1968), the Dodgers (22 innings against the Expos in 1989), the Pirates (21 innings against the Braves in 1918), and the Giants (21 innings against the Reds in 1967). During Blue's game, he left after 11 innings and was relieved by Hall of Famer Rollie Fingers, who allowed just two hits over seven innings. The final two innings were hurled by Bob Locker and Darold Knowles. Oakland won in the bottom of the 20th when Angel Mangual knocked a two-out single that drove home Curt Blefary, who had reached base when he was hit by a pitch leading off the inning.

Of course, all the games listed above are extra-inning affairs. To make a more conventional comparison of the best-pitched games, here's a list of the highest Game Scores of 10 innings or less thrown by an Athletics pitcher:

Table 15-5. Athletics Highest Game Scores of 10 innings or less

Rank	Pitcher (Team Home)	Date Score	Opponent	GSc	IP, Hits, Runs, ERs, Walks, Strikeouts
1	Bobby Witt (Oakland)	6/23/1994 Oak 4-0	Kansas City Royals	99	9.0 IP, 1 Hit, 0 Runs, 0 ERs, 0 BBs, 14 Ks
2	Catfish Hunter (Oakland)	5/8/1968 Oak 4-0	Minnesota Twins	98	9.0 IP, 0 Hits, 0 Runs, 0 ERs, 0 BBs, 11 Ks
3 (tie)	Rube Waddell (Philadelphia)	7/1/1902 Phi 2-0	Baltimore Orioles	96	9.0 IP, 2 Hits, 0 Runs, 0 ERs, 0 BBs, 13 Ks
3 (tie)	Dave Stewart (Oakland)	6/29/1990 Oak 5-0	Toronto Blue Jays	96	9.0 IP, 0 Hits, 0 Runs, 0 ERs, 3 BBs, 12 Ks
5 (tie)	Vida Blue (Oakland)	9/21/1970 Oak 6-0	Minnesota Twins	95	9.0 IP, 0 Hits, 0 Runs, 0 ERs, 1 BB, 9 Ks
5 (tie)	Sean Manaea (Oakland)	4/21/2018 Oak 3-0	Boston Red Sox	95	9.0 IP, 0 Hits, 0 Runs, 0 ERs, 2 BBs, 10 Ks
7 (tie)	Rube Waddell (Philadelphia)	8/22/1907 Phi 2-0	Chicago White Sox	94	9.0 IP, 3 Hits, 0 Runs, 0 ERs, 0 BBs, 13 Ks
7 (tie)	Mark Mulder (Oakland)	7/6/2001 Oak 3-0	Arizona D-backs	94	9.0 IP, 1 Hit, 0 Runs, 0 ERs, 0 BBs, 9 Ks
9 (tie)	Bullet Joe Bush (Philadelphia)	8/26/1916 Phi 5-0	Cleveland Indians	93	9.0 IP, 0 Hits, 0 Runs, 0 ERs, 1 BB, 7 Ks
9 (tie)	Lefty Grove (Philadelphia)	5/19/1928 Phi 2-0	Chicago White Sox	93	9.0 IP, 2 Hits, 0 Runs, 0 ERs, 1 BB, 11 Ks
9 (tie)	Dallas Braden (Oakland)	5/9/2010 Oak 4-0	Tampa Bay Rays	93	9.0 IP, 0 Hits, 0 Runs, 0 ERs, 0 BBs, 6 Ks
21 (tie)	Mike Fiers (Oakland)	5/7/2019 Oak 2-0	Cincinnati Reds	91	9.0 IP, 0 Hits, 0 Runs, 0 ERs, 2 BBs, 6 Ks
32 (tie)	Charles Bender (Philadelphia)	5/12/1910 Phi 4-0	Cleveland Naps	90	9.0 IP, 0 Hits, 0 Runs, 0 ERs, 1 BB, 4 Ks
46 (tie)	Dick Fowler (Philadelphia)	9/9/1945 (2) Phi 1-0	St. Louis Browns	89	9.0 IP, 0 Hits, 0 Runs, 0 ERs, 4 BBs, 6 Ks

Rank	Pitcher (Team Home)	Date Score	Opponent	GSc	IP, Hits, Runs, ERs, Walks, Strikeouts
46 (tie)	Bill McCahan (Philadelphia)	9/3/1947 Phi 3-0	Washington Senators	89	9.0 IP, 0 Hits, 0 Runs, 0 ERs, 0 BBs, 2 Ks
46 (tie)	Mike Warren (Oakland)	9/29/1983 Oak 3-0	Chicago White Sox	89	9.0 IP, 0 Hits, 0 Runs, 0 ERs, 3 BBs, 5 Ks
132 (tie)	Weldon Henley (Philadelphia)	7/22/1905 (1) Phi 6-0	St. Louis Browns	86	9.0 IP, 0 Hits, 0 Runs, 0 ERs, 3 BBs, 2 Ks
1142 (tie)	Rube Waddell (Philadelphia)	8/15/1905 Phi 2-0 (5 inn)	St. Louis Browns	76	5.0 IP, 0 Hits, 0 Runs, 0 ERs, 0 BBs, 9 Ks
---	*Rube Vickers (Philadelphia)*	*10/5/1907 (2) Phi 4-0 (5 inn)*	*Washington Nationals*	70	*5.0 IP, 0 Hits, 0 Runs, 0 ERs, 0 BBs, 9 Ks*
---	Vida Blue +3 (Oakland)	9/28/1975 Oak 5-0	California Angels	67	5.0 IP, 0 Hits, 0 Runs, 0 ERs, 2 BBs, 2 Ks

METHODOLOGY: This table includes the highest Game Scores of 10 innings or less thrown by an Athletics pitcher from 1901-2021. Games are ranked by Game Score (GSc) and consider all franchise regular season and postseason games. For comparison purposes, all thirteen no-hitters are included in this table. Game Score (GSc) measures a pitcher's performance in any given game started. Introduced by baseball writer/statistician Bill James in the 1980s, Game Score is presented as a figure between 0-100 — except for extreme outliers — and usually falls between 40-70.

LEGEND: Dates are shown as month/day/year (for example, June 12, 2018, is shown as 6/12/2018). The Athletics (frequently known just as the "A's") have played in three different cities since the team's entrance into the American League in 1901. From 1901-1954 the Athletics played in Philadelphia. They moved to Kansas City in 1955 and stayed there through the 1967 season. In 1968, the Athletics went further west and became the Oakland Athletics, where they remain to this day (2022). "Team Home" indicates where the team was located during the season the particular game was thrown. IP = innings pitched. One-third of an inning pitched has 0.1 added and two-thirds of an inning pitched has 0.2 added (for example, 9 1/3 innings pitched is displayed as 9.1). BB(s) = base(s) on balls; K(s) = strikeout(s); ER(s) = earned run(s); inn = innings (associated with the length of extra-inning games); and (1) or (2) = first or second game of a doubleheader. *The Athletics perfect games (thrown by Catfish Hunter and Dallas Braden) are shown in italics. Rube Vickers' 1907 five-inning effort is also italicized. Even though it is no longer officially considered a perfect game because it was called after five innings due to darkness, it had been listed as a perfect game prior to the 1991 ruling on what constitutes a no-hitter.*

NOTE 1: While not included in the table above, the two highest postseason Game Scores of 10 innings or less by an Athletic pitcher was a score of 90 by George Earnshaw in Game 4 of the 1931 World Series against the St. Louis Cardinals, and by Vida Blue in Game 3 of the 1974 ALCS against Baltimore. Earnshaw's two-hit shutout resulted in a 3-0 victory that tied the World Series at two games apiece against the Cardinals. St. Louis would go on to win the series in seven games. Blue's win was also a two-hit shutout, as the A's squeaked by the Orioles 1-0 in Baltimore for a two games to one series lead. Oakland would close out the 1974 ALCS with a 2-1 victory the next day and go on to defeat the Los Angeles Dodgers in the World Series.

NOTE 2: There are no games from the Kansas City era (1955-1967) included in this table. Losers of 100+ games four out of the 13 seasons they were in Missouri, the team never had a winning record while playing in Kansas City. Their best season was a 73-81 effort in 1958, good enough for seventh place in the eight-team American League. The highest Game Score of 10 innings or less was an 89, achieved by Diego Segui on June 15, 1965, during a two-hit, 5-0 shutout against the California Angels. The closest any Kansas City pitcher ever came to throwing a no-hitter was a one-hit effort by Ralph Terry on August 22, 1958, against the Washington Senators. The only Washington baserunner during that entire game was the result of a two-out single in the third inning by opposing Senator pitcher Russ Kemmerer.

NOTE 3: On September 28, 1975, the Athletics threw a multi-pitcher no-hitter against California in a 5-0 win. This game was the last of the season as the three-time World Champion A's were headed to their fifth straight ALCS, this time against the Boston Red Sox. As such, the game was seen as more of a tune-up, since the 97-win Oakland team had already clinched the division title over the Kansas City Royals days earlier. Vida Blue started the game with five innings of no-hit ball, earning a Game Score of 67 for his effort. Glenn Abbott and Paul Lindblad threw an inning each, with Rollie Fingers finishing the game with two innings of no-hit ball. Oakland took an early lead en route to a 5-0 win to close out the regular season. The combined statistics of Blue, Abbott, Lindblad, and Fingers would have yielded a Game Score of 90 if a single pitcher had thrown the game.

NOTE 4: The highest nine-inning Game Score by an Athletic pitcher was a one-hitter by Bobby Witt against Kansas City in 1994. The only Royal baserunner came on a bunt single by Greg Gagne with one out in the sixth inning. While walking none, Witt struck out 14 batters, 11 of them swinging, in his 120-pitch effort. Witt would win 142 games over a solid 16-year career, mostly with Texas, and this was easily his best game. Witt was only with Oakland for all or part of three seasons from 1992-1994. Of note, while Witt struck out a very impressive 14 batters in his best game, the highest number of strikeouts achieved by an Athletic pitcher in a game that didn't go into extra innings was 16. That was accomplished by Jose Rijo against the Seattle Mariners over eight innings in a 1986 game won by Oakland 7-2.

NOTE 5: Dave Stewart's no-hitter against the Blue Jays was one of two thrown on June 29, 1990. The other was by Fernando Valenzuela of the Dodgers against the St. Louis Cardinals. While both games started around 7:30 local time, Stewart completed his first since it was played in the Eastern time zone in Toronto. Valenzuela's no-hitter started three hours later in Los Angeles (Pacific Time).

NOTE 6: Vida Blue's 1970 no-hitter against the Twins was his third career win and eighth start. He had lost a no-hitter with two outs in the eighth inning two starts earlier against Kansas City. The only baserunner he allowed during his no-hitter was a fourth inning walk to Hall of Famer Harmon Killebrew.

NOTE 7: In Sean Manaea's 2018 game, Boston was no-hit for the first time since 1993. The Red Sox came into the game with a record of 17-2, the best winning percentage by a team who had a no-hitter thrown against them in history. It was also the first time since 1988 that a no-hitter was thrown against that season's World Series champions.

NOTE 8: The only Arizona batter to reach base in Mark Mulder's 2001 one-hitter was Diamondback right fielder Danny Bautista. He hit a single to lead off the eighth inning.

NOTE 9: In his 1916 no-hitter against Cleveland, Leslie "Bullet Joe" Bush retired 27 batters in a row after a leadoff walk in the first inning. He also started against the Indians a day earlier and gave up five runs in just three innings. The Athletics went 36–117 that season – Bush went 15-24, leading the majors in losses – making them the worst team to ever pitch a no-hitter. This was also the final game in the career of future Hall of Famer Nap Lajoie.

NOTE 10: Mike Fiers's 2019 no-hitter against the Reds was one of two he would pitch. The other was in 2015 as a member of the Astros, when he threw a no-hitter against the Dodgers. Both of his no-hitters were interleague games.

NOTE 11: Hall of Famer Charles "Chief" Bender nearly threw a perfect game in his 1910 no-hitter. He faced just 27 hitters as the lone man to reach, shortstop Terry Turner, was caught stealing after a walk.

NOTE 12: Dick Fowler's 1945 no-hitter against the Browns was unusual since it was a walk-off no-hitter. Fowler was in the dugout, as he had thrown nine innings of no-hit ball in a 0-0 tie game. Philadelphia scored the winning run in the bottom of the ninth when right fielder Hal Peck tripled to lead off the inning and the next hitter (second baseman Irv Hall) singled to knock him in. This was also the first no-hitter by a Canadian-born pitcher. Fowler was making his first start in nearly three years after serving in World War II. This was his only victory of the season.

NOTE 13: During Bill McCahan's 1947 no-hitter against the Washington Senators, the only baserunner he allowed was on a one-out throwing error by first baseman (and future All-Star) Ferris Fain. Apart from that one batter, McCahan retired every other Senator.

NOTE 14: Rube Waddell and Rube Vickers threw shortened, five-inning no-hitters that were called because of rain or darkness. In both cases, no hits or walks were allowed, but one runner reached base in Waddell's game when he made an error fielding the ball due to the wet field conditions. His game was called because of rain after five innings. Vickers' perfect game was the second game of a doubleheader on the last day of the 1907 season and stopped after five innings due to darkness. By that point in the season, Ty Cobb and the Detroit Tigers had already nosed out second-place Philadelphia for the American League pennant.

Mike Warren's accomplishment should be celebrated, as he has etched his name among the best performances for any Athletics pitcher in the team's 121-season history. Another factor that makes Warren's performance so notable is that he achieved his no-hitter in only his ninth career start. This places him in the Top 10 earliest no-hitters – in terms of least experience as a starter -- among all pitchers who ever threw one. He's in with some impressive company:

Table 15-6. Lowest Number of Career Starts by a No-Hit Pitcher

Rank	Pitcher	Team	Date Score	Opponent	Career Start Number
1 (tie)	Bobo Holloman	St. Louis Browns	5/6/1953 StL 6-0	Philadelphia Athletics	1
1 (tie)	Tyler Gilbert	Arizona Diamondbacks	8/14/2021 Ari 7-0	San Diego Padres	1
3 (tie)	Wilson Alvarez	Chicago White Sox	8/11/1991 Chi 7-0	Baltimore Orioles	2
3 (tie)	Clay Buchholz	Boston Red Sox	9/11/2007 Bos 10-0	Baltimore Orioles	2
5	Nick Maddox	Pittsburgh Pirates	9/20/1907 Pit 2-1	Brooklyn Superbas	3
6 (tie)	*Charlie Robertson*	*Chicago White Sox*	*4/30/1922 Chi 2-0*	*Detroit Tigers*	*4*
6 (tie)	Bo Belinsky	Los Angeles Angels	5/5/1962 LA 2-0	Baltimore Orioles	4
6 (tie)	Burt Hooton	Chicago Cubs	4/16/1972 Chi 4-0	Philadelphia Phillies	4
9	Vida Blue	Oakland Athletics	9/21/1970 Oak 6-0	Minnesota Twins	8
10	Mike Warren	Oakland Athletics	9/29/1983 Oak 3-0	Chicago White Sox	9

METHODOLOGY: This table lists the pitchers who had the fewest career starts when they threw their no-hitter and covers the period 1900-2021. No-hit games are ranked in ascending order by the fewest number of starts. For example, both Bobo Holloman in 1953 and Tyler Gilbert in 2021 threw a no-hitter the very first time they started a major league game. The number "1" indicates their no-hitter occurred in their first start.

LEGEND: Dates are shown as month/day/year (for example, June 12, 2018, is shown as 6/12/2018). Career Start Number is the number of starts a pitcher had in his career at the time he threw his no-hitter. The number includes that day's start. *Charlie Robertson's perfect game in 1922 is shown in italics. He threw his perfect game in just his fourth start, holding the record in that category.*

Not only did Mike Warren turn in one of the most extraordinary underdog no-hit performances of all time by blanking a team that far outmatched his own, he was also one of the youngest and most inexperienced pitchers to ever throw a no-hitter. His performance that night in Oakland was truly remarkable.

Like many ballplayers, Mike Warren had to beat the odds to play in the major leagues. For starters, the Detroit Tigers chose him in the 12th round of the major league draft with the 299th pick overall. Historically, just a handful of players selected that late in the draft ever make it to the big leagues, and 1979 was no different. Of the 26 players chosen in the 12th round that year, only four (15%) played in the majors. Warren was also drafted directly out of high school, which decreases the odds of him making the major leagues by 50% when compared to college players who were drafted.

Warren was shuffled around a bit as a minor league player. Drafted by the Tigers in 1979, he was released early in the 1981 season after struggling with the team's Bristol (Rookie) and Lakeland (Class A) farm teams. Oakland picked him up and Warren turned things around with success at the A's Modesto (Class A) club to the point the Milwaukee Brewers drafted him in the 1981 Rule 5 draft. The A's clearly wanted Warren back and they traded for him early in the 1982 season. From that point on, Warren blossomed, rising rapidly through Oakland's AA (Albany) and AAA (Tacoma) teams.

Debuting with the parent club in June 1983, Warren had two disastrous relief appearance – one against the same Chicago White Sox he would no-hit three months later – before being sent down for more seasoning. Recalled by Oakland in mid-August, Warren finally settled down. He started and won the last four games he pitched, including three complete game victories at the end of the season – even one that lasted 10 innings.

After his emergence as a solid starting pitcher during the last couple months of the 1983 season, Warren began suffering serious control issues as the 1984 season began. As a result, he not only was removed from the rotation, he also lost his place on the roster. He was sent down to the minors, recalled as part of the September roster expansion in 1984, and briefly reappeared in 1985 as a spot starter and a mop-up reliever. By that point, it was apparent Warren had lost his effectiveness, and Oakland released him.

The Kansas City Royals signed him to a minor league contract in 1986 and Warren began the season by making impressive progress at Kansas City's AAA club in Omaha. Unfortunately, Warren injured his arm during his comeback – even undergoing Tommy John surgery to try to correct the situation – and he never appeared in the majors again. By the end of the year, his big-league playing career was over at the age of 25.

While Mike Warren's career was short, he made the most of it while it lasted. He reached the pinnacle of his game as a rookie starter for Oakland in September of 1983, culminating in a dominating no-hit performance against the best team in baseball that season. He etched his name in the record books and his David vs. Goliath performance – a young 22-year-old rookie facing down the mighty White Sox – was one for the ages. For this alone, he and his achievement that night should be celebrated.

I'd also like to acknowledge one other hero of this game, Oakland catcher Mike Heath. For nine innings on a cold Bay Area night that built toward a pressure-filled climax, Heath was there with Warren every step of the way. By 1983, the 28-year-old Heath was already an established veteran presence, having broken in with the World Champion New York Yankees in 1978. Heath would go on to a distinguished 14-year career in the major leagues.

Mike Heath's guidance and steady presence were key that no-hit night in September. Mike Warren gave him credit as well, giving Heath an autographed picture of the two of them hugging on the field after the last out. Warren signed it with the inscription "Thanks for giving me enough confidence to pitch up in the bigs. I'll remember this day forever."

I had the very enjoyable privilege of interviewing Mike Heath recently. I encourage you to read the transcript below.

Mike Heath Interview
Conducted by Kevin Hurd on May 14, 2021

Kevin Hurd (KH): Would you consider yourself to be the best catcher on your Little League, high school, college, or minor league teams?

Mike Heath (MH): It's funny; I was pretty much a shortstop through Little League and high school. I was drafted in the second round (in 1973) as a shortstop at age 18, then played in the minors as a shortstop, second baseman, and third baseman until age 21 (in 1976). At that point, my coaches talked to me and said I could make it to MLB quicker if I switched positions to catcher. In 1978, I made it with the Yankees.

KH: Did you feel any different, good or bad, on the day of Mike Warren's no-hitter?

MH: Not really – in many ways it just felt like another game, except that around the fifth or sixth inning I started thinking, *"He's still got a no-no."*

KH: What pitches – fastball, curve, slider, or something else – were working best for Mike Warren that day?

MH: Mike had an average fastball, but with great location. He had three different breaking balls: in-zone, out-of-zone to get hitters to chase bad pitches, and a change-up curve that disrupted their timing. For the change-up he would take a little off and got the hitters off-balance which would get them out front of the ball which led to fly outs.

KH: What was the best defensive play, or the closest Mike came to losing the no-hitter?

MH: I don't remember that there were any great defensive plays that day. As far as the closest the White Sox came to a hit, in the eighth inning Mike Squires hit a deep fly ball to right field that was caught by Mike Davis.

KH: Did Mike shake off your signs much during the game?

MH: I'm don't remember an exact number. It wasn't that many times.

KH: Do you have any memorabilia/souvenirs, such as a baseball, plaque, uniform, or something like that from the game in your house?

MH: I've got a picture of (Oakland third baseman) Wayne Gross and myself hugging Mike after the no-hitter. Mike autographed the picture and also wrote, "Thanks for giving me enough confidence to pitch up in the bigs. I'll remember this day forever. Thanks, Mike Warren."

KH: You played 13 years and played for eight managers: Bob Lemon, Jim Marshall, Billy Martin, Steve Boros, Jackie Moore, Whitey Herzog, Sparky Anderson, and Bobby Cox. Was there one or two of them that you liked playing for the most?

MH: First, Billy Martin. He showed confidence in me. I'd run through a wall for him. Also, Sparky Anderson. They were all good, though.

KH: Do you think the number of pitches Mike threw that day led to him getting a sore arm?

MH: I don't think we had readily available pitch counts back then. I never heard of the number of pitches he threw. Nowadays, teams invest a lot with these young pitchers and are pretty religious about not exceeding pitch count limits, especially early in their career. We didn't really have strength and conditioning training before 1989. When Bo Schembechler joined the front office of the Tigers in 1989, he helped initiate that training.

KH: Did Mike Warren request you as a catcher for this game?

MH: No, he did not.

KH: Do you still stay in contact with Mike?

MH: Usually not. Last year on Facebook I touched base.

KH: Did the A's give you a bonus for catching the game?

MH: No (laughs).

KH: During the game when did you think, *"He's got a real shot at a no-hitter?"*

MH: The sixth inning. Starting about that time nobody mentioned no-hitters to Mike, either. That superstition is usually always followed.

KH: Were you able to get a follow-on job in baseball after your playing days were over? In the majors, minors, college, high school, or media?

MH: In 1996-1997 I managed two years in the minors (Birmingham and Winston-Salem). I didn't have any coaching, scouting or front-office jobs. I wanted to be a catching instructor, but that never happened. I didn't like being a manager. Players have agents and complaints.

KH: You retired from playing in 1991. What other things have you worked at?

MH: I got my real-estate license and sold real estate for two years. I didn't like it. I've worked at the Ostingers Baseball Academy here in Florida. It is run by Jimmy Osting who pitched in the majors from 2001-2002. We have a travel ball team which is gone a lot of the time, but I also get to do a lot of coaching, specifically with the catchers. I've been with the Academy for 10-12 years. I also ride motorcycles a lot and play golf.

KH: Since you did get a job in baseball, do you think having caught a no-hitter helped you get the job?

MH: What helped me get the 1996 managerial job was that I knew Kenny Williams, who was the Director of Minor League Operations for the Chicago White Sox. He liked my mental makeup and attitude.

KH: Do you have any kids or grandkids who have pursued or will pursue baseball as a career?

MH: I have a daughter who's 33. She was born in Detroit. She's a great athlete. Growing up, she was good at swimming, volleyball, and basketball. She went to Warner College (NAIA school) in Florida on a basketball scholarship and scored 1,100 points in her career. She is married to Fabio Tamayo, an ex-soccer player from Columbia. They have two children who are excellent soccer players.

KH: Was the no-hitter the highlight of your career?

MH: Well, it was great playing 14 years in MLB. It was great playing on the 1978 Yankees, getting into a World Series game as a rookie, and getting a full World Series share. However, I would have to say the highlight was the day in 1987 during the season when my daughter was born in Detroit.

KH: What was your best season?

MH: That would be either 1984 or 1985 with Oakland. I hit 13 HRs both seasons.

KH: Have you been to the section of the Baseball Hall of Fame that focuses on no-hitters?

MH: I went there once in the 1990s as part of a motorcycle trip with Gordon Balker.

KH: Did you take pictures and/or spend much time there?

MH: No, I didn't.

Chapter 16

Joe Cowley: Effectively Wild

September 19, 1986
Undrafted journeyman Joe Cowley walks seven and allows a run as he no-hits the AL West Division Champion California Angels (92-70)

"I almost yanked him five different times. I'll tell you, I've never seen an uglier no-hitter."
Chicago White Sox Manager Jim Fregosi on Joe Cowley's no-hitter (Frank Lidz, "Flashes in the Pan," *Sports Illustrated*, May 4, 1992).

"Joe had control problems. This game he threw 138 pitches – half were balls. His ball always moved a lot. He overthrew a lot of the time."
Chicago White Sox Catcher Ron Karkovice (Interview with the author, May 13, 2021).

"I was having some trouble with my release point. I was racing too much in the stretch and I was trying to keep the ball down as much as I could."
Joe Cowley commenting on his control problems during the game (Mike Terry, *San Bernardino Sun*, September 20, 1986).

"He was either two feet outside or right on the black (the corner). He did his job. He got 27 outs. But he wasn't tough at all, he wasn't. We didn't get a hit, that's all that happened. If you guys don't look up at the scoreboard, you'd think he gave up eight or nine hits. When he was around the

plate, he was barely around it. I'm not even frustrated. It wasn't impressive, it wasn't. Not to put Joe Cowley down, but it wasn't impressive."

California Angels First Baseman Wally Joyner providing his perspective on Cowley's no-hitter (Gene Wojciechowski, *Los Angeles Times*, September 20, 1986).

"He had good stuff, an excellent fastball. The ball was in on you fast. And he's not easy to pick up."

California Angels' Second Baseman Bobby Grich offering a different opinion on Cowley's performance (Gene Wojciechowski, *Los Angeles Times*, September 20, 1986).

"I started to think no-hitter in the seventh inning. The bad inning I had in the sixth was on my mind, but I shut them down in the seventh and I started thinking I could do it. But now, I can't believe it. You just go out and throw as hard as you can for as long as you can. The whole world knows I was in Buffalo earlier this year. I've come a long way since spring training."

Joe Cowley reflecting on his no-hitter and his baseball journey after the game (Gene Wojciechowski, *Los Angeles Times*, September 20, 1986).

Joe Cowley was wild that day. Really wild. He walked seven batters, including the first three hitters he faced in the sixth inning (Bob Boone, Gary Pettis, and the always dangerous Wally Joyner). Manager Jim Fregosi shared the feeling that Cowley was having difficulty throwing strikes. In the sixth inning, after walking the first three hitters, Cowley got California's #3 hitter in the lineup, Brian Downing, to pop out to Jack Perconte at second base. Next up was future Hall of Famer Reggie Jackson, the Angels' #4 hitter.

While Fregosi later acknowledged that Cowley "had great stuff tonight," he also remembered thinking "if Cowley walks Jackson, he's not going to see DeCinces (the next hitter)." Even though the White Sox were leading 3-0 and his pitcher (Cowley) was throwing a no-hitter, Fregosi was so concerned with his pitcher's lack of control that he was prepared to pull Cowley if he allowed a run by walking Jackson with the bases loaded.

Cowley himself realized his precarious position. "I debated whether to throw Reggie a curve. I decided to throw a heater, keep it down and low. Once I got out of the sixth, I had a good feeling." As it turned out, Jackson flew out to Darryl Boston in deep center field, allowing Bob Boone to score, advancing Gary Pettis to third, and cutting Chicago's lead down to just two runs. With runners on first and third, Doug DeCinces ended the inning by popping out to Perconte at second.

The outcome of the game after the sixth inning was never in doubt. Cowley only walked one batter in his last three innings. No other hitter reached base for the Angels from that point forward. The White Sox added three runs in the eighth and another in the ninth for a final score of 7-1. Cowley's batterymate that day, 22-year-old rookie catcher Ron Karkovice, contributed offensively by scoring Chicago's fourth run in the eighth and hitting a solo home run in the ninth.

There were other close calls to Cowley's no-hitter late in the game. Reggie Jackson played a role in what might have been the biggest threat, when Boston again chased down Jackson's fly ball in deep center field with one out in the ninth inning. The no-hitter was also in jeopardy with two outs in the eighth, when slick-fielding White Sox shortstop Ozzie Guillen snagged a Wally Joyner line drive to end the inning. Through it all, Joe Cowley powered through the 7-1 White Sox victory, and he and Ron Karkovice had a no-hitter to their credit. Karkovice would also catch a second no-hitter – that one by Wilson Alvarez in 1991.

Cowley threw his no-hitter against a tough team. Before this game, California had an 85-60 record. The Angels won the AL West Division in 1986 with 92 wins and came within a pitch of winning the American League pennant. Boston's Dave Henderson hit a two-run home run off Angels' closer Donnie Moore with two outs in the top of the ninth during Game 5 of the ALCS. That tied the game at 5-5 and the Red Sox would win it in the 11th. The series went back to Boston and the Red Sox won Games 6 and 7 running away.

For Chicago, it was a disappointing year. The White Sox finished 85-77 in 1985, good enough for third place in the AL West Division. By the time this game was played in 1986, Chicago was 65-81 and well out of the pennant race, despite having stars like Guillen, Baines, and Hall of Fame pitchers Tom Seaver and Steve Carlton on their staff.

Joe Cowley was one of the unlikeliest no-hit pitchers ever. Signed by the Atlanta Braves in July 1976 as an undrafted free agent, Cowley was in the minors from 1976-1982, pitching for six different teams throughout the South in the

Atlanta organization. In 1982, he was called up briefly by Atlanta and went 1-2. He returned to the minors from 1983-1984 with both the Braves and the Yankees organizations. He was called up by the Yankees in 1984 and went 21-8 with a 3.81 ERA over the next two years for New York. Cowley was traded to the White Sox after the end of the 1985 season, and went 11-11 for Chicago in 1986, the year he pitched his no-hitter.

After this game, Cowley's career came to a screeching halt. He went 0-2 for the rest of the year. He was traded to the Phillies before the 1987 season but didn't last long with them. He never won another game and lost four in the process. He finished with an astronomical ERA of 15.43 in just over 11 innings pitched. Cowley retired after the 1987 season.

One of the first questions that comes to mind is what happened to Joe Cowley? Why did he go from being a no-hit pitcher to completely falling off the map as an effective pitcher? After no-hitting an outstanding Angels team, he never won another game, and he was especially bad with the Phillies the following season.

The first thing that appears as a possible cause of his professional downfall is arm problems. For a guy who hadn't pitched long at the major-league level, throwing 138 pitches in a high-stress game seems like a lot of wear and tear in a very short period of time. Was it too much? Did he blow out his arm? The short answer seems to be "no."

Frank Lidz of Sports Illustrated wrote an outstanding article in May 1992 ("Flashes in the Pan") that told the stories of four baseball players who had meteoric careers that flashed brightly in the 1980s and then went dark just as quickly. Joe Cowley was the headline player for the article. For the record, the other three were Joe Charboneau, Roger Moret, and Jeff Stone, although Cowley appears to be the most extreme example of this "fell off a cliff" syndrome.

It seems that Cowley's issues were not physical. Instead, he appears to have come down with a severe case of "Steve Blass disease." For those who haven't heard this term, Steve Blass disease refers to the sudden loss of ability in baseball players to throw accurately. It's named after Pittsburgh pitcher Steve Blass, who went from being a World Champion starter in 1971 and National League All-Star and Cy Young runner-up in 1972, to being completely unable to find the strike zone in 1973, ending the season with a 6.82 ERA and leading the league with 12 hit batsmen in just 88 innings. Blass would later become a beloved color commentator for the Pirates over a 20+-year broadcasting career.

While Joe Cowley was not as big of a star as Steve Blass, his fall from grace was every bit as dramatic. He's the first to admit that one day, he simply lost the ability to throw the ball accurately. And while he attributes many of his troubles to allowing himself to get out of shape, he recognizes that an almost paralyzing fear of failure overcame him. The worse he pitched, the more afraid he'd become. And the booing fans in Philadelphia, his last stop as a player, made things even worse. While many other Level 5 pitchers in this book did have to retire due to arm problems, Joe Cowley wasn't one of them.

As I've described earlier, the metric I use to define a player's career value is JAWS (the Jaffe WAR Score system). JAWS is a means to measure a player's Hall of Fame worthiness by comparing him to the players at his position who are already enshrined – this allows players from different eras to be compared to each other fairly. Using JAWS, Joe Cowley has a career score of 4.3. This places him in the lowest (Level 5) category, meaning that he is among the least likely pitchers to throw a no-hitter based on career performance. Despite his short career and his meteoric rise and fall, Cowley is not the least likely pitcher to throw a no-hitter. Not even close. There are 22 others who have lower career scores than Joe.

Using the Game Score (GSc) metric, we can see how dominating a pitcher's performance was during his no-hit game. GSc was developed by renowned baseball statistician Bill James. For example, if a pitcher pitches nine innings, allows no hits, no runs, and strikes out the same number of players as he walks, he'll have a GSc of 87. For his game, Joe Cowley had a GSc of 84, which is actually very low for a no-hitter. Specifically, he allowed one earned run (-4 points), walked 7 batters (-7), and had 8 strikeouts (+8), which places him at #251 out of 257 no-hit Game Scores ranked from highest to lowest. The biggest subtractions were his seven walks and one earned run allowed, which – as described earlier – came on three consecutive walks and a sacrifice fly. Furthermore, it is uncommon for the no-hit team to score a run – this has happened in only 15 games (less than 6%).

To see how Cowley's efforts compare to others, we can look at the top Game Scores throughout the team's history. The White Sox as a team have a rich history of pitching excellence. This can be demonstrated by looking at the top Game Scores achieved by Chicago pitchers since the team began in 1901.

Table 16-1. White Sox Highest Game Scores

Rank	Pitcher	Date Score	Opponent	GSc	IP, Hits, Runs, ERs, Walks, Strikeouts
1	Ed Walsh	8/4/1910 0-0 Tie (16 inn)	Philadelphia Athletics	117	16.0 IP, 6 Hits, 0 Runs, 0 ERs, 3 BBs, 10 Ks
2	Jim Scott	4/20/1912 0-0 Tie (15 inn)	St. Louis Browns	116	15.0 IP, 6 Hits, 0 Runs, 0 ERs, 2 BBs, 13 Ks
3 (tie)	Lefty Williams	5/15/1918 Was 1-0 (18 inn)	Washington Senators	109	17.1 IP, 8 Hits, 1 Run, 1 ER, 2 BBs, 3 Ks
3 (tie)	Jack Harshman	8/13/1954 Chi 1-0 (16 inn)	Detroit Tigers	109	16.0 IP, 9 Hits, 0 Runs, 0 ERs, 7 BBs, 12 Ks
5	Jimmy Callahan	5/18/1902 2-2 Tie (17 inn)	St. Louis Browns	106	17.0 IP, 8 Hits, 2 Runs, 2 ERs, 2 BBs, 5 Ks
6	Pat Caraway	8/29/1930 Chi 3-0 (13 inn)	Cleveland Indians	104	13.0 IP, 3 Hits, 0 Runs, 0 ERs, 2 BBs, 5 Ks
7	Joe Benz	7/25/1914 Chi 1-0 (13 inn)	New York Yankees	101	13.0 IP, 6 Hits, 0 Runs, 0 ERs, 3 BBs, 9 Ks
8	Billy Pierce	8/6/1959 1-1 Tie (18 inn)	Baltimore Orioles	100	16.0 IP, 11 Hits, 1 Run, 1 ER, 3 BBs, 7 Ks
9 (tie)	Nick Altrock	10/1/1906 Chi 1-0 (13 inn)	St. Louis Browns	99	13.0 IP, 6 Hits, 0 Runs, 0 ERs, 1 BB, 5 Ks
9 (tie)	Wilbur Wood	5/7/1974 Chi 1-0 (11 inn)	Detroit Tigers	99	11.0 IP, 2 Hits, 0 Runs, 0 ERs, 4 BBs, 10 Ks
9 (tie)	Lucas Giolito	8/25/2020 Chi 4-0	Pittsburgh Pirates	99	9.0 IP, 0 Hits, 0 Runs, 0 ERs, 1 BB, 13 Ks

METHODOLOGY: This table includes the highest Game Scores thrown by a White Sox pitcher from 1901-2021. Games are ranked by Game Score (GSc) and consider all franchise regular season and postseason games. Table 16-2 below limits the eligible games to those pitching performances that were 10 innings or less. Game Score (GSc) measures a pitcher's performance in any given game started. Introduced by baseball writer/statistician Bill James in the 1980s, Game Score is presented as a figure between 0-100 — except for extreme outliers — and usually falls between 40-70.

LEGEND: Dates are shown as month/day/year (for example, June 12, 2018, is shown as 6/12/2018). IP = innings pitched. One-third of an inning pitched has 0.1 added and two-thirds of an inning pitched has 0.2 added (for example, 9 1/3 innings pitched is displayed as 9.1). BB(s) = base(s) on balls; K(s) = strikeout(s); ER(s) = earned run(s); inn = innings (associated with the length of extra-inning games); and (1) or (2) = first or second game of a doubleheader.

NOTE 1: The highest postseason Game Score ever achieved by a White Sox pitcher was a score of 94 by 25-year-old Ed Walsh in Game 3 of the 1906 World Series against the Chicago Cubs. Tied for seventh best Game Score among any White Sox game of nine innings or less, Walsh threw a two-hit shutout against the heavily favored Cubs in a battle of the Titans. He also set a then-record for the highest number of strikeouts in a World Series game with 12. Led by Hall of Famers Joe Tinker, Johnny Evers, and Frank Chance, the Cubs – with an all-time best .763 winning percentage – racked up a record-setting 116 wins over a 152-game schedule, as they won the National League pennant by 20 games over the second-place Giants. Walsh, meanwhile, led the American League in shutouts with 10 and finished near the top of the league with an ERA of 1.88. His victory in Game 3 put the White Sox ahead of the Cubs two games to one. The White Sox – nicknamed "The Hitless Wonders" because of their American League-worst team batting average of .230 – would go on to finish their remarkable upset victory in the 1906 World Series by beating the Cubs four games to two, with Walsh recording a victory in Game 5 as well.

Future Hall of Famer Walsh would achieve a career ERA of 1.82, placing him at the top of all qualifying pitchers in baseball history. He also recorded the top Game Score (117) in Chicago White Sox history in his 16-inning shutout of the World Champion Philadelphia Athletics in 1910. Walsh dueled Philadelphia's Jack Coombs to a scoreless tie in that game. The two teams managed just nine hits between them, while striking out a combined 28 times. For his efforts, Coombs recorded an extraordinary Game Score of 128, the fourth highest score of all time.

NOTE 2: 23-year-old pitcher Jim "Death Valley" Scott recorded the second-highest White Sox Game Score ever for his 15 innings of shutout ball in an April 1912 game against the St. Louis Browns. The contest ended in a 0-0 tie despite the White Sox having numerous chances to score. Chicago had nine hits and eight walks off Browns starter George Baumgardner over 15 innings. The Browns also made five errors, yet Chicago was unable to scratch out a single run. Unfortunately, Scott's 15-inning herculean effort developed into a case of rheumatism afterward that limited him to only six games that season, as he missed May through August because of injury. Scott recovered and was the team's ace in 1913-1915, setting a major league record that lasted over 100 years by pitching 39 consecutive starts in which he allowed three or fewer earned runs. When the U.S. went to war in 1917, the patriotic Scott left baseball and became a supply officer in the Army. After World War I, he pitched briefly for the San Francisco Seals in the Pacific Coast League, umpired for several years, and became a movie director.

NOTE 3: As part of his August 2020 no-hitter, Lucas Giolito recorded the highest Game Score (99) of any White Sox Game of nine innings or less. Tied for ninth place, his is the only game in this table that wasn't an extra-inning contest. The only batter Giolito allowed to reach base was Pittsburgh leadoff hitter Erik Gonzalez, who drew a four-pitch walk in the fourth inning. There were no fans in attendance for this game due to Covid restrictions.

Comparing Game Scores of White Sox pitchers who threw 10 innings or less can be considered a measure of pitching excellence that's set apart from the length of extra-inning games. Using these parameters, Giolito's game comes out on top. For comparison purposes, I've included all 20 White Sox no-hitters in this table.

Table 16-2. White Sox Highest Game Scores of ten innings or less

Rank	Pitcher	Date Score	Opponent	GSc	IP, Hits, Runs, ERs, Walks, Strikeouts
1	Lucas Giolito	8/25/2020 Chi 4-0	Pittsburgh Pirates	99	9.0 IP, 0 Hits, 0 Runs, 0 ERs, 1 BB, 13 Ks
2 (tie)	Gary Peters	7/15/1963 Chi 4-0	Baltimore Orioles	98	9.0 IP, 1 Hit, 0 Runs, 0 ERs, 0 BBs, 13 Ks
2 (tie)	Jim O'Toole	5/13/1967 Chi 1-0 (10 inn)	California Angels	98	10.0 IP, 2 Hits, 0 Runs, 0 ERs, 1 BB, 11 Ks
4	Philip Humber	4/21/2012 Chi 4-0	Seattle Mariners	96	*9.0 IP, 0 Hits, 0 Runs, 0 ERs, 0 BBs, 9 Ks*
5 (tie)	Billy Pierce	6/4/1957 Chi 1-0 (10 inn)	Boston Red Sox	95	10.0 IP, 2 Hits, 0 Runs, 0 ERs, 0 BBs, 7 Ks
5 (tie)	Floyd Bannister	9/13/1987 Chi 2-0	Seattle Mariners	95	9.0 IP, 1 Hit, 0 Runs, 0 ERs, 0 BBs, 10 Ks
7 (tie)	Frank Smith	8/31/1905 Chi 2-0	Washington Senators	94	9.0 IP, 1 Hit, 0 Runs, 0 ERs, 0 BBs, 9 Ks

Rank	Pitcher	Date / Score	Opponent	GSc	IP, Hits, Runs, ERs, Walks, Strikeouts
7 (tie)	Ed Walsh	10/11/1906 White Sox 3-0	Chicago Cubs	94	9.0 IP, 2 Hits, 0 Runs, 0 ERs, 1 BB, 12 Ks
7 (tie)	Ed Walsh	8/11/1910 Chi 1-0	Boston Red Sox	94	9.0 IP, 3 Hits, 0 Runs, 0 ERs, 2 BBs, 15 Ks
7 (tie)	Frank Lange	9/20/1910 Chi 3-0	New York Highlanders	94	9.0 IP, 2 Hits, 0 Runs, 0 ERs, 2 BBs, 13 Ks
7 (tie)	Ed Walsh	8/27/1911 Chi 5-0	Boston Red Sox	94	9.0 IP, 0 Hits, 0 Runs, 0 ERs, 1 BB, 8 Ks
7 (tie)	Billy Pierce	6/27/1958 Chi 3-0	Washington Senators	94	9.0 IP, 1 Hit, 0 Runs, 0 ERs, 0 BBs, 9 Ks
7 (tie)	Mark Buehrle	4/18/2007 Chi 6-0	Texas Rangers	94	9.0 IP, 0 Hits, 0 Runs, 0 ERs, 1 BB, 8 Ks
7 (tie)	Zach Stewart	9/5/2011 (2) Chi 4-0	Minnesota Twins	94	9.0 IP, 1 Hit, 0 Runs, 0 ERs, 0 BBs, 9 Ks
7 (tie)	Carlos Rodon	4/14/2021 Chi 8-0	Cleveland Indians	94	9.0 IP, 0 Hits, 0 Runs, 0 ERs, 0 BBs, 7 Ks
16 (tie)	*Charlie Robertson*	*4/30/1922 Chi 2-0*	*Detroit Tigers*	*93*	*9.0 IP, 0 Hits, 0 Runs, 0 ERs, 0 BBs, 6 Ks*
16 (tie)	*Mark Buehrle*	*7/23/2009 Chi 5-0*	*Tampa Bay Rays*	*93*	*9.0 IP, 0 Hits, 0 Runs, 0 ERs, 0 BBs, 6 Ks*
25 (tie)	Frank Smith	9/6/1905 (2) Chi 15-0	Detroit Tigers	92	9.0 IP, 0 Hits, 0 Runs, 0 ERs, 3 BBs, 8 Ks
36 (tie)	Joel Horlen	9/10/1967 (1) Chi 6-0	Detroit Tigers	91	9.0 IP, 0 Hits, 0 Runs, 0 ERs, 0 BBs, 4 Ks
49 (tie)	Bill Dietrich	6/1/1937 Chi 8-0	St. Louis Browns	90	9.0 IP, 0 Hits, 0 Runs, 0 ERs, 2 BBs, 5 Ks
67 (tie)	Eddie Cicotte	4/14/1917 Chi 11-0	St. Louis Browns	89	9.0 IP, 0 Hits, 0 Runs, 0 ERs, 3 BBs, 5 Ks
67 (tie)	Wilson Alvarez	8/11/1991 Chi 7-0	Baltimore Orioles	89	9.0 IP, 0 Hits, 0 Runs, 0 ERs, 5 BBs, 7 Ks
89 (tie)	Frank Smith	9/20/1908 Chi 1-0	Philadelphia Athletics	88	9.0 IP, 0 Hits, 0 Runs, 0 ERs, 1 BB, 2 Ks
89 (tie)	Ted Lyons	8/21/1926 Chi 6-0	Boston Red Sox	88	9.0 IP, 0 Hits, 0 Runs, 0 ERs, 1 BB, 2 Ks

Rank	Pitcher	Date Score	Opponent	GSc	IP, Hits, Runs, ERs, Walks, Strikeouts
89 (tie)	Vern Kennedy	8/31/1935 Chi 5-0	Cleveland Indians	88	9.0 IP, 0 Hits, 0 Runs, 0 ERs, 4 BBs, 5 Ks
122 (tie)	James Callahan	9/20/1902 (1) Chi 3-0	Detroit Tigers	87	9.0 IP, 0 Hits, 0 Runs, 0 ERs, 2 BBs, 2 Ks
161 (tie)	Joe Benz	5/31/1914 Chi 6-1	Cleveland Naps	86	9.0 IP, 0 Hits, 1 Run, 0 ERs, 2 BBs, 3 Ks
161 (tie)	Bob Keegan	8/20/1957 (2) Chi 6-0	Washington Senators	86	9.0 IP, 0 Hits, 0 Runs, 0 ERs, 2 BBs, 1 K
283 (tie)	Joe Cowley	9/19/1986 Chi 7-1	California Angels	84	9.0 IP, 0 Hits, 1 Run, 1 ER, 7 BBs, 8 Ks
---	Melido Perez	7/12/1990 Chi 8-0 (6 inn)	New York Yankees	77	6.0 IP, 0 Hits, 0 Runs, 0 ERs, 4 BBs, 9 Ks
---	Ed Walsh	5/26/1907 Chi 8-1 (5 inn)	New York Highlanders	62	5.0 IP, 0 Hits, 1 Run, 1 ER, 2 BBs, 1 K
---	Blue Moon Odom +1	7/28/1976 Chi 2-1	Oakland Athletics	59	5.0 IP, 0 Hits, 1 Run, 0 ERs, 9 BBs, 3 Ks

METHODOLOGY: This table includes the highest Game Scores of 10 innings or less thrown by a White Sox pitcher from 1901-2021. Games are ranked by Game Score (GSc) and consider all franchise regular season and postseason games. For comparison purposes, all 20 franchise no-hitters are included in this table. Game Score (GSc) measures a pitcher's performance in any given game started. Introduced by baseball writer/statistician Bill James in the 1980s, Game Score is presented as a figure between 0-100 — except for extreme outliers — and usually falls between 40-70.

LEGEND: Dates are shown as month/day/year (for example, June 12, 2018, is shown as 6/12/2018). IP = innings pitched. One-third of an inning pitched has 0.1 added and two-thirds of an inning pitched has 0.2 added (for example, 9 1/3 innings pitched is displayed as 9.1). BB(s) = base(s) on balls; K(s) = strikeout(s); ER(s) = earned run(s); inn = innings (associated with the length of extra-inning games); and (1) or (2) = first or second game of a doubleheader. The White Sox played well over 18,000 games from 1901-2021; although many of the earliest games do not have Game Scores attributed to them because of the inability to determine whether a run was earned or unearned. *Philip Humber's, Mark Buehrle's, and Charlie Robertson's perfect games in 2012, 2009, and 1922 are italicized.*

NOTE 1: The White Sox are tied with the Yankees for the most perfect games thrown by a franchise (with three). Humber's perfect game had the highest Game Score of the three at 96 (fourth best for any nine-inning game in White Sox history) yet that was his only career complete game. In the ninth inning of Buehrle's perfect game – his second no-hitter – defensive replacement center fielder DeWayne Wise leapt over the wall to take a potential home run away from Tampa Bay's Gabe Kapler. Buehrle retired the first 17 batters in his next start to set the record for consecutive batters retired at 45 spanning three starts. His record was later broken by San Francisco's Yusmeiro Petit in 2014 (46 batters). Charlie Robertson and Mark Buehrle share the same Game Score (93) in their perfect games. They had the exact same line score, too, with 9.0 innings pitched, 27 batters faced, no hits, no runs, no walks, and six strikeouts.

NOTE 2: While Joe Cowley's 84 Game Score is the lowest among all White Sox no-hit pitchers, his isn't the lowest score in a no-hit game. On July 28, 1976, the White Sox threw a multi-pitcher no-hitter against Oakland in a 2-1 win. Blue Moon Odom started the game with 5.0 innings of no-hit ball, earning a Game Score of 59. His very low score was a result of the nine walks and one unearned run he allowed, as Odom only struck out three batters. The Athletics scored their only run in the bottom of the fourth inning when Billy Williams walked to lead off the inning, followed by a Gene Tenace walk two batters later. Claudell Washington then hit into a fielder's choice that sent Williams to third, with Washington ending up on first base. With two outs and runners on first and third in a 1-0 game, Washington stole second and Williams scored when Chicago catcher Jim Essian made a throwing error trying to catch Washington stealing. The White Sox went ahead for good when first baseman Jim Spencer hit a two-out solo shot off Oakland reliever Paul Lindblad in the top of the sixth. Chicago's Francisco Barrios entered the game in the bottom of the sixth after Odom walked the leadoff hitter. Barrios earned his second save of the season, as he allowed two walks and struck out two Oakland batters over four innings of no-hit ball. Primarily because of the 11 walks and one unearned run allowed, the combined statistics of Odom and Barrios would have yielded an extraordinarily low no-hitter Game Score of 79 if the game had been thrown by a single pitcher.

NOTE 3: Gary Peters is tied for the second-highest nine-inning Game Score (98) due to his one-hit shutout against the Orioles in 1963. The only baserunner he allowed was the opposing pitcher Robin Roberts, who hit a two-out single in the top of the third. In his 1987 one-hitter against Seattle, Floyd Bannister faced the minimum 27 batters. Harold Reynolds of the Mariners hit a two-out single in the bottom of the third inning, but was thrown out by Chicago left fielder Gary Redus trying to advance to second base on the hit.

NOTE 4: Hall of Famer Ed Walsh is on the list four times, three of his games with the same Game Score of 94. His fourth game on the list is a rain-shortened no-hitter – no longer considered official – of five innings. Melido Perez also had a rain-shortened, six-inning no-hitter against the Yankees in 1990. Frank "Piano Mover" Smith has the second-most listings of any White Sox pitcher, with three mentions in the table. Walsh also is tied with two other White Sox pitchers (Chris Sale and Jim Scott) for the second-most strikeouts in a single game with 15. Twenty-six-year-old rookie Jack Harshman set the White Sox strikeout record as he fanned 16 Red Sox batters in a nine-inning game in 1954. Harshman is also tied for the team's third-best Game Score (109) with a 16-inning shutout of the Detroit Tigers during that same season. Finishing the year with a 14-8 record and a 2.95 ERA, Harshman had established himself as a big leaguer that season. He spent the next seven seasons with the White Sox, Orioles, and Indians and finished his career with 69 wins and a solid 3.50 ERA.

NOTE 5: Frank Smith threw two no-hitters for the White Sox, one in 1905 against the Tigers, and the second in 1908 versus the Athletics. The late September 1908 game was an exciting contest, as the White Sox were deep into a three-way race with Detroit and Cleveland for the American League pennant. Chicago won 1-0 with one out in the bottom of the ninth when shortstop Freddy Parent drove in first baseman Frank Isbell on a fielder's choice. Parent hit a grounder to second when he managed to make contact with a ball that was too close to the plate during an intentional walk. Smith was in the dugout during the walk off no-hitter win. His first no-hitter was a blowout, though, as the White Sox beat the Tigers 15-0 for the most one-sided no-hitter until Jake Arrieta's 16-0 win over the Reds in 2016. Smith's third game on the list may very well have been his best. In 1905, Smith struck out nine Senators and walked no one, as he shut down Washington 2-0. Facing just 28 batters, the only baserunner Smith allowed was a single by Washington first baseman

Jake Stahl. Smith's 94 Game Score ties him for seventh place on the White Sox highest 10-inning or less game scores.

NOTE 6: Perennial White Sox All-Star Billy Pierce is also on the list twice. His highest Game Score (95) is tied with Floyd Bannister for fifth place on this list and was achieved during a 10-inning, 1-0 shutout of the Boston Red Sox in 1957. Both Red Sox hits were recorded before the ninth inning – these were the only baserunners Pierce allowed. Light-hitting Boston shortstop Billy Klaus was the only Red Sox hitter who made it past first base when he led off with a double in the top of the third. The next three batters were retired in order. Pierce also achieved a Game Score of 94 in 1958 for his one-hitter against the Senators. Pierce retired the first 26 batters he faced in the 3-0 win. Washington's lone baserunner was pinch-hitter Ed FitzGerald, who doubled with two outs in the bottom of the ninth inning.

NOTE 7: The only baserunner allowed in Carlos Rodon's 2021 no-hitter was Cleveland catcher Roberto Perez, who was hit by a pitch with one out in the bottom of the ninth. Likewise, Zach Stewart allowed only one baserunner in his 2011 effort against the Twins. Minnesota third baseman Danny Valencia led off the bottom of the eighth with a double in an eight-pitch at bat.

NOTE 8: In 1967, the White Sox, Red Sox, Tigers, and Twins were involved in a very tight pennant race that went to the very last day of the season, with Boston coming out on top. In that environment, Chicago ace Joel Horlen threw a September no-hitter against the Tigers. The only Detroit batters to reach base were catcher Bill Freehan (hit by a pitch in the third inning) and third baseman Eddie Mathews (reached first base on an error by Chicago first baseman Ken Boyer). Mathews was subsequently retired on a double play grounder back to the pitcher Horlen.

Beyond his pitching a no-hitter – a remarkable feat unto itself – Joe Cowley had an exceptional start to his career – he came to the majors as an undrafted pitcher at a time when the draft went through 40 rounds. Players drafted after the first few rounds typically had a very small chance to make it to the majors, much less an undrafted high-school pitcher. Cowley signed as a free agent with Atlanta in 1976 after graduating from Lafayette High School in Lexington, Kentucky. Of course, many no-hit pitchers weren't drafted because they were born outside of the United States, began playing before there even was a draft, or – like Cowley – weren't drafted at all.

Table 16-3. No-hit Pitcher Draft Round and JAWS Level Breakdown

Draft Round	Number of No-hit Pitchers	No-hit Pitcher JAWS Level	Number of No-hit Pitchers
Round 1	29	Level 1 (JAWS = 50.0 & up)	16
Rounds 2-5	25	Level 2 (JAWS = 30.0 to 49.9)	25
Rounds 6-39	26	Level 3 (JAWS = 20.0 to 29.9)	24
Undrafted American Born	4	Level 4 (JAWS = 10.0 to 19.9)	23
Ineligible Foreign Born	16	Level 5 (JAWS = 9.9 & below)	22
No Draft At the time	10	N/A	0
Total	110	Total	110

METHODOLOGY: This table represents an analysis of the draft round and career JAWS value of all pitchers who threw a no-hitter from 1965 through 2021. 110 no-hit pitchers are included in this analysis. Pitchers are divided into groups based on draft round and levels of career JAWS achievement.

LEGEND: JAWS = Jaffe Wins Above Replacement Score. JAWS is a sabermetric baseball statistic developed to evaluate the strength of a player's career and merit for induction into the Baseball Hall of Fame. It is created by averaging a player's career Wins Above Replacement (WAR) with their 7-year peak WAR.

NOTE 1: Roughly speaking, a quarter of the no-hit pitchers were drafted in the first round, a quarter in the next four rounds, and a quarter in all the remaining rounds. The remaining quarter represents pitchers who weren't drafted at all. No pitcher drafted after the 39th round has pitched a no-hitter. The lowest draft pick ever to throw a no-hitter, 39th-Rounder Kenny Rogers of the Texas Rangers, threw a perfect game against the California Angels in 1994. The remaining 30 pitchers who threw no-hitters from 1965-2021 mostly began their pro baseball career before the draft was initiated or were foreign- born pitchers who weren't eligible for the draft. Only four no-hit pitchers in that timeframe were pitchers who weren't drafted by any teams even though they were eligible to participate – Joe Cowley was one of those four.

NOTE 2: As described earlier, the number of pitchers in each of the five JAWS levels decreases substantially as the level of accomplishment gets higher and exponentially more difficult to achieve. For example, only around 2% of major league pitchers are in JAWS Level 1, whereas almost 75% of major league pitchers are in Level 5. Despite this enormous numbers imbalance, the two levels have almost the same number of no-hitters thrown. While this is somewhat intuitive, of course – better pitchers are going to throw more no-hitters – it really emphasizes the rarity of the lower-level pitchers, like Joe Cowley, throwing one. This is further broken out in this table that compares draft round and JAWS level for the 80 drafted pitchers.

Table 16-4. Drafted No-hit Pitcher Career Success Analysis

No-hit Pitcher JAWS Level	Number in Round 1	Number in Rounds 2-5	Number in Rounds 6-39	Total Pitchers
Level 1 (JAWS = 50.0 & up)	6	5	2	13
Level 2 (JAWS = 30.0 to 49.9)	6	8	3	17
Level 3 (JAWS = 20.0 to 29.9)	4	7	6	17
Level 4 (JAWS = 10.0 to 19.9)	8	3	5	16
Level 5 (JAWS = 9.9 & below)	5	2	10	17
Total Pitchers	29	25	26	80

METHODOLOGY: This table compares the career JAWS value and draft round of all drafted pitchers who threw a no-hitter from 1965 through 2021. Eighty no-hit pitchers are included in this analysis. Pitchers are grouped based on draft round and levels of career JAWS achievement.

LEGEND: JAWS = Jaffe Wins Above Replacement Score. JAWS is a sabermetric baseball statistic developed to evaluate the strength of a player's career and merit for induction into the Baseball Hall of Fame. It is created by averaging a player's career Wins Above Replacement (WAR) with their 7-year peak WAR.

NOTE 1: This chart further compares the expected career accomplishment by no-hit pitchers who were drafted. If a pitcher went in the earlier rounds, especially in the First Round, the likelihood of throwing a no-hitter increases markedly over those who were chosen later ... or not chosen at all. Again, this is somewhat intuitive, since more talented players are going to be drafted and the most talented are going to be drafted first.

NOTE 2: Making the likelihood of success even smaller for an undrafted pitcher like Joe Cowley, he signed with a pro team right out of high school. Of the drafted pitchers who threw a no-hitter, the large majority (62%) were drafted out of college. The remaining 38% were high-school graduates. This large disparity reflects several things. First, it's logical to assume that there's a selection process that goes with playing college ball, i.e., college players are going to be more talented as a group simply because they were competitively chosen to play for their schools. It's also safe to assume that college players have several years to develop their skills at a high level of competition before having to perform in the make-or-break professional leagues. For an undrafted high school player like Joe Cowley, the simple chances of success in the major leagues – much less the chances of throwing a no-hitter — were very small.

Starting with Bill Stoneman – the first drafted no-hit pitcher – the vast majority of no-hitters were thrown by players who were drafted, entered the majors before the draft, or were foreign-born pitchers who weren't eligible for the draft. To be more specific, through 2021 there have been only four American no-hit pitchers who were not drafted, like Joe Cowley. Analyzing this even further, players drafted in the first five rounds had a 40% chance of making it to MLB, with players drafted from round 6 and later having an 8% chance.

As displayed in the tables above, players who are undrafted have a microscopic chance of playing in the majors. From this vantage point, Joe Cowley is an enormous success. Not only did he beat the odds by making it to the majors with the Braves in 1982, and then with the Yankees from 1984-1985, he threw a no-hitter against Reggie Jackson and the mighty California Angels in 1986. Joe Cowley should be celebrated for this.

Catcher Ron Karkovice is another success story, in a different way. A career member of the Chicago White Sox, Karkovice spent his entire 12-year stint in the major leagues with the same team. He was called up in mid-August of 1986 and quickly became the team's starting catcher due to his impressive hitting and his maturity behind the plate. His role as a starter didn't last, though. His 1987 and 1988 seasons were disasters at the plate, hitting .071 and .174 respectively as he bounced between the majors and AAA. By 1989, he had reestablished himself as a full-time major leaguer, primarily as an often-used backup to Hall-of-Famer Carlton Fisk. Later in his career, he would be Chicago's primary starting catcher.

Karkovice was renowned for his defensive prowess and poise behind the plate. In particular, his throwing arm was legendary. In 1991, *Inside Sports* magazine summed it up this way: "The much-in-demand back-up to Carlton Fisk is said to own the most powerful catcher's arm in the bigs. He (Ron Karkovice) caught 17 of 34 base-stealers, an inhuman success rate in this day and age. Luckily for would-be thieves, Karkovice plays only twice a week."

On that September day in 1986, 27-year-old Joe Cowley and 22-year-old rookie catcher Ron Karkovice worked well together, and the result was a game for the record books.

Ron Karkovice Interview
Conducted by Kevin Hurd on May 13, 2021

Kevin Hurd (KH): Would you consider yourself to be the best player or catcher on your Little League, American Legion, High School, or Minor League teams?

Ron Karkovice (RK): In Little League from ages 8-14, I played pitcher and first base. At 15, I started playing catcher. I also played catcher in American Legion Ball, and in high school. I was the best catcher on my team in both the American Legion and in high school (Boone High School in Orlando, Florida). In high school my junior year, we won the state title, and in my senior year we made it to the final four in the state.

In the minors, I was on a team (Birmingham at the AA level) in 1986 where many of the players on the team were prospects. There were four players that hit over 20 home runs. I was the starting catcher.

KH: Did you feel any different, good or bad, on the day of Joe Cowley's no-hitter?

RK: It was great catching a no-hitter. The next day Joe was popping off to the Angels before the game. Our teammates were saying to him, "Joe, don't pop off to the Angels." I didn't say anything because I was a rookie and had only been with the team for a month.

KH: What pitches, such as the fastball, curve, or slider, were working best for Joe that day?

RK: The slider. The Angels hitters were chasing it a lot. The pitch would start off good, came right up to the plate, then dipped out of the strike zone and their hitters chased it.

KH: What was the best defensive play or the closest you came to losing the no-hitter?

RK: There were several plays, but I remember Reggie Jackson hitting a long fly to center field – I think it was the ninth inning – that Daryl Boston was able to chase down and catch.

KH: Did Joe shake off your signs much during the game?

RK: Actually, yes, he did. I was a rookie who had been on the team for a month. Joe had been pitching for four years and knew the hitters better than I did. I remember my first major league game (August 17), and I caught Steve Carlton who was pitching his first American League game. Steve shook me off a lot the first few innings, then we got more synchronized after that. After the game he told me, "Good game, kid."

KH: Did you catch any no-hitters in Little League, American Legion, high school or the minors?

RK: No, although I did catch a second no-hitter in the majors (on August 11, 1991). The pitcher was Wilson Alvarez.

KH: Do you have any memorabilia or souvenirs, such as a baseball, plaque, uniform, or something else, from the game in your house?

RK: For that game, no. Usually what the Hall of Fame requests is a signed ball and a signed uniform from the pitcher, and a signed ball from the catcher.

KH: From reading baseball-reference.com, I see you have the nickname "Officer." How'd you get that nickname?

RK: With the White Sox, we did a commercial with several players. I played a trooper carrying a gun which signified I had a gun for an arm. Ken Harrelson (General Manager) gave me the nickname.

KH: You were a 22-year-old rookie when the no-hitter happened. How big of a deal was it?

RK: It was a big, big deal. The first four or five games I caught in August I was very nervous. I was still very new to the big leagues, and then this happened.

KH: You played from 1986-1998 with the White Sox. You played for managers Jim Fregosi, Jeff Torborg, Gene Lamont, and Terry Bevington. Who'd you like playing for the most?

RK: Jeff Torborg. He was very much of a player's manager. Not that the other managers weren't, but Jeff seemed to have more standing with the front office if a problem with a player came up.

KH: Do you think the number of pitches Joe Cowley threw that day (138 pitches) led to him having a short career?

RK: Well, Joe didn't get a sore arm. He had control problems. This game he threw 138 pitches – half were balls. His ball always moved a lot. He overthrew a lot of the time. Like I said, he always had control problems.

KH: Did Joe request you as his catcher before this game?

RK: No, Jim Fregosi (the White Sox manager) would always decide who was going to catch every game. I've seen circumstances where a star pitcher tells the manager or pitching coach that he wants a specific catcher to catch him every game. When Charlie Hough pitched for us on the White Sox, he would request me because I was good at catching the knuckleball. I would let the knuckler come to me rather than stab at it.

KH: Do you still stay in contact with Joe Cowley?

RK: No, I haven't talked to him in years.

KH: Did your team give you a bonus for catching the no-hitter?

RK: Well, Joe Cowley got a watch and $1,500. I got $500. I've heard that with other teams the pitcher will get $1,500 and he will then take out $200-$300 and give it to his catcher.

KH: During the game, when did you think, *"He's got a real shot at a no-hitter?"* Was it the fifth inning, sixth inning, or later?

RK: It was about the sixth or seventh inning. In keeping with superstition, nobody said anything to Joe about it so they wouldn't jinx him.

KH: Were you able to get a follow-on job in baseball after your playing days were over? For example, in the majors, minors, college, high school, or working in the media?

RK: Well, I was a manager in 2000 in the Gulf Coast League, and in 2009 I was a minor league coach in Newark. In 2012-13, I coached and managed in Camden, New Jersey.

KH: What kind of work do you do outside of baseball? Do you enjoy it?

RK: From 2001-2008 I owned a lawn maintenance business. Since 2015, I've worked at and owned Maschmeyer Concrete. I like it – it gives me something to do. Also, I've got six kids, two living with me now. Unlike when I was in baseball, I can come home every day after work and see my kids instead of being gone six months a year.

KH: You were able to get a job in baseball. Do you think having caught a no-hitter helped you get the job?

RK: Not really. It didn't hurt. Many of the jobs in baseball, such as minor league coach and manager, and major league coach, are really dependent on who you know. For a major league manager position, the manager really has to know his stuff and he picks guys he knows to fill the coaching positions.

KH: Do you have any kids or grandkids who have or will pursue baseball as a career? Do you encourage them to do so?

RK: I've got four girls and two boys. My two oldest girls were into cheerleading in high school. My youngest girls are into horses. My boys played baseball in high school, then switched to playing football. I supported their decisions.

KH: Was the no-hitter the highlight of your career? If not, what was?

RK: A couple of other events were my highlights:

(1) The other no-hitter I caught (by pitcher Wilson Alvarez on August 11, 1991). Alvarez was a rookie, and it was his second career start. Before the game, the pitching coach told Alvarez, "Whatever Karkovice calls, you throw."

(2) Number two was the first home run I hit in the majors (on August 27, 1986). I had been up for about a week and a half, and I hit it off Danny Jackson of Kansas City.

KH: What was your best season?

RK: That would be 1993. We made the ALCS playoffs, I hit 20 HRs, and if I hadn't got injured right before the All-Star game, I probably would have been on the All-Star team.

KH: Have you been to the section of the Baseball Hall of Fame that focuses on no-hitters?

RK: No, I haven't.

KH: Which pitcher was the hardest for you to hit?

RK: Dave Stieb. He threw from a lot of different angles. I could never pick up the ball.

KH: Have you spent time signing autographs in Las Vegas, or Florida, or Arizona during spring training?

RK: I did sign autographs in Arizona with the White Sox, along with Ron Kittle and Daryl Boston. I have also signed autographs a couple times in Chicago.

KH: Do you have any favorite stories regarding any of these experiences?

RK: For autographs: I like that people will keep up with you, and not just when you played. They know what you're doing in your post-playing career. It's good to have people still remember you. For my playing career, I remember playing in my first game. I flew in the night before, the plane was late, so I didn't catch that night. Hall of Famer Steve Carlton was going to be the pitcher on August 17, and I was scared. I was told "You'll be catching tomorrow." We won 7-4, I got a hit, everything worked out well.

CHAPTER 17

ERIC MILTON: FACING THE "B" TEAM

September 11, 1999
Eric Milton throws a brilliant game against
an Angels team that had clearly given up

"I gave it everything I had; it's probably the greatest day of my life. It's not about who's at the plate."
Twins pitcher Eric Milton describing his reaction to throwing a no-hitter (Scott Miller, "Morning Glory," *St. Paul Pioneer Press*, September 12, 1999).

"I did a lot of following with (Dave Stewart). (With) Milton, however, I'm the veteran. I was more nervous than he was in the seventh, eighth, and ninth innings. He's going to pretty much throw what I call, so I felt a tremendous amount more pressure not to blow it."
Veteran Minnesota catcher Terry Steinbach comparing his first no-hitter in 1990 with Dave Stewart and the Oakland A's to his no-hitter with Eric Milton (Interview with author Stew Thornley, "September 11, 1999: Eric Milton no-hits the Angels," *Society for American Baseball Research (Sabr.org)*, February 15, 2008).

"You don't want to see your team get no-hit. It's a frustrating thing, whether you're in the game or not. All of us were in the dugout, watching after the fifth inning . . . you don't want that to happen. I don't care what the score is, we're getting no-hit. I guess (manager Joe Maddon) decided

we were going to get the day off. It's amazing some of the things you see in this game."

Veteran Angels' slugger Mo Vaughn expressing his frustration at not being called upon to hit during a no-hit game (Mike DiGiovanna, "Milton Finds Paradise Won in No-Hitter," *Los Angeles Times*, September 12, 1999).

"Due in large part to the pathetic lineup the Angels trotted into the batter's box, Milty's no-no often gets discounted as a "fluke" or somehow undeserving of praise. What is incredibly impressive, however, are the 13 strikeouts on just 122 pitches. Usually, a high K number results in a high pitch count, but not here. This wasn't just Milton getting lucky against inferior opponents — it was him dominating those inferior opponents."

Sportswriter Zach Koenig ("If you throw a no-hitter and no one sees it, does it count? Eric Milton's, twenty years ago does," *SB Nation (twinkietown.com)*, September 12, 2019).

"I knew what was going on. The fans really got behind me from the seventh inning on. That kind of ovation really got you going. It's a miracle. I had the opportunity. I gave it all I had and it was able to work out."

Eric Milton describing his reaction as he realized he had a no-hitter going ("Milton tosses fourth no-hitter in Twins' history," *ESPN.com*, September 11, 1999).

The 70-win Anaheim Angels of 1999 were a poor-hitting team. They were dead last (14th out of 14 teams) in the American League in hits, doubles, batting average, and on-base percentage. They were also next to last in runs scored, slugging percentage, and OPS. Even so, they had some individual stars who were recognized as hitting threats. Up-and-coming players like Troy Glaus, Darin Erstad, Jim Edmonds, and Garrett Anderson had either been named to the American League All-Star team recently or would be chosen soon. In addition, solid veterans Randy Velarde, Orlando Palmeiro, Tim Salmon, and former MVP Mo Vaughn were regulars that year.

This was not the lineup Eric Milton and the Twins faced the day of his no-hitter. Except for Troy Glaus and Orlando Palmeiro, the Anaheim lineup was composed entirely of substitutes and late-season call-ups. In place of the future stars and seasoned veterans on the Angels, Milton and the Twins faced players like rookie Brett Hemphill (21 career at bats, batting average of .143), second-year Matt Luke (269 total at bats over two seasons as a part-time player), rookie Trent Durrington (235 career at bats, .196 batting average), utility infielder Andy Sheets (.197 batting average in 1999), and rookie Jerry DaVanon with one career plate appearance to his name. Light-hitting backup catcher Steve Decker was the designated hitter that day in place of slugger Mo Brooks.

The wholesale replacement of substitutes in the Anaheim lineup undoubtedly contributed to the team's hitless performance that day. The Angels unintentionally set a record that afternoon in the Metrodome. With seven substitutes inserted in place of the nine usual starters, they set the record for the most lineup substitutes ever for a no-hit game. The table below shows the 15 games where four or more players were substitutes for the usual starters. Thirteen of the 15 teams were in a similar position as the Angels, as they had been or were just about to be eliminated from postseason consideration and they wanted to rest their starters and try out younger players who had spent most of the season in the minor leagues. The other two teams, the 1958 New York Yankees and 2013 Detroit Tigers, had already punched their tickets to the postseason and were resting their regulars.

Table 17-1. September No-hitters with four or more substitutes

Rank	Date/Score Pitcher(s)	Opponent (Status)	Regular Player (Position)	Substitute Player	# Sub
1	9/11/1999 Min 7-0 Eric Milton (Minnesota Twins)	Anaheim Angels (Eliminated)	M. Waldeck (C) D. Erstad (1B) R. Velarde (2B) G. Disarcina (SS) O. Palmeiro (LF) G. Anderson (CF) T. Salmon (RF) M. Vaughn (DH)	B. Hemphill M. Luke T. Durrington A. Sheets T. Greene O. Palmeiro* J. DaVanon S. Decker	7 of 9
2 (tie)	9/22/1977 Tex 6-0 Bert Blyleven (Texas Rangers)	California Angels (Eliminated)	T. Humphrey (C) T. Salata (1B) J. Remy (2B) D. Chalk (3B) R. Mulliniks (SS) J. Rudi (LF) G. Flores (CF) B. Bonds (RF) D. Baylor (DH)	A. Etchebarren W. Aikens D. Chalk* R. Jackson M. Guerrero T. Bosley K. Landreaux D. Baylor* B. Bonds*	6 of 9

Rank	Date/Score Pitcher(s)	Opponent (Status)	Regular Player (Position)	Substitute Player	# Sub
2 (tie)	9/2/1990 Tor 3-0 Dave Stieb (Toronto Blue Jays)	Cleveland Indians (Eliminated)	S. Alomar (C) K. Hernandez (1B) B. Jacoby (3B) F. Fermin (SS) C. Maldonado (LF) M. Webster (CF) R. Jefferson (DH)	J. Skinner B. Jacoby* T. Brookens C. Baerga D. James A. Cole M. Ramirez	6 of 9
4 (tie)	9/20/1908 Chi 1-0 Frank Smith (Chicago White Sox)	Philadelphia Athletics (Eliminated)	O. Schrecongost (C) H. Davis (1B) E. Collins (2B) J. Collins (3B) T. Hartsell (OF) D. Murphy (OF)	J. Lapp D. Murphy* S. Bar F. Manush J. Coombs S. Seybold	5 of 8
4 (tie)	9/16/1960 Mil 4-0 Warren Spahn (Milwaukee Braves)	Philadelphia Phillies (Eliminated)	J. Coker (C) T. Taylor (2B) A. Dark (3B) B. Smith (LF) B. Del Greco (CF)	C. Neeman B. Malkmus J. Woods J. Callison T. Gonzalez	5 of 8
6	9/28/1975 Oak 5-0 Blue (5) Abbott (1) Lindblad (1) Fingers (2) (Oak A's)	California Angels (Eliminated)	E. Rodriguez (C) M. Miley (SS) D. Collins (LF) M. Rivers (CF) L. Stanton (RF) T. Harper (DH)	B. Allietta I. Hampton R. Jackson L. Stanton* J. Balaz P. Dade	5 of 9
7 (tie)	9/20/1958 Bal 1-0 Hoyt Wilhelm (Baltimore Orioles)	New York Yankees (Clinched AL pennant 9/13/1958)	Y. Berra (C) B. Skowron (1B) G. McDougald (2B) A. Carey (3B) T. Kubek (SS)	E. Howard M. Throneberry B. Richardson B. Skowron* J. Lumpe	4 of 8
7 (tie)	9/29/1976 SF 9-0 John Montefusco (SF Giants)	Atlanta Braves (Eliminated)	V. Correl (C) J. Wynn (LF) R. Office (CF) K. Henderson (RF)	D. Murphy D. May B. Asselstine T. Paciorek	4 of 8
7 (tie)	9/8/1993 Hou 7-1 Darryl Kile (Hou Astros)	New York Mets (Eliminated)	T. Bogar (SS) H. Johnson (3B) V. Coleman (LF) B. Bonilla (RF)	J. McKnight B. Huskey J. Orsulak J. Burnitz	4 of 8

Rank	Date/Score Pitcher(s)	Opponent (Status)	Regular Player (Position)	Substitute Player	# Sub
7 (tie)	9/14/2008 Chi 5-0 Carlos Zambrano (Chi Cubs)	Houston Astros (Eliminated)	B. Ausmus (C) K. Matsui (2B) T. Wiggington (3B) C. Lee (LF)	H. Quintero D. Newhan G. Blum D. Erstad	4 of 8
7 (tie)	9/29/2013 Mia 1-0 Henderson Alvarez III (Miami Marlins)	Detroit Tigers (Clinched AL Central 9/28/2013)	A. Avila (C) M. Cabrera (3B) J. Peralta (SS) A. Dirks (LF) A. Jackson (CF) T. Hunter (RF)	B. Pena R. Santiago J. Iglesias J. Peralta* D. Kelly A. Dirks*	4 of 8
7 (tie)	9/28/2014 Was 1-0 Jordan Zimmerman (Wash Nationals)	Miami Marlins (Eliminated)	J. Saltalamacchia (C) G. Jones (1B) C. Yelich (LF) M. Ozuna (CF) G. Stanton (RF)	J.T. Realmuto J. Bour R. Johnson C. Yelich* G. Jones	4 of 8
13 (tie)	9/4/1993 NY 4-0 Jim Abbott (New York Yankees)	Cleveland Indians (Eliminated)	P. Sorrento (1B) A. Espinoza (3B) W. Kirby (RF) R. Jefferson (DH)	R. Milligan J. Thome C. Maldonado M. Ramirez	4 of 9
13 (tie)	9/1/2019 Hou 2-0 Justin Verlander (Houston Astros)	Toronto Blue Jays (Eliminated)	D. Jansen (C) F. Galvis (SS) L. Gurriel Jr. (LF) T. Hernandez (CF) R. Grichuk (RF)	R. McGuire B. Bichette B. Drury R. Grichuk* B. McKinney	4 of 9
13 (tie)	9/11/2021 Mil 3-0 Burnes (8) Hader (1) (Milwaukee Brewers)	Cleveland Indians (Nearly eliminated from WC)	C. Hernandez (2B) A. Rosario (SS) E. Rosario (LF) J. Naylor (RF)	O. Miller A. Gimenez H. Ramirez B. Zimmer	4 of 9

METHODOLOGY: This table tabulates and ranks no-hit games based on the number of substitutions in the starting lineup of the team who was no-hit. Only games during the final month of the regular season (September) were considered, as that is when rosters expand to 40 players and teams eliminated from competition or teams who have already clinched postseason berths will freely substitute players.

The timeframe examined was 1900-2021. Rankings are determined based upon the total number of substitutions as compared to the number of non-pitchers in the lineup. For example, a team that substituted four players in a lineup that only has eight non-pitchers ranks higher than a team that substituted four players in a lineup that has nine non-pitchers (i.e., where a designated hitter is used). Regular starters who are in the lineup but not playing in their usual position are not counted as substitutes.

LEGEND: Dates are shown as month/day/year (for example, June 12, 2018, is shown as 6/12/2018). None of the games in this table were either the first or second game of a doubleheader, and all games were nine inning contests. Instead, numbers in parentheses identify the number of innings thrown by a specific pitcher in a multi-pitcher no-hitter. For example, Vida Blue threw five (5) innings of no-hit ball in 1975, and Corbin Burnes threw eight (8) innings in his 2021 no-hitter. "Eliminated" designates a team who has already been eliminated from postseason consideration. "Nearly eliminated" represents a team not mathematically eliminated from postseason consideration, but on the verge of elimination with no realistic chance of contention. "Clinched" identifies a team headed to the postseason as a league or division champion. "Position" is the standard abbreviation for the fielding position for a player on the no-hit team. Substitute players are listed to the right of the player who normally started in the position. For example, "M. Waldeck (C)" indicates that he typically started at catcher for the Angels. In the next column to the right, "B. Hemphill" shows that Hemphill started at catcher that day. An asterisk ("*") identifies a player who was regularly in the team's lineup but starting at a different position on the day in question. Players in these circumstances do not count as a substitute for the purposes of this analysis. "# Sub" shows how many substitutes were in the starting lineup and the number of non-pitcher spots in the lineup ("of 8" or "of 9").

The 1999 Angels were a team in turmoil. After coming close to winning the American League West Division title in 1997 and 1998, the 1999 season turned into a disaster. By the time September rolled around, Anaheim was hopelessly out of the playoff race. Anaheim manager Terry Collins was fired on September 3rd. The next day, replacement manager Joe Maddon and the Angels were mathematically eliminated from the division title race. At that point, the Angels began looking to the future, playing younger players as part of their September call-ups. With a record of 56-84 going into the game on September 11, new manager Joe Maddon had nothing to lose by trying out new players, as the expectations for him and his Angels were not very high.

Adding to the strangeness of the game that day, the start time had been moved up to 11:00 AM to accommodate the University of Minnesota football game against the University of Louisiana at Monroe that evening. Because of the early start following on the heels of a Friday night game, batting practice the next day was curtailed for both teams. While the lack of practice clearly didn't hurt the Minnesota batters, it may have affected the Anaheim hitters.

As it turned out, the game outcome was little in doubt after the second inning. The Twins struck in the bottom of the first with a Terry Steinbach triple driving in right fielder Matt Lawton to open the scoring. In the bottom of the second, the Twins tallied three more runs on three singles, a walk, and a Ramon Ortiz balk to give Minnesota a 4-0 lead. The Twins would add two more in the bottom of the fifth when shortstop Denny Hocking hit a two-run home run. The Twins finished their scoring in the eighth inning when third baseman Corey Koskie knocked in Terry Steinbach for Minnesota's seventh and final run of the game.

On the other side of things, Eric Milton was dominating the Anaheim hitters, compiling 13 strikeouts while only walking two batters. There were only two occasions during the game where Milton's no-hitter was in doubt. Leading off the fifth inning, Anaheim designated hitter Steve Decker hit a towering drive to left field, where it was caught by fleet-footed Torii Hunter at the wall. With two outs in the eighth, catcher Bret Hemphill hit a broken bat infield blooper. Second baseman Cleatus Davidson made a nice running catch of the weak pop fly near the mound in what almost certainly would have been a single if it had dropped. Milton got stronger as the game went on, too, retiring the last 18 batters he faced.

Despite the fact Milton was clearly pitching against a substandard lineup, his accomplishment shouldn't be minimized. He achieved the highest game score (98) of any Twins pitcher since the franchise moved from Washington DC to Minnesota in 1961. The top Game Scores by franchise pitchers are shown in the table below.

Table 17-2. Senators and Twins Highest Game Scores

Rank	Pitcher (Team Home)	Date Score	Opponent	GSc	IP, Hits, Runs, ERs, Walks, Strikeouts
1	Walter Johnson (Washington)	5/15/1918 Was 1-0 (18 inn)	Chicago White Sox	120	18.0 IP, 10 Hits, 0 Runs, 0 ERs, 1 BB, 9 Ks
2	Walter Johnson (Washington)	7/28/1908 Was 2-1 (16 inn)	St. Louis Browns	113-115	16.0 IP, 9 Hits, 1 Run, ? ERs, 2 BBs, 15 Ks

Rank	Pitcher (Team Home)	Date Score	Opponent	GSc	IP, Hits, Runs, ERs, Walks, Strikeouts
3 (tie)	Walter Johnson (Washington)	4/13/1926 Was 1-0 (15 inn)	Philadelphia Athletics	111	15.0 IP, 6 Hits, 0 Runs, 0 ERs, 3 BBs, 9 Ks
3 (tie)	Walt Masterson (Washington)	6/8/1947 (1) Was 1-0 (18 inn)	Chicago White Sox	111	16.0 IP, 6 Hits, 0 Runs, 0 ERs, 6 BBs, 7 Ks
5	Walter Johnson (Washington)	7/25/1918 Was 1-0 (15 inn)	St. Louis Browns	110	15.0 IP, 4 Hits, 0 Runs, 0 ERs, 2 BBs, 3 Ks
6	Casey Patten (Washington)	7/22/1904 0-0 Tie (13 inn)	Detroit Tigers	109	13.0 IP, 4 Hits, 0 Runs, 0 ERs, 0 BBs, 10 Ks
7	Walter Johnson (Washington)	5/11/1919 0-0 Tie (12 inn)	New York Yankees	106	12.0 IP, 2 Hits, 0 Runs, 0 ERs, 1 BB, 9 Ks
8 (tie)	Walter Johnson (Washington)	9/5/1914 Was 4-1 (13 inn)	New York Yankees	101	13.0 IP, 4 Hits, 1 Run, 1 ER, 3 BBs, 9 Ks
8 (tie)	Eric Erickson (Washington)	8/20/1921 Was 1-0 (13 inn)	Chicago White Sox	101	13.0 IP, 3 Hits, 0 Runs, 0 ERs, 4 BBs, 4 Ks
10 (tie)	Wyatt Lee (Washington)	8/14/1903 (1) Was 1-0 (15 inn)	St. Louis Browns	100	15.0 IP, 10 Hits, 0 Runs, 0 ERs, 1 BB, 4 Ks
10 (tie)	Walter Johnson (Washington)	9/21/1914 Was 6-1 (13 inn)	Chicago White Sox	100	13.0 IP, 6 Hits, 1 Run, 1 ER, 3 BBs, 12 Ks
10 (tie)	Harry Harper (Washington)	5/24/1918 2-2 Tie (16 inn)	Detroit Tigers	100	16.0 IP, 6 Hits, 2 Runs, 2 ERs, 5 BB, 3 Ks
10 (tie)	G. Mogridge (Washington)	7/1/1921 (2) Was 1-0 (12 inn)	Philadelphia Athletics	100	12.0 IP, 3 Hits, 0 Runs, 0 ERs, 1 BB, 5 Ks
10 (tie)	Dutch Leonard (Washington)	5/4/1938 1-0 (13 inn)	Cleveland Indians	100	13.0 IP, 6 Hits, 0 Runs, 0 ERs, 0 BB, 5 Ks

METHODOLOGY: This table includes the highest Game Scores thrown by an (original franchise) Senators or Twins pitcher from 1901-2021. Games are ranked by Game Score (GSc) and consider all franchise regular season and postseason games. Table 17-3 below limits the eligible games to those pitching performances that were 10 innings or less. Game Score (GSc) measures a pitcher's performance in any given game started. Introduced by baseball writer/statistician Bill James in the 1980s, Game Score is presented as a figure between 0-100 — except for extreme outliers — and usually falls between 40-70.

LEGEND: Dates are shown as month/day/year (for example, June 12, 2018, is shown as 6/12/2018). The franchise was based in Washington and was known as the Senators when the team began as part of the newly created American League in 1901. The team was officially named the Senators during 1901–1904, the Nationals during 1905–1955, and the Senators again during 1956–1960, but nonetheless was commonly referred to as the Senators throughout its history. The team moved to Minneapolis-St. Paul in 1961, as the Washington Senators then became the Minnesota Twins. A new expansion franchise based in Washington, also known as the Senators, was established in the American League in 1961. That franchise moved to the Dallas-Fort Worth area in 1972 and was renamed the Texas Rangers. "Team Home" in the table above indicates whether the team was based in Washington or Minnesota during the season the game was thrown. IP = innings pitched. One-third of an inning pitched has 0.1 added and two-thirds of an inning pitched has 0.2 added (for example, 9 1/3 innings pitched is displayed as 9.1). BB(s) = base(s) on balls; K(s) = strikeout(s); ER(s) = earned run(s); inn = innings (associated with the length of extra-inning games); and (1) or (2) = first or second game of a doubleheader.

NOTE 1: The highest postseason Game Score ever achieved by a franchise pitcher was a score of 84 by Minnesota's Jack Morris in the decisive 10-inning Game 7 of the 1991 World Series against the Braves. In one of the most suspenseful games in postseason history, Morris outdueled John Smoltz and the Atlanta staff in an extra-inning thriller that was scoreless after nine innings. While this was not Morris's most dominating game ever – he achieved a 92 Game Score in a 1986 two-hit shutout against the Rangers, and he has a 1984 no-hitter versus the Red Sox (both games when he was with Detroit) – he never pitched in a more high-pressure situation during his 18-year major league career. With his team's season on the line, Hall of Famer Morris held the National League Champion Braves scoreless, as he scattered seven hits and allowed two walks. Routinely pitching with runners in scoring position – including a bases-loaded, one-out jam in the eighth inning – he managed to keep Atlanta off the scoreboard for 10 innings. Minnesota finally won with a one-out, walk off single in the bottom of the 10th.

NOTE 2: The highest postseason Game Score for the Senators was an 82, achieved by Hall of Famer Walter Johnson in the opening game of the 1925 World Series against the Pirates. Washington won by the score of 4-1, as Pittsburgh's lone run was the result of a Pie Traynor home run to lead off the fifth inning. Pittsburgh would win the series four games to three, as the Pirates came back from a three-games-to-one deficit and rallied for five runs against Johnson in the seventh and eighth innings to win the decisive seventh game by the score of 9-7.

NOTE 3: Walter Johnson features prominently in the list of the franchise's highest Game Scores, occupying four of the five highest scores in the team's history, including the top score of 120 in a 1-0 complete game shutout against the White Sox in 1918. His 18 innings pitched during that game was also the most ever thrown by a Senator or Twin in franchise history. In total, Johnson dominates this list, as he holds seven of the top 14 Game Scores for the Washington/Minnesota franchise. No other pitcher is on the list twice, and – unlike Johnson – none of the other pitchers listed has thrown a no-hitter.

The second highest Game Score for a franchise pitcher is also held by Walter Johnson for his 16-inning victory over the St. Louis Browns in 1908 at the age of 20. His 113 or 115 score is an unofficial tally because game records can't definitively determine whether the one run he allowed was earned or unearned that day. His 15 strikeouts are tied for second-most among Minnesota/Washington pitchers for most strikeouts in a game.

NOTE 4: The franchise record of 17 strikeouts in a game is held by Minnesota pitcher Johann Santana for his eight innings of work against the Texas Rangers in 2007. In that remarkable game, Santana averaged more than two strikeouts per inning, as he struck out three batters in three of the innings. Santana walked no one, and only allowed two hits. He was pulled at the end of the eighth after three Texas batters struck out swinging that inning. To that point, Santana had thrown 112 pitches, and the Twins were clinging to a 1-0 lead. Closer Joe Nathan finished the game by shutting out the Rangers in the ninth. Santana's Game Score of 95 is tied for fifth place among all franchise pitchers for highest score in a nine-inning or less game (see Table 17-3 below). Santana's remarkable game also places him in second place, with Dave Boswell, for highest score in a nine-inning game among all Minnesota pitchers.

NOTE 5: Tied for third on the franchise all-time leaderboard was Johnson's 15-inning Opening Day win in Washington against Connie Mack's Philadelphia Athletics in 1926. The ceremonial first pitch was thrown out by Vice President Charles Dawes, as President Calvin Coolidge was away. This game was Johnson's ninth Opening Day win, still a major league record. It was also the sixth and last time he threw 15 innings or more in a game. In Johnson's 1919 game against New York, he retired 28 straight Yankees after he allowed a one-out single to shortstop

Roger Peckinpaugh in the first inning. The 12-inning game ended in a 0-0 tie that was prematurely stopped due to a mistaken perception that Sunday games had to end by 6:00 in New York.

NOTE 6: Tied with Walter Johnson for third place on the all-time list is Walt Masterson. Masterson threw 16 scoreless innings in a 1-0, 18-inning shutout over the Philadelphia Athletics in 1947. Hall of Famer Early Wynn threw the last two innings in relief to close out the game for the win. Masterson was a stalwart for the Washington pitching staff throughout the 1940s, except during his two-year service during World War II. During his time with the team, the Senators had a winning record only once, and were often at the bottom of the American League. Masterson, though, was a bright spot for Washington, as he was selected for the American League All-Star team in 1947 and 1948. He even started the 1948 game for the AL in their 5-2 win over the National League.

As described earlier, Eric Milton's game registers as being tied for the best among all franchise pitchers in a game of 10-innings or less during the team's 121-season history. The complete list is included below in Table 17-3. For comparison purposes, I've included all the team's no-hitters in this table.

Table 17-3. Senators and Twins Highest Game Scores of 10 Innings or Less

Rank	Pitcher (Team Home)	Date Score	Opponent	GSc	IP, Hits, Runs, ERs, Walks, Strikeouts
1 (tie)	Walter Johnson (Washington)	5/23/1924 Was 4-0	Chicago White Sox	98	9.0 IP, 1 Hit, 0 Runs, 0 ERs, 1 BB, 14 Ks
1 (tie)	Eric Milton (Minnesota)	9/11/1999 Min 7-0	Anaheim Angels	98	9.0 IP, 0 Hits, 0 Runs, 0 ERs, 2 BBs, 13 Ks
3	Walter Johnson (Washington)	7/1/1920 Was 1-0	Boston Red Sox	97	9.0 IP, 0 Hits, 0 Runs, 0 ERs, 0 BBs, 10 Ks
4	Walter Johnson (Washington)	9/25/1910 (2) Was 3-0	St. Louis Browns	96	9.0 IP, 1 Hit, 0 Runs, 0 ERs, 0 BBs, 11 Ks
5 (tie)	Dave Boswell (Minnesota)	7/30/1966 Min 7-0	Baltimore Orioles	95	9.0 IP, 1 Hit, 0 Runs, 0 ERs, 1 BB, 11 Ks
5 (tie)	Johan Santana (Minnesota)	8/19/2007 Min 1-0	Texas Rangers	95	8.0 IP, 2 Hits, 0 Runs, 0 ERs, 0 BBs, 17 Ks
7 (tie)	Walter Johnson (Washington)	5/11/1912 Was 8-0	Cleveland Indians	94	9.0 IP, 2 Hits, 0 Runs, 0 ERs, 0 BBs, 11 Ks

Rank	Pitcher (Team Home)	Date Score	Opponent	GSc	IP, Hits, Runs, ERs, Walks, Strikeouts
7 (tie)	Jim Merritt (Minnesota)	5/30/1967 (2) Min 3-0	New York Yankees	94	9.0 IP, 2 Hits, 0 Runs, 0 ERs, 0 BBs, 11 Ks
9 (tie)	Bert Blyleven (Minnesota)	8/1/1986 Min 10-1	Oakland Athletics	93	9.0 IP, 2 Hits, 1 Run, 1 ER, 1 BB, 15 Ks
9 (tie)	Kevin Tapani (Minnesota)	6/24/1992 Min 11-0	California Angels	93	9.0 IP, 2 Hits, 0 Runs, 0 ERs, 0 BBs, 10 Ks
9 (tie)	Scott Baker (Minnesota)	8/31/2007 (2) Min 5-0	KC Royals	93	9.0 IP, 1 Hit, 0 Runs, 0 ERs, 1 BB, 9 Ks
33 (tie)	Bobby Burke (Washington)	8/8/1931 Was 5-0	Boston Red Sox	90	9.0 IP, 0 Hits, 0 Runs, 0 ERs, 5 BBs, 8 Ks
46 (tie)	Jack Kralick (Minnesota)	8/26/1962 Min 1-0	KC Athletics	89	9.0 IP, 0 Hits, 0 Runs, 0 ERs, 1 BB, 3 Ks
66 (tie)	Scott Erickson (Minnesota)	4/27/1994 Min 6-0	Milwaukee Brewers	88	9.0 IP, 0 Hits, 0 Runs, 0 ERs, 4 BBs, 5 Ks
128 (tie)	Dean Chance (Minnesota)	8/25/1967 (2) Min 2-1	Cleveland Indians	86	9.0 IP, 0 Hits, 1 Run, 1 ER, 5 BBs, 8 Ks
289 (tie)	Francisco Liriano (Minnesota)	5/3/2011 Min 1-0	Chicago White Sox	83	9.0 IP, 0 Hits, 0 Runs, 0 ERs, 6 BBs, 2 Ks
---	Walter Johnson (Washington)	8/25/1924 Was 2-0 (7 inn)	St. Louis Browns	77	7.0 IP, 0 Hits, 0 Runs, 0 ERs, 2 BBs, 2 Ks
---	Carl Cashion (Washington)	8/20/1912 (2) Was 2-0 (6 inn)	Cleveland Indians	73	6.0 IP, 0 Hits, 0 Runs, 0 ERs, 1 BB, 2 Ks
---	*Dean Chance (Minnesota)*	*8/6/1967 Min 2-0 (5 inn)*	*Boston Red Sox*	*71*	*5.0 IP, 0 Hits, 0 Runs, 0 ERs, 0 BBs, 4 Ks*

METHODOLOGY: This table includes the highest Game Scores of 10 innings or less thrown by an (original franchise) Senators or Twins pitcher from 1901-2021. Games are ranked by Game Score (GSc) and consider all franchise regular season and postseason games. For comparison purposes, all seven franchise no-hitters are included in this table. Game Score (GSc) measures a pitcher's performance in any given game started. Introduced by baseball writer/statistician Bill James in the 1980s, Game Score is presented as a figure between 0-100 — except for extreme outliers — and usually falls between 40-70.

LEGEND: Dates are shown as month/day/year (for example, June 12, 2018, is shown as 6/12/2018). The franchise was based in Washington and was known as the Senators when the team began as part of the newly created American League in 1901. The team was officially named the Senators during 1901–1904, the Nationals during 1905–1955, and the Senators again during 1956–1960, but nonetheless was commonly referred to as the Senators throughout its history in Washington. The team moved to Minneapolis-St. Paul in 1961, as the Washington Senators then became the Minnesota Twins. A new expansion franchise based in Washington, also known as the Senators, was established in the American League in 1961. That franchise moved to the Dallas-Fort Worth area in 1972 and was renamed the Texas Rangers. "Team Home" in the table above indicates whether the team was based in Washington or Minnesota during the season the game was thrown. IP = innings pitched. One-third of an inning pitched has 0.1 added and two-thirds of an inning pitched has 0.2 added (for example, 9 1/3 innings pitched is displayed as 9.1). BB(s) = base(s) on balls; K(s) = strikeout(s); ER(s) = earned run(s); inn = innings (associated with the length of extra-inning games); and (1) or (2) = first or second game of a doubleheader.

NOTE 1: Walter Johnson tops this list in a tie with Minnesota's Eric Milton. Johnson achieved a Game Score of 98 for his 1924 one-hit, 14-strikeout shutout against the White Sox in 1924. Hall of Famer Harry Hooper was the only Chicago batter who reached base that day. Hooper walked with one out in the first inning (he was subsequently doubled off first on a line drive). He also hit a one-out single in the fourth inning. Johnson recorded an impressive 14 strikeouts that afternoon. It was one of four occasions when he struck out 14 or more batters in a game.

NOTE 2: Much like the franchise all-time high scores with no innings limit, Walter Johnson dominates the 10-inning or less list, too. He holds four of the 11 top scores, including three of the top four scores. The only batter Johnson allowed to reach base in his 1920 no-hitter against the Red Sox – at 97, the third-highest Game Score on this franchise list – was on an error by Hall of Famer second baseman Bucky Harris to the leadoff hitter in the seventh inning (Harry Hooper strikes again). In Johnson's 1910 one-hitter against the St. Louis Browns – at 96, the fourth highest Game Score on the list – the only baserunner he allowed was a single by second baseman and lifetime .220 hitter Frank Truesdale.

NOTE 3: Dave Boswell's one-hit gem against the soon-to-be World Champion Orioles in 1966 – tied with Johann Santana's 17-strikeout performance for fifth place score in a nine-inning game – was remarkable. Not only did Boswell dominate three future Hall of Famers – MVP Frank Robinson, Brooks Robinson, and Luis Aparicio – he also had to overcome the ever-dangerous Boog Powell and Davey Johnson en route to blanking Baltimore. While Aparicio managed to draw a walk to lead off the game, the only Oriole hit was a single by right fielder Russ Snyder to lead off the seventh inning.

NOTE 4: Scott Baker – tied for ninth place with a 93 score – threw a perfect game for eight innings in his 2007 game against the Royals. Kansas City's John Buck drew a walk to lead off the top of the ninth inning, and Mike Sweeney hit a line drive single to center field with one out. Baker retired the last two batters for a 5-0 complete game victory. He threw 111 pitches in this effort.

NOTE 5: Jack Kralick only allowed one baserunner in his 1962 no-hitter against the Kansas City Athletics – pinch-hitter George Alusik drew a one-out walk in the top of the ninth inning. Dean Chance got off to a rather inauspicious start in his 1967 no-hitter versus the Indians. The Indians scored a first inning run on two walks, an error by third baseman Cesar Tovar to load the bases, and a wild pitch. Chance settled down after that, as he retired the last two batters in the inning. After that, he only allowed two more baserunners, both on walks, in a 2-1 Minnesota win. Francisco Liriano's 2011 no-hitter against the White Sox was his first complete game in 95 starts. He would throw two more complete games in his 300-start career, neither of which were shutouts.

NOTE 6: Carl Cashion (six innings in 1912), Walter Johnson (seven innings in 1924), and Dean Chance (five innings in 1967) would throw no-hit games that were officially counted at the time, but ended before nine innings were complete. Cashion's game against the Cleveland Naps was the second game of a doubleheader. It ended after only six innings because the teams had agreed prior to the first game to conclude the second contest early so that the Naps could catch a train to Boston, where they had a game against the Red Sox the next afternoon. Johnson's seven-inning no-hit game against the Browns was called due to rain with Washington leading 2-0. Dean Chance threw five perfect innings against the Boston Red Sox. His game was called due to rain in the bottom of the fifth with the Twins batting and leading 2-0. All three games were official contests, but do not count as no-hitters using modern, minimum nine innings criteria.

With 93 wins — more wins than any Twins pitcher in this century – and one of the highest Game Scores of any franchise pitcher, Johan Santana was a standout pitcher for Minnesota during his eight seasons with the team from 2000-2007. A two-time Cy Young winner and three-time All-Star with the Twins, Santana is also arguably the best pitcher from a long line of outstanding hurlers to ever come from Venezuela. Here's the top 10 list covering the period from 1900-2021:

Table 17-4. Best Pitchers Born in Venezuela

Rank	Pitcher (Home)	Team	Season(s)	Career IP	WAR (per 200 IP)	Wins (per season)
1	Johan Santana (Tovar)	Min Twins NY Mets	2000-2007 2008-2012	2,025.2	51.1 (5.04)	139 (11.6)
2	Felix Hernandez (Valencia)	Sea Mariners	2005-2019	2,729.2	49.9 (3.66)	169 (11.3)
3	Carlos Zambrano (Puerto Cabello)	Chi Cubs Mia Marlins	2001-2011 2012	1,959.0	38.3 (3.91)	132 (11.0)
4	Freddy Garcia (Caracas)	Sea Mariners Chi White Sox Phi Phillies Det Tigers Chi White Sox NY Yankees Bal Orioles Atl Braves	1999-2004 2004-2006 2007 2008 2009-2010 2011-2012 2013 2013	2,264.0	34.4 (3.04)	156 (10.4)
5	Anibal Sanchez (Maracay)	Fla Marlins Det Tigers Atl Braves Was Nationals	2006-2012 2012-2017 2018 2019-2020	1,948.1	29.1 (2.99)	116 (7.7)
6	Wilson Alvarez (Maracaibo)	Tex Rangers Chi White Sox SF Giants TB D-Rays LA Dodgers	1989 1991-1997 1997 1998-2002 2003-2005	1,747.2	25.0 (2.86)	102 (7.3)
7	Kelvim Escobar (La Guaira)	Tor Blue Jays LA Angels	1997-2003 2004-2009	1,507.0	24.6 (3.26)	101 (8.4)

Rank	Pitcher (Home)	Team	Season(s)	Career IP	WAR (per 200 IP)	Wins (per season)
8	Francisco Rodriguez (Caracas)	LA Angels NY Mets Mil Brewers Bal Orioles Mil Brewers Det Tigers	2002-2008 2009-2011 2011-2013 2013 2014-2015 2016-2017	976.0	24.2 (4.96)	52 Wins (3.3) 437 Saves (27.3)
9	Carlos Carrasco (Barquisimeto)	Cle Indians NY Mets	2009-2020 2021	1,296.0	20.7 (3.19)	89 (7.4)
10	Jhoulys Chacín (Maracaibo)	Col Rockies Ari D-backs Atl Braves LA Angels SD Padres Mil Brewers Bos Red Sox Atl Braves Col Rockies	2009-2014 2015 2016 2016 2017 2018-2019 2019 2020 2021	1,388.1	19.7 (2.84)	81 (6.2)

METHODOLOGY: To qualify for inclusion in this table, pitchers had to be of Venezuelan heritage and born in Venezuela. Pitchers are ranked from 1-10 based upon their career Wins Above Replacement (WAR) between 1900-2021. WAR measures a player's value in all facets of the game by deciphering how many more wins he's worth than a replacement-level player at his same position.

LEGEND: Home = the place a pitcher was born in Venezuela. Team and season(s) are the teams a pitcher played for and the season(s) they were with each team listed in chronological order. Career IP = career innings pitched. Career WAR = the pitcher's accumulated WAR over his career. Career Wins = the number of wins each pitcher accumulated over his career. Because pitchers had different career lengths, I included two rate measures (WAR per 200 innings pitched and wins per season). Because Francisco Rodriguez was a career reliever, his career saves and save rate per season are included as well. Multiple pitchers missed entire seasons for various reasons. Therefore, those missed seasons don't count as part of the wins per season calculation. Specifically, Johan Santana missed the 2011 season, Wilson Alvarez missed 1990 and 2000-2001, Kelvim Escobar missed 2008, and Carlos Carrasco missed 2012.

NOTE 1: This group of extremely talented pitchers authored multiple no-hitters. Johan Santana threw a no-hitter for the Mets in 2012 – it was the franchise's first no-hitter after being in existence for over 50 seasons. Felix Hernandez hurled a perfect game for the Mariners against Tampa Bay in 2012. Carlos Zambrano pitched a no-hitter for the Cubs against the Astros in 2008. That game was played at Miller Park in Milwaukee because Hurricane Ike was pounding Houston at the time. It's the only occasion where a no-hitter was thrown at a neutral site. Anibal Sanchez threw a no-hitter for the Marlins against the Diamondbacks in 2006.

NOTE 2: Besides Johan Santana winning the Cy Young Award in 2004 and 2006, he was an All-Star in 2005-2007 and 2009. Felix Hernandez was the Cy Young winner in 2010 and was a six-time All-Star with the Mariners in 2009 and 2011-15. Many of the other impressive pitchers on this list were also named as All-Stars during their playing careers: Carlos Zambrano in 2004, 2006, and 2008 with the Cubs; Freddy Garcia in 2001 and 2002 as a Mariner; Wilson Alvarez in 2004 with the White Sox; and Francisco Rodriguez in 2004 and 2007-2009 as a closer with the Angels and Mets. Carlos Carrasco and Jhoulys Chacin are still active beyond 2021. These pitchers have helped their clubs to postseason success as well. Francisco Rodriguez was a big part of the Anaheim Angels championship run in 2002 as a rookie closer, Freddy Garcia was a World Series champion with the White Sox in 2005, and Anibal Sanchez helped the Nationals win their first title in 2019.

NOTE 3: Venezuela has been highly competitive during the World Baseball Classic, reaching the semifinal round in 2009. Freddy Garcia (2006), Francisco Rodriguez (2006, 2009 & 2013), Carlos Zambrano (2006), Kelvim Escobar (2006), Johan Santana (2006), Felix Hernandez (2009 & 2017), Jhoulys Chacin (2013 & 2017), Carlos Zambrano (2013), and Anibal Sanchez (2013) were all chosen to be part of the national team during the WBC Tournament.

The focus of this chapter, Eric Milton, was a star in his own right. His franchise-best nine-inning performance was no fluke, either. With a Game Score of 92 in a 2002 shutout he pitched against the Chicago White Sox, he is also tied for ninth place on the list of highest scores by a Minnesota pitcher (1961-2021), During that game, he walked no one while striking out 11 and allowing only three hits. Named to the 2001 American League All-Star team, Milton excelled in the postseason, going 1–0 with a 1.65 ERA in the 2002 and 2003 playoffs against the Athletics, Angels, and Yankees. In 2004 with the Phillies, Milton came close to throwing a second no-hitter. He took the game into the ninth inning before giving up a leadoff double to Michael Barrett of the Cubs in a 3-2 Philadelphia win. Overall, Milton completed his 11-year major league career with a record of 89-85 and an ERA of 4.99 with the Twins, Phillies, Reds, and Dodgers as he retired after the 2009 season.

Milton stayed in baseball after his playing days, joining the University of Maryland in September 2011 as an assistant coach. In 2012 he was named interim head coach, and in 2013, he became the head coach at Severna Park High School in Maryland.

Veteran catcher Terry Steinbach finished out his 14-year career with the Twins in 1999 after having spent his first 11 seasons with the Athletics, being named part of the American League All-Star team three times with Oakland. In 1988, Steinbach hit a solo home run and a sacrifice fly in the All-Star game, accounting for both American League runs in a 2-1 victory, He was named All-Star MVP that year. He was also a key part of the World Champion 1989 Oakland team.

Since retiring, Steinbach was a bench coach with the Twins in 2013-14, coached some high school ball, and did a short stint as a Twins announcer. I invite you to enjoy the interview with Terry Steinbach below.

Terry Steinbach Interview
Conducted by Kevin Hurd on June 4, 2021

Kevin Hurd (KH): Would you consider yourself to be the best catcher on your Little League, American Legion, High School, college, or minor league teams?

Terry Steinbach (TS): Well, I usually played infield from Little League through college, with infield being third base and second base. Sometimes I pitched. When I was drafted by the A's in 1983, it was as a third baseman. My first two years in the minors (in 1983 and 1984) I mostly played first base and third base, and near the end of the season they started catching me. The coaches explained to me that I wasn't fast, and first base, third base, and catcher were the positions I should play, with catcher being number one. In 1985, I caught about 25-30 games. That year there were two catchers – Charlie O'Brien and Brian Dorset – who were ranked ahead of me on the organizational chart, so I was basically backing up prospects. In 1986, I was the catcher the whole season at Huntsville (AA) and hit .325. I then got a September-call-up to Oakland.

KH: Did you catch any no-hitters before you came into the majors?

TS: No, I did not.

KH: Did you feel any different – good or bad – on the day of Eric Milton's no-hitter?

TS: When the game started it felt about the same as always. The difference came as the game progressed. The further we went into the game, the pressure built up. I felt the same kind of pressure during Dave Stewart's no-hitter in 1990. After a certain point you really don't want to lose the no-hitter.

KH: What pitches – fastball, curve, slider, or something else – were working best for Eric that day?

TS: The fastball. Definitely. The curve and slider were working well, also. What made the difference was that Eric's control was way above average. He was able to hit my target consistently.

KH: What was the best defensive play or the closest Eric came to losing the no-hitter?

TS: I don't recall there being any great plays during the game.

KH: Which pitcher during your career was the hardest for you to hit?

TS: There were a lot of them (laughs). I would say Nolan Ryan, Roger Clemens, and Pedro Martinez. There were other pitchers. The ones who threw side-armed, like Jeff Nelson (a 6'8" right-hander), were difficult for me to hit.

KH: Did Eric shake off your signs much during the game?

TS: Yes, but not that much. There was more pressure on me, being the veteran, than there was on Eric. Neither of us wanted to see the no-hitter broken up. Sometimes the pitcher will shake off a sign if he's got a new ball and he feels he can throw a better curve than a fastball. So yes, sometimes pitchers will shake off the sign, but they'll usually have a good reason.

KH: Do you have any memorabilia or souvenirs, such as a baseball, plaque, uniform, or something else, from the game in your house?

TS: Yes. We have a framed picture that is signed by Eric Milton. It's a picture drawn in charcoal and has two ticket stubs from the game. The picture was drawn by renowned Minneapolis charcoal artist Thomas Fogerty.

KH: You played 14 seasons (1986-1999) and for five managers (Jackie Moore, Jeff Newman, Tony La Russa, Art Howe, and Tom Kelly). Who did you like playing for the most?

TS: I would say I had the most team success playing for La Russa, because we won. I did enjoy playing for him, also. I will say Tom Kelly was a close second.

KH: Do you think the number of pitches Eric threw that day (122) led to him getting a sore arm?

TS: Not really a factor in Eric's case. He won 13 games in 2000, 15 in 2001, 13 in 2002 and 14 in 2004. Tom Kelly used tell me that he would make mental notes if a pitcher had a high pitch count. Usually, if a pitcher was affected by a high pitch count it wouldn't affect him the next start but on his second start after the high pitch count.

KH: Do you stay in contact with Eric Milton?

TS: Yes, we do on Facebook. Our families swap pictures of our kids.

KH: Did the Twins give you a bonus for catching the no-hitter?

TS: No, they didn't (laughs).

KH: During the game, when did you think *"He's got a real shot at a no-hitter?"* Was it in the fifth inning, sixth inning, or later?

TS: It was around the fifth or sixth, but I also kept thinking there is never a guarantee, a no-hitter takes luck, too.

KH: Were you able to get a follow-on job in baseball after your playing days were over? Such as working in the majors, minors, college, high school, or media?

TS: I have coached high school, and I was a bench coach with the Twins from 2013-2014. I also spent one season part-time (15-20 games) with the Twins as an announcer. The University of Minnesota offered me positions as a part-time coach several times, but I have turned them down. If they already have full-time coaches and I come in there giving the players different advice then what their regular hitting, catching, or pitching coach is saying it's confusing and it makes it harder for the regular coach.

KH: What non-baseball work have you done? Do you enjoy it?

TS: Well, I have been a handyman, landscaper, and electrician, but that was all in a non-paid capacity (laughs).

KH: Since you got a post-playing career job in baseball, do you think having caught two no-hitters helped you get the job?

TS: Well, it didn't hurt but usually to get the coaching or management jobs you really got to know your stuff and know how to deal with personalities.

KH: Do you have kids or grandkids who have or will pursue baseball as a career? Do you encourage them to do so?

TS: I've got three kids: two boys and a girl. The two boys played college baseball. When I've given talks in front of youth or high school baseball teams, I've emphasized remembering the friendships they'll make and that everybody can't make it to the major leagues.

KH: Was the no-hitter the highlight of your career? If not, what was?

TS: No, that would be winning the 1989 World Series. My best season was 1996 when I hit 35 home runs. Interesting thing about the 1996 season was that the Oakland Coliseum had been reconfigured before the season because the Raiders had moved back from Los Angeles. They still hadn't completed it when the season began, so the first seven games we played our home games in Las Vegas. When the configuration was completed, the ball just carried a lot better. Balls I hit that would have been in the gap for a double were now going over the fence. That definitely helped me to get to 35 home runs that year.

KH: Have you been to the section of the Hall of Fame that focuses on no-hitters?

TS: No, I haven't.

KH: Have you spent time signing autographs in Las Vegas, or in Florida or Arizona during Spring Training?

TS: Not specifically Las Vegas, Florida, or Arizona. I have done autograph signings about 6-10 times at the annual Twinsfest which raises money for good causes.

KH: Do you have any favorite stories regarding any of these experiences?

TS: Early in my career when I was in the minors, one winter my wife and I stayed with my in-laws. I needed a car for the winter, so I bought a used car for two months. When I headed out for Spring Training, I sold the car for $1,000. Fifteen years later I was signing autographs at Twinsfest, and a guy came up to me and started yelling "the car you sold me was junk, the engine blew up, you ruined my life!" And this was after I told him 15 years prior to take the car to any service station you want before you buy it. Anyway, while this guy was getting upset, some security guards came down and escorted him out.

KH: Any last things to say about your career?

TS: It was a lot of fun. It's a great game with a lot to offer. There are lots of ups and downs, and you've got to learn how to deal with failure.

Chapter 18

Jonathan Sanchez: Journeymen Battery No-Hitter

July 10, 2009
Last-minute Giants' starter Jonathan Sanchez and backup catcher Eli Whiteside combine to create one of the unlikeliest duos to ever produce a no-hitter

"Maybe this is just going to be one of those miracle, unexplainable, unfathomable seasons for the Giants. What else is there to think after watching Jonathan Sanchez, of all people, throw the Giants' first no-hitter in 33 years? Prior to beating the San Diego Padres 8-0 Friday night, he had been terrible. He was justifiably pulled from the rotation, and only got this start because of Randy Johnson's injury."

Sportswriter Tim Kawakami ("Sanchez's night just the latest sign of Giants' magic," *San Jose Mercury News*, July 10, 2009).

"To center field! Hit well! Hit very well! Rowand on the move! ROWAND MAKES THE CATCH! Two down in the ninth!"

Giants play-by-play announcer Duane Kuiper describing Aaron Rowand's thrilling ninth inning catch as he slammed into the center field wall on the run (*Comcast SportsNet (CSN)*, July 9, 2009).

"I was going to go up and over and land on the other side of the fence if I had to, to try to make the catch."

Center fielder Aaron Rowand ("Sanchez makes most of opportunity, throws no-hitter in front of father," *ESPN.com*, July 11, 2009).

"(I didn't realize Sanchez had a no-hitter) until the eighth inning, when the Padres got their only baserunner on an error. After the error, I looked over at Bochy in the dugout for run (stealing) defense positioning, and then realized the Padres didn't have any hits."

Giants Catcher Eli Whiteside describing the moment he recognized Sanchez was on the verge of throwing a no-hitter (interview with the author, August 16, 2021).

"On film he throws the ball hard, but it looks like he doesn't know where it's going. Today he looked exactly like he knew where it was going."

San Diego center fielder Tony Gwynn, Jr. describing Sanchez's pitching effectiveness that night ("Sanchez makes most of opportunity, throws no-hitter in front of father," *ESPN.com*, July 11, 2009).

"I think if you looked at the staff, he wouldn't be the one you picked. He came out throwing 94-96 (mph). He just had incredible stuff."

Giants' Manager Bruce Bochy ("Sanchez makes most of opportunity, throws no-hitter in front of father," *ESPN.com*, July 11, 2009).

Jonathan Sanchez, having recently been removed from the 2009 Giants' starting rotation with a record of 2-8 and an ERA of 5.30, threw a very unexpected no-hitter for a team that hadn't thrown one for 33 years. The last Giants' no-hitter was accomplished at the very end of the 1976 season against the last-place Atlanta Braves by John "The Count" Montefusco. With three games left in that season, both teams were way below .500, long since out of contention, and simply playing out the string.

Sanchez's 110-pitch no-hitter was no fluke, either. He struck out 11 and walked no one en route to a dominating victory with a Game Score of 98. When he wasn't striking out the Padres, Sanchez induced them to fly out eight times, ground out five times, and pop out twice, with one lineout to Travis Ishikawa at first base. The Padres had some dangerous hitters in the lineup that day, too, led by perennial All-Star first baseman Adrian Gonzalez, an up-and-coming Chase Headley playing left field, power-hitting third baseman Kevin Kouzmanoff batting third, and young center fielder Tony Gwynn, Jr. in the number two position. Sanchez, though, got even stronger as the game went along, registering swinging strikeouts of the number 1-2-3 hitters in the lineup – Everth Cabrera, Tony Gwynn, Jr., and Kevin Kouzmanoff — in order in the seventh inning.

The only San Diego baserunner the entire evening was on a one-out eighth inning error by San Francisco third baseman Juan Uribe on a weak groundball to the left side of the infield. Uribe had been shifted from his usual position at second base when San Francisco's sharp-fielding regular third baseman Pablo Sandoval was lifted because of a back injury in the top of the seventh.

There was plenty of excitement keeping the 30,000+ fans charged up throughout the game. The San Francisco lineup provided Sanchez with lots of run support, starting with a leadoff triple by Travis Ishikawa in the second inning, followed by a walk and three singles to give the Giants a 4-0 lead. San Francisco would pad its lead with a three-run Pablo Sandoval home run in the fifth inning and an Aaron Rowand RBI single in the eighth, giving the Giants a very comfortable 8-0 lead heading into the ninth.

There were some defensive gems, too. The closest the no-hitter came to being broken up came with one out in the ninth inning. Gold Glove center fielder Aaron Rowand provided the most exciting play of the evening when he raced back to the wall to grab a screaming fly ball off the bat of pinch-hitter Edgar Gonzalez (Adrian's brother). Rowand leaped and caught the ball just as he crashed into the fence on a dead run. At the crack of the bat, everyone in the stadium and those watching at home knew it was going to be trouble, especially when they saw Rowand take off like a bullet to try and track the ball down. At first, it looked like there was no way he was going to get there on time, but his routing and speed saved the day.

The one other close call was a warning-track fly ball hit by All-Star Adrian Gonzalez leading off the eighth inning that was snagged by San Francisco left fielder John Bowker. For the Padres, it was more of the same frustration. Sanchez's gem was the seventh time the San Diego team had been no-hit since their entry into the National League forty years earlier. It would be another 12 years before San Diego-raised Joe Musgrove would throw the team's first-ever no-hitter in

2021. The Padres would be the last of all 14 teams that began in the Expansion Era (1961-1998) to record a no-hitter. From when the team began in 1969 to the end of the 2021 season, San Diego has had 10 no-hitters thrown against them.

This was also the first no-hitter thrown in the Giants' new ballpark (named AT&T Park at the time). After Jonathan Sanchez's 2009 no-hitter, the Giants would record four more no-hitters in a three-year span: Matt Cain's perfect game versus the rebuilding Astros in 2012; Tim Lincecum's two no-hitters against the Padres in 2013 and 2014; and rookie Chris Heston's no-hitter against the Mets in 2015.

Sanchez's game would mark the start of an extraordinarily successful span of time for the franchise as well. Lasting through the 2014 season, San Francisco would win three World Series championships in 2010, 2012, and 2014 – the only three titles since the team moved west in 1958. Jonathan Sanchez played a critical role in securing the 2010 championship, easily his best year ever, compiling a 13-9 win-loss record and sporting an excellent 3.07 ERA. Crucially, he was called upon to start the 162nd game of the season against the Padres, in what was perhaps the most important game he ever started.

On October 3, 2010, San Francisco was hosting the second-place Padres with the National League West title on the line. If San Diego won, the Giants, Padres, and Atlanta Braves would play a series of tiebreaker games to determine who was the NL West champion (the Giants or Padres), who was the Wild Card (any of the three teams), and who was eliminated from the post-season. If the Giants won, they were the NL West champions, the Braves were the NL Wild Card, and the Padres' season was over. Making things worse for the Giants was the fact that San Diego had won the first two games of the three-game series at AT&T Park. All the momentum was in San Diego's favor heading into the last game of the season. For Giants fans, it looked like the team's typical late season collapse we had all gotten used to over the years.

The pressure was on, and Jonathan Sanchez was brilliant. He threw five innings of scoreless ball before the expert San Francisco relief corps took over to finish the game in what ended up as a 3-0 shutout, division-winning victory for the Giants. Sanchez helped with the bat, too. With one out in the third and the score still at 0-0, Sanchez lined a ball down the right field line for a stand-up triple – the only triple of his entire career. He would come around to score later in the inning on a single by second baseman Freddy Sanchez (no relation to Jonathan) to give the Giants a 1-0 lead.

Jonathan Sanchez had bright spots in the 2010 postseason, too. He secured a critical Game Three 3-2 victory in Atlanta against the Braves in the National League Division Series with a 7.1-inning, two-hit, one-run performance. He also pitched admirably in a National League Championship Series (NLCS) Game Two loss in Philadelphia, giving up just two earned runs over six innings in a game where the Giants only scored one run off Phillies' ace Roy Oswalt. Sanchez's last two starts against the Phillies in NLCS Game Six and a Game Three loss to the Rangers in the World Series were less than stellar, proving he was human, after all.

There were other remarkable events surrounding Jonathan Sanchez's no-hitter, also. Sanchez became just the second native Puerto Rican to ever throw a no-hitter, with the first being Juan Nieves of the Milwaukee Brewers in 1987. This was also a very special day for Jonathan Sanchez on a personal level, too. His father, Sigfredo, had flown in from Puerto Rico to watch the game at AT&T Park. It was the first time Sigfredo had ever seen Jonathan pitch a major-league game. The emotion between father and son captured on camera at the conclusion of the game put an exclamation point on how incredible this day was for both of them.

There is no denying this was a very unexpected no-hitter. As it stands now, the Jonathan Sanchez-Eli Whiteside battery may be the least accomplished of all pitcher-catcher duos to put together a no-hitter since 1906. If the JAWS of starting pitcher Sanchez and catcher Whiteside are combined, they have the second lowest combined career value than any battery ever to throw a no-hitter. For comparison, here are the lowest combined career JAWS values from no-hit batteries.

Table 18-1. Lowest Pitcher-Catcher Career JAWS Totals

Rank	No-hitter Date	Pitcher	JAWS	Catcher	JAWS	Total JAWS	Team
1	7/20/1906	Mal Eason	-1.1	Lew Ritter	-1.2	-2.3	Brooklyn Superbas
2	7/10/2009	Jonathan Sanchez	3.2	Eli Whiteside	-0.7	2.5	SF Giants
3	5/8/1907	Big Jeff Pfeffer	2.4	Sam Brown	0.2	2.6	Boston Doves
4	5/6/1953	Bobo Holloman	0.0	Les Moss	3.0	3.0	St. Louis Browns

Rank	No-hitter Date	Pitcher	JAWS	Catcher	JAWS	Total JAWS	Team
5	7/10/1947	Don Black	-1.9	Jim Hegan	5.4	3.5	Cle Indians
6	9/19/1914	Ed Lafitte	2.4	Yip Owens	1.2	3.6	Brooklyn Tip-Tops
7	9/16/1965	Dave Morehead	3.1	Bob Tillman	0.6	3.7	Boston Red Sox
8	6/25/1999	Jose Jimenez	2.3	Alberto Castillo	1.7	4.0	St. Louis Cardinals
9	4/23/1946	Ed Head	5.0	Ferrell Anderson	-0.2	4.8	Brooklyn Dodgers
10	*5/9/2010*	*Dallas Braden*	*5.0*	*Landon Powell*	*0.2*	*5.2*	*Oakland Athletics*

METHODOLOGY: This table lists the lowest combined career JAWS for the pitcher-catcher batteries that threw a no-hitter during the period from 1900-2021. No-hit batteries are ranked from lowest to highest using the combined total of pitcher and catcher JAWS. The lowest 10 combined scores are included in this table.

LEGEND: Dates are shown as month/day/year (for example, June 12, 2018, is shown as 6/12/2018). JAWS = Jaffe Wins Above Replacement Score. JAWS is a sabermetric baseball statistic developed to evaluate the strength of a player's career and merit for induction into the Baseball Hall of Fame. It is created by averaging a player's career Wins Above Replacement (WAR) with their 7-year peak WAR. Total JAWS = the combined score. *Dallas Braden's no-hitter is italicized because it was a perfect game.*

NOTE 1: Mal Eason threw his no-hitter as a member of the Brooklyn Superbas. The National League Superbas became the Robins in 1914, and officially became the Dodgers in 1932. After moving to Los Angeles in 1958, they became the Los Angeles Dodgers. Big Jeff Pfeffer's team was known as the Boston Doves from 1907-1910. After that they were called the Boston Rustlers in 1911 and changed their name to the Boston Braves in 1912. When the franchise moved, they became the Milwaukee Braves in 1953 and the Atlanta Braves in 1966. Ed Lafitte and the Brooklyn Tip-Tops played in the Federal League, a major league which existed from 1914-1915.

NOTE 2: Mal Eason has the third lowest career JAWS (-1.1) of all pitchers to ever throw a no-hitter, right between Mike Warren (-0.9) and Iron Davis (-1.7). Don Black (-1.9) has the lowest career JAWS of all no-hit pitchers. Eason's catcher, Lew Ritter (-1.2), is ranked #178 of 194 catchers on the list. Bill Bergen, an unusually poor hitting catcher with a .395 OPS over an 11-year career, has by far the lowest JAWS (-5.2) of any no-hit catcher. Bergen caught Nap Rucker's no-hitter with the Brooklyn Superbas in 1908.

Of note, one of the pitchers listed in the table above was primarily used as a relief pitcher during his major league career: the Cardinals' Jose Jimenez (1999). Apart from Hall-of-Fame closer Hoyt Wilhelm, Jose Jimenez has the highest percentage of his game appearances in a relief role (89%). With only 38 starts to his career, Jimenez has a higher percentage of relief appearances than everyone else on this list, including Hall of Fame closer Dennis Eckersley and All-Star closer Dave Righetti. The only time Jimenez was ever incorporated in a team's starting rotation was with St. Louis in 1999, the year he threw his no-hitter. The Cardinals understandably didn't feel this experiment was working out – Jimenez finished the season with a 5-14 record and 5.95 ERA – and traded Jimenez to the Rockies after the season. Jimenez became a fixture in the Colorado relief staff as their primary closer for the next four seasons. The full list of the 12 no-hit pitchers who had more relief appearances than starts is included below.

Table 18-2. Relief Pitchers who Threw No-hitters

Rank	Pitcher (JAWS)	Team	Date Score	Opponent	Relief Apps	Total Apps	Relief Pct
1	Hoyt Wilhelm (36.7)	Bal Orioles	9/20/1958 Bal 1-0	NY Yankees	1,018	1,070	95%
2	Jose Jimenez (2.3)	St. Louis Cardinals	6/25/1999 StL 1-0	Arizona D-backs	291	328	89%
3	Dave Righetti (21.1)	NY Yankees	7/4/1983 NY 4-0	Boston Red Sox	629	718	88%
4	George Culver (5.2)	Cin Reds	7/29/1968 Cin 6-1	Phi Phillies	278	335	83%
5	Clyde Shoun (10.0)	Cin Reds	5/15/1944 Cin 1-0	Boston Braves	369	454	81%

Rank	Pitcher (JAWS)	Team	Date Score	Opponent	Relief Apps	Total Apps	Relief Pct
6	Kent Mercker (11.7)	Atlanta Braves	4/8/1994 Atl 6-0	LA Dodgers	542	692	78%
7	Don Nottebart (9.8)	Houston Colt .45s	5/17/1963 Hou 4-1	Phi Phillies	207	296	70%
8	Dennis Eckersley (49.9)	Cle Indians	5/30/1977 Cle 1-0	Cal Angels	710	1071	66%
9	Bobby Burke (7.7)	Was Senators	8/8/1931 Was 5-0	Boston Red Sox	166	254	65%
10	Don Larsen (17.4)	NY Yankees	10/8/1956 NY 2-0	Bro Dodgers	241	412	58%
11	Ed Head (5.0)	Brooklyn Dodgers	4/23/1956 Bro 5-0	Boston Braves	65	118	55%
12	Terry Mulholland (12.8)	Phi Phillies	5/15/1990 Phi 6-0	SF Giants	353	685	52%

METHODOLOGY: This table includes all 12 no-hit pitchers from 1900-2021 who had more than 50% of their game appearances as a reliever during their career. Pitchers are ranked in order of relief appearance percentage as calculated by the number of relief appearances divided by the total number of career appearances. For example, Hoyt Wilhelm (#1 on the list) appeared as a reliever in 95% of the games he entered.

LEGEND: Dates are shown as month/day/year (for example, June 12, 2018, is shown as 6/12/2018). JAWS = a pitcher's Jaffe Wins Above Replacement Score compiled over the course of his career. JAWS is a sabermetric baseball statistic developed to evaluate the strength of a player's career and merit for induction into the Baseball Hall of Fame. It is created by averaging a player's career Wins Above Replacement (WAR) with their 7-year peak WAR. Relief Apps = Career relief appearances (i.e., the number of games a player entered as a relief pitcher during his career). Total Apps = Total career appearances as a pitcher. Relief Pct = The percentage of games a pitcher entered as a reliever compared to the total number of games a player pitched.

NOTE 1: Elected to the Hall of Fame in 1985, Hoyt Wilhelm is the most extreme example of a pitcher who was primarily used in a relief mode throwing a no-hitter. Bursting onto the scene as a 29-year-old rookie in 1952, Wilhelm spent his first six seasons as a full-time reliever. In 1958, the Indians experimented with him as a part-time starter and released him mid-season. The Orioles picked him up near the end of the year and started him against Don Larsen and the American League champion Yankees. New York had already clinched the title, and it was only the ninth start of Wilhelm's career. Wilhelm become a full-time starter – and an All-Star – with Baltimore in 1959 before reverting to being a reliever midway through the 1960 season. Wilhelm would retire in 1971 after setting the then-record for most appearances by a pitcher (1,070), breaking the record of 906 games set by Cy Young in 1905. Wilhelm's record was broken by Dennis Eckersley in 1998 (1,071) and is now held by Jesse Orosco (1,252).

NOTE 2: The other Hall of Famer on this list, Dennis Eckersley, spent the first 12 years of his career as an accomplished starter before being traded by the Chicago Cubs to the Oakland Athletics in 1987. It was then the Athletics converted him into the most feared closer of his time, winning the Cy Young and MVP Awards in 1992 as a 37-year-old relief pitcher. Reinforcing his credentials as one of the greatest relievers of all time, Eckersley has the most saves (390) of any pitcher to have ever thrown a no-hitter.

NOTE 3: Similar to Eckersley who began his career as a starter, 1981 Rookie of the Year Dave Righetti spent his first three seasons in the Yankee rotation before New York converted him to their closer in 1984. He would spend the next 11 seasons as a full-time reliever, being selected twice to the American League All-Star team because of his performance as the Yankee closer. Despite the legions of outstanding Yankee pitchers throughout the years, Righetti's Fourth of July no-hitter in 1983 was the first thrown by a Yankee hurler since Don Larsen's perfect game in the 1956 World Series.

NOTE 4: The Reds' George Culver was primarily a reliever during his career, also. In 1968, though, Culver was a spot starter with Cincinnati. This was the only season out of a nine-year career where he started more than 13 games or logged more than 101 innings. His no-hitter was the second game of a doubleheader during a stretch in which the Reds played nine games over eight days. Clyde Shoun of the Reds was primarily a reliever over his 14-year career, too, although he was sporadically used as a spot starter throughout this time. He threw his 1944 no-hitter at a time when the team's pitching staff was depleted due to military call-ups and injuries. He began his service in the Navy later that year as part of the ongoing World War II mobilization.

NOTE 5: Two pitchers on this list (Ed Head and Bobby Burke) were part-time starters during an era when full-time relievers were a relative rarity on rosters. Don Larsen broke in as a starter with the St. Louis Browns in 1953, and went on to compile a 3-21 record with the fledgling 100-loss Baltimore Orioles the next year. After being traded to the Yankees prior to the 1955 season, Larsen was used as a frequent starter, gathering between 13-20 starts each season until 1961. It was during this period when he threw his perfect game in the 1956 World Series against the star-studded Brooklyn Dodgers. Starting in 1961, Larsen became a full-time, non-closer reliever with an occasional start.

NOTE 6: Terry Mulholland was nearly a full-time starter for the first 11 years of his career, including being named to the 1993 National League All-Star team as a member of the National League Champion Phillies. Mulholland transitioned to primarily a relief role at the age of 36 in 1999. He then racked up a large number of game appearances – including an occasional start – in his role as a non-closer relief pitcher over the next nine seasons, retiring in 2006 at the age of 43.

In Jonathan Sanchez's case, he was recognized as not being a great late-inning pitcher. Specifically, it was apparent he would tire and become less effective as the game went on. The fact that Bruce Bochy and Dave Righetti agreed ahead of time that Sanchez would only throw 60 pitches during his July 10 start emphasizes this. Ultimately, this no-hitter was the only complete game of Sanchez's career 137 starts. On a percentage basis, this makes him the least likely no-hit pitcher ever to throw a complete game. Without the emphasis of trying to finish out his no-hit pitching gem, it's doubtful that Sanchez would have ever thrown a complete game.

Table 18-3. No-hit pitchers with lowest complete game percentage

Rank	Pitcher	Career Duration	Career Starts	Complete Games	Complete Game Pct.
1	Jonathan Sanchez	2006-2013	137	1	0.73
2	Hisashi Iwakuma	2012-2017	136	1	0.74
3	Francisco Liriano	2005-2019	300	3	1.00
4	Mike Fiers	2011-2021	199	2	1.01

Rank	Pitcher	Career Duration	Career Starts	Complete Games	Complete Game Pct.
5	Kent Mercker	1989-2008	150	2	1.33
6	Edwin Jackson	2003-2019	318	5	1.57
7	*Philip Humber*	*2006-2013*	*51*	*1*	*1.96*
8	Derek Lowe	1997-2013	377	10	2.65
9	Anibal Sanchez	2006-2020	327	9	2.75
10 (tie)	Ubaldo Jimenez	2006-2017	315	9	2.86
10 (tie)	Homer Bailey	2008-2020	245	7	2.86

METHODOLOGY: No-hit pitchers are ranked in order of complete game percentage from lowest to highest. The complete game percentage is calculated by taking the number of career complete games thrown by a pitcher and dividing that by the total number of games started by a pitcher during his career.

LEGEND: Career Duration = The time frame between when a pitcher first appeared in the major leagues and when a pitcher last appeared. Any breaks in service are not identified. For example, Francisco Liriano began his Major League career in 2005 and retired in 2019 but did not play in the majors in 2007. His career is identified as 2005-2019. Career Starts = The number of regular season games a pitcher started during his career. Complete Games = The number of regular season complete games a pitcher threw during his career. A pitcher earns a complete game if he pitches the entire game for his team regardless of how long it lasts. Complete Game Pct = Complete Games divided by Career Starts expressed in terms of a percentage carried to two decimal points. For example, Jonathan Sanchez threw one Complete Game out of 137 Career Starts. This equates to 1/137 or 0.0073, expressed as 0.73 percent. *Philip Humber's line is italicized as he threw a perfect game for his no-hitter.*

NOTE 1: Bobo Holloman threw a no-hitter in his first major league start in 1953, which was also the only complete game in his career (like Jonathan Sanchez, Hisashi Iwakuma, and Philip Humber on this list). Holloman, though, just had 10 starts total (all in the 1953 season), so he had a 10% complete game percentage compared to his number of starts. Bud Smith of the St. Louis Cardinals threw a no-hitter in 2001, which was also the only complete game of his career over 24 starts, giving him a complete game percentage of 4.17%.

NOTE 2: Numerous active no-hit pitchers have only one complete game to their credit. Since their starts and complete game totals are likely to change, they aren't included in this analysis. This includes John Means (Baltimore Orioles, 63 starts through the 2021 season), Spencer Turnbull (Detroit Tigers, 53 starts), Alec Mills (Chicago Cubs, 37 starts), and Tyler Gilbert (Seattle Mariners, 6 starts). Using statistics through the end of the 2021 season, John Means would be in seventh place (1.57%) and Spencer Turnbull would be in eighth place (1.89%) on this list.

NOTE 3: Mike Fiers has thrown two no-hitters, both of which are his only complete games. The first no-hitter was with Houston in 2015, and the second with Oakland in 2019. While Fiers has not pitched in the majors since 2021, he is still active in independent leagues, so his numbers may change. Because he has already played 11 seasons and has established a very defined pattern over 199 starts, it's almost certain he will be near the top of this chart when he decides to retire, which is why he's included in this analysis.

NOTE 4: Homer Bailey also has two no-hitters to his credit. His no-hitters at the very end of 2012 and the middle of the 2013 season were #279 and #280 thrown in MLB history. Homer Bailey is technically still active, so his numbers might change based on his career accomplishments; however, he didn't play in the majors in 2021, and he was 36 years old at the beginning of the 2022 season. It's unlikely his statistics will change much, if at all.

The island of Puerto Rico has a rich history of baseball excellence. Besides Jonathan Sanchez, one other Puerto Rican has thrown a no-hitter: Juan Nieves in 1987. His story, including interviews with him and his catcher (Bill Schroeder), is told in Chapter 2 of Volume I of this book. There's no shortage of highly accomplished Puerto Rican pitchers. Here's the top 10 list covering the period from 1900-2021:

Table 18-4. Best Pitchers Born in Puerto Rico

Rank	Pitcher (Home)	Team	Season(s)	Career IP	WAR (per 200 IP)	Wins (per season)
1	Javier Vazquez (Ponce)	Mon Expos NY Yankees Ari D-backs Chi White Sox Atl Braves NY Yankees Fla Marlins	1998-2003 2004 2005 2006-2008 2009 2010 2011	2,840.0	43.4 (3.06)	165 (11.8)
2	Roberto Hernandez (Santurce)	Chi White Sox SF Giants TB D-Rays KC Royals Atl Braves Phi Phillies NY Mets Pit Pirates Cle Indians LA Dodgers	1991-1997 1997 1998-2000 2001-2002 2003 2004 2005-2006 2006 2007 2007	1,071.1	18.5 (3.45)	67 Wins (3.9) 326 Saves (19.2)
3	Willie Hernandez (Aguada)	Chi Cubs Phi Phillies Det Tigers	1977-1983 1983 1984-1989	1,044.2	16.5 (3.16)	70 Wins (5.4) 147 Saves (11.3)
4	Juan Pizarro (Santurce)	Mil Braves Chi White Sox Pit Pirates Bos Red Sox Cle Indians Oak Athletics Chi Cubs Hou Astros Pit Pirates	1957-1960 1961-1966 1967-1968 1968-1969 1969 1969 1970-1973 1973 1974	2.034.1	16.2 (1.59)	131 (7.3)
5	Ed Figueroa (Ciales)	Cal Angels NY Yankees Tex Rangers Oak Athletics	1974-1975 1976-1980 1980 1981	1,309.2	15.9 (2.43)	80 (10.0)
6	Ruben Gomez (Arroyo)	NY Giants Phi Phillies Cle Indians Min Twins Phi Phillies	1953-1958 1959-1960 1962 1962 1967	1,454.0	13.9 (1.91)	76 (7.6)

Rank	Pitcher (Home)	Team	Season(s)	Career IP	WAR (per 200 IP)	Wins (per season)
7	Jose Guzman (Santa Isabel)	Tex Rangers " " Chi Cubs	1985-1988 1991-1992 1993-1994	1,224.1	13.4 (2.19)	80 (10.0)
8	Joel Pineiro (Rio Piedras)	Sea Mariners Bos Red Sox StL Cardinals LA Angels	2000-2006 2007 2007-2009 2010-2011	1,754.1	13.3 (1.52)	104 (8.7)
9	Omar Olivares (Mayaguez)	StL Cardinals Col Rockies Phi Phillies Det Tigers Sea Mariners Ana Angels Oak Athletics Pit Pirates	1990-1994 1995 1995 1996-1997 1997 1998-1999 1999-2000 2001	1,591.2	13.2 (1.66)	77 (6.4)
10	Jose Berrios (Bayamon)	Min Twins Tor Blue Jays	2016-2021 2021	851.2	11.5 (2.70)	60 (10.0)

METHODOLOGY: To qualify for inclusion in this table, pitchers had to be of Puerto Rican heritage and born in Puerto Rico. Pitchers are ranked from 1-10 based upon their career Wins Above Replacement (WAR) between 1900-2021. WAR measures a player's value in all facets of the game by deciphering how many more wins he's worth than a replacement-level player at his same position.

LEGEND: Home = the place a pitcher was born in Puerto Rico. Team and season(s) are the teams a pitcher played for and the season(s) they were with each team listed in chronological order. Career IP = career innings pitched. Career WAR = the pitcher's accumulated WAR over his career. Career Wins = the number of wins each pitcher accumulated over his career. Because pitchers had different career lengths, I included two rate measures (WAR per 200 innings pitched and wins per season). Because Roberto Hernandez and Willie Hernandez were career relievers, their career saves and save rate per season are included as well. Two pitchers missed entire seasons for various reasons. Therefore, those missed seasons don't count as part of the wins per season calculation. Specifically, Ruben Gomez missed the 1961 season and did not play in the majors from 1963-1966, and Jose Guzman missed the 1989-1990 seasons.

NOTE 1: Perhaps the greatest season ever experienced by a Puerto Rican pitcher was achieved by Detroit closer Willie Hernandez, as he led the Tigers to a World Series championship in 1984. Pitching in 80 regular season games, Hernandez racked up 32 saves and a 1.92 ERA while winning the American League Cy Young Award and Most Valuable Player Award. Hernandez is one of only three relievers to be awarded the MVP trophy. The other MVPs are Oakland's Dennis Eckersley (1992) and Philadelphia's Jim Konstanty (1950). There was no Cy Young Award in 1950, so it was more common at that time for a pitcher (like Konstanty) to be named MVP since there was no pitcher-specific award for excellence. Willie Hernandez was also named to the American League All-Star team in 1984, 1985, and 1986.

NOTE 2: In addition to Willie Hernandez, several other Puerto Rican pitchers on this list have been named as All-Stars: Javier Vazquez in 2004 as a Yankee; Roberto Hernandez with the White Sox in 1996 and Tampa Bay in 1999; Juan Pizarro in 1963-1964 with the White Sox; and Jose Berrios in 2018-2019 with Minnesota.

NOTE 3: Along with Willie Hernandez, other pitchers listed have helped their teams go all the way to a World Series championship. Ed Figueroa was a member of the World Champion Yankee teams of 1977-1978. Juan Pizarro helped Milwaukee win the city's first title as a member of the 1957 Braves. Ruben Gomez was key to the New York Giants winning the World Series in 1954, starting and winning Game 3 in Cleveland en route to a four-game sweep of the Indians.

NOTE 4: Puerto Rico has also been highly competitive during the World Baseball Classic, reaching the finals in 2013 and 2017. Javier Vazquez (2006, 2009), Jose Berrios (2013), Joel Pineiro (2017), and Jonathan Sanchez (2009) were all chosen to be part of the national team during the WBC Tournament.

Jonathan Sanchez, the focus of this chapter, was drafted in the 27th round by the Giants in the 2004 June draft. As described in previous chapters, the odds of someone chosen so late in the draft having a significant career of any type are overwhelming. The chances of that pitcher throwing a no-hitter are infinitesimal.

Sanchez developed in the Giants minor-league system from 2004-2007. Before that, he was a successful college pitcher at Ohio Dominican University, where he threw four no-hitters. He broke into the big leagues with the San Francisco Giants in 2006, going 3-1 over 40 innings with 33 strikeouts. He appeared again briefly in 2007, and in 2008 he was an important part of the rotation on an underperforming Giants team that boasted a superb young pitching staff led by Cy Young winner Tim Lincecum, Matt Cain, and veteran All-Star Barry Zito. That year, Sanchez went 9-12 over 158 innings, gathering 157 strikeouts in the process.

In 2009, Sanchez started off in the rotation, but then developed some real control problems, as he began the season with a won-loss record of 2-8. This led to his eventually being dropped from a regular starting slot to work on his mechanics in a relief role. By the time Sanchez started on July 10, he hadn't won a game since May 25.

To reduce the stress on his arm, and because Sanchez seemed less effective in later innings, manager Bruce Bochy and pitching coach Dave Righetti decided Sanchez was going to be limited to 60 pitches. As the game progressed and the Giants lead grew, it became apparent that Sanchez was in complete control. So, Bochy and Righetti decided to throw the pitch limit out the window.

Eli Whiteside, the starting catcher that night, was a late-minute substitution because Bengie Molina, the Giants' regular catcher, was with his wife as she was giving birth to their child. Like Sanchez – starting in place of injured Hall of Famer Randy Johnson – Whiteside wasn't originally intended to play that evening.

Eli Whiteside was, in many ways, the definition of a journeyman catcher. The most playing time he had by far came from 2009-2012 when he was a backup to starters Bengie Molina and then Buster Posey. His single season playing time was highest in 2011, when he appeared in 82 games after Posey was lost early in the season when he was injured in a horrific home plate collision.

While Whiteside collected modest statistics over his six years of playing time, his real value wasn't as much his offensive punch (career .210 batting average over a total of 514 at bats), as it was the mature, veteran presence he provided to the younger pitchers he was guiding. This was completely in evidence the night of July 10, 2009.

Whiteside has also been recognized by his hometown of New Albany, Mississippi. After Whiteside was on the team that won the 2010 World Series, New Albany declared an "Eli Whiteside Day" in February 2011 and presented Whiteside with a key to the city.

From Randy Johnson to Dallas Braden

I invite you to enjoy the interview I had with Eli Whiteside below.

Eli Whiteside Interview
Conducted by Kevin Hurd on August 16, 2021

Kevin Hurd (KH): Would you consider yourself to be the best player on your Little League, American Legion, high school, college, or minor league teams?

Eli Whiteside (EW): Yes. I started off as a catcher in Little League, and mostly played catcher although as I got older my coaches would have me play other positions as well.

KH: When you were in Little League, were some players head and shoulders above the rest of the league. In other words, did they produce home runs and no-hitters consistently?

EW: Yes, there were a couple guys like that. Not home runs for every at-bat, but pretty often.

KH: When you caught in games growing up, in school, and in the minors, did you catch any no-hitters?

EW: I caught two no-hitters in the minors while playing for the Bowie Bay Sox (AA) from 2002-2004. In one of the games, it was a combined no-hitter, with three pitchers accomplishing the no-hitter.

KH: Did you feel any different, either good or bad on the day of Jonathan Sanchez's no-hitter?

EW: Not different physically, but when I showed up before the game, I found out I was going to catch because the regular starting catcher (Bengie Molina), had a situation where his wife had gone into labor, and he joined her at the hospital.

KH: What pitches, fastball, curve, slider, or something else, were working best for Jonathan that day?

EW: His breaking balls, his slider curve, or slurve, was working very well, along with his changeup. Jonathan had an injury, was coming back, had made a few relief appearances, then he got his start. During the rehabilitation/relief appearances he developed a good changeup. I found out later he was on a 60-pitch limit until he allowed a hit, which he never did this night.

KH: What was the best defensive play or the closest you came to losing the no-hitter?

EW: In the ninth inning with one out, Padres' hitter Edgar Martinez hit a long fly ball to center field where Aaron Rowand ran back and caught it right up against the fence.

KH: Did Jonathan shake off your signs much during the game?

EW: Not much, maybe two times. Many of the Giants pitchers – Sanchez, Ryan Vogelsong, Matt Cain — trusted me to call the game and didn't shake me off very much.

KH: You played minor league ball, off and on, from 2001-2014. You played for 14 minor league managers. Assuming you liked them all, was there any that you liked the most or felt you would be like if you ever got a manager job?

EW: In 2014, I played for the Iowa Cubs (AAA). The manager was Marty Pevey. He was great, a real player's manager.

KH: In the majors, you played for four managers: Lee Mazzilli, Sam Perlozzo, Bruce Bochy, and Rick Renteria. Which one did you like playing for the most?

EW: That would be Bruce Bochy. "Boch" was awesome, always a step ahead of the other team.

KH: Do you have any memorabilia or souvenirs, such as a baseball, plaque, uniform, or something else, from the game in your house?

EW: I've got some catcher's gear, plus the catcher's glove.

KH: Do you stay in contact with Sanchez?

EW: Not really. I haven't been in contact with him for years.

KH: Did the Giants give you a bonus for catching the no-hitter? I've heard from several catchers on this topic. Some got a bonus, some got nothing, and with some their pitcher got a bonus and shared part of it. Any of these fit you?

EW: I didn't get a bonus. I don't know if Jonathan got one, but some of the players on the team good-naturedly gave him a hard time, saying he should have got me a Rolex watch. I didn't care, no big deal.

KH: During the game, when did you think *"He's got a real shot at a no-hitter?"* Was it in the fifth inning, sixth inning, or later?

EW: Not until the eighth inning, when the Padres got their only baserunner on an error. After the error, I looked over at Bochy in the dugout for run (stealing) defense positioning, and suddenly realized the Padres didn't have any hits.

KH: Were you able to get a follow-on job in baseball after your playing days were over? If so, was it working in Major League Baseball, the minors, college, high school, or the media?

EW: Yes. From 2015-2018, I was a minor league coach. I worked as a pitching coach and bullpen coach. From 2019-2020, I was a roving catching instructor.

KH: Do you want to be a manager, either in the minors or majors, someday?

EW: I don't know. I kind of like what I'm doing now. I'm able to see my kids a lot more now.

KH: What kind of work do you do now? Do you enjoy it?

EW: My wife and I have an event venue catering business. We started it last year but obviously there was a problem with getting business jobs and other events because of the pandemic. We like the business. More control and can see our kids.

KH: Do you think having caught a no-hit game helped you get the coaching job in 2015? If not, what did?

EW: The no-hitter didn't hurt, but what helped get me the job was my relationships with the guys in the front office and around the organization. I had been with the Giants for six years and they knew me.

KH: Do you have kids who have/will pursue baseball as a career?

EW: I have two sons, 11 and 9. The older one has no interest in baseball. The younger one has been on a Soccer Travel Team and is looking to be on a Baseball Travel Team. I don't know about a career. My feeling is let them do whatever they want to do regarding sports. I'll just encourage them whatever path they take.

KH: Was the no-hitter the highlight of your career? If not, what was?

EW: It is number two. Number one is being a member of the Giants in 2010 and playing on a winning World Series team.

KH: Have you been to the section of the baseball Hall of Fame that focuses on no-hitters?

EW: No, I've never been to the Hall of Fame yet.

KH: Have you spent any time signing autographs in Las Vegas, or in Florida/Arizona for Spring Training?

EW: I haven't done autographs in those places. In 2011, the team had us sign autographs during the season on an off day in the Convention Center in San Francisco, celebrating our 2010 World Series win.

KH: Any last thoughts on the game?

EW: It was great that Jonathan's dad could make the game – the first time he had seen him pitch in the majors. They hugged after the game. It was great to see that.

KH: Any last thoughts on your career?

EW: I got to live out my dream, got to be a major league player, got to be on a World Series champion team, and I caught a no-hitter.

Chapter 19

Edwin Jackson:
One Hell of a Long Night

June 25, 2010

Ultimate journeyman Edwin Jackson throws a record-breaking 149-pitch no-hitter as he leads the struggling Diamondbacks to a 1-0 victory over the mighty Tampa Bay Rays

> *"It just proves that no one can dictate your future. I've had a lot of people say this and say that, but I've always said that a pen and paper can't dictate my future. Nobody can write anything and predict what can happen in my career. The only person that can dictate that is me. Either I can go out and get the job done, or I can listen to what's being said and stay buried. Or you can fight and find a way to get up."*

Arizona pitcher Edwin Jackson describing his approach toward pitching and what this game meant to him (as reported by Jim McLennan, *azsnakepit.com* (SBNation), June 26, 2010).

> *"He kept saying, 'I'm fine. I'm not coming out. I'm not coming out. I'm not coming out.' You do want to make smart decisions, but you do have a chance at history and you don't want to take it away from him. And that's for everybody involved, from the team, to the fans, to anybody that was included in this game. It was the most bizarre no-hitter you'll ever be around."*

Arizona manager A.J. Hinch, describing Edwin Jackson's performance and why he kept him in the game (Senior sportswriter Bob McManaman, "Jackson Gem is Remarkable," *The Arizona Republic*, June 26, 2010).

"It would probably be the 8th inning. With EJ walking eight batters, there were always runners on base. We got one run on an Adam LaRoche HR in the second and held onto the lead the rest of the game. The emphasis was on winning the game, so thinking about the no-hitter didn't really happen until the 8th inning."

Arizona catcher Miguel Montero describing when he first started thinking about this game being a no-hitter (Interview with the author, August 31, 2021).

"You've got to give him a lot of credit. He's a horse and a great athlete. He's a great kid and he deserved to do that tonight. Hats off to him; he's a wonderful man."

Tampa Bay manager Joe Maddon summing up his feelings on Edwin Jackson's performance (Senior sportswriter Bob McManaman, "Jackson Gem is Remarkable," *The Arizona Republic*, June 26, 2010).

"We got three guys work(ing) tonight on the side, so I was kind of kidding that we got three guys up who got their sides in. It's always a tough decision. Obviously, he had a high pitch count. The guy's a warrior, and he battles."

Arizona pitching coach, Mel Stottlemyre talking about how they constantly had someone warming up in the late innings of the game (Senior sportswriter Bob McManaman, "Jackson Gem is Remarkable," *The Arizona Republic*, June 26, 2010).

"It's one of those moments where you're just caught up in the moment. It's one of the craziest games I've had, especially the game starting off how it did. Not being able to find the strike zone with the fastball. Good thing I could throw the slider for strikes in any count. It just resurrected my game."

Edwin Jackson describing his struggles with control early on (*ESPN.com / AP*, June 25, 2010).

"All's well that ends well. We stopped (pitch) counting at 115. You do want to make smart decisions. You do have a chance at history, and you don't want to take it away from him."

A.J. Hinch talking about his decision to let Jackson continue despite his high pitch count ("Not a Masterpiece, but Still a No-Hitter for Arizona's Jackson," *New York Times*, June 25, 2010).

Edwin Jackson is a "horse" and a "great athlete." Those are the words of Tampa Bay manager Joe Maddon, but everyone involved with Jackson's no-hitter that day felt the same. He battled through nine full innings and refused to give up despite control problems early in the game.

Jackson walked a total of eight batters, a remarkably high number for a no-hit game. Even more astounding was that seven of the walks occurred during the first three innings. Arizona manager A.J. Hinch and pitching coach Mel Stottlemyre were so concerned about Jackson's control issues and skyrocketing pitch count they had relievers warming up in the bullpen every inning from the sixth on. After walking two hitters each in the first and second innings, Jackson walked the first three hitters in the third inning. After a short flyout by Tampa Bay's Matt Joyce, the dangerous B.J. Upton came to the plate.

On the first pitch, Upton hit a very difficult grounder to Arizona third baseman Mark Reynolds. Reynolds fielded the ball, spun around, and threw home for a force out just ahead of Rays' runner Ben Zobrist. The final hitter of the inning, Hank Blalock, grounded to Arizona second baseman Tony Abreu.

While Upton's grounder in the third was the closest Tampa Bay came to getting a hit all game, Reynolds made another big play on a sharp line drive from the Rays' Jason Bartlett leading off the seventh. That ball would likely have gone for extra bases if Reynolds hadn't snagged it.

Jackson's no-hitter is easily the most memorable part of this game, but that wasn't everyone's primary focus for much of the contest. Until the last out of the ninth inning, this was a one-run game that could have turned on one swing of the bat. One of the key plays cited as part of the Arizona win occurred in the eighth inning when Arizona catcher Miguel Montero caught speedy pinch runner Carl Crawford trying to steal second base. During the 2010 season, Crawford successfully stole 47 bases, while being caught only 10 times. If Crawford had been successful, he would have been standing on second with highly capable hitter B.J. Upton at the plate in a 1-0 game. As it turned out, Crawford caught stealing was the final out of the inning.

Arizona managed to collect seven hits over nine innings, but they only threatened to stage a meaningful rally in the top of the sixth inning when Kelly Johnson, Stephen Drew, and Justin Upton led off with three singles to load the bases with no one out. Unfortunately for them, the next batter (Miguel Montero) struck out and Chris Young hit into an inning-ending double play. It was the only time during the entire game Arizona moved any runners past first base.

Except . . .

When veteran first baseman Adam LaRoche parked a 2-0 offering from Tampa Bay starter Jeff Niemann into the right field bleachers for a solo home run in the second inning. This gave the Diamondbacks a 1-0 lead, which remarkably ended up as the final score. LaRoche's homer wasn't an unusual event, though. It was LaRoche's 11th of the year on his way to 25 home runs over the course of the season.

Overall, the two teams were on different trajectories early in the 2010 season. Arizona was struggling with a record of 28-45 before going into this game. This put them 10+ games behind all four teams in the National League West Division. Manager A.J. Hinch would only last five more games after this one, being fired from the job. His replacement, Kirk Gibson, didn't fare much better, as the Diamondbacks would finish the season with a 65-97 record, 27 games behind the division champion San Francisco Giants.

Tampa Bay, on the other hand, was in the middle of a very successful stretch. Having won the American League title in 2008, the 2010 team finished the season at 96-66, giving the Rays the best record in the American League. The Rays were a solid-hitting team, led by B.J. Upton and All-Stars Evan Longoria, Carlos Pena, and Carl Crawford.

Beating Tampa Bay would be a tall order for this Arizona team under any circumstances. The minus-31 game differential between the two teams' final records is one of the highest negative differences for any no-hit game ever, as displayed in a chapter on Randy Johnson in Volume I. Because of all the different team and individual dynamics going on, throwing a no-hitter against the Rays was a minor miracle. Despite all the walks and the lack of control in the early innings, Edwin Jackson did a remarkable job that day.

The end result was a no-hitter from Edwin Jackson and a win for Arizona. Over the course of the game, Jackson threw 149 pitches, setting a record for pitch count in a nine-inning, no-hit game. While there are some pitch counts available for games prior to that, pitch counts did not become an official statistic until 1988, so the data is not comprehensive prior to that season.

Jackson's 149-pitch effort is higher than any nine-inning no-hitter for the last 34 seasons, as shown in the table below.

Table 19-1. Highest Pitch Count in a Nine-Inning No-hitter

Rank	Pitcher	Team	Date Score	Opponent	Pitch Count	IP, Runs, Walks, Strikeouts
1	Edwin Jackson	Arizona D-backs	6/25/2010 Ari 1-0	TB Rays	149	9.0 IP, 0 Runs, 8 BBs, 6 Ks
2	Tim Lincecum	SF Giants	7/13/2013 SF 9-0	SD Padres	148	9.0 IP, 0 Runs, 4 BBs, 13 Ks
3 (tie)	Sandy Koufax	LA Dodgers	6/30/1962 LA 5-0	NY Mets	138	9.0 IP, 0 Runs, 5 BBs, 13 Ks
3 (tie)	Randy Johnson	Seattle Mariners	6/2/1990 Sea 2-0	Detroit Tigers	138	9.0 IP, 0 Runs, 6 BBs, 8 Ks
5 (tie)	Dwight Gooden	NY Yankees	5/14/1996 NY 2-0	Seattle Mariners	134	9.0 IP, 0 Runs, 6 BBs, 5 Ks
5 (tie)	Bud Smith	St. Louis Cardinals	9/3/2001 StL 4-0	SD Padres	134	9.0 IP, 0 Runs, 4 BBs, 7 Ks
5 (tie)	Johann Santana	NY Mets	6/1/2012 NY 8-0	St. Louis Cardinals	134	9.0 IP, 0 Runs, 5 BBs, 8 Ks
5 (tie)	Mike Fiers	Houston Astros	8/21/2015 Hou 3-0	LA Dodgers	134	9.0 IP, 0 Runs, 3 BBs, 10 Ks
9 (tie)	Kent Mercker	Atlanta Braves	4/8/1994 Atl 6-0	LA Dodgers	131	9.0 IP, 0 Runs, 4 BBs, 10 Ks
9 (tie)	Mike Fiers	Oakland Athletics	5/7/2019 Oak 2-0	Cincinnati Reds	131	9.0 IP, 0 Runs, 2 BBs, 6 Ks

METHODOLOGY: This table includes those nine-inning, single-pitcher no-hitters with the highest pitch counts. Pitchers are ranked in descending order of the pitch count they accumulated during their no-hitter. Pitch count became an official statistic in 1988 for all games. A relatively small number of games prior to that have pitch counts available. When a pitch count has been calculated prior to 1988, those games are included here. All games displayed in the table are from 1988 through the 2021 season. The one exception to this is Sandy Koufax's no-hitter against the New York Mets in 1962, which has a pitch count associated with it. For comparison, the average pitch count for no-hitters thrown between 1988-2021 is 114.5.

LEGEND: Dates are shown as month/day/year (for example, June 12, 2018, is shown as 6/12/2018). Pitch count = The number of pitches thrown by the no-hit pitcher during the game. IP = The number of innings the pitcher threw during the game. BB(s) = base(s) on balls, or walks. K(s) = strikeout(s).

These high pitch count games are frequently accompanied by a large number of walks and strikeouts. This isn't a big surprise, of course, since at bats that end in a walk or strikeout often have higher number of pitches associated with them. The top four games in Table 19-1 have at least fourteen combined strikeouts plus walks.

Intuitively, we would also think that a high number of walks specifically would result in higher pitch counts. After all, when a batter walks, a runner is generated, and the next batter must be faced. But when a strikeout is made, the inning is closer to being over.

Edwin Jackson's eight walks in a no-hitter is also close to being a major league record. While it's expected that a pitcher throwing a no-hitter would be in firm control of his game, that wasn't the case with Jackson, and with many of the other pitchers on the list below.

Table 19-2. Most Walks Allowed in a No-hitter

Rank	Pitcher	Team	Date Score	Opponent	BBs	IP, Runs, Ks, HBPs
1	Jim Maloney	Cincinnati Reds	8/19/1965 (1) Cin 1-0 (10 inn)	Chi Cubs	10	10.0 IP, 0 Run, 12 Ks, 1 HBP
2	A.J. Burnett	Florida Marlins	5/12/2001 Fla 3-0	SD Padres	9	9.0 IP, 0 Runs, 7 Ks, 1 HBP
3 (tie)	Johnny Vander Meer	Cincinnati Reds	6/15/1938 Cin 6-0	Bro Dodgers	8	9.0 IP, 0 Runs, 7 Ks, 0 HBPs
3 (tie)	Cliff Chambers	Pittsburgh Pirates	5/6/1951 (2) Pit 3-0	Bos Braves	8	9.0 IP, 0 Runs, 4 Ks, 0 HBPs
3 (tie)	Dock Ellis	Pittsburgh Pirates	6/12/1970 (1) Pit 2-0	SD Padres	8	9.0 IP, 0 Runs, 6 Ks, 1 HBP
3 (tie)	Nolan Ryan	California Angels	9/28/1974 Cal 4-0	Min Twins	8	9.0 IP, 0 Runs, 15 Ks, 0 HBPs

Rank	Pitcher	Team	Date Score	Opponent	BBs	IP, Runs, Ks, HBPs
3 (tie)	Edwin Jackson	Arizona D-backs	6/25/2010 Ari 1-0	TB Rays	8	9.0 IP, 0 Runs, 6 Ks, 1 HBP
8 (tie)	Ed Lafitte	Brooklyn Tip-Tops	9/19/1914 (1) Bro 6-2	KC Packers	7	9.0 IP, 2 Runs, 1 K, 1 HBP
8 (tie)	Sad Sam Jones	Chicago Cubs	5/12/1955 Chi 4-0	Pit Pirates	7	9.0 IP, 0 Runs, 6 Ks, 0 HBPs
8 (tie)	Burt Hooton	Chicago Cubs	4/16/1972 Chi 4-0	Phi Phillies	7	9.0 IP, 0 Runs, 7 Ks, 0 HBPs
8 (tie)	Bill Stoneman	Montreal Expos	10/2/1972 (1) Mon 7-0	NY Mets	7	9.0 IP, 0 Runs, 9 Ks, 0 HBPs
8 (tie)	Joe Cowley	Chicago White Sox	9/19/1986 Chi 7-1	Cal Angels	7	9.0 IP, 1 Run, 8 Ks, 0 HBPs
8 (tie)	Tommy Greene	Phi Phillies	5/23/1991 Phi 2-0	Mon Expos	7	9.0 IP, 1 Run, 10 Ks, 0 HBPs

METHODOLOGY: This table lists single-pitcher no-hitters with the most walks from 1900-2021. Pitchers are ranked in descending order based on how many walks they issued during their no-hitter.

LEGEND: Dates are shown as month/day/year (for example, June 12, 2018, is shown as 6/12/2018). Pitch count = the number of pitches thrown by the no-hit pitcher during the game. IP = the number of innings the pitcher threw during the game. BB(s) = base(s) on balls, or walks. K(s) = strikeout(s). HBP(s) = the number of batters that reached base on a hit by pitch. (1) or (2) indicates the first or second game of a doubleheader. inn = innings, indicating how many innings a game went.

NOTE: Ed Lafitte's 1914 game was a Federal League contest. The Federal League is recognized as a major league that existed from 1914-1915. All other games in this table were American League, National League, or interleague games.

At eight walks allowed, Jackson is tied for third place overall for a no-hit pitcher. If Jim Maloney's 10-inning effort is excluded, Jackson is tied for second place, right behind A.J. Burnett in 2001. It can be fair to say that all the pitchers on this list had control issues of some sort as they often recorded more walks than strikeouts. The one glaring exception to this is Nolan Ryan's 15-strikeout no-hitter in 1974.

With Edwin Jackson's eight-walk game, it's fair to wonder how the quality of his performance stacks up compared to other no-hitters. Using Game Score (GSc) as a metric, we can determine where he would fit in. The table below shows where he stands compared to other low-GSc no-hitters.

Table 19-3. Lowest Game Score of any No-hitters

Rank	Pitcher Team	Team	Date Score	Opponent	GSc	IP, Runs, ERs, Walks, Strikeouts
1	Ed Lafitte	Bro Tip-Tops	9/19/1914 (1) Bro 6-2 (FL)	KC Packers	77	9.0 IP, 2 Runs, 0 ERs, 7 BBs, 1 K
2 (tie)	Pete Dowling	Cle Blues	6/30/1901 Cle 7-0	Mil Brewers	83	9.0 IP, 0 Runs, 0 ERs, 4 BBs, 0 Ks
2 (tie)	Earl Hamilton	StL Browns	8/30/1912 StL 5-1	Det Tigers	81-83	9.0 IP, 1 Run, ? ERs, 2 BBs, 0 Ks
2 (tie)	Cliff Chambers	Pit Pirates	5/6/1951 (2) Pit 3-0	Bos Braves	83	9.0 IP, 0 Runs, 0 ERs, 8 BBs, 4 Ks
2 (tie)	Francisco Liriano	Min Twins	5/3/2011 Min 1-0	Chi W. Sox	83	9.0 IP, 0 Runs, 0 ERs, 6 BBs, 2 Ks
6 (tie)	Ernie Koob	StL Browns	5/5/1917 StL 1-0	Chi W. Sox	84	9.0 IP, 0 Runs, 0 ERs, 5 BBs, 2 Ks
6 (tie)	George Culver	Cin Reds	7/29/1968 (2) Cin 2-1	Phi Phillies	84	9.0 IP, 1 Run, 0 ERs, 5 BBs, 4 Ks
6 (tie)	Ken Holtzman	Chi Cubs	8/19/1969 Chi 3-0	Atl Braves	84	9.0 IP, 0 Runs, 0 ERs, 3 BBs, 0 Ks
6 (tie)	Joe Cowley	Chi W. Sox	9/19/1986 Chi 7-1	Cal Angels	84	9.0 IP, 1 Run, 1 ER, 7 BBs, 8 Ks
10 (tie)	Bob Rhoads	Cle Naps	9/18/1908 Cle 2-1	Bos Red Sox	83-85	9.0 IP, 1 Run, ? ERs, 2 BBs, 2 Ks
10 (tie)	Frank Allen	Pit Rebels	4/24/1915 Pit 2-0 (FL)	StL Terriers	85	9.0 IP, 0 Runs, 0 ERs, 4 BBs, 2 Ks
10 (tie)	George Mogridge	NY Yankees	4/17/1924 NY 2-1	Bos Red Sox	85	9.0 IP, 1 Run, 0 ERs, 3 BBs, 3 Ks
10 (tie)	Ed Head	Bro Dodgers	4/23/1946 Bro 5-0	Bos Braves	85	9.0 IP, 0 Runs, 0 ERs, 3 BBs, 1 K
10 (tie)	Bobo Holloman	StL Browns	5/6/1953 StL 6-0	Phi A's	85	9.0 IP, 0 Runs, 0 ERs, 5 BBs, 3 Ks

Rank	Pitcher Team	Team	Date Score	Oppo-nent	GSc	IP, Runs, ERs, Walks, Strikeouts
10 (tie)	Dock Ellis	Pit Pirates	6/12/1970 (1) Pit 2-0	SD Padres	85	9.0 IP, 0 Runs, 0 ERs, 8 BBs, 6 Ks
10 (tie)	Clyde Wright	Cal Angels	7/3/1970 Cal 4-0	Oak A's	85	9.0 IP, 0 Runs, 0 ERs, 3 BBs, 1 K
10 (tie)	Steve Busby	KC Royals	4/27/1973 KC 3-0	Det Tigers	85	9.0 IP, 0 Runs, 0 ERs, 6 BBs, 4 Ks
10 (tie)	Jim Abbott	NY Yankees	9/4/1993 NY 4-0	Cle Indians	85	9.0 IP, 0 Runs, 0 ERs, 5 BBs, 3 Ks
10 (tie)	A.J. Burnett	Fla Marlins	5/12/2001 Fla 3-0	SD Padres	85	9.0 IP, 0 Runs, 0 ERs, 9 BBs, 7 Ks
10 (tie)	Edwin Jackson	Ari D-backs	6/25/2010 Ari 1-0	TB Rays	85	9.0 IP, 0 Runs, 0 ERs, 8 BBs, 6 Ks

METHODOLOGY: This table lists single-pitcher no-hitters from 1900-2021 with the lowest Game Scores. Pitchers are ranked in ascending Game Score (GSc) order. GSc measures a pitcher's performance in any given game started. Introduced by baseball writer/statistician Bill James in the 1980s, Game Score is presented as a figure between 0-100 -- except for extreme outliers -- and usually falls between 40-70.

LEGEND: Dates are shown as month/day/year (for example, June 12, 2018, is shown as 6/12/2018). IP = innings pitched. BB(s) = base(s) on balls; K(s) = strikeout(s); ER(s) = earned run(s); ERs with a "?" in front indicate the number of earned runs is undetermined. (1) or (2) = the first or second game of a doubleheader. FL = Federal League game.

NOTE 1: Ed Lafitte's 1914 and Frank Allen's 1915 games were Federal League contests. The Federal League is recognized as a major league that existed from 1914-1915. All other games in this table were American League, National League, or interleague games.

NOTE 2: Pete Dowling's 1901 no-hitter is not officially recognized by Major League Baseball because there is some discrepancy over whether there was a hit in this game. Baseball-Reference and Retrosheet, two authoritative baseball resources, both credit Dowling with giving up no hits. Newspaper accounts, however, state that Milwaukee's Wid Conroy reached on an infield single in the seventh inning. Conroy's career statistics, though, do not credit him with a hit in this game. Dowling pitched for the Cleveland Blues in 1901 in the first year of the brand-new American League. Cleveland would change its nickname to the Bronchos in 1902, and then the Naps in 1903. In 1915 the team became the Cleveland Indians. The team name was changed to the Cleveland Guardians before the start of the 2022 season.

NOTE 3: Dowling's opponent for his 1901 no-hitter, the Milwaukee Brewers, only lasted in that city for one season. In 1902, the team moved to St. Louis and became the Browns. In 1954, the St. Louis Browns moved to Baltimore and became the Orioles, where they have been ever since. There was a different Baltimore Orioles franchise in the brand-new American League from 1901-1902. In 1903, the franchise was transferred to New York and played as the New York Highlanders until 1912. The team changed its name to the Yankees in 1913 and has been known as the New York Yankees since then. There was also another Baltimore Orioles franchise that played in the American Association and National League from 1882-1899. After 1899, the National League contracted from 12 teams to eight, and the Orioles were one of the teams that was removed prior to the 1900 season.

NOTE 4: Bob "Dusty" Rhoads does not have an official Game Score for his 1908 no-hitter. At the time, runs allowed weren't differentiated between "earned" runs and "unearned" runs. Since Rhoads allowed two walks and a hit batsman, and his Cleveland Naps teammates (second baseman Nap Lajoie and third baseman Bill Bradley) committed errors, it can't be determined with certainty whether the run allowed was earned or unearned. There were also four sacrifice hits, but no RBIs recorded for Boston hitters. Descriptions of the game are incomplete at best. It is very likely the run was unearned since the lack of an RBI indicates an error was probably involved in the run scoring. If the run was an earned run, that's minus four points for Rhoads' Game Score. An unearned run subtracts two points. Therefore, his Game Score is either 83 or 85, with the likelihood of it being an 85. Either way, Rhoads qualifies for inclusion in this table.

NOTE 5: Earl Hamilton is in the same situation as Bob Rhoads, in that he does not have an official Game Score in his 1912 no-hitter because of the indeterminate nature of the run scored (earned or unearned). In Hamilton's case, though, there's sufficient evidence from a contemporary newspaper write-up that the run was unearned. The Tigers scored a fourth inning run after Ty Cobb walked and Sam Crawford was safe at first when Browns rookie second baseman Del Pratt booted Crawford's groundball. Cobb raced around to third on the error, drawing the throw attempting to tag him out. After Cobb was called safe, third baseman Jimmy Austin then threw the ball to second, trying to catch the trailing runner (Crawford) as he advanced to second. When Austin made his throw, Cobb took off for home and scored on a close play at the plate. To summarize, Ty Cobb scored from first because of a sequence of events that started due to an infield error. Based on the narrative in the Grand Rapids newspaper, it's apparent this was an unearned run, which would determine that Hamilton's Game Score was 83. Since this isn't an official ruling, it's important to note that Hamilton's GSc could only be either 83 (if the run was unearned) or 81 (if the run was earned), so both scores are listed in the table.

Edwin Jackson's game finishes in a tie for 10th place with a game score of 85. His comparatively low score, like almost all the pitchers on this chart, is driven by allowing more walks than strikeouts in his no-hit game.

Completely unrelated to his pitching performance that day against Tampa Bay, Jackson would eventually set a record that stands to this day. He is not only the no-hit pitcher who played for the most teams during his career (14), but also the current record holder for any player in major league baseball in this category.

The table below shows the Top 13 no-hit pitchers in this category, and it's not even close. Playing for 14 teams spanning 16 different assignments, Edwin Jackson towers over his nearest competitor, David Wells, who played for nine teams.

Table 19-4. No-hit Pitchers who Played for the Most Teams

Rank	No-Hit Pitcher	No of Teams	No-Hitter Date	Teams	Seasons
1	Edwin Jackson	14	6/25/2010	Los Angeles Dodgers Tampa Bay (Devil) Rays Detroit Tigers I Arizona Diamondbacks Chicago White Sox St. Louis Cardinals Washington Nationals I Chicago Cubs Atlanta Braves Miami Marlins San Diego Padres Baltimore Orioles Washington Nationals II Oakland Athletics Toronto Blue Jays Detroit Tigers II	2003-2005 2006-2008 2009 2010 2010-2011 2011 2012 2013-2015 2015 2016 2016 2017 2017 2018 2019 2019

Rank	No-Hit Pitcher	No of Teams	No-Hitter Date	Teams	Seasons
2	*David Wells*	9	*5/17/1998*	Toronto Blue Jays I Detroit Tigers Cincinnati Reds Baltimore Orioles *New York Yankees I* Toronto Blue Jays II Chicago White Sox New York Yankees II San Diego Padres I Boston Red Sox San Diego Padres II Los Angeles Dodgers	1987-1992 1993-1995 1995 1996 *1997-1998* 1999-2000 2001 2002-2003 2004 2005-2006 2006-2007 2007
3 (tie)	Gaylord Perry	8	9/17/1968	San Francisco Giants Cleveland Indians Texas Rangers I San Diego Padres Texas Rangers II New York Yankees Atlanta Braves Seattle Mariners Kansas City Royals	1962-1971 1972-1975 1975-1977 1978-1979 1980 1980 1981 1982-1983 1983
3 (tie)	Jerry Reuss	8	6/27/1980	St. Louis Cardinals Houston Astros Pittsburgh Pirates I Los Angeles Dodgers Cincinnati Reds California Angels Chicago White Sox Milwaukee Brewers Pittsburgh Pirates II	1969-1971 1972-1973 1974-1978 1979-1987 1987 1987 1988-1989 1989 1990
3 (tie)	John Candelaria	8	8/9/1976	Pittsburgh Pirates I California Angels New York Mets New York Yankees Montreal Expos Minnesota Twins Toronto Blue Jays Los Angeles Dodgers Pittsburgh Pirates II	1975-1985 1985-1987 1987 1988-1989 1989 1990 1990 1991-1992 1993

Rank	No-Hit Pitcher	No of Teams	No-Hitter Date	Teams	Seasons
6 (tie)	Bullet Joe Bush	7	8/26/1916	Philadelphia Athletics I Boston Red Sox New York Yankees St. Louis Browns Washington Senators Pittsburgh Pirates New York Giants Philadelphia Athletics II	1912-1917 1918-1921 1922-1924 1925 1926 1926-1927 1927 1928
6 (tie)	Vern Kennedy	7	8/31/1935	Chicago White Sox Detroit Tigers St. Louis Browns Washington Senators Cleveland Indians Philadelphia Phillies Cincinnati Reds	1934-1937 1938-1939 1939-1941 1941 1942-1944 1944-1945 1945
6 (tie)	Sad Sam Jones	7	5/12/1955	Cleveland Buckeyes Cleveland Indians Chicago Cubs St. Louis Cardinals I San Francisco Giants Detroit Tigers St. Louis Cardinals II Baltimore Orioles	1947-1948 1951-1952 1955-1956 1957-1958 1959-1961 1962 1963 1964
6 (tie)	Ken Johnson	7	4/23/1964	Kansas City Athletics Cincinnati Reds Houston Colt .45s/Astros Milwaukee Braves I Atlanta Braves II New York Yankees Chicago Cubs Montreal Expos	1958-1961 1961 1962-1965 1965 1966-1969 1969 1969 1970
6 (tie)	Hideo Nomo	7	4/4/2001	Los Angeles Dodgers I New York Mets Milwaukee Brewers Detroit Tigers Boston Red Sox Los Angeles Dodgers II Tampa Bay Devil Rays Kansas City Royals	1995-1998 1998 1999 2000 2001 2002-2004 2005 2008

Rank	No-Hit Pitcher	No of Teams	No-Hitter Date	Teams	Seasons
6 (tie)	Derek Lowe	7	4/27/2002	Seattle Mariners Boston Red Sox Los Angeles Dodgers Atlanta Braves Cleveland Indians New York Yankees Texas Rangers	1997 1997-2004 2005-2008 2009-2011 2012 2012 2013
6 (tie)	Kevin Millwood	7	4/27/2003	Atlanta Braves Philadelphia Phillies Cleveland Indians Texas Rangers Baltimore Orioles Colorado Rockies Seattle Mariners	1997-2002 2003-2004 2005 2006-2009 2010 2011 2012
6 (tie)	Edinson Volquez	7	6/3/2017	Texas Rangers I Cincinnati Reds San Diego Padres Los Angeles Dodgers Pittsburgh Pirates Kansas City Royals Miami Marlins Texas Rangers II	2005-2007 2008-2011 2012-2013 2013 2014 2015-2016 2017 2019-2020

METHODOLOGY: This table lists no-hit pitchers from 1900-2021 who have played for the most teams. Pitchers are ranked in descending order based on the number of teams they have played for. Having more than one stint with the same team is still only counted as having played for one team.

LEGEND: Dates are shown as month/day/year (for example, June 12, 2018, is shown as 6/12/2018). No of Teams = the number of different franchises a pitcher played for. If that pitcher played for the same franchise more than once, the first time he played for the team has a roman numeral "I" after the team name, and the second time has a roman numeral "II" after the team name. The date of the pitcher's no-hitter is listed on the same line as the team he played for and the years he was with that team. Seasons = the seasons the pitcher played for the team listed. The years listed can be either full seasons or partial seasons. *David Wells' no-hitter with the Yankees in 1998 was a perfect game. It is italicized to signify that.*

NOTE 1: The Tampa Bay Devil Rays changed their nickname to the Rays prior to the start of the 2008 season. As such, the team is listed as the "Tampa Bay (Devil)

Rays" for Edwin Jackson, since he played for them for three seasons (2006-2008) that spanned the name change.

NOTE 2: The Milwaukee Braves moved to Atlanta in 1966. Therefore, Ken Johnson has two listings: "Milwaukee Braves I" for the 1965 season, and "Atlanta Braves II" for the 1966-1969 seasons. This still counts as only one team for him in this ranking. Ken Johnson was also on the Houston team when it changed its nickname from the Colt .45s to the Astros in 1965. This team is listed as the "Houston Colt .45s/Astros" for his 1962-1965 stint. Johnson's no-hitter in 1964 was when the team referred to itself as the Colt .45s, often shortened to the "Colts."

NOTE 3: "Sad Sam" Jones started his major league career with the Cleveland Buckeyes of the Negro American League. He was signed by the Cleveland Indians prior to the 1950 season. The Negro Leagues are considered major leagues, and their teams are included in this tally.

NOTE 4: Hideo Nomo played for the Osaka Kintetsu Buffaloes of the Japan Pacific League from 1990-1994. Since the Japanese leagues are not yet designated as major leagues, his time on Osaka doesn't count for this analysis. If it did, Nomo would have played for eight teams, and he would be tied for third place on this list with Gaylord Perry, Jerry Reuss, and John Candelaria.

NOTE 5: No-hit pitchers Jim Wilson and Lew Burdette were on the Braves in both 1952 and 1953 when the team made the move from Boston to Milwaukee. While they played in seven different locations, they only played for six different franchises and are not included in this table.

It's important to note that this is a very distinguished list of pitchers. Every pitcher in this table has been an All-Star at least once during their career, with many of them being selected multiple times. There's even one Hall of Famer who is also a Cy Young Award winner (Gaylord Perry).

Edwin Jackson also has the distinction of being on both the giving and receiving end of a no-hit game. He is one of only 10 no-hit pitchers who have been the losing pitcher in a no-hitter. In Jackson's case, he was the pitcher of record for the White Sox when Minnesota's Francisco Liriano no-hit Chicago.

Even though the Diamondbacks share being the youngest baseball franchise with the Tampa Bay Rays, they have an enviable record of having outstanding pitching. The two Arizona pitchers who stand out most prominently are Randy Johnson and Curt Schilling, as they dominate the list of highest Game Scores ever thrown by an Arizona pitcher. Unlike many Game Score lists from older teams, the Diamondbacks don't have any pitchers who have gone deep into extra-inning games on their list of top scores. More notably, despite playing in their share of extra-inning games over the years, Arizona has never had a pitcher throw more than nine innings in a game.

Table 19-5. Diamondbacks Highest Game Scores

Rank	Pitcher	Date Score	Opponent	GSc	IP, Hits, Runs, ERs, Walks, Strikeouts
1 (tie)	Curt Schilling	4/7/2002 Ari 2-0	Milwaukee Brewers	100	9.0 IP, 1 Hit, 0 Runs, 0 ERs, 2 BBs, 17 Ks
1 (tie)	*Randy Johnson*	*5/18/2004* *Ari 2-0*	*Atlanta Braves*	*100*	*9.0 IP, 0 Hits, 0 Runs, 0 ERs, 0 BBs, 13 Ks*
3 (tie)	Randy Johnson	5/8/2001 Ari 4-3 (11 inn)	Cincinnati Reds	97	9.0 IP, 3 Hits, 1 Run, 1 ER, 0 BBs, 20 Ks
3 (tie)	Randy Johnson	4/21/2002 Ari 7-1	Colorado Rockies	97	9.0 IP, 2 Hits, 1 Run, 0 ERs, 1 BB, 17 Ks
5 (tie)	Randy Johnson	9/14/2002 Ari 5-0	Milwaukee Brewers	96	9.0 IP, 3 Hits, 0 Runs, 0 ERs, 2 BBs, 17 Ks
5 (tie)	Randy Johnson	9/14/2003 Ari 5-0	Colorado Rockies	96	9.0 IP, 1 Hit, 0 Runs, 0 ERs, 1 BB, 12 Ks
5 (tie)	Curt Schilling	5/14/2003 Ari 2-0	Philadelphia Phillies	96	9.0 IP, 2 Hits, 0 Runs, 0 ERs, 1 BB, 14 Ks
8	Curt Schilling	4/10/2001 Ari 2-0	Los Angeles Dodgers	93	9.0 IP, 2 Hits, 0 Runs, 0 ERs, 0 BBs, 10 Ks
9 (tie)	Randy Johnson	8/5/2002 Ari 2-0	New York Mets	92	9.0 IP, 2 Hits, 0 Runs, 0 ERs, 2 BBs, 11 Ks
9 (tie)	Patrick Corbin	4/17/2018 Ari 1-0	San Francisco Giants	92	9.0 IP, 1 Hit, 0 Runs, 0 ERs, 1 BB, 8 Ks
19 (tie)	Tyler Gilbert	8/14/2021 Ari 7-0	San Diego Padres	89	9.0 IP, 0 Hits, 0 Runs, 0 ERs, 3 BBs, 5 Ks
48 (tie)	Edwin Jackson	6/25/2010 Ari 1-0	Tampa Bay Rays	85	9.0 IP, 0 Hits, 0 Runs, 0 ERs, 8 BBs, 6 Ks
59 (tie)	Madison Bumgarner	4/25/2021 (2) Ari 7-0 (7 inn)	Atlanta Braves	84	7.0 IP, 0 Hits, 0 Runs, 0 ERs, 0 BBs, 7 Ks

METHODOLOGY This table includes the highest Game Scores thrown by a Diamondbacks pitcher from 1998-2021. Games are ranked by Game Score (GSc) and consider all franchise regular season and postseason games. For comparison purposes, all three Arizona no-hitters are included in this table. Game Score (GSc) measures a pitcher's performance in any given game started. Introduced by baseball writer/statistician Bill James in the 1980s, Game Score is presented as a figure between 0-100 — except for extreme outliers — and usually falls between 40-70.

LEGEND: Dates are shown as month/day/year (for example, June 12, 2018, is shown as 6/12/2018). The Arizona Diamondbacks were created as an expansion team in the National League West Division in 1998 and have remained there under the same name since then. IP = innings pitched. One-third of an inning pitched has 0.1 added and two-thirds of an inning pitched has 0.2 added (for example, 9 1/3 innings pitched is displayed as 9.1). BB(s) = base(s) on balls; K(s) = strikeout(s); ER(s) = earned run(s); inn = innings (associated with the length of games that went less than or more than nine innings); and (1) or (2) = first or second game of a doubleheader. *Randy Johnson's no-hitter is italicized, as it is the only perfect game thrown by a Diamondback pitcher.*

NOTE 1: The highest postseason Game Score by a Diamondback pitcher was a score of 91 by Randy Johnson in two games of the 2001 postseason. The first time he achieved this score was in the opening game of the 2001 NLCS against the Atlanta Braves. Arizona won that game by the score of 3-0 on the strength of Johnson's three-hit, 11-strikeout performance. Johnson would also be the winning pitcher in the deciding fifth game of the NLCS, outdueling fellow Hall of Famer Tom Glavine in a 3-2 win. The second time Johnson achieved a postseason Game Score of 91 was in the second game of the 2001 World Series against the Yankees, when he shut out New York 4-0 behind another dominating three-hit 11-strikeout performance. Johnson was again the starter and winner in the must-win Game 6 of the series, when he threw seven innings in a 15-2 blowout over the Yankees. Johnson was also called upon to relieve in the eighth inning of the deciding Game 7 as New York was leading 2-1. Johnson would retire all four batters he faced, as Arizona would rally for two runs in the bottom of the ninth against the legendary Yankee closer Mariano Rivera in a stirring 3-2 game and series win. For his three-win effort, Johnson would be named 2001 World Series MVP.

For Arizona fans, 2001 is rightfully seen as the high-water mark for the Diamondbacks over their 24 seasons from 1998-2021. That was the year they won the World Series, of course, as they beat the three-time World Champion Yankees with a ninth inning come-from-behind walk-off win. The Diamondbacks won more than 92 regular season games in 2001. They have surpassed that win total four other times – including a 100-win season in 1999 – but they have never won a single game beyond the NLDS in any of the other five times they went to the postseason. A big reason for the team's 2001 success was the extraordinary pitching they received from the superb duo of Randy Johnson and Curt Schilling. Of the 42 postseason games Arizona has ever played, the seven top Game Scores were all achieved in 2001, and they were all thrown by Johnson or Schilling.

NOTE 2: Randy Johnson and Curt Schilling are also featured prominently in Arizona's top regular season Game Scores, as the two pitchers hold all eight of the highest scores. Johnson's 2004 perfect game is discussed in detail in Chapter 4 in Volume I, which includes an interview with him. Tied with Johnson for a top score of 100 is Schilling and his 17-strikeout one-hitter against the Brewers in 2002. In that game, Schilling allowed only three baserunners: a one-out line drive single to catcher Raul Casanova in the third inning and walks to Jeffrey Hammonds in the fourth and seventh innings.

NOTE 3: Achieving a Game Score of 100 or more in a nine-inning game is an extraordinary accomplishment, as it has happened only 16 times since 1900, and most teams have never had a pitcher score that well. Nolan Ryan has done it three times, and Max Scherzer twice. No one else has achieved this level of excellence more than once. Only four teams have pitchers who have done it more than once. The Dodgers have the most 100+ Game Scores, having done it three times: Nap Rucker with Brooklyn in 1908, Sandy Koufax in 1965, and Clayton Kershaw in 2014. Nolan Ryan did it with the Angels in 1972 and 1973, and Max Scherzer accomplished it twice in 2015 with the Nationals. As shown in the table above, Arizona's Randy Johnson and Curt Schilling both did it, too.

NOTE 4: Randy Johnson's 20-strikeout effort in 2001 was very impressive for quite a few reasons. First, his 20 strikeouts in a nine-inning game are the most ever achieved by a Diamondback pitcher. Perhaps more impressive than that, Johnson is tied with Roger Clemens (accomplished twice), Kerry Wood, and Max Scherzer for the most strikeouts in a nine-inning game. The only pitcher to strike out more than 20 batters in a single game is Tom Cheney of the Washington Senators, but it took him 16 innings to strike out 21 hitters. Perhaps most impressive of all was that no Arizona pitcher besides Curt Schilling came within six strikeouts of Johnson (Robbie

Ray struck out 14 in a 2017 game) – and Schilling only did that once with 17 in his 2002 one-hitter against the Brewers. Meanwhile, Johnson struck out 14 or more batters 23 separate times as a member of the Diamondbacks. Johnson dominates all Arizona pitchers in strikeouts, having accrued 2,077 during his tenure as a Diamondback. The next closest pitcher is Brandon Webb (2003-2009), who struck out a total of 1,065 batters. No one else has more than 1,000 strikeouts for Arizona.

NOTE 5: Randy Johnson also came close to throwing a no-hitter against Colorado in September 2003. He allowed just two baserunners – a one-out walk to Garrett Atkins in the fourth inning, and a one-out single to Rene Reyes in the fifth. Johnson only faced 28 batters that game, as Reyes was picked off first base for the third out of the inning. Similarly, Patrick Corbin only allowed one hit and one walk in his one-hitter, where he is tied for ninth place on the all-time list with a Game Score of 92. Corbin came close to his own no-hitter, allowing a walk in the fourth inning to Joe Panik and a two-out infield single to Brandon Belt in the eighth inning, just four outs away from completing a no-hitter.

NOTE 6: 27-year-old rookie Tyler Gilbert threw his no-hitter in the first start of his Major League career. He had pitched in three games previously, throwing a total of 3.2 innings of relief during the previous 11 days. Gilbert gave up three walks, all of which were to San Diego leadoff hitter Tommy Pham. Pham never made it past first base, and he also made the final out of the game on a deep fly to Diamondback center fielder Ketel Marte.

NOTE 7: Madison Bumgarner's unofficial seven-inning no-hitter was the second game of a doubleheader against the future World Champion Atlanta Braves. Under the rules instituted for the 2021 season, games played as part of a doubleheader would be limited to seven innings, unless the game was tied. The Braves had won the first game 5-0 on a Zac Gallen one-hitter. Bumgarner would only allow one baserunner during his game, and that was on a throwing error by shortstop Nick Ahmed in the bottom of the second inning. Ozzie Albies, the Atlanta runner, was forced out on a double-play grounder on the next play. Bumgarner would only face the minimum 21 batters during the game and not allow a hit or a walk, yet his achievement is not recorded as a no-hitter. Under the rules established in 1991, a no-hitter is "a game in which a pitcher, or pitchers, gives up no hits while pitching at least nine innings," and this game didn't qualify because it was only a seven-inning game.

Edwin Jackson was born in Neu-Ulm, West Germany where his father was stationed in the Army. In high school, Jackson played basketball, football, and baseball until his sophomore year. He was drafted by the Los Angeles Dodgers in the sixth round of the 2001 Amateur Draft. As described earlier, he spent his career with a record-setting number of teams. Along the way, he won 107 games, was named to the 2009 American League All-Star team with the Detroit Tigers and threw his 2010 no-hitter while with the Arizona Diamondbacks. Jackson also played for the silver medal-winning U.S. Olympic team in the 2021 games.

Miguel Montero, Jackson's catcher that day, had a distinguished 13-year major league career, primarily with the Diamondbacks (nine seasons) and the Chicago Cubs (three seasons). Named to the National League All-Star teams in 2011 and 2014 while with Arizona, he was also one of two primary catchers, along with David Ross, on the 2016 World Champion Chicago Cubs. He finished his major league career with 126 home runs, a batting average of .256 and an OPS of .751. Additionally, he played for the Venezuelan national baseball team at the 2013 World Baseball Classic.

Montero was very well-regarded for his catching skills throughout his playing days. In 2017, Miguel and his wife created the Miguel and Vanessa Montero Foundation, which aims to provide medical assistance to seriously ill children from Venezuela.

I invite you to enjoy my interview with him below.

Miguel Montero Interview
Conducted by Kevin Hurd on August 31, 2021

Kevin Hurd (KH): Would you consider yourself to be the best catcher on your Little League team, a travel team, your high school team, or minor league teams?

Miguel Montero (MM): That's hard to say. When I started off, from ages 8-13 I basically played everywhere. When I turned 13, at the beginning of the season there seemed to be many guys competing for positions ... except for catcher. So, I became a catcher (laughs).

KH: When you were in Little League, did your league have some guys who were outliers, meaning that they hit home runs or threw no-hitters most of the time?

MM: There were guys like that who were tall when they were 13. Unfortunately for these players, by the time they were 16, they hadn't grown any and numerous players had surpassed them.

KH: Did you ever catch a no-hitter in Little League, on a traveling team, in high school, or in the minors?

MM: No, although I did catch a game at Knoxville (AA) where the pitcher had a perfect game with two outs in the ninth and two strikes on the batter, then the batter got a hit and broke it up.

KH: During Edwin Jackson's no-hitter, did you feel any different – good or bad – on the day of his no-hitter?

MM: No, everything was pretty normal. As the game progressed, I got more anxious because I didn't want to make mistakes and overthink.

KH: What pitches, such as the fastball, curve, slider, or something else, were working best for Edwin Jackson that day?

MM: Nothing was consistent. He was everywhere. His fastball was hard but all over the place. There were good plays behind him, and he made good pitches when he needed them.

KH: What was the best defensive play or the closest you came to losing the no-hitter?

MM: A line drive where second baseman Tony Abreu made a diving stop of a hard grounder, then threw the runner out at first.

KH: What pitcher did you have the hardest time hitting?

MM: That would be John Smoltz, although there were several pitchers I had a hard time hitting (laughs).

KH: Do you have any memorabilia souvenirs, such as a baseball, plaque, uniform, or something else, from the game in your house?

MM: (I have) a replica of the lineup card and a watch Edwin gave me which described the no-hitter and had the number of pitches.

KH: Assuming all of them were good, which minor league managers that you played for (Jack Howell, Tony Perezchica, Bill Plummer, and Chip Hale) did you enjoy playing for the most?

MM: That would be Tony Perezchica and Bill Plummer.

KH: Which Major League Managers you played for (Bob Melvin, AJ Hinch, Kirk Gibson, Alan Trammel, Joe Maddon, John Gibbons and Dave Martinez) did you enjoy playing for the most?

MM: Bob Melvin, AJ Hinch, and Kirk Gibson, although all of them were good.

KH: Do you think the number of pitches Edwin Jackson threw that day (149) hurt his arm during that season?

MM: No, I don't think so. After the no-hitter, he was given an additional two days off for recovery. I never heard him complain about having a sore arm.

KH: Did he request you as his catcher for this game?

MM: No (laughs). The manager made those decisions.

KH: Do you still stay in contact with Edwin?

MM: Yes, absolutely, he lives here in Arizona.

KH: Did your team give you a bonus for catching the no-hitter?

MM: No (laughs).

KH: During the game, when did you start *thinking "Jackson has a real shot at a no-hitter?"* Was it in the fifth inning, sixth inning, or later?

MM: It would probably be the eighth inning. With Jackson walking eight batters, there were always runners on base. We got one run on an Adam LaRoche home run in the second and held onto the lead the rest of the game. The emphasis was on winning the game, so thinking about the no-hitter didn't really happen until the eighth inning.

KH: Were you able to get a follow-on job in baseball after your playing days were over? Did you work in the majors, minors, college, high school ball, or the media?

MM: No, I didn't get one of those jobs.

KH: What kind of work do you do? Do you enjoy it?

MM: My wife Vanessa and I had a foundation/charity that brought sick kids from Venezuela to the USA. We wound up shutting it down. I've also got a sports agency (ZT Sports) where I work as a player's agent.

KH: What coaches or managers in minors helped you the most on your climb up to the majors?

MM: That would be Bill Plummer, by far.

KH: Do you have any kids who are participating in baseball? Do you encourage them to do so?

MM: I've got two sons, ages 10 and three. The 10-year-old plays Little League and the three-year-old will start tee-ball next year. If they chose to pick another sport to participate in in the future, I'll support their decision.

KH: Was the no-hitter the highlight of your career? If not, what was?

MM: The 2016 season which ended with my team (the Chicago Cubs) winning the World Series was the highlight. I also caught a second no-hitter on August

30, 2015, with Jake Arietta as the pitcher. Jake's no-hitter was easier to catch (116 pitches versus 149) but both no-hitters were special.

KH: Have you been to the section of the Baseball Hall of Fame that focuses on no-hitters?

MM: No, I haven't.

KH: Have you spent time in Las Vegas, or in Florida during spring training signing autographs?

MM: I've done some of that.

KH: Do you have any favorite stories regarding any of these experiences?

MM: Not really. They were usually quick, sign-and-go experiences.

KH: Any last things you'd like to say about the game?

MM: The party afterwards was great (laughs).

KH: Any last things you'd like to say regarding your career?

MM: I'm happy with my career. I started as a backup, I moved up, no regrets, I'm happy.

Chapter 20
Henderson Alvarez III: Walk-off No-hitter

September 29, 2013

Henderson Alvarez III sees his team win and his no-hitter become official on a walk-off wild pitch in the last game of the season

"I was ready to go back out there for the 10th inning, but I'll take that wild pitch."

Henderson Alvarez III describing his determination to continue his no-hitter into extra innings if his team couldn't score in the bottom of the ninth (Paul White, "Walk-off, wild pitch no-hitter for Marlins," *USA Today*, September 30, 2013).

"I don't know that, in your life, you can envision a no-hitter ending like that."

Marlins manager Mike Redmond describing the walk-off wild pitch that ended the game in a Miami victory ("Henderson Alvarez closes Miami Marlins season with no-hitter," *Miami Herald*, September 29, 2013).

"Probably the middle of the game, around the sixth inning. Henderson's ball was still jumping – he didn't appear tired at all."

Miami catcher Koyie Hill talking about when he realized Alvarez had a no-hitter going (Interview with author, September 12, 2021).

"I thought to myself, 'God, give me this inning, a hit or whatever, to win and get the no-hitter.'"

Henderson Alvarez reflecting on his thoughts in the dugout while watching his team bat in the bottom of the ninth in a scoreless game ("Henderson Alvarez closes Miami Marlins season with no-hitter," *Miami Herald*, September 29, 2013).

"I want to play this game, I want to win this game, but I want to get this over with and get home. Guys are anxious. They want to get to the postseason."

Playoff-bound Detroit manager Jim Leyland reflecting on his team's attitude towards the game ("Rangers, Rays to have one-game playoff," *New York Post/AP*, September 29, 2013).

"It was like nothing all year, to be honest. It really hasn't been that exciting all year for us."

Miami slugger Giancarlo Stanton reflecting on the team's last-game-of-the-year, no-hit win that finished out the Marlins' 100-loss 2013 season ("Henderson Alvarez closes Miami Marlins season with no-hitter," *Miami Herald*, September 29, 2013).

Henderson Alvarez III was in the on-deck circle, waiting for his turn to bat, as he saw Detroit relief pitcher Luke Putkonen uncork his second wild pitch in the bottom of the ninth inning. Unlike Putkonen's first one, though, this pitch led to a run, as Giancarlo Stanton scampered home from third base. His two-out run broke a scoreless tie and the hometown Marlins had just won the game. They also made Alvarez a no-hit pitcher.

The game itself was tight. Detroit's Justin Verlander, Doug Fister, and Rick Porcello held the Marlins scoreless for eight innings as Alvarez shut out the Tigers for nine frames. The closest Detroit came to getting a hit was when Miami shortstop Adeiny Hechavarria made a terrific snag on a line drive off the bat of Ramon Santiago leading off the top of the third inning.

Alvarez also helped himself with his glove. He made at least four plays on the defensive end that helped keep the ball from getting past him and becoming a potential hit. Particularly impressive were the two plays he made on consecutive batters leading off the top of the ninth inning. Alex Avila hit a sharp grounder that Alvarez fell to his knees to grab and quickly toss to first base for the first out of the inning. The following batter, Don Kelly, also hit a ball up the middle that Alvarez leaped for and snagged out of the air. By cutting it off and throwing to first himself, he prevented a potentially difficult throw from second base.

As happened regularly throughout the 2013 season, Miami's offense was mostly ineffective. Through the first eight innings, the team scored no runs and only managed four singles and a walk. The only Miami batter to make it past first base before the eighth was Justin Ruggiano, who reached first on a two-out single. Ruggiano was then picked off first by Verlander, but an error on the throw by the pitcher allowed him to reach second. That was it until the Marlins loaded the bases in the bottom of the ninth and finally scored a run to win the game.

Despite the lack of offense from both teams, this game was different from other no-hitters in many ways. To begin with, it was the last game in a disappointing 100-loss season for the Marlins. Everyone was glad the year was over, including the Miami fans. Despite the team having finished the season on a four-game winning streak, they still had the worst record in the National League. While their team pitching was middle-of-the-pack decent, their hitting was atrocious. With a team batting average of .236 and an OPS of .642, the Marlins only scored 513 runs the entire year. This total was 89 runs less than the next closest team, the almost-as-miserable Chicago Cubs (losers of 96 games).

This doesn't take away from the remarkable achievement of Miami's pitcher. Henderson Alvarez had just thrown the first no-hitter ever at Marlins Park, Miami's beautiful brand-new baseball-only stadium. His no-hitter was also one of only six "walk-off" no-hitters since 1900. In each of these cases, the no-hit pitcher was in the dugout watching his team score the winning run in the bottom of the ninth or 10th inning of a 0-0 game.

Alvarez and the other no-hit pitchers had to be prepared to come out to pitch again in the top of the 10th or 11th inning. Because each game was very likely headed into (or further into) extra innings, it was entirely possible that a hit by the visiting team would ruin the no-hitter – and potentially cost the home team a win. The pressure was still on, even as the home team batted.

Along with that, there would be no "mobbing of the pitcher" like there is at the end of almost all no-hitters. By arriving in the bottom of the ninth inning in a tie game, the hometown pitcher's team would finish the game at the plate. No matter how many innings it took, the home team would either win the game or fail to overcome a visiting team lead in the last half of the inning. In either case, the pitcher would be watching his team bat. That's what happened to Alvarez. As Giancarlo Stanton crossed the plate, the game was over. The season was also over for the Marlins, even though the Tigers were continuing in the postseason. And Henderson Alvarez III had his no-hitter.

Walk-off no-hit games are rare. The list below displays all six of them since the beginning of the modern baseball era in 1900. Two of them occurred in the same year (1908), yet Alvarez's walk-off no-no is the only one since 1997, 24 seasons ago. It's also just the second one since 1952, almost 70 seasons ago.

Table 20-1. Walk-off No-hit Games

Pitcher	Team	Date Score	Opponent	Game Story
Hooks Wiltse	New York Giants	7/14/1908 (1) NY 1-0 (10 inn)	Philadelphia Phillies	Giants scored in the bottom of the tenth on a leadoff single and two errors. All scoring came with no outs.
Frank Smith	Chicago White Sox	9/20/1908 Chi 1-0	Philadelphia Athletics	Chicago scored in the bottom of the ninth on a leadoff single, a stolen base, a passed ball, and a fielder's choice at home plate.
Dick Fowler	Philadelphia Athletics	9/9/1945 Phi 1-0	St. Louis Browns	The A's scored in the bottom of the ninth on a triple by Hal Peck and a single by Irv Hall. There were no outs at the time.
Virgil Trucks	Detroit Tigers	5/15/1952 Det 1-0	Washington Senators	Detroit scored in the bottom of the ninth on a two-out solo home run by right fielder Vic Wertz.

Pitcher	Team	Date Score	Opponent	Game Story
Francisco Cordova (9) Ricardo Rincon (1)	Pittsburgh Pirates	7/12/1997 Pit 3-0 (10 inn)	Houston Astros	Pittsburgh scored three runs in the bottom of the tenth on two walks and a three-run HR by pinch hitter Mark Smith.
Henderson Alvarez III	Miami Marlins	9/29/2013 Mia 1-0	Detroit Tigers	Miami scored in the bottom of the ninth on a couple of singles, a wild pitch, a walk, and another wild pitch.

METHODOLOGY: This table lists all walk-off no-hitters from 1900-2021. Pitchers and games are listed in chronological order.

LEGEND: Dates are shown as month/day/year (for example, June 12, 2018, is shown as 6/12/2018). (1) = first game of a doubleheader. A (9) or a (1) next to a pitcher's name indicates how many innings the pitcher threw in a multi-pitcher no-hitter. In the table above, Francisco Cordova threw nine innings of the 1997 Pittsburgh no-hitter, while Ricardo Rincon threw the last one inning. The notation "(10 inn)" identifies games that were 10-inning no-hitters.

NOTE: Many of the teams in this table moved or changed names over the years. The Philadelphia Athletics, St. Louis Browns, and Washington Senators were teams in the original American League when it started in 1901. The Athletics moved to Kansas City in 1955 and then to Oakland in 1968. The Browns started as the Milwaukee Brewers in 1901 but moved to St. Louis in 1902. The team moved to Baltimore and became the Orioles in 1954. The Washington Senators moved to Minneapolis-St. Paul and became the Minnesota Twins when the American League expanded that year. A new team was established in Washington and was called the Senators. That Washington Senators team moved to the Dallas-Ft. Worth area in 1972 and was renamed the Texas Rangers. The New York Giants moved to San Francisco in 1958.

The first five games in the table above were decided by singles or home runs from the home team. Alvarez's win was the result of a walk-off wild pitch, a relative rarity. There are 242 identified games from 1916 through 2021 that have been won on a walk-off wild pitch. There are likely more than that since play-by-play documentation in the early twentieth century was sporadic at best. Still, what this number represents is an average of approximately 2-3 walk-off wild pitches every season. This is roughly the same tiny percentage of games that are no-hitters. To have both a no-hitter and a walk-off wild pitch in the same game is truly extraordinary.

Not all walk-off wild pitches are the same, either. Some come in much higher leverage situations, as represented by the Win Probability Added (WPA) of the winning play. WPA specifically tells us how a particular play affects a team's win expectancy. For example, the highest WPA in a postseason game (+.870) came during the 1988 World Series when the Dodgers' Kirk Gibson hit a two-out, two-run HR in the ninth inning to give Los Angeles a come-from-behind 5-4 walk-off win over the Oakland Athletics in Game 1. That "+.870" figure represents an increase from a 13% chance of winning to a 100% chance on that single play.

There have been two walk-off wild pitches in the postseason, both of which happened to be the final, decisive play of the series. In the 1927 World Series, the Babe Ruth-led New York Yankees were dominating the Pittsburgh Pirates three games to none. The fourth game was tied 3-3 going into the bottom of the ninth inning in New York. Pirates' reliever Johnny Miljus loaded the bases with a walk, a single, a wild pitch, and then an intentional walk to Babe Ruth. With no outs, he proceeded to strike out the great Lou Gehrig and slugging outfielder Bob Meusel.

With two outs and the game on the line, 23-year-old future Hall of Famer Tony Lazzeri came to the plate and fouled off the first pitch he saw from Miljus deep into the left field bleachers. On the next pitch, Miljus uncorked his second wild pitch of the inning and Earle Combs, the runner on third base, raced home. The Yankees won the game, and completed the first four-game sweep of a World Series by an American League team, as they put an exclamation point on one of the greatest seasons a baseball team has ever had. The WPA for the decisive wild pitch from Miljus was +.337.

The second postseason walk-off wild pitch was far more decisive for the outcome of the series. In 1972, the Cincinnati Reds and the Pittsburgh Pirates were battling it out in the five-game NLCS for the National League pennant. Going into the final, decisive Game 5 in Cincinnati, the series was tied at two games apiece. The defending World Champion Pirates were leading 3-2 as they entered the bottom of the ninth. Pittsburgh closer Dave Giusti promptly gave up a solo HR to the formidable Johnny Bench leading off the inning. With the score tied 3-3, Giusti then gave up singles to slugger Tony Perez and veteran infielder Denis Menke.

At that point, manager Bill Virdon brought in ace Bob Moose to try and put out the fire. Moose got Cesar Geronimo to fly out and Darrell Chaney to pop out; although, pinch runner George Foster advanced to third base on Geronimo's fly to right field. With two outs and runners on first and third in the bottom of the ninth of a tied game, Moose faced Cincinnati pinch-hitter Hal McRae. On a 1-1 pitch, Bob Moose threw it past catcher Manny Sanguillen. Foster ran home and scored. The stadium erupted. The Reds had won the National League pennant and were going to the World Series for the first time since 1961 where they would face the up-and-coming Oakland Athletics. The WPA for the decisive wild pitch from Moose was +.375.

Walk-off plays, of course, have higher WPAs than the same plays occurring in less critical situations. The table below shows the Top 10 highest WPAs for walk-off wild pitches.

Table 20-2. Highest WPA for Wild Pitch Walk-off Wins

Rank	Visiting Pitcher Team	Home Team	Date Score	Situation and Outcome (WPA on wild pitch)
1	Larry Benton Boston Braves	Brooklyn Robins	5/27/1923 Bos 5-4	Bottom 9th inning, two outs, runners on 2nd and 3rd. Both runners scored on WP (+.751). Brooklyn wins 6-5.
2	Hugh Mulcahy Philadelphia Phillies	Pittsburgh Pirates	7/25/1939 Phi 4-3	Bottom 10th inning, two outs, bases loaded. Two runners scored on WP (+.730). Pittsburgh wins 5-4.
3	Michael Jackson Seattle Mariners	Minnesota Twins	4/25/1991 Sea 3-2	Bottom 10th inning, one out, bases loaded. Two runners scored on WP (+.458). Minnesota wins 4-3.
4	Milt Watson Philadelphia Phillies	Cincinnati Reds	5/24/1918 1-1 tie	Bottom 11th inning, two outs, man on 2nd. Runner scored on WP (+.403). Cincinnati wins 2-1.
5	Joe Hesketh Montreal Expos	Los Angeles Dodgers	8/20/1988 3-3 tie	Bottom 9th inning, two outs, man on 2nd. Runner scored on WP (+.401). Los Angeles wins 4-3.

Rank	Visiting Pitcher Team	Home Team	Date Score	Situation and Outcome (WPA on wild pitch)
6	Fred Toney New York Giants	St. Louis Cardinals	7/12/1920 3-3 tie	Bottom 10th inning, two outs, man on 2nd. Runner scored on WP (+.400). St. Louis wins 4-3.
7	Dick Selma Philadelphia Phillies	Pittsburgh Pirates	5/20/1970 2-2 tie	Bottom 14th inning, two outs, man on 2nd. Runner scored on WP (+.394). Pittsburgh wins 3-2.
8	Buzz Capra Atlanta Braves	Cincinnati Reds	4/4/1974 6-6 tie	Bottom 11th inning, two outs, men on 1st and 2nd. Runner scored on WP (+.393). Cincinnati wins 7-6.
9 (tie)	Charlie Williams San Francisco Giants	Cincinnati Reds	4/22/1975 4-4 tie	Bottom 9th inning, two outs, man on 2nd. Runner scored on WP and E2 (+.392). Cincinnati wins 5-4.
9 (tie)	Blake Treinen Los Angeles Dodgers	Miami Marlins	7/6/2021 1-1 tie	Bottom 10th inning, two outs, man on 2nd. Runner scored on WP and E2 (+.392). Miami wins 2-1.

METHODOLOGY: This table lists the walk-off wins with the highest Win Probability Added (WPA) where a wild pitch was the last play of the game. The games considered were from 1918-2021 and are ranked in descending order based upon WPA. WPA quantifies the percent change in a team's chances of winning from one event to the next. It does so by measuring the importance of a given plate appearance in the context of the game. For instance: a homer in a one-run game is worth more than a homer in a blowout. Using the top entry in this table as an example, the Brooklyn Robins had a 24.9% win probability as Brooklyn's Gene Bailey batted in the bottom of the ninth inning with runners on second and third, two outs, and the Boston Braves leading 5-4. After Boston pitcher Larry Benton threw a wild pitch that allowed both runners to score, Brooklyn won the game 6-5 (win probability became 100%). Therefore, the WPA of that play was 75.1%. Win probability is calculated by comparing the current game situation -- with the score, inning, number of outs, men on base and run environment all considered – to similar historical situations.

LEGEND: Dates are shown as month/day/year (for example, June 12, 2018, is shown as 6/12/2018). WP = wild pitch. E2 = throwing error by catcher on the same play, typically allowing the runner to score all the way from second on the same play. WPA = win probability added. WPA is expressed as a fraction of 1.0 and is displayed in parentheses incorporating a "+" sign. For example, a WPA increase of 75.1% is shown as (+.751).

NOTE: The walk-off wild pitch in Henderson Alvarez's game had a WPA of +.347, ranking 88th out of the 242 games that have ended in a wild pitch.

Another unusual aspect of Alvarez's no-hitter was that it occurred on the last day of the season. There have only been three no-hitters thrown in the last game of the season. All games were decided by a final score of 1-0. Henderson Alvarez's no-hitter was the only one that was an end-of-season, walk-off victory.

Table 20-3. No-hitters on Last Day of the Season

No-hit Pitcher Team	Date Score	Opposing Pitcher Team	No-hit Pitcher Performance
Mike Witt *California Angels*	*9/30/1984* *Cal 1-0*	*Charlie Hough* *Texas Rangers*	*9.0 IP, 0 Hits, 0 Runs,* *0 BBs, 10 Ks, 0 HBPs*
Henderson Alvarez III Miami Marlins	9/29/2013 Mia 1-0	Justin Verlander Detroit Tigers	9.0 IP, 0 Hits, 0 Runs, 1 BB, 4 Ks, 1 HBP
Jordan Zimmermann Washington Nationals	9/28/2014 Was 1-0	Henderson Alvarez III Miami Marlins	9.0 IP, 0 Hits, 0 Runs, 1 BB, 10 Ks, 0 HBPs

METHODOLOGY: No-hit games thrown on the last day of the season from 1900-2021 are listed in chronological order.

LEGEND: Dates are shown as month/day/year (for example, June 12, 2018, is shown as 6/12/2018). IP = Innings Pitched, BB = Base on Balls (Walk), K = Strikeout, HBP = Hit by Pitch. *Mike Witt's no-hitter is italicized to indicate it was a perfect game.*

NOTE 1: Mike Witt's perfect game was thrown against a 92-loss Texas Rangers team; although, most of the regular starters were in the lineup that day. Both Henderson Alvarez and Jordan Zimmerman threw their last-day no-hitters against lineups that had 50% of their starters benched in favor of playing September call-ups. Interestingly, Henderson Alvarez was involved in both of those games. He was the no-hit pitcher in 2013 and he opposed Jordan Zimmermann on the mound for the final game of the season in 2014.

NOTE 2: There has been only one no-hitter on Opening Day. On April 16, 1940, 21-year-old Cleveland pitcher and future Hall of Famer Bob Feller no-hit the Chicago White Sox as the Indians won their first game of the season by a final score of 1-0.

Henderson Alvarez's no-hitter compares well with the other Marlin no-hit games. With a game score of 90, his performance ranks as #4 behind Edinson Volquez (95), Kevin Brown (94), and Al Leiter (91). Volquez's and Brown's no-hitters are also the two highest Game Scores in Marlins history. The list of the team's highest Game Scores is included in Table 20-4 (below). For comparison purposes, I've included all the team's no-hitters in this table.

Table 20-4. Marlins Highest Game Scores

Rank	Pitcher (Team Name)	Date Score	Opponent	GSc	IP, Hits, Runs, ERs, Walks, Strikeouts
1	Edinson Volquez (Miami)	6/3/2017 Mia 3-0	Arizona Diamondbacks	95	9.0 IP, 0 Hits, 0 Runs, 0 ERs, 2 BBs, 10 Ks
2	Kevin Brown (Florida)	6/10/1997 Fla 9-0	San Francisco Giants	94	9.0 IP, 0 Hits, 0 Runs, 0 ERs, 0 BBs, 7 Ks
3 (tie)	Alex Fernandez (Florida)	4/10/1997 Fla 1-0	Chicago Cubs	93	9.0 IP, 1 Hit, 0 Runs, 0 ERs, 0 BBs, 8 Ks
3 (tie)	Josh Beckett (Florida)	10/12/2003 Fla 4-0	Chicago Cubs	93	9.0 IP, 2 Hits, 0 Runs, 0 ERs, 1 BB, 11 Ks
3 (tie)	Ricky Nolasco (Florida)	8/19/2008 Fla 6-0	San Francisco Giants	93	9.0 IP, 2 Hits, 0 Runs, 0 ERs, 1 BB, 11 Ks
3 (tie)	Anibal Sanchez (Florida)	9/10/2011 Fla 3-0	Pittsburgh Pirates	93	9.0 IP, 1 Hit, 0 Runs, 0 ERs, 3 BBs, 11 Ks
7 (tie)	Brad Penny (Florida)	6/26/2001 Fla 3-0	Montreal Expos	92	8.0 IP, 1 Hit, 0 Runs, 0 ERs, 1 BB, 13 Ks
7 (tie)	Dontrelle Willis (Florida)	6/16/2003 Fla 1-0	New York Mets	92	9.0 IP, 1 Hit, 0 Runs, 0 ERs, 1 BB, 8 Ks
7 (tie)	Dontrelle Willis (Florida)	9/10/2006 Fla 3-0	Philadelphia Phillies	92	9.0 IP, 3 Hits, 0 Runs, 0 ERs, 1 BB, 12 Ks
7 (tie)	Anibal Sanchez (Florida)	7/29/2010 Fla 5-0	San Francisco Giants	92	9.0 IP, 1 Hit, 0 Runs, 0 ERs, 1 BB, 8 Ks
11 (tie)	Al Leiter (Florida)	5/11/1996 Fla 11-0	Colorado Rockies	91	9.0 IP, 0 Hits, 0 Runs, 0 ERs, 2 BBs, 6 Ks

Rank	Pitcher (Team Name)	Date Score	Opponent	GSc	IP, Hits, Runs, ERs, Walks, Strikeouts
13 (tie)	H. Alvarez III (Miami)	9/29/2013 Mia 1-0	Detroit Tigers	90	9.0 IP, 0 Hits, 0 Runs, 0 ERs, 1 BB, 4 Ks
18 (tie)	Anibal Sanchez (Florida)	9/6/2006 Fla 2-0	Arizona Diamondbacks	89	9.0 IP, 0 Hits, 0 Runs, 0 ERs, 4 BBs, 6 Ks
40 (tie)	AJ Burnett (Florida)	5/12/2001 Fla 3-0	San Diego Padres	85	9.0 IP, 0 Hits, 0 Runs, 0 ERs, 9 BBs, 7 Ks

METHODOLOGY: This table includes the highest Game Scores thrown by a Marlins pitcher from 1993-2021. Games are ranked by Game Score (GSc) and consider all franchise regular season and postseason games. For comparison purposes, all six franchise no-hitters are included in this table. Games are ranked by pitcher Game Score (GSc) in descending order. Game Score measures a pitcher's performance in any given game started. Introduced by baseball writer/statistician Bill James in the 1980s, Game Score is presented as a figure between 0-100 — except for extreme outliers — and usually falls between 40-70.

LEGEND: Dates are shown as month/day/year (for example, June 12, 2018, is shown as 6/12/2018). The Florida Marlins became an expansion team in the National League East Division in 1993. In 2012, the team physically moved from their home field at the football-oriented Sun Life Stadium (located in Miami Gardens) to the brand-new Marlins Park in downtown Miami. As a condition of the move, the team was renamed the Miami Marlins, and adopted a new logo and colors. "Team Name" indicates the name of the team when the pitcher threw the no-hitter. IP = innings pitched; BB(s) = base(s) on balls; K(s) = strikeout(s); ER(s) = earned run(s).

NOTE 1: Josh Beckett's two-hit shutout against the Cubs (tied for #3 all-time) was Game 5 of the 2003 NLCS. After dropping Game 1 against the Marlins in an 11-inning thriller, Chicago won three straight and were on the verge of going to the World Series for the first time since 1945. They just needed to win one more game. Beckett pitched masterfully in the fifth game of the series, as he only allowed two singles and a walk, with none of the Cub runners moving past first base.

With that win, the momentum swung toward Florida, and the Marlins won the final two games at Wrigley Field, including the infamous "Bartman Game." With Chicago leading 3-0 in that game, with one out in the eighth inning, a well-intended Cub fan reached for a foul ball in the stands that could possibly have been caught.

That second out would have helped shut down a potential Marlin rally. Instead, the Cub defense and pitching seemed to be shaken by this incident, as Florida went on to score eight runs in the inning en route to a shocking 8-3 win. Florida went on to seal the pennant with a 9-6 win the next night. Beckett would also star in the World Series that year, shutting out the powerful Yankees 6-0 in Game 6 (achieving a GSc of 84 with five hits and two walks allowed). The Marlins clinched their second championship in a six-year timespan. For his efforts, Beckett would be named 2003 World Series MVP, allowing only two runs over 16.1 innings pitched.

NOTE 2: Another notable postseason game for the Marlins was Game 5 of the 1997 NLCS. Florida starter Livan Hernandez beat Atlanta 2-1, allowing just three hits while striking out 15 Brave batters. His GSc of 90 ties him for 13th place all-time for Marlin pitchers, and his 15 strikeouts in a game is second highest among all Marlin pitchers. In that game, he also threw 143 pitches, which is the highest-ever for a Marlin pitcher. The most strikeouts ever achieved by a Marlin pitcher was 16 by Ricky Nolasco in 7.2 innings of work during a 2009 regular season win over the Braves.

NOTE 3: With a GSc of 95, the no-hitter thrown by Edinson Volquez has the highest score of any game in Marlins' history. Volquez was dominant in this 3-0 victory over a very good Arizona team that would win 93 games that season (2017). He only faced the minimum 27 batters, as the two runners who reached base on walks were quickly erased by double-play grounders. Volquez retired the last three Diamondback hitters – two of whom were pinch-hitters – on swinging strikeouts.

NOTE 4: Kevin Brown's 1997 no-hitter came very close to being a perfect game. After retiring the first 23 batters he faced, Brown hit San Francisco's Marvin Benard on a 1-2 count with two outs in the bottom of the eighth inning. Benard was the only baserunner for the Giants in the Marlins' blowout 9-0 win. Brown's no-hitter was no easy feat, as the 1997 West Division Campion Giants had a lineup that featured All-Stars Barry Bonds, Jeff Kent, and J.T. Snow.

NOTE 5: Alex Fernandez briefly held the record for highest Marlins Game Score (93) when he threw his one-hitter in April 1997. He was surpassed by Kevin Brown and his no-hitter exactly two months later. While Fernandez walked no one and struck out eight, the only hit he allowed was an infield single to Chicago's Dave Hansen with one out in the ninth inning of a 1-0 game. Taking a one-run lead in the top of the first, the Marlins' victory was uncertain throughout the game, as the Cubs threatened to score a couple of times because of four Florida errors.

NOTE 6: Anibal Sanchez has two one-hitters among the top Marlins games in Table 20-4. In his 2010 no-hitter, Sanchez outdueled rookie sensation Madison Bumgarner as he handcuffed the resurging Giants. Pablo Sandoval collected the only hit for San Francisco when he reached first on a one-out single in the fifth inning. Only two other Giants reached base that game: Juan Uribe on a throwing error and Aubrey Huff on a seventh-inning walk. The hard-hitting 2010 Giants would win their first World Series Championship since their move to the West Coast that season. The only hit Anibal Sanchez allowed in his other one-hitter, a 3-0 victory over Pittsburgh in 2011, was on a one-out Neil Walker double in the second inning. The Pirates would load the bases on an error and a walk before Sanchez struck out Jeff Locke to end the inning in a 0-0 game. No other Pirate batter would make it past first base after that. Of course, Sanchez is the only Marlins' pitcher included in this table three times, as he had previously achieved a no-hitter in September 2006 against the struggling Arizona Diamondbacks.

NOTE 7: The only other Marlin pitcher listed more than once in this table is Dontrelle Willis, who twice achieved Game Scores of 92. His 2003 one-hitter against Hall of Famer Tom Glavine and the New York Mets might have been his best-pitched game ever. The only baserunner he allowed was Ty Wigginton, who worked a two-out walk in the first inning and reached first on a one-out single through the left side of the infield in the fourth. The game was tightly contested throughout, as the Marlins managed just a solo home run by the legendary catcher Ivan Rodriguez in the fourth inning.

NOTE 8: 16-game winner Al Leiter threw the first Marlin no-hitter in 1996, only the team's fourth season in existence. It was also the year that Florida began being taken seriously, as the team finished the 1996 season just under .500 with a record of 80-82. The Marlins would win the World Series the very next season. Besides reaching the height of pitching achievement by throwing a no-hitter, AJ Burnett set a record that day in 2001 against the Padres. He recorded the most walks in a nine-inning no-hitter with nine.

The Marlins (1993 expansion team) compare well to the other 13 expansion teams with six no-hitters. Only the Colts/Astros (1962 team, 13 no-hitters), Angels (1961 team, 12 no-hitters), and Expos/Nationals (1969 team, 7 no-hitters) are ahead of them.

While explored more deeply in other chapters, Alvarez's no-hit game was also notable in that it involved one of the largest negative win/loss differentials between the no-hit team (Miami) and their opponent (Detroit) at -31 games. Additionally, the Henderson Alvarez/Koyie Hill battery had one of the lowest combined career JAWS scores (+5.9) of any pitcher/catcher combination to ever throw a no-hitter.

A native of Venezuela, Henderson Alvarez was signed by the Toronto Blue Jays in 2006. He would break in with the Jays in 2011 and become an established member of their rotation the next year. He was traded as part of a huge deal with the Marlins after the end of the 2012 season. His major-league career blossomed in 2014, when he compiled a 12-7 record and finished with a 2.65 ERA. He would also be named to the 2014 National League All-Star team, along with Giancarlo Stanton. An arm injury early in the 2015 season resulted in season-ending surgery. Alvarez would appear briefly with the Philadelphia Phillies in 2017, but that would be it for his time in the majors. Overall, he compiled a record of 27-35 with an ERA of 3.82 in the major leagues. Since leaving the majors, Alvarez has continued to play professional baseball in the Mexican League and the independent American Association.

Miami's catcher that day, Koyie Hill, had an 11-year major-league career with the Dodgers, Diamondbacks, Cubs, Marlins, and Phillies. Most of his time was spent with the Cubs from 2007-2012, primarily being used in a backup or platoon role where his switch-hitting skills were useful. He finished his major league career in 2014 with 1,049 plate appearances, a .207 batting average, and eight home runs. In 2013, his only year with the Marlins, he appeared in just 18 games.

Taken in the fourth round of the 2000 draft by the Dodgers, Hill broke into the majors with Los Angeles in 2003. Hill was briefly a coach in the Phillies' organization in 2015. Tired of traveling, he decided to go into a different career field, and in 2016 he became a real-estate developer.

I invite you to enjoy his interview below.

Koyie Hill Interview
Conducted by Kevin Hurd on September 12, 2021

Kevin Hurd (Kevin): Would you consider yourself to be the best player on your Little League, American Legion, High School, College and minor league teams?
Koyie Hill (Koyie): Yes, pretty much at all those levels. At all the levels before the minor leagues I mostly played 2B, 3B and Shortstop. I started mostly catching in 2001 in the minors in Wilmington, NC.

Kevin: When you played in Little League, were there several guys or even one guy who was an outlier, i.e., hit home runs/threw no-hitters all the time?

Koyie: Yes, there were several guys like that. One guy was 6 feet tall at age 12 and nobody could touch him. Growing up in Lawton, Oklahoma, we had several Indian towns around us and there were some outstanding athletes that came out of those small towns.

Kevin: Did you feel any different (good or bad) on the day of your pitcher's no-hitter?

Koyie: No, physically I was the same as normal. What was different was that it was the last game of the season, we just wanted to get the game/season over with so we could catch a departing flight and be with our families. Detroit was going to the playoffs and sat Miguel Cabrera for the game; other than that, all their starters were in the lineup. After the game was different, though. Since it was the last game of the season, everybody kind of went their own separate ways. I wound up watching the highlights of the no-hitter at a sports bar in Miami by myself (Laughs). Additionally, when you have a no-hitter at night, you'll have your local sportswriters asking you questions the next day. Since we were all leaving the next day, that didn't happen.

Kevin: Did you ever catch a no-hitter in Little League, American Legion, High School, College or the minors?

Koyie: Yes, in the minors with Las Vegas (Nevada) in 2003 in the Pacific Coast League.

Kevin: What pitches (fastball, curve, slider, etc.) were working best for your pitcher (Henderson Alvarez III) that day?

Koyie: Henderson had a feel for everything that day. His fastball and slider were especially good, but everything he threw moved around a lot.

Kevin: What was the best defensive play/closest you came to losing the no-hitter?

Koyie: It was the third inning. Our short stop (Adeiny Hechavarria) made a great leaping catch on a line drive over his head.

Kevin: Did Henderson shake off your catcher signs much during the game?

Koyie: Not a whole lot. It didn't really matter to him that day — everything he was throwing was working/moving that day.

Kevin: Do you have any memorabilia/souvenirs (baseball, plaque, uniform, etc.) from the game in your house?

Koyie: Yes, I have my jersey from the game, plus some pictures in frames I got from the Marlins.

Kevin: From 2000-2005 you played off and on in the minor leagues. The managers you played for were Butch Hughes, Dino Ebel, John Shoemaker, Terry Kennedy and Chip Hale. Assuming they were all good, was there one manager who you enjoyed playing for the most?

Koyie: Yes, that would be Dino Ebel. He was a real student of the game. He was kind of a combination big brother/father figure. He was a players' manager, but he didn't let people take advantage of him.

Kevin: From 2004-14 you were in the majors off and on. The managers you played for were Bob Brenly, Al Pedrique, Bob Melvin, Lou Piniella, Mike Quade, Dale Sveum, Mike Redmond and Ryne Sandberg. As before, was their one manager you enjoyed playing for the most?

Koyie: That would be Lou Piniella. He was a players' coach but he could be a tough guy if needed. He had the ability to make good players better.

Kevin: Did Henderson request you as his catcher before this game?

Koyie: No, our manager usually made those assignments.

Kevin: Do you still stay in contact with Henderson?

Koyie: No, not really. It's been a while since I talked to him.

Kevin: Did the Marlins give you a bonus for catching the no-hit game?

Koyie: No (laughs).

Kevin: During the game, when did you think *"He's got a real shot at a no-hitter?"* Fifth inning, sixth inning, etc.?

Koyie: Probably the middle of the game, around the sixth inning. Henderson's ball was still jumping — he didn't appear tired at all.

Kevin: Were you able to get a follow-on job in baseball after your playing days were over? MLB, minors, college, high school, media?

Koyie: My last playing season was 2014. In 2015 I was a coach in the Philadelphia minor-league system with Clearwater. I had several other opportunities, I turned them down. I was tired of traveling at that point.

Kevin: What kind of work do you do now?

Koyie: I've been in real estate development since 2016. I've been interested in this for a while. My dad was a master carpenter and builder. I've had an interest in real estate, and this business didn't require me to be on the road a lot each year.

Kevin: Which coaches/managers helped you the most in minor-league baseball, college baseball, etc., in your climb to the majors.

Koyie: That would be Dino Ebel (minors) and my old coach at Wichita State University, Gene Stephenson.

Kevin: You were able to get a post-playing career job in the minors. Do you think having caught a no-hitter helped you get the job?

Koyie: Not really. My last year playing was 2014 with Philadelphia. I got the coaching job in 2015 because the Philadelphia organization knew me.

Kevin: Do you have any kids who will pursue baseball/softball as a career? Do you encourage them to do so?

Koyie: I've got two daughters. Currently the youngest is heavily into basketball and wants to be in the WNBA someday. The oldest is into golf but doesn't have high expectations — she just likes playing it. Neither is into softball and that's okay.

Kevin: Was the no-hitter the highlight of your career? If not, what was?

Koyie: Every day in the big leagues was great. As far as a record that will be in the record books forever, then it would be the no-hitter. However, I also had a stretch in 2009 when the regular catcher (Geovany Soto) was injured and I played in 27 consecutive games. That was my favorite time in my career.

Kevin: Have you been to the section of the baseball HOF that focuses on no-hitters?

Koyie: No, I haven't. I haven't been to the Hall of Fame yet.

Kevin: Have you spent time signing autographs in Las Vegas, or in Florida or Arizona during spring training? Any other places?

Koyie: I haven't done those places, but I have been at the Cubs Convention in Chicago 3-4 times. They hold it every year in Chicago in late January a couple of weeks before spring training starts.

Kevin: Do you have any last words regarding the no-hitter?

Koyie: I was proud to be part of it, a sliver of history.

Kevin: Do you have any last words regarding your career?

Koyie: I had a blast. (laughs)

CHAPTER 21

GAYLORD PERRY: CLASH OF THE TITANS

September 17, 1968
Gaylord Perry wins pitching duel against Bob Gibson 1-0 in San Francisco

"The best thing I had going was my control. I was hitting the corners consistently and I was keeping the ball down. The hard slider was my best pitch."

Gaylord Perry talking about his control being the key to his pitching success that day (Neal Russo, "Perry Cuts Short Cardinal Celebration," *St. Louis Post-Dispatch*, September 18, 1968).

"He should be in the Hall of Fame with a tube of K-Y Jelly attached to his plaque."

Major league manager Gene Mauch expressing his frustration at Perry's alleged use of foreign substances – later confirmed by Perry himself — to make his ball move in an unpredictable manner (Dennis Corcoran, *Induction Day at Cooperstown: A History of the Baseball Hall of Fame Ceremony*, November 3, 2010).

"I watched Gaylord like a hawk. I've never found anything. I'll tell you what he's got: a good curve, a fine fastball, a good change, and a fine sinker. I'll tell you what Perry is: He's one helluva pitcher, and a fine competitor."

Legendary American League umpire Bill Haller describing his admiration for Gaylord Perry's pitching skills ("Gaylord Perry," *www.baseballhall.org*, 1991).

"Not until they get a hit off of him."

Giants manager Herman Franks, responding to a question of whether Perry should be pulled in the eighth inning when the pitching coach was concerned Perry might be losing his stuff (Gaylord Perry, *Me and the Spitter: An Autobiographical Confession*, 1974).

"It's a hard slider."

Allison Perry, Gaylord's five-year-old daughter, not missing a beat as she responded to a reporter's question "Does your daddy throw a grease ball?" during the 1971 National League playoffs (Mark Amour, "Gaylord Perry," www.sabr.org, February 1, 2011).

"He had a little trouble catching the high pitches but was great with the low ones. I didn't pitch high anyway, so we got along great."

Gaylord Perry expressing appreciation for his catcher Dick Dietz (David Bush, San Francisco Chronicle sportswriter, "DICK DIETZ: 1941-2005 / 'Mule' starred with '70 Giants," www.sfgate.com, June 30, 2005).

It was a titanic pitching match-up that day at Candlestick Park. San Francisco's Gaylord Perry was on the hill for the home team. By 1968, the 29-year-old All-Star was already a fixture in the Giants' rotation right behind ace Juan Marichal and 1967 Cy Young winner Mike McCormick.

Facing Perry that day was the Cardinals' extraordinary Bob Gibson, currently sporting a 1.13 ERA on his way to a dominating Cy Young season as he led St. Louis to a National League pennant. While the Giants would finish in second place, the title race had already been decided a couple days earlier when the Cardinals clinched in Houston.

Despite the fact they were looking ahead to the World Series, the Cardinals had their "A" team in the lineup that day. Led by Hall of Famer Orlando Cepeda, the St. Louis lineup was full of dangerous hitters, such as Bobby Tolan, Curt Flood, Roger Maris, and Mike Shannon. Even in the "Year of the Pitcher," when the league ERA dropped to a remarkably sparse 2.98, the Cardinals were near the top of the league in runs scored, hits, and slugging percentage. Perry had his work cut out for him in what everyone expected would be a low-scoring game.

The Perry vs. Gibson matchup was indeed remarkable. It is one of only five no-hitters that featured two future Hall of Famers squaring off against each other. The table below shows those five no-hitters ranked by total combined JAWS of the two starting pitchers.

Table 21-1. No-hitters Featuring Opposing Hall of Fame Starters

Rank	Date Score	No-hit Pitcher (JAWS) Team	Opposing Starter (JAWS) Team	Total JAWS
1	5/5/1904 Bos 3-0	Cy Young (120.8) Boston Americans	Rube Waddell (53.8) Philadelphia Athletics	174.6
2	9/17/1968 SF 1-0	Gaylord Perry (71.2) San Francisco Giants	Bob Gibson (75.2) St. Louis Cardinals	146.4
3	6/13/1905 NY 1-0	Christy Mathewson (87.9) New York Giants	Mordecai Brown (51.0) Chicago Cubs	138.9
4	10/2/1908 Cle 1-0	Addie Joss (42.7) Cleveland Naps	Ed Walsh (64.1) Chicago White Sox	106.8
5	5/11/1963 LA 8-0	Sandy Koufax (47.4) Los Angeles Dodgers	Juan Marichal (57.4) San Francisco Giants	104.8

METHODOLOGY: This table lists the five no-hitters from 1900-2021 when two Hall of Fame starting pitchers opposed each other. The games are ranked in order of highest combined JAWS of the two pitchers. JAWS = Jaffe Wins Above Replacement Score. JAWS is a sabermetric baseball statistic developed to evaluate the strength of a player's career and merit for induction into the Baseball Hall of Fame. It is created by averaging a player's career Wins Above Replacement (WAR) with their 7-year peak WAR. WAR measures a player's value in all facets of the game by deciphering how many more wins he's worth than a replacement-level player at his same position.

LEGEND: Dates are shown as month/day/year (for example, June 12, 2018, is shown as 6/12/2018). Total JAWS = the combined total of both starting pitchers' JAWS.

NOTE: Some of the teams in this table moved or changed names over the years. The Boston Americans became the Boston Red Sox in 1908. The Cleveland Naps changed their name to the Cleveland Indians in 1915. The team has been known as the Cleveland Guardians since 2022. The Dodgers and Giants began in Brooklyn and

New York, respectively. The two teams moved to Los Angeles and San Francisco before the start of the 1958 season.

Since Cy Young's epic no-hitter against fellow Hall of Famer Rube Waddell, Perry's no-hitter has the highest total JAWS of the two opposing starters. The Top 15 Total JAWS in a no-hit game in the modern era are shown in the table below.

Table 21-2. Highest Starting Pitchers JAWS in a No-hit Game

Rank	Date Score	No-hit Pitcher (JAWS) Team	Opposing Pitcher (JAWS) Team	Total JAWS
1	5/5/1904 Bos 3-0	Cy Young (120.8) Boston Americans	Rube Waddell (53.8) Philadelphia Athletics	174.6
2	9/17/1968 SF 1-0	Gaylord Perry (71.2) San Francisco Giants	Bob Gibson (75.2) St. Louis Cardinals	146.4
3	7/1/1920 Was 1-0	Walter Johnson (127.2) Washington Senators	Harry Harper (12.5) Boston Red Sox	139.7
4	6/13/1905 NY 1-0	Christy Mathewson (88.4) New York Giants	Mordecai Brown (51.0) Chicago Cubs	139.4
5	6/30/1908 Bos 8-0	Cy Young (120.8) Boston Red Sox	Rube Manning (3.3) New York Highlanders	124.1
6	6/16/1978 Cin 4-0	Tom Seaver (84.6) Cincinnati Reds	John Denny (30.9) St. Louis Cardinals	115.5
7	5/18/2004 Ari 2-0	Randy Johnson (81.3) Arizona Diamondbacks	Mike Hampton (26.7) Atlanta Braves	108.0
8	10/2/1908 Cle 1-0	Addie Joss (42.7) Cleveland Naps	Ed Walsh (64.1) Chicago White Sox	106.8
9	5/1/1991 Tex 3-0	Nolan Ryan (62.2) Texas Rangers	Jimmy Key (42.7) Toronto Blue Jays	104.9
10	5/11/1963 LA 8-0	Sandy Koufax (47.4) Los Angeles Dodgers	Juan Marichal (57.4) San Francisco Giants	104.8
11	6/18/1967 Hou 2-0	Don Wilson (27.2) Houston Astros	Phil Niekro (75.1) Atlanta Braves	102.3
12	7/15/1901 NY 5-0	Christy Mathewson (88.4) New York Giants	Willie Sudhoff (13.6) St. Louis Cardinals	102.0
13	8/19/1969 Chi 3-0	Ken Holtzman (25.8) Chicago Cubs	Phil Niekro (75.1) Atlanta Braves	100.9

Rank	Date Score	No-hit Pitcher (JAWS) Team	Opposing Pitcher (JAWS) Team	Total JAWS
14	7/15/1973 Cal 6-0	Nolan Ryan (62.2) California Angels	Jim Perry (36.0) Detroit Tigers	98.2
15	5/30/1977 Cle 1-0	Dennis Eckersley (49.9) Cleveland Indians	Frank Tanana (47.6) California Angels	97.5

METHODOLOGY: This table lists the top 15 no-hit games ranked in order of highest combined JAWS of the two starting pitchers. JAWS = Jaffe Wins Above Replacement Score. JAWS is a sabermetric baseball statistic developed to evaluate the strength of a player's career and merit for induction into the Baseball Hall of Fame. It is created by averaging a player's career Wins Above Replacement (WAR) with their 7-year peak WAR. WAR measures a player's value in all facets of the game by deciphering how many more wins he's worth than a replacement-level player at his same position.

LEGEND: Dates are shown as month/day/year (for example, June 12, 2018, is shown as 6/12/2018). Total JAWS = the combined total of both starting pitchers' JAWS.

NOTE 1: Some of the teams in this table moved or changed names over the years. The Boston Americans became the Boston Red Sox in 1908. The New York Highlanders changed their name to the New York Yankees in 1913. The Cleveland Naps changed their name to the Cleveland Indians in 1915. The team has been known as the Cleveland Guardians since 2022. The Dodgers and Giants began in Brooklyn and New York, respectively. The two teams moved to Los Angeles and San Francisco before the start of the 1958 season.

NOTE 2: With a combined JAWS of 146.4, the Perry-Gibson matchup dwarfs all the others in the past 100 years. Of course, there are quite a few other Hall-of-Fame no-hit pitchers in the Top 15, including Cy Young (twice), Christy Mathewson (twice), Nolan Ryan (twice), Walter Johnson, Addie Joss, Tom Seaver, Randy Johnson, Sandy Koufax, and Dennis Eckersley. Rube Waddell, Mordecai Brown, Juan Marichal, and Phil Niekro (twice) are on this list, also, because they had a no-hitter thrown against them and their team. Gaylord Perry's brother Jim is there, as well.

Gaylord Perry racked up a lot of WAR during his career largely due to his longevity, throwing for eight different teams over 22 seasons from 1962-1983. His best years were from 1966-1979, a span in which he was selected for five All-Star teams and won the Cy Young Award with Cleveland in 1972 and San Diego in 1978. Even though his no-hitter happened during the 1960s, his best decade was the 1970s, where he was clearly one of the top pitchers of that era. For comparison purposes, the best pitchers of the 1970s are listed in Table 21-3 (below).

Table 21-3. Best Pitchers of the 1970s

Rank	Pitcher (Team(s))	Seasons Pitched	Innings Pitched	WAR (per 200 IP)	Wins (per Season)
1	Tom Seaver (Mets, Reds)	1970-1979	2,652.1	67.1 (5.06)	178 (17.8)
2	Phil Niekro (Braves)	1970-1979	2,881.0	64.6 (4.48)	164 (16.4)
3	Gaylord Perry (Giants, Indians, Rangers, Padres)	1970-1979	2,905.0	59.0 (4.06)	184 (18.4)
4	Bert Blyleven (Twins, Rangers, Pirates)	1970-1979	2,624.2	57.9 (4.41)	148 (14.8)
5	Jim Palmer (Orioles)	1970-1979	2,745.0	54.2 (3.95)	186 (18.6)
6	Ferguson Jenkins (Cubs, Rangers, Red Sox)	1970-1979	2,706.2	52.6 (3.89)	178 (17.8)
7	Steve Carlton (Phillies, Cardinals)	1970-1979	2,747.0	44.6 (3.25)	178 (17.8)
8	Wilbur Wood (White Sox)	1970-1978	2,150.1	43.3 (4.03)	136 (15.1)
9	Nolan Ryan (Mets, Angels)	1970-1979	2,465.0	41.4 (3.36)	155 (15.5)
10	Rick Reuschel (Cubs)	1972-1979	1,834.1	40.8 (4.45)	114 (14.3)
11	Luis Tiant (Twins, Red Sox, Yankees)	1970-1979	2,063.0	39.5 (3.83)	142 (14.2)
12	Vida Blue (Athletics, Giants)	1970-1979	2,398.2	35.3 (2.94)	155 (15.5)

METHODOLOGY: Pitchers are ranked in order of Wins Above Replacement (WAR) achieved from 1970-1979. WAR measures a player's value in all facets of the game by deciphering how many more wins he's worth than a replacement-level player at his same position. Another measure of merit I wanted to include was the number of wins each pitcher accumulated as well. Because a number of pitchers were only present for a portion of the decade, I included two rate measures (WAR per 200 innings pitched and wins per season).

LEGEND: Team(s) = the team(s) a player played for during the 1970s. If a pitcher played for more than one team, teams are listed in chronological order. IP = innings pitched. One-third of an inning is designated as ".1" and two-thirds of an inning is designated as ".2"

NOTE: Gaylord Perry wasn't the only multi-year winner of the Cy Young Award in the 1970s. Steve Carlton was a four-time winner. He won it twice in the 1970s (1972 and 1977) and twice in the 1980s (1980 and 1982). Jim Palmer won the award three times in a four-year period (1973, 1975, and 1976). Tom Seaver won the award three times, also. His first was in 1969 and the last two were in the 1970s (1973 and 1975). All four of these pitchers are included in Table 21-3.

The game itself played out as one might have expected. It was a 1-0 shutout, with the Giants collecting just four hits and two walks. One of those hits, though, was a solo home run to left field in the first inning by Ron Hunt. He was the second hitter for the Giants and, even though San Francisco threatened to score in the second, sixth, and eighth innings, they couldn't get any more runners across home plate.

Meanwhile, Gaylord Perry was masterful. Only two Cardinals ever reached base – both on two-out walks – and they never went past first. Perry struck out nine and induced the St. Louis batters to ground out 10 times in a game he controlled from the beginning. The remaining outs were relatively routine fly balls and pop outs.

While the Cardinals never had a runner in scoring position, Perry's no-hitter was noticeably threatened twice. Light-hitting Dal Maxvill led off the top of the sixth by sending a shot to the left of Perry, who gloved it and threw out the shortstop. Two batters later, Bobby Tolan hit a sharp grounder in between first baseman Willie McCovey and the first base bag. McCovey scooped it up and led Perry with the toss to get the speedy Tolan in a force-out. Beyond that, it was pretty routine for Perry and the Giants.

Ron Hunt, the offensive hero of the game, deserves some special attention. It's important to note that he was overmatched by Bob Gibson that day, like many hitters, and hitting a home run against him was an extraordinary achievement. Hunt had limited power. He only hit two home runs in 1968 in 650 plate appearances. By that measure alone, his home run was a rarity. Against Bob Gibson, though, Hunt had a career of general futility.

During Hunt's career, he faced Bob Gibson a whopping 126 times – 26 more times than any other pitcher. With just 18 hits – all but five were singles — Hunt batted .177 against the St. Louis ace. He hit just one home run against Gibson, which happened to be this day. On the positive side, Hunt knew how to get on base, even facing the Cardinal hurler. Against Gibson, he collected 16 walks and reached base another six times by getting hit by a pitch, giving him a relatively decent on-base-percentage of .323.

The six HBPs against the fireballer Gibson was extraordinary – and it had to hurt a lot. It was also the most HBPs against any pitcher in Hunt's career. Hunt himself made something of a specialty of using the HBP to get on base, as he was hit 243 times during his 12-year career. This works out to be a remarkable 20+ times per season.

Hunt led baseball in HBPs every year from 1968-1973, setting the post-1900 major league record in 1971 for most HBPs in a single season (50) while playing with the Montreal Expos. His enormous total of career HBPs is the fourth highest in baseball history from 1900 to the present as displayed in the table below.

Table 21-4. Career Hit By Pitch Leaders

Rank	Batter (Career Length)	Career HBP	Plate Appearances	HBP per 1,000 PAs	OBP, SLG, OPS, OPS+
1	Craig Biggio (1988-2007)	285	12,504	22.79	.363, .433, .796, 112
2	Don Baylor (1970-1988)	267	9,401	28.40	.342, .436, .777, 118
3	Jason Kendall (1996-2010)	254	8,702	29.19	.366, .378, .744, 95
4	Ron Hunt (1963-1974)	243	6,158	39.46	.368, .347, .715, 105
5	Chase Utley (2003-2018)	204	7,863	25.94	.358, .465, .823, 117
6	Frank Robinson (1956-1976)	198	11,744	16.86	.389, .527, .926, 154
7	Minnie Minoso (1946-1980)	197	8,233	23.92	.387, .461, .848, 130
8	Jason Giambi (1995-2014)	180	8,908	20.21	.399, .516, .916, 139

Rank	Batter (Career Length)	Career HBP	Plate Appearances	HBP per 1,000 PAs	OBP, SLG, OPS, OPS+
9 (tie)	Andres Galarraga (1985-2004)	178	8,916	19.96	.347, .499, .846, 119
9 (tie)	Anthony Rizzo (2011-2021)	178	5,992	29.71	.369, .481, .850, 127

METHODOLOGY: This table includes batters who reached base by being hit by a pitch (HBP) the most times during their career. This table covers the seasons from 1900-2021 and batters are ranked by the number of times they were hit by a pitch.

LEGEND: Career length = the span of time between a player's first appearance in the Major Leagues and his last appearance. This span does not account for gaps during that period. For example, Hall of Famer Minnie Minoso began his career in 1946, playing for the New York Cubans of the Negro National League. From 1946-1964, Minoso played nearly continuously for the Cubans, White Sox, Cardinals, and Senators. He made cameo appearances for the White Sox in 1976 and 1980 (when he was in his fifties), therefore, his career length is listed as 1946-1980. HBP = Hit by pitch, PA = Plate appearance, OBP = On-base percentage, SLG = Slugging percentage, OPS = On-base percentage plus slugging percentage. OPS+ takes a player's on-base plus slugging percentage and normalizes the number across the entire league. It accounts for external factors like ballparks. It then adjusts so a score of 100 is league average, and 150 is 50 percent better than the league average. HBP per 1,000 PAs measures the rate of a batter's HBP by dividing career HBP by plate appearances and multiplying by 1,000.

NOTE 1: Dan McGann, an infielder who played from 1896-1908, had a total of 230 HBPs. He accumulated 149 of them from 1900 on.

NOTE 2: Hall of Famer Hughie Jennings played from 1891-1910; although the large majority of his value as a player came during his prime years of 1891-1902. During his career he accumulated 287 HBPs, leading the majors in five straight seasons from 1894-1898, and setting the all-time season high HBP mark at 51 in 1896 with the Baltimore Orioles of the National League. Since these statistics come from the pre-1900 era, he does not qualify to be included on this table. If he did, he would be in the #1 position, slightly ahead of Craig Biggio.

NOTE 3: Anthony Rizzo is still an active player as of the beginning of the 2022 season, so his total HBPs will likely increase.

Even more impressive for Ron Hunt, the rate at which he accumulated HBPs was much higher than any player who appeared as often as he did. The table below shows the highest rates of getting hit by a pitch for all batters with more than 1,000 plate appearances and with a minimum of 50 career HBPs.

Hunt has far more plate appearances (PAs) than all batters on the list and has more than twice as many PAs than any batter in the top four HBP rates. It's important to note that Hunt is the only player who appears on both the career total HBPs list and the highest HBP rate list depicted in this chapter.

Table 21-5. Hit By Pitch Highest Rate

Rank	Batter (Career Length)	Career HBP	Plate Appearances	HBP per 1,000 PAs	OBP, SLG, OPS, OPS+
1	Brandon Guyer (2011-2018)	85	1,487	57.16	.339, .388, .727, 101
2	Derek Dietrich (2013-2020)	123	2,513	48.95	.335, .428, .762, 107
3	Victor Robles (2017-2021)	54	1,268	42.59	.317, .375, .692, 83
4	F.P. Santangelo (1995-2001)	83	2,075	40.00	.364, .351, .715, 89
5	Ron Hunt (1963-1974)	243	6,158	39.46	.368, .347, .715, 105
6	Carlos Quentin (2006-2014)	127	3,247	39.11	.347, .484, .831, 120
7	Craig Wilson (2001-2007)	90	2,311	38.94	.353, .474, .827, 113
8	Jason LaRue (1999-2010)	107	3,103	34.48	.315, .396, .712, 84
9	Reed Johnson (2003-2015)	134	3,992	33.57	.335, .405, .740, 94
10	Fernando Vina (1993-2004)	157	4,742	33.11	.348, .379, .728, 89

METHODOLOGY: Batters are ranked by the highest rate they were hit by a pitch during their career. To qualify for inclusion in this table, a player has to have a minimum of 50 HBPs and 1,000 plate appearances during their career from 1900-2021.

LEGEND: Career length = the span of time between a player's first appearance in the Major Leagues and his last appearance. This span does not account for gaps during that period. HBP = Hit by pitch, PA = Plate appearance, OBP = On-base percentage, SLG = Slugging percentage, OPS = On-base percentage plus slugging percentage. OPS+ takes a player's on-base plus slugging percentage and normalizes the number across the entire league. It accounts for external factors like ballparks. It then adjusts so a score of 100 is league average, and 150 is 50 percent better than the league average. HBP per 1,000 PAs measures the rate of a batter's HBP by dividing career HBP by plate appearances and multiplying by 1,000.

NOTE 1: Dan McGann, an infielder who played from 1896-1908, had an HBP/1000 PA rate of 37.97 over 6,057 total plate appearances. He had an HBP/1000 PA rate of 32.02 from 1900 on.

NOTE 2: Victor Robles was still an active player as of the beginning of the 2022 season, so his statistics could change by the time he retires.

Ron Hunt was not a flash-in-the-pan, either. Selected for the National League All-Star team in both 1964 and 1966 when he was with the Mets, he came in second in the NL Rookie of the Year voting in 1963. The Giants thought so highly of Hunt, they traded All-Star catcher Tom Haller to the rival Los Angeles Dodgers before the 1968 season to get him. Hunt even received a handful of MVP votes in 1969 while playing with the Giants.

In addition to the high caliber of the starting pitchers and the uniqueness of Ron Hunt's accomplishments, the game highlighted in this chapter was a rarity in that it was the first of two no-hitters thrown on consecutive days. Even more remarkably, the consecutive no-hitters involved the same two teams – the second one was thrown by the Cardinals' Ray Washburn. The table below shows the shortest time in days between two no-hitters.

Table 21-6. Shortest Time Between Two No-hit Games

Rank	No-hitter #1 Score	No-hitter #1 Pitcher/Team	No-hitter #2 Score	No-hitter #2 Pitcher/Team	Days
1	6/29/1990 LA 6, StL 0	F. Valenzuela LA Dodgers	6/29/1990 Oak 5, Tor 0	Dave Stewart Oak Athletics	0
2 (tie)	5/5/1917 StL 1, Chi 0	Ernie Koob StL Browns	5/6/1917 StL 3, Chi 0	Bob Groom StL Browns	1

Rank	No-hitter #1 Score	No-hitter #1 Pitcher/Team	No-hitter #2 Score	No-hitter #2 Pitcher/Team	Days
2 (tie)	9/17/1968 SF 1, StL 0	Gaylord Perry SF Giants	9/18/1968 StL 2, SF 0	Ray Washburn StL Cardinals	1
2 (tie)	4/30/1969 Cin 10, Hou 0	Jim Maloney Cincinnati Reds	5/1/1969 Hou 4, Cin 0	Don Wilson Houston Astros	1
2 (tie)	5/18/2021 Det 5, Sea 0	Spencer Turnbull Detroit Tigers	5/19/2021 NY 2, Tex 0	Corey Kluber NY Yankees	1
6 (tie)	9/18/1908 Cle 2, Bos 1	Bob Rhoads Cleveland Naps	9/20/1908 Chi 1, Phi 0	Frank Smith Chi White Sox	2
6 (tie)	5/5/2021 Bal 6, Sea 0	John Means Baltimore Orioles	5/7/2021 Cin 3, Cle 0	Wade Miley Cincinnati Reds	2
8 (tie)	5/2/1917 Cin 1, Chi 0	Fred Toney Cincinnati Reds	5/5/1917 StL 1, Chi 0	Ernie Koob StL Browns	3
8 (tie)	9/4/1923 NY 2, Phi 0	Sad Sam Jones NY Yankees	9/7/1923 Bos 4, Phi 0	Howard Ehmke Boston Red Sox	3
8 (tie)	9/26/1983 StL 3, Mon 0	Bob Forsch StL Cardinals	9/29/1983 Oak 3, Chi 0	Mike Warren Oak Athletics	3
11 (tie)	6/30/1908 Bos 8, NY 0	Cy Young Boston Red Sox	7/4/1908 NY 1, Phi 0	Hooks Wiltse NY Giants	4
11 (tie)	8/26/1916 Phi 5, Cle 0	Bullet Joe Bush Phi Athletics	8/30/1916 Bos 4, StL 0	Dutch Leonard Boston Red Sox	4
11 (tie)	6/11/1938 Cin 3, Bos 0	J. Vander Meer Cincinnati Reds	6/15/1938 Cin 6, Bro 0	J. Vander Meer Cincinnati Reds	4
11 (tie)	6/26/1962 Bos 2, LA 0	Earl Wilson Boston Red Sox	6/30/1962 LA 5, NY 0	Sandy Koufax LA Dodgers	4
11 (tie)	9/4/1993 NY 4, Cle 0	Jim Abbott NY Yankees	9/8/1993 Hou 7, NY 1	Darryl Kile Houston Astros	4
11 (tie)	5/3/2011 Min 1, Chi 0	Francisco Liriano Minnesota Twins	5/7/2011 Det 9, Tor 0	Justin Verlander Detroit Tigers	4

METHODOLOGY: This table shows the pairs of no-hitters from 1900-2021 that had the shortest time between the first and second no-hitter. Game pairs are ranked by the shortest number of days between consecutive no-hitters thrown in the Major Leagues. "0" indicates the two-no-hitters were thrown on the same day, with the one occurring earlier in the day being listed first.

LEGEND: Dates are shown as month/day/year (for example, June 12, 2018, is shown as 6/12/2018). Scores listed are for the no-hitter thrown that day. Team abbreviations are standard designations used for the home city of the teams involved. Since teams routinely share hometowns, clarification may be necessary in some cases:

- Ernie Koob, Bob Groom, Mike Warren, and Francisco Liriano threw their no-hitters against the Chicago White Sox.
- Bob Rhoads threw his no-hitter against the Boston Red Sox.
- Frank Smith, Sad Sam Jones, and Howard Ehmke threw their no-hitters against the Philadelphia Athletics. The team moved to Kansas City in 1955 and to Oakland in 1968.
- Fred Toney threw his 10-inning no-hitter against the Chicago Cubs.
- Cy Young threw his no-hitter against the New York Highlanders, who became the Yankees in 1913.
- Hooks Wiltse threw his 10-inning no-hitter against the Philadelphia Phillies.
- Dutch Leonard threw his no-hitter against the St. Louis Browns. The Browns moved to Baltimore and became the Orioles in 1954.
- Johnny Vander Meer threw his first no-hitter against the Boston Braves. The Braves would later become the Milwaukee Braves (1953) and Atlanta Braves (1966). Vander Meer's second no-hitter was thrown against the Brooklyn Dodgers. The Dodgers would move to Los Angeles in 1958.
- Earl Wilson threw his no-hitter against the Los Angeles Angels. The Angels have also been known as the California Angels (1965) and Anaheim Angels (1997).
- Sandy Koufax and Darryl Kile threw their no-hitters against the New York Mets.

NOTE 1: Ranked number one in Table 21-6 are the two no-hitters thrown by the Dodgers' Fernando Valenzuela and the Athletics' Dave Stewart on the exact same day (June 29, 1990). Tied for second are four pairs of pitchers who threw no-hitters on consecutive days. Like the Perry-Washburn duo in San Francisco, two other pairs of no-hitters were thrown in games involving the same two teams on consecutive days: the Browns-White Sox games in 1917, and the Reds-Astros games in 1969. It's also remarkable to note that Cincinnati pitcher Johnny Vander Meer threw no-hitters on consecutive starts (four days apart) in 1938.

NOTE 2: Ernie Koob's no-hitter is listed twice in this table. Fred Toney threw a no-hitter against the Cubs on May 2, 1917. Three days later, Ernie Koob threw a no-hitter against the White Sox. The following day, Koob's teammate Bob Groom threw another no-hitter against the White Sox. Throwing three no-hitters in the span of four days is also a record.

While Gaylord Perry had just turned 30 when he threw his no-hitter, most of his value as a pitcher came after that milestone. He is among the top no-hit pitchers who achieved the majority of their career value after they turned 30, with over 78% of his replacement value (WAR) coming after his 30th birthday. His post-30 accomplishments include two Cy Young Awards (one in each league) and multiple All-star team selections.

Table 21-7. No-hit Pitchers Who Excelled After Turning 30

Rank	Pitcher (Career Length)	Innings Before 30 After 30	Wins-Losses Before 30 After 30	Strikeouts Before 30 After 30	WAR Before 30 (pct) After 30 (pct)
1	Dazzy Vance (1915-1935)	33 **2934**	0-4 **197-136**	18 **2027**	-0.4 (-0.6%) **63.3 (100.6%)**
2	Phil Niekro (1964-1987)	603 **4800**	31-27 **287-247**	343 **2999**	8.6 (8.9%) **88.4 (91.1%)**
3	Randy Johnson (1988-2009)	1073 **3062**	68-56 **235-110**	1126 **3749**	11.1 (10.7%) **92.4 (89.3%)**
4	Kenny Rogers (1989-2008)	736 **2567**	53-44 **166-112**	540 **1428**	6.9 (13.7%) **43.6 (86.3%)**
5	David Wells (1987-2007)	687 **2752**	47-37 **192-120**	449 **1752**	8.2 (15.3%) **45.4 (84.7%)**
6	Gaylord Perry (1962-1983)	1360 **3990**	76-70 **238-195**	1001 **2533**	20.1 (21.6%) **72.9 (78.4%)**
7	Warren Spahn (1942-1965)	1283 **3960**	86-58 **277-187**	653 **1930**	25.6 (27.7%) **66.9 (72.3%)**
8	Bob Gibson (1959-1975)	1449 **2435**	91-69 **160-105**	1210 **1907**	25.5 (31.2%) **56.2 (68.8%)**
9	Nolan Ryan (1966-1993)	2085 **3451**	122-116 **202-176**	2085 **3629**	28.8 (34.4%) **54.8 (65.6%)**

METHODOLOGY: This table lists no-hit pitchers from 1900-2021 who have achieved the highest Wins Above Replacement (WAR) after turning 30 years old. WAR measures a player's value in all facets of the game by deciphering how many more wins he's worth than a replacement-level player at his same position. Players in this table are ranked by the highest percentage of WAR they compiled after turning 30. This percentage is indicated in the entry entitled "After 30 (pct)" in the WAR column.

LEGEND: Career length = the span of time between a player's first appearance in the Major Leagues and his last appearance. This span does not account for gaps during that period. The columns labeled "Innings," "Wins-Losses," "Strikeouts," and "WAR" list a pitcher's accomplishments in those categories. *"Before 30" (in italics) shows what a pitcher achieved before they turned 30.* **"After 30" (in bold) shows what a pitcher achieved after their 30th birthday.** The term "(pct)" refers to the percentage of their career WAR a pitcher achieved either before or after their 30th birthday. For example, Dazzy Vance (#1 entry on this list) had a career WAR of 62.9. He achieved minus 0.4 WAR before he turned 30 and 63.3 WAR after his 30th birthday. Therefore, his (pct) before 30 was *(-0.6%)* and his (pct) after 30 was **(100.6%)**.

NOTE: In terms of total value (WAR) provided after 30, Hall of Famers Randy Johnson and Phil Niekro dwarf all the other great pitchers on this list. Johnson, Nolan Ryan, and Niekro eclipsed the others in the number of strikeouts they registered, and Niekro, Perry, Warren Spahn, and Ryan threw the most innings of this group. Niekro, Johnson, Perry, Spahn, and Ryan all won over 200 games after their 30th birthdays, too.

This is an incredibly accomplished list of pitchers. Seven of the nine are Hall of Famers, with the only exceptions being Kenny Rogers and David Wells, two of the very best pitchers of their era. Of course, the one eye-popping example is Hall of Famer Dazzy Vance, who achieved virtually all his value after he turned 30. This included a National League MVP Award with the Brooklyn Dodgers in 1924 at the age of 33 (note: there was no Cy Young Award for best pitcher at that time).

Gaylord Perry had a long and highly productive career with eight different teams. While he was with the Giants the longest (10 years), he excelled with his other teams, including winning the 1972 Cy Young Award with the Cleveland Indians, and the 1978 Cy Young Award with the San Diego Padres.

A notoriously bad hitter – like many pitchers of his time – there is an oft-told story about Gaylord Perry when he was a young pitcher. In it, Giants' manager Alvin Dark once suggested that man would walk on the moon before Gaylord hit a home run. In fact, Neil Armstrong did step on the moon one-hour prior to Perry's first home run in 1969. Perry would go on to hit five more home runs during his career, including his last one at the age of 42 with the Atlanta Braves in 1981.

Dick Dietz, Gaylord Perry's catcher the day he threw a no-hitter, was a valued teammate and a great hitter. He played for eight seasons from 1966-1973, six of which were for the Giants. Platooning from 1966 to 1969, Dietz became the primary catcher on the Giants in 1970 and 1971. His best year was 1970, when he was selected for the National League All-Star team. Dietz's home run leading off the bottom of the ninth inning in that game ignited a game-tying rally. Eventually the National League won in 12 innings. Dietz was also the primary catcher for the 1971 West Division champion Giants, playing every day down the last stretch of the pennant drive despite a head injury.

Dietz was challenged as a fielder, though, as he led the National League in passed balls (25) and stolen bases allowed (92) during the 1970 season – no other catcher was even close. He was also in the top 10 of those categories, even when he was a platoon player. Additionally, controversy surrounded Dietz early in the 1972 season when he was acting as the player representative for the Giants as the players union went on strike. Giants' ownership didn't appreciate his active role in the process and offloaded him to the Dodgers for a song.

After brief, very successful stints with the Dodgers and Braves in 1972 and 1973, Dietz was not signed by any team for the 1974 season. Rumors of being blackballed by notorious Giants owner Horace Stoneham surfaced. After Dietz's death from a heart attack in 2005, other players came forward to express support for the viewpoint that Dietz had been treated unfairly by management at that time.

After his playing years were done, the relationship between Dietz and the Giants healed – Stoneham sold the club in 1976. Dietz very successfully managed the San Jose Giants, San Francisco's High-A farm team, in 1993 and 1994. He also managed the independent league Sioux Falls Canaries in 1995 and the Sonoma County Crushers from 1996 to 1999.

Dietz still has the distinction of ranking third overall in career on-base percentage among major league catchers (.385), placing him behind only Joe Mauer and Gene

Tenace. Dietz is also one of the featured players on the Giants' Wall of Fame outside of Oracle Park.

On a personal note, this no-hitter has a special place in my heart. My oldest brother Dave and a couple of his friends were at this game. Afterwards, they went to the Giants locker room and waited in line for one hour to shake Gaylord Perry's hand. They were totally impressed by him. The following day, my next older brother Drew went to the game with some friends and saw the Cardinals' Ray Washburn throw his no-hitter against the Giants. Remarkable.

CHAPTER 22

BOB GIBSON: HALL OF FAME COMBINATION

August 14, 1971

Bob Gibson and Ted Simmons combine for the only Hall of Fame no-hit battery

"You keep looking up at that big scoreboard and see they don't have any hits. Starting in the seventh, I was really concentrating ... In the last two innings, I was bearing down extra hard. I was trying not to make bad pitches. Even when I was getting behind in the count, I was careful not to groove the ball."

Hall of Famer Bob Gibson describing his increasing intensity as the game reached its final stages (Neil Russo, "Gibson Fires First No-Hitter," *St. Louis Post-Dispatch*, August 15, 1971).

"That was the greatest thrill of my life, catching a no-hitter. Man, he was throwing fire."

Cardinal catcher and fellow Hall of Famer Ted Simmons describing his emotions surrounding this historic game (Neil Russo, "Gibson Fires First No-Hitter," *St. Louis Post-Dispatch*, August 15, 1971).

"I didn't think that I'd ever throw a no-hitter. I'm a high-ball pitcher and not many high-ball pitchers throw no-hitters."

Bob Gibson giving his earlier assessment of his chances of ever throwing a no-hitter (Neil Russo, "Gibson Fires First No-Hitter," *St. Louis Post-Dispatch*, August 15, 1971).

"All those people who said that Gibson was washed up should have had to bat against him tonight."

Pittsburgh slugger Willie Stargell offering his opinion of how difficult it was to hit Bob Gibson that evening (Neil Russo, "Gibson Fires First No-Hitter," *St. Louis Post-Dispatch*, August 15, 1971).

"It thrilled me. I felt as if we'd won the seventh game of the World Series."

Bob Gibson's post-game reaction to his momentous accomplishment (Neil Russo, "Gibson Fires First No-Hitter," *St. Louis Post-Dispatch*, August 15, 1971)

Thirty-five-year-old Bob Gibson had already crafted a Hall of Fame career by the time he took the mound in Pittsburgh that evening to face the division-leading – and eventual World Series champion – Pirates. A two-time Cy Young Award winner, two-time World Series MVP, and seven-time All-Star by the start of 1971, Gibson had over 200 wins and was the record holder for the lowest ERA in an entire season, an otherworldly 1.12 in 1968 ("The Year of the Pitcher"). A fierce competitor, Gibson was renowned for not giving an inch to anyone.

Despite his years of success, his 1971 season had not gone particularly well up to that point (by Bob Gibson standards). After losing to the Dodgers by the score of 6-5 in his last start five days earlier, Gibson's record stood at 10-10 with an ERA of 3.39. Part of this was due to a sore leg injury that affected him throughout May, eventually placing him on the Disabled List (DL) for three weeks starting at the end of the month. By the time he came off the DL in June, his record was 4-5 and his ERA had ballooned to a very un-Gibson-like 4.27. Gibson then promptly lost his next two starts, closing out the month of June with a 4-7 record. Rumors began circulating that the fastball-throwing Gibson was all washed up at 35 years old.

At the other end of the pitcher-catcher battery this day was 21-year-old Ted Simmons in his second year as the Cardinals' regular catcher. Simmons was in the midst of a breakout season, finishing with a batting average of .304 and even earning a few down-ballot votes for Most Valuable Player. Simmons would collect almost 2,500 hits over a distinguished 21-year career, being named to eight different All-Star teams and winning the Silver Slugger Award. Simmons would be selected for the Hall of Fame in 2020 as the only player chosen on the Veterans Committee ballot.

The outcome of the game was never in much doubt after the first inning. The Cardinals jumped on Pittsburgh starter Bob Johnson for five runs in the first inning, with a walk, three singles, and a three-run home run over the centerfield fence by Joe Hague. St. Louis would add to its lead with a three-run fifth inning, punctuated by a two-run double from Ted Kubiak and a Bob Gibson sacrifice fly. The Cardinals would cap their scoring with a three-run eighth inning, featuring a bases-loaded walk followed by a two-run single from Bob Gibson. With a final score of 11-0, the only real drama in this game would center around whether Gibson would be able to finally chalk up a no-hitter.

The Pittsburgh Pirates of 1971 were a powerful hitting team. Featuring All-Stars Manny Sanguillen, Al Oliver, Willie Stargell, and Roberto Clemente, along with up-and-coming stars like Bob Robertson and Richie Hebner, the Pirates led the National League in runs, hits, home runs, slugging, and OPS – and the runner-up teams in these categories typically weren't close. Even though Sanguillen, Clemente, and Hebner were not in the starting lineup, Pittsburgh had plenty of firepower facing Gibson.

As it turned out, only four Pirate batters got on base that day: a strikeout/wild pitch in the second inning where Milt May reached first; a walk to Jackie Hernandez leading off the third; a one-out walk to Willie Stargell in the fourth; and a two-out walk to Bob Robertson in the seventh. None of those runners ever advanced beyond first base in this lopsided contest, as Gibson struck out 10 Pirate batters and otherwise dominated the rest.

While the game's eventual outcome was pretty much sealed by the late innings, there were two especially close plays late in the game that threatened Gibson's no-hitter. After Willie Stargell struck out to lead off the seventh, Milt May followed with the first hard-hit ball of the game for the Pirates. His drive sent Jose Cruz deep into center field where he made a running catch at the warning track. May thought he had hit a home run, while Gibson knew it would either go over the fence or the swift Cruz would catch up to it and get the out. May's drive was a few feet short of going over the wall.

The one play "that really scared" Bob Gibson happened in the eighth inning. With Dave Cash batting with two outs in an 11-0 game, third baseman Joe Torre was playing in at third to defend against the bunt. Instead, Cash hit a high chopper that Torre had to leap to snag to keep the ball from bouncing into the outfield. Once it was clear he had it, Torre made the throw to Matty Alou at first for the third out.

While Gibson would spend his entire illustrious career with St. Louis, Simmons split his time primarily between the Cardinals and the Milwaukee Brewers of the American League. In what must be seen as an extraordinarily lopsided trade, Simmons, future Hall of Famer Rollie Fingers, and future Cy Young Award winner Pete Vuckovich were traded by St. Louis after the 1980 season to Milwaukee for David Green, Dave LaPoint, Sixto Lezcano, and Lary Sorensen.

The three newly acquired Brewers would be key elements of the 1982 American League pennant-winning Milwaukee team. Ironically, it would be the Cardinals who would come out on top in the 1982 World Series as they defeated "Harvey's Wallbangers" (nicknamed after manager Harvey Kuenn) in an exciting seven-game series.

Bob Gibson's no-hitter, with Ted Simmons as his batterymate, has the distinction of being the only no-hitter ever thrown that involved a pitcher and a catcher who were both members of the Hall of Fame. Unsurprisingly, the Gibson/Simmons duo also has the highest combined JAWS of any battery going back to at least 1950. The Top 10 combined scores since 1950 are included in the table below.

Table 22-1. Pitcher-catcher Highest Combined JAWS

Rank	Date Score	Team (Opponent)	Pitcher Catcher	JAWS	Total JAWS
1	8/14/1971 StL 11-0	St. Louis Cardinals (Pittsburgh Pirates)	Bob Gibson Ted Simmons	75.2 42.6	117.8
2	6/12/2007 Det 4-0	Detroit Tigers (Milwaukee Brewers)	Justin Verlander Ivan Rodriguez	61.9 54.2	116.1
3	9/22/1977 Tex 6-0	Texas Rangers (California Angels)	Bert Blyleven Jim Sundberg	72.4 34.6	107.0
4	9/16/1960 Mil 4-0	Milwaukee Braves (Philadelphia Phillies)	Warren Spahn Del Crandall	75.8 26.3	102.1
5	4/30/1969 Cin 10-0	Cincinnati Reds (Houston Astros)	Jim Maloney Johnny Bench	37.2 61.2	98.4
6	7/28/1994 Tex 4-0	Texas Rangers (California Angels)	Kenny Rogers Ivan Rodriguez	42.4 54.2	96.6
7	9/17/1968 SF 1-0	San Francisco Giants (St. Louis Cardinals)	Gaylord Perry Dick Dietz	71.2 12.7	83.9

Rank	Date Score	Team (Opponent)	Pitcher Catcher	JAWS	Total JAWS
8	9/21/1970 Oak 1-0	Oakland Athletics (Minnesota Twins)	Vida Blue Gene Tenace	41.7 40.9	82.6
9	6/15/1963 SF 1-0	San Francisco Giants (Houston Colt .45s)	Juan Marichal Ed Bailey	57.4 25.1	82.5
10	5/1/1991 Tex 3-0	Texas Rangers (Toronto Blue Jays)	Nolan Ryan Mike Stanley	62.2 20.2	82.4

METHODOLOGY: This table includes those pitcher/catcher batteries with the highest combined career Jaffe Wins Above Replacement Score (JAWS) from 1950-2021. No-hit pitcher/catcher batteries are ranked in descending order by combined JAWS. JAWS is a sabermetric baseball statistic developed to evaluate the strength of a player's career and merit for induction into the Baseball Hall of Fame. It is created by averaging a player's career Wins Above Replacement (WAR) with their 7-year peak WAR. WAR measures a player's value in all facets of the game by deciphering how many more wins he's worth than a replacement-level player at his same position.

LEGEND: Dates are shown as month/day/year (for example, June 12, 2018, is shown as 6/12/2018). JAWS = Jaffe Wins Above Replacement Score. WAR = Wins Above Replacement. JAWS values for each pitcher and catcher are listed next to their name. Combined JAWS = the combined JAWS value for the pitcher and catcher involved in the no-hitter listed. *Italicized game (Kenny Rogers/Ivan Rodriguez in 1994) was a perfect game.*

NOTE 1: Justin Verlander's career WAR and JAWS continue to climb – this table reflects his JAWS before the 2022 season started. It is highly likely that by the time Verlander retires he and Ivan Rodriguez will be at the top of the list. With three-time Cy Young Award winner Justin Verlander's inevitable selection for the Hall of Fame, they will also become the second Hall of Fame no-hitter duo ever.

NOTE 2: Of note, almost all the Top 10 JAWS combinations in Table 22-1 have at least one Hall of Famer. The single exception is the Vida Blue/Gene Tenace no-hitter. While the game involved two outstanding players, neither of them is in the Hall of Fame. Blue and Tenace are also the most evenly matched teammates as measured by JAWS, with Vida Blue at 41.7 and Gene Tenace at 40.9.

As might be expected, Bob Gibson features prominently in the list of best-pitched games in Cardinal history. He is the only pitcher since 1900 who is listed twice in the top ten St. Louis pitcher performances of 10 or less innings. His no-hit game in this chapter is tied for sixth with a game score of 94, and it is the highest-ranked Cardinal no-hitter of the nine that have been thrown. Surprisingly, the St. Louis no-hitter total is among the lowest of the 16 original baseball franchises (non-expansion teams), with only the Tigers, Senators/Twins, and Pirates having thrown fewer. For comparison purposes, I've included all the team's no-hitters in this table.

Table 22-2. Cardinals Highest Game Scores of 10 innings or Less

Rank	Pitcher	Date Score	Opponent	GSc	IP, Hits, Runs, ERs, Walks, Strikeouts
1	Shelby Miller	5/10/2013 StL 3-0	Colorado Rockies	98	9.0 IP, 1 Hit, 0 Runs, 0 ERs, 0 BBs, 13 Ks
2 (tie)	Ernie Broglio	7/15/1960 StL 6-0	Chicago Cubs	97	9.0 IP, 1 Hit, 0 Runs, 0 ERs, 2 BBs, 14 Ks
2 (tie)	Jaime Garcia	4/14/2016 StL 7-0	Milwaukee Brewers	97	9.0 IP, 1 Hit, 0 Runs, 0 ERs, 1 BB, 13 Ks
4	Bob Gibson	6/17/1970 StL 8-0	San Diego Padres	96	9.0 IP, 1 Hit, 0 Runs, 0 ERs, 2 BBs, 13 Ks
5	Red Ames	9/19/1915 (2) StL 1-0 (10 inn)	Philadelphia Phillies	95	10.0 IP, 1 Hit, 0 Runs, 0 ERs, 2 BBs, 7 Ks
6 (tie)	Steve Carlton	6/19/1968 StL 4-0	Chicago Cubs	94	9.0 IP, 1 Hit, 0 Runs, 0 ERs, 0 BBs, 9 Ks
6 (tie)	Bob Gibson	8/14/1971 StL 11-0	Pittsburgh Pirates	94	9.0 IP, 0 Hits, 0 Runs, 0 ERs, 3 BBs, 10 Ks
6 (tie)	Matt Morris	9/3/2004 StL 3-0	Los Angeles Dodgers	94	9.0 IP, 2 Hits, 0 Runs, 0 ERs, 0 BBs, 11 Ks
6 (tie)	Chris Carpenter	6/14/2005 StL 7-0	Toronto Blue Jays	94	9.0 IP, 1 Hit, 0 Runs, 0 ERs, 1 BB, 10 Ks
6 (tie)	Adam Wainwright	5/20/2014 StL 5-0	Arizona Diamondbacks	94	9.0 IP, 1 Hit, 0 Runs, 0 ERs, 0 BBs, 9 Ks
11 (tie)	Bob Gibson	10/2/1968 StL 4-0	Detroit Tigers	93	9.0 IP, 5 Hits, 0 Runs, 0 ERs, 1 BB, 17 Ks

Rank	Pitcher	Date Score	Opponent	GSc	IP, Hits, Runs, ERs, Walks, Strikeouts
11 (tie)	Bob Forsch	9/26/1983 StL 3-0	Montreal Expos	93	9.0 IP, 0 Hits, 0 Runs, 0 ERs, 0 BBs, 6 Ks
11 (tie)	Jose Jimenez	6/25/1999 StL 1-0	Arizona Diamondbacks	93	9.0 IP, 0 Hits, 0 Runs, 0 ERs, 2 BBs, 8 Ks
20 (tie)	Paul (Daffy) Dean	9/21/1934 (2) StL 3-0	Brooklyn Dodgers	92	9.0 IP, 0 Hits, 0 Runs, 0 ERs, 1 BB, 6 Ks
35 (tie)	Ray Washburn	9/18/1968 StL 2-0	San Francisco Giants	90	9.0 IP, 0 Hits, 0 Runs, 0 ERs, 5 BBs, 8 Ks
35 (tie)	Bud Smith	9/3/2001 StL 4-0	San Diego Padres	90	9.0 IP, 0 Hits, 0 Runs, 0 ERs, 4 BBs, 7 Ks
60 (tie)	Jesse Haines	7/17/1924 StL 5-0	Boston Braves	89	9.0 IP, 0 Hits, 0 Runs, 0 ERs, 3 BBs, 5 Ks
84 (tie)	Lon Warneke	8/30/1941 StL 2-0	Cincinnati Reds	88	9.0 IP, 0 Hits, 0 Runs, 0 ERs, 1 BB, 2 Ks
84 (tie)	Bob Forsch	4/16/1978 StL 5-0	Philadelphia Phillies	88	9.0 IP, 0 Hits, 0 Runs, 0 ERs, 2 BBs, 3 Ks
784 *(tie)*	*Ed* *Karger*	*8/11/1907 (2)* *StL 4-0 (7 inn)*	*Boston* *Doves*	*79*	*7.0 IP, 0 Hits, 0 Runs,* *0 ERs, 0 BBs, 2 Ks*
---	Stoney McGlynn	9/24/1906 (2) 1-1 Tie (7 inn)	Brooklyn Superbas	75	7.0 IP, 0 Hits, 1 Run, 0 ERs, 2 BBs, 2 Ks
---	Johnny Lush	8/6/1908 StL 2-0 (6 inn)	Brooklyn Superbas	70	6.0 IP, 0 Hits, 0 Runs, 0 ERs, 5 BBs, 3 Ks

METHODOLOGY: This table includes the highest Game Scores of 10 innings or less thrown by a Cardinals pitcher from 1900-2021. Games are ranked by Game Score (GSc) and consider all franchise regular season and postseason games. For comparison purposes, all nine post-1900 St. Louis no-hitters are included in this table. Games are ranked by pitcher Game Score (GSc) in descending order. Game Score measures a pitcher's performance in any given game started. Introduced by baseball writer/statistician Bill James in the 1980s, Game Score is presented as a figure between 0-100 — except for extreme outliers — and usually falls between 40-70.

LEGEND: Dates are shown as month/day/year (for example, June 12, 2018, is shown as 6/12/2018); IP = innings pitched. BB(s) = base(s) on balls. K(s) =

strikeout(s). ER(s) = earned run(s). inn = innings (associated with the length of games that were more or less than nine innings). (2) indicates the game is the second game of a doubleheader.

NOTE 1: The highest Cardinals postseason Game Score was a 93 achieved by Bob Gibson in Game 1 of the 1968 World Series against the Detroit Tigers. Facing off against American League Cy Young, MVP, and 31-game winner Denny McLain, Gibson shut out a powerful Detroit lineup that featured Hall of Famer Al Kaline, and All-Stars Bill Freehan, Willie Horton and Norm Cash. Gibson held the Tigers to just five hits and one walk, while he struck out a remarkable 17 Tigers. Gibson beat McLain and the Tigers again in Game 4, but was the losing pitcher in Game 7, as World Series MVP Mickey Lolich prevailed in a 4-1 game.

NOTE 2: With 17 strikeouts in Game 1 of the 1968 World Series, Gibson is tied with legendary Hall of Famer Dizzy Dean for the second-most strikeouts ever achieved by a Cardinal pitcher in a single game. Dean achieved his 17 strikeouts in the first game of a July 1933 doubleheader against the Cubs. The most ever strikeouts by a St. Louis pitcher was 19 by Hall of Famer Steve Carlton in a 1969 game against the Mets. While throwing a complete game, Carlton lost to New York 4-3, as he allowed four runs on nine hits, two of which were home runs.

NOTE 3: In his 2013 game, Shelby Miller allowed a first-inning leadoff single on a 3-1 pitch to Eric Young, Jr. After Young stole second, Miller then retired the next 27 batters in a row for a 3-0 win over the Rockies in St. Louis.

NOTE 4: Ernie Broglio's only hit allowed was a one-out single in the second inning by Ed Bouchee. Jaime Garcia's only hit allowed was a two-out single to Domingo Santana with two outs in the sixth inning. Glenn Beckert led off the fourth inning with a single for the only hit in Steve Carlton's 1968 game.

NOTE 5: In his 1970 game, Bob Gibson's only hit allowed was a two-out single in the top of the eighth inning by San Diego's Ivan Murrell. Prior to that, he had walked Nate Colbert to lead off the fifth inning for the first Padres baserunner of the game.

NOTE 6: There were two Montreal baserunners in Bob Forsch's 1983 no-hitter, preventing it from becoming a perfect game. Gary Carter was hit by a pitch with two outs in the second inning. Immediately following that, Chris Speier reached first base on an error by second baseman Ken Oberkfell.

NOTE 7: St. Louis pitcher Ed Karger threw a seven-inning perfect game against the Boston Doves in 1907. While no Boston runner ever reached base, this game isn't officially recognized as a no-hitter because it did not go a full nine innings. Both the Cardinals and Doves agreed to only play seven innings in the second game of a doubleheader so they would be able to catch a train to Boston where they would start a four-game series in the following days. The Boston team had been known as the Beaneaters until they changed their name to the Doves prior to the 1907 season. They were known as the Boston Rustlers for one season (1911) before settling on the Braves in 1912. Still known as the Braves today, the team moved to Milwaukee in 1953 and Atlanta in 1966.

NOTE 8: The second game of a doubleheader, Stoney McGlynn's seven inning no-hit effort ended in a 1-1 tie due to darkness. While officially there is no Game Score associated with this because earned runs weren't a statistic in 1906, newspaper write-ups indicate the Brooklyn run scored on an errant throw by the St. Louis first baseman. Designating that run as an unearned run gives McGlynn a Game Score of 75.

NOTE 9: Cardinals' pitcher Johnny Lush threw a no-hitter against Brooklyn for six innings in 1908 before the game was called due to rain. Because St. Louis was leading 2-0 at the time, the game counted as a win for the Cardinals, but is not included as an official no-hitter since it only went six innings. The last three games in this table – shortened no-hit efforts from Ed Karger, Stoney McGlynn, and Johnny Lush over a three-season span – were all thrown for some pretty bad Cardinal teams who racked up 98, 101, and 105 losses and finished 50 or more games behind the pennant-winning Chicago Cubs those years. Karger, McGlynn, and Lush were bright spots during an otherwise bleak stretch. The Cardinals would finally turn things around in the 1920s, and even win the 1926 World Series against Babe Ruth's New York Yankees behind legendary players Rogers Hornsby and Grover Cleveland Alexander. Alexander was a star in the 1926 series, winning Games 2 and 6 as a starter, and being called in to get the save with the bases loaded in the seventh inning of the deciding seventh game. Alexander's story was portrayed in the 1952 film *The Winning Team*, starring future president Ronald Reagan and Doris Day.

There have been quite a few Cardinal games where the Game Score is higher than any of the games listed in Table 22-2. These games are typically from an earlier era where relievers were infrequently used and starting pitchers often stayed in the game no matter how many innings it lasted. Those St. Louis pitchers who have achieved a Game Score of 100 or better are listed below. Note that Bob Gibson is included with his 13-inning game against the San Francisco Giants from 1969.

Table 22-3. Cardinals Highest Game Scores

Rank	Pitcher	Date Score	Opponent	GSc	IP, Hits, Runs, ERs, Walks, Strikeouts
1	Roy Parmelee	4/29/1936 StL 2-1 (17 inn)	New York Giants	116	17.0 IP, 6 Hits, 1 Run, 1 ER, 4 BBs, 9 Ks
2	Kid Nichols	8/11/1904 StL 4-3 (17 inn)	Brooklyn Superbas	110-112	17.0 IP, 9 Hits, 3 Runs, ? ERs, 1 BB, 14 Ks
3	Tex Carleton	7/2/1933 (1) NY 1-0 (18 inn)	New York Giants	106	16.0 IP, 8 Hits, 0 Runs, 0 ERs, 7 BBs, 7 Ks
4	Jack Taylor	6/24/1905 Chi 2-1 (18 inn)	Chicago Cubs	105-109	18.0 IP, 11 Hits, 2 Runs, ? ERs, 4 BBs, 7 Ks
5	Harry Brecheen	4/30/1950 StL 1-0 (13 inn)	Chicago Cubs	104	13.0 IP, 5 Hits, 0 Runs, 0 ERs, 1 BB, 8 Ks
6	Buster Brown	5/3/1906 (1) StL 4-2 (15 inn)	Chicago Cubs	103-107	15.0 IP, 3 Hits, 2 Runs, ? ERs, 8 BBs, 8 Ks
7	Jose DeLeon	8/30/1989 Cin 2-0 (13 inn)	Cincinnati Reds	103	11.0 IP, 1 Hits, 0 Runs, 0 ERs, 0 BBs, 8 Ks
8	Lee Meadows	9/22/1917 0-0 Tie (14 inn)	Boston Braves	102	14.0 IP, 10 Hits, 0 Runs, 0 ERs, 0 BBs, 10 Ks
9 (tie)	Bill Doak	6/11/1917 StL 5-4 (15 inn)	Philadelphia Phillies	100	15.0 IP, 6 Hits, 4 Runs, 2 ERs, 3 BBs, 10 Ks
9 (tie)	Bob Gibson	7/25/1969 StL 2-1 (13 inn)	San Francisco Giants	100	13.0 IP, 6 Hits, 1 Run, 1 ER, 2 BBs, 11 Ks

METHODOLOGY: This table includes the highest Game Scores thrown by a Cardinals pitcher from 1900-2021. Games are ranked by Game Score (GSc) and consider all franchise regular season and postseason games. Table 22-2 above limits the eligible games to those pitching performances that were 10 innings or less. Games are ranked by pitcher Game Score (GSc) in descending order. Game Score measures a pitcher's performance in any given game started. Introduced by baseball writer/statistician Bill James in the 1980s, Game Score is presented as a figure between 0-100 — except for extreme outliers — and usually falls between 40-70.

LEGEND: Dates are shown as month/day/year (for example, June 12, 2018, is shown as 6/12/2018). IP = innings pitched; BB(s) = base(s) on balls; K(s) = strikeout(s); ER(s) = earned run(s). inn = innings and is used to indicate how many innings a game went if it was other than a standard nine-inning game. (1) = first game of a doubleheader

NOTE 1: Roy Parmelee, facing Hall of Famer Carl Hubbell, matched him inning for inning through 17 innings. St. Louis won the game in the bottom of the 17th when Terry Moore knocked in Spud Davis on a fielder's choice. Parmelee hit for himself in the 17th with one out and runners on first and second, so he intended to pitch again in the 18th inning if the Cardinals did not score.

NOTE 2: Tex Carleton threw 16 innings of shutout ball in an 18-inning, 1-0 loss to Carl Hubbell and the New York Giants. Hubbell pitched all 18 innings for New York, earning a Game Score of 132 as he struck out 12, walked none, and allowed just six hits.

NOTE 3: Jose DeLeon threw 11 innings of shutout ball in a 2-0 loss to the Cincinnati Reds. By the end of the ninth inning, DeLeon had allowed no runs, only one hit (a one-out single by Luis Quinones in the fourth inning), zero walks, and struck out seven batters. If the game had ended at the conclusion of nine innings, DeLeon would have had a game score of 92 – tied for 18th place on the list of the best nine-inning game scores in Cardinal history.

NOTE 4: Lee Meadows' 14-inning effort in 1917 was a well-pitched game, as he managed to strike out 10, walk none, and not allow a run over the course of the game. Ending in a 0-0 tie wasn't all that unusual in that era, though. From 1901-1920, 46 games ended in 0-0 ties. Overall, 66 games had a final score of 0-0, with nearly half (32) being extra-inning games. The longest 0-0 game ever was a 19-inning contest on September 11, 1946, when the Reds and Dodgers battled to a scoreless tie in Brooklyn. Reportedly, the game was called on account of darkness; however, Ebbets Field had lights installed in 1938, so this is a little questionable.

NOTE 5: Bob Gibson's Game Score of 100 in the 13-inning contest in 1969 is the highest of his career. His second highest is a Game Score of 97 in an 11-inning, 2-1 win against the Mets on May 6, 1968. Beyond that, his two Game Scores of 96 and 94 in nine-inning, complete game victories listed in the earlier table are his next two highest.

NOTE 6: There are three games listed in the table above thrown during the period when earned runs didn't count as a statistic (before 1912). As such, the Game Score cannot be determined precisely for Kid Nichols, Jack Taylor, and Buster Brown. A range of possible Game Scores was calculated by analyzing each game and determining a high end score if the runs allowed were unearned and a low end score if they were earned.

Bob Gibson also shares a special distinction with 15 other pitchers who have thrown no-hitters since 1966. Along with them, he has both thrown a no-hitter and lost a game where his team was no-hit when he was the starting pitcher. In Gibson's case, he was the losing pitcher when San Francisco's Gaylord Perry threw a no-hitter against the Cardinals in 1968. The list of all 16 is shown below.

Table 22-4. Pitchers who won and lost no-hitters

No-hit Pitcher/Date	Date Pitcher's Team No-hit	Opposing No-hit Pitcher	Score
Sonny Siebert 6/10/1966	8/25/1967 (2)	Dean Chance	Minnesota 2, Cleveland 1
Clyde Wright 7/3/1970	6/19/1974	Steve Busby	KC Royals 2, Milwaukee 0
Vida Blue 9/21/1970	7/30/1973 6/27/1980	Jim Bibby Jerry Reuss	Texas 6, Oakland 0 LA Dodgers 8, SF Giants 0
Bob Gibson 8/14/1971	9/17/1968	Gaylord Perry	SF Giants 1, St. Louis 0
Phil Niekro 8/5/1973	6/18/1967 8/19/1969	Don Wilson Ken Holtzman	Houston 2, Atlanta 0 Chicago Cubs 3, Atlanta 0
Randy Johnson 1990 & 2004	6/25/1999	Jose Jimenez	St. Louis 1, Arizona 0
A.J. Burnett 5/12/2001	9/28/2012 5/25/2014	Homer Bailey Josh Beckett	Cincinnati 1, Pittsburgh 0 LA Dodgers 6, Philadelphia 0
Kevin Millwood 4/27/2003	4/18/2007	Mark Buehrle	Chicago W. Sox 6, Texas 0
Edwin Jackson 6/25/2010	5/3/2011	Francisco Liriano	Minnesota 1, Chi W. Sox 0
Francisco Liriano 5/3/2011	6/20/2015	Max Scherzer	Washington 6, Pittsburgh 0
Tim Lincecum 2013 & 2014	7/2/2013	Homer Bailey	Cincinnati 3, SF Giants 0
H. Alvarez III 9/29/2013	9/28/2014	J. Zimmermann	Washington 1, Miami 0

No-hit Pitcher/Date	Date Pitcher's Team No-hit	Opposing No-hit Pitcher	Score
Max Scherzer 2015 twice	7/26/2010	Matt Garza	Tampa Bay 5, Detroit 0
Jake Arrieta 2015 & 2016	7/25/2015	Cole Hamels	Philadelphia 5, Chi Cubs 0
Edinson Volquez 6/3/2017	10/6/2010 7/13/2013	Roy Halladay Tim Lincecum	Philadelphia 4, Cincinnati 0 SF Giants 9, San Diego 0
Joe Musgrove 4/9/2021	8/14/2021	Tyler Gilbert	Arizona 7, San Diego 0

METHODOLOGY: This table displays all pitchers from 1966-2021 who have thrown a no-hitter and have also been the starting pitcher on the losing end of a no-hitter thrown against their team. Pitchers are listed in chronological order based on the date they threw their no-hitter.

LEGEND: Dates are shown as month/day/year (for example, June 12, 2018, is shown as 6/12/2018). (2) = second game of a doubleheader. "No-hit Pitcher" and "Date of No-hitter" in the first column show the pitcher who threw a no-hitter and the date he threw his no-hitter. Randy Johnson, Max Scherzer, and Jake Arrieta have each thrown two no-hitters, so their no-hitters are indicated by the year in which they were thrown. "Date Pitcher's Team was No-hit" in the second column indicates the date the no-hit pitcher in the first column had a no-hitter thrown against their team when they were the opposing starting pitcher. "Opposing No-hit Pitcher" (third column) and "Score" (fourth column) show the pitcher who threw the no-hitter on that date and the score of the game. Vida Blue, Phil Niekro, A.J. Burnett, and Edinson Volquez have each had two no-hitters thrown against their teams when they were the opposing starter.

NOTE: Roy Halladay's 2010 no-hitter against Edinson Volquez and the Cincinnati Reds was in the first game of the 2010 NLDS. Halladay's Phillies would beat the Reds in the NLDS but lose to the Giants in the NLCS. The Giants would win the 2010 World Series against the Rangers for their first championship since they moved to San Francisco in 1958.

Bob Gibson was a dominating pitcher in the 1960s, crafting what is arguably the best pitcher's season ever in 1968, when he went 22-9 with a 1.12 ERA. During that season, he threw 13 shutouts, the most since Grover Cleveland Alexander threw

16 in 1916. Alexander started 45 games that year. Gibson started 34 games in 1968. With his otherworldly performance, Gibson features prominently in the list of the top pitchers of the 1960s (Table 22-5).

Table 22-5. Best Starting Pitchers of the 1960s

Rank	Pitcher (Team(s))	Seasons Pitched	Innings Pitched	WAR (per 200 IP)	Wins (per Season)
1	Juan Marichal (Giants)	1960-1969	2,549.2	55.3 (4.34)	191 (19.1)
2	Bob Gibson (Cardinals)	1960-1969	2,447.0	54.2 (4.43)	164 (16.4)
3	Sandy Koufax (Dodgers)	1960-1966	1,807.2	47.9 (5.30)	137 (19.6)
4	Jim Bunning (Tigers, Phillies, Pirates, Dodgers)	1960-1969	2,590.1	46.3 (3.58)	150 (15.0)
5	Don Drysdale (Dodgers)	1960-1969	2,629.2	44.7 (3.40)	158 (15.8)
6	Larry Jackson (Cardinals, Cubs, Phillies)	1960-1968	2,335.2	35.9 (3.07)	141 (15.7)
7	Jim Maloney (Reds)	1960-1969	1,802.0	35.3 (3.92)	134 (13.4)
8	Dean Chance (Angels, Twins)	1961-1969	1,900.2	33.6 (3.54)	115 (12.8)
9	Sam McDowell (Indians)	1961-1969	1,590.0	30.2 (3.80)	89 (9.9)
10	Chris Short (Phillies)	1960-1969	1,843.2	28.8 (3.13)	115 (11.5)
11	Whitey Ford (Yankees)	1960-1967	1,608.2	27.3 (3.39)	115 (14.4)
12	Gaylord Perry (Giants)	1962-1969	1,685.2	27.1 (3.22)	95 (11.9)

METHODOLOGY: Pitchers are ranked in order of Wins Above Replacement (WAR) achieved from 1960-1969. WAR measures a player's value in all facets of the game by deciphering how many more wins he's worth than a replacement-level player at his same position. Another measure of merit I wanted to include was the number of wins each pitcher accumulated as well. Because a number of pitchers were only present for a portion of the decade, I included two rate measures (WAR per 200 innings pitched and wins per season).

LEGEND: Team(s) = the team(s) a player played for during the 1960s. If a pitcher played for more than one team, teams are listed in chronological order. IP = innings pitched. One-third of an inning is designated as ".1" and two-thirds of an inning is designated as ".2."

NOTE: Bob Gibson was a two-time winner of the Cy Young Award. He first won the award, along with the MVP Award, in 1968. His second Cy Young Award came in 1970. There are other Cy Young Award winners in this table too. Most notably, Sandy Koufax won the award three times (1963, 1965, and 1966). Each time he won, Koufax was the unanimous choice among Cy Young voters. What makes his three awards especially impressive is that at the time there was only one Cy Young Award presented for all of baseball, with two awards given (one for the National League and one for the American League) starting in 1967. Other Cy Young winners in this table include Dean Chance (1964) and Don Drysdale (1962). Juan Marichal, the WAR leader during the 1960s, had the misfortune of playing during an era when other pitchers had extraordinary individual seasons when he was consistently great. Of note, the top five pitchers in Table 22-5, including Bob Gibson, are all Hall of Famers.

Bob Gibson was born in Omaha, Nebraska, where he starred in basketball, track, and baseball in high school. He also played basketball and baseball at Creighton University. He was signed as a free agent before the 1957 season by St. Louis. He was in the St. Louis minor league system from 1957-1959, compiling a record of 23-22. After the 1957 baseball season, he played with the incredibly talented Harlem Globetrotters basketball team in the winter of 1957-1958. While he enjoyed that experience, it convinced him he wanted to focus on baseball for his athletic career. Gibson debuted with St. Louis in 1959. He was elected to the Hall of Fame in 1981 with 84% on his first ballot.

Gibson was a coach for the New York Mets in 1981 and for Atlanta from 1982-1984. He hosted a Cardinals' pregame and postgame show for KMOX from 1985-1989 and was on the ESPN baseball broadcast team in 1990. In 1995, Gibson again served as pitching coach, this time returning to the Cardinals.

In 1992, Ted Simmons was hired as general manager of the Pittsburgh Pirates. Later, he became Director of Player Development for both the Cardinals and San Diego Padres, and a scout at the Major League level for the Cleveland Indians. He was named the bench coach for the Milwaukee Brewers starting the 2008 season.

In November 2008 Simmons was named bench coach for the Padres under manager Bud Black. In 2010 he became a senior advisor to the Seattle Mariners. In 2015, Simmons rejoined the Braves – where he ended his major league playing career – as a scout.

Chapter 23

Joe Musgrove:
The Padres Have a No-Hitter

April 9, 2021
San Diego product Joe Musgrove throws the first-ever no-hitter for San Diego

"Just a San Diego kid that made it to the big leagues. So it feels even better to be able to do it in a Padres' uniform — and, selfishly, be able to do it for my city and have everyone know that the kid from Grossmont High threw the first no-hitter."

Joe Musgrove reflecting on what his no-hitter means to him (Tyler Kepner, "A 'San Diego Kid' Gives the Padres Their First No-Hitter," *The New York Times*, April 9, 2021).

"Yes, the streak of 8,205 games played over 52 seasons plus a week is no more. The Padres are no longer the only team to have never thrown a no-hitter."

Sportswriter Kevin Acee tallying up the record-breaking streak that Joe Musgrove happily ended (Kevin Acee, "NO-HITTER! Padres' Joe Musgrove throws first in team history," *San Diego Union-Tribune*, April 9, 2021).

"The curveball and the cutter backdoor weren't really working for me early on. We were getting decent results because we were using them in the right situations. I found something in the seventh inning with the

curveball. I felt like my last two, three innings with the curveball were really, really sharp and that helped me get through those last couple innings."

Joe Musgrove describing his pitching strategy (Kevin Acee, "NO-HITTER! Padres' Joe Musgrove throws first in team history," *San Diego Union-Tribune*, April 9, 2021).

"He was in control. After the seventh inning, that's when we kind of put all the chips in. For Joe, for the team, for the organization, for the city that hadn't had a no-hitter before, at that point you throw everything out the window and you roll with it and see where it lays out."

Padres' manager Jayce Tingler describing his decision to let Musgrove "roll with it." (Tyler Kepner, "A 'San Diego Kid' Gives the Padres Their First No-Hitter," *The New York Times*, April 9, 2021).

"I've always wanted to throw a no-hitter. I never even threw one in high school, Little League, all through the minor leagues. I've come close but never anything past the sixth or seventh. It feels really good to do that but more to prove to yourself you're capable of doing it. ... Pretty crazy it comes on a big-league stage and I'm in a Padres' uniform."

Joe Musgrove talking about his lifelong desire to throw a no-hitter (Kevin Acee, "NO-HITTER! Padres' Joe Musgrove throws first in team history," *San Diego Union-Tribune*, April 9, 2021).

In April 2021, the Padres were just beginning their 53rd season. While they had never won a World Series championship, they had stretches of success, including two trips to the World Series: once in 1984 vs. the Tigers and again in 1998 against the Yankees. They also had extraordinary individual achievers. Ken Caminiti was the National League MVP in 1996, and San Diego racked up four Cy Young Award winners: closer Mark Davis in 1989, and starters Randy Jones (1976), Gaylord Perry (1978), and Jake Peavy (2007).

Despite the solid achievements by the team and its individual players, there was one accomplishment that had eluded them all this time: alone among all major league teams, the Padres had never thrown a no-hitter. Every other team, including the other 13 teams that were established during the Expansion Era from 1961 on, had at least one. Making things worse was the fact that the Padres had been no-hit nine times, more than any other expansion team, and tied with the long-established St. Louis Cardinals and the Washington/Minnesota franchise. At 52+ seasons without a no-hitter when Joe Musgrove took the mound that day, San Diego set a new record every day for the longest period of time it took for an expansion franchise to throw its first no-hitter.

Table 23-1. Time from Expansion Team Start to First No-Hitter

Rank	Team	Est. (# NHs)	No-hit Pitcher	No-hit Date Score	Opponent	Time
1	Montreal Expos	1969 (7)	Bill Stoneman	4/17/1969 Mon 7-0	Philadelphia Phillies	9 days
2	Los Angeles Angels	1961 (11)	Bo Belinsky	5/5/1962 LA 2-0	Baltimore Orioles	1 year 24 days
3	Houston Colt .45s	1962 (13)	Don Nottebart	5/17/1963 Hou 4-1	Philadelphia Phillies	1 year 37 days
4	Florida Marlins	1993 (6)	Al Leiter	5/11/1996 Fla 11-0	Colorado Rockies	3+ years
5	Kansas City Royals	1969 (4)	Steve Busby	4/27/1973 KC 3-0	Detroit Tigers	4+ years
6	Arizona D-backs	1998 (3)	Randy Johnson	5/18/2004 Ari 2-0	Atlanta Braves	6+ years
7	Texas Rangers	1961 (5)	Jim Bibby	7/30/1973 Tex 6-0	Oakland Athletics	12 years 111 days
8	Tampa Bay Rays	1998 (1)	Matt Garza	7/26/2010 TB 5-0	Detroit Tigers	12 years 117 days
9	Seattle Mariners	1977 (6)	Randy Johnson	6/2/1990 Sea 2-0	Detroit Tigers	13 years 57 days
10	Toronto Blue Jays	1977 (1)	Dave Stieb	9/2/1990 Tor 3-0	Cleveland Indians	13 years 148 days
11	Colorado Rockies	1993 (1)	Ubaldo Jimenez	4/17/2010 Col 4-0	Atlanta Braves	17+ years
12	Milwaukee Brewers	1969 (2)	Juan Nieves	4/15/1987 Mil 7-0	Baltimore Orioles	18+ years

Rank	Team	Est. (# NHs)	No-hit Pitcher	No-hit Date Score	Opponent	Time
13	New York Mets	1962 (1)	Johann Santana	6/1/2012 NY 8-0	St. Louis Cardinals	50+ years
14	San Diego Padres	1969 (1)	Joe Musgrove	4/9/2021 SD 3-0	Texas Rangers	52+ years

METHODOLOGY: This table includes all expansion teams established from 1961 on. The first no-hitter thrown by each expansion franchise is ranked in ascending order based upon the time span between the franchise's first game and the no-hitter.

LEGEND: "Est" is the year the franchise was established and first played as a modern expansion team. "(#NHs)" is the number of no-hitters the franchise has thrown since it became a major league team up through the 2021 season – this total includes both single- and multiple-pitcher no-hitters. "Time" is the span of time between the franchise's first game and its first no-hitter. All games listed above were single-pitcher, nine-inning games. None of the games were played as part of a doubleheader.

NOTE: Of interest, many expansion franchises have moved and/or changed names since they became Major League teams:

1) The Washington Senators joined the American League in 1961 and played in the AL East division from 1969-1971. In 1972, the team moved to the Dallas-Fort Worth area and became the Texas Rangers. As part of this franchise move the Rangers joined the AL West and the Milwaukee Brewers switched from the western division to the AL East. The logic behind this move was that it geographically made more sense for a Texas-based team to be in the western division than a Milwaukee-based team.

2) The Angels were known as the Los Angeles Angels from 1961-1964. In 1965, they changed their name to the California Angels. They kept the "California" designation through the 1996 season. In 1997, they changed their name to the Anaheim Angels, which they kept through the end of the 2004 season. Starting in 2005, the team was officially known as the Los Angeles Angels of Anaheim. In 2015, the team shortened its name to the Los Angeles Angels. Since the end of the 1965 season and the construction of Angels Stadium, the team has played its games in Anaheim. Prior to

that, they shared Dodger Stadium with the Los Angeles Dodgers. When the American League split into divisions in 1969, the Angels joined the AL West and have remained there since then.

3) The Houston franchise was originally known as the Houston Colt .45s (often just shortened to "Colts") when they joined the National League in 1962. In September 1965, the team changed its name to the Houston Astros when it moved into the Astrodome. Originally part of the NL West Division when it was created in 1969, the Astros moved to the NL Central Division when it was established in 1994. In 2013, the Astros became one of just two teams to ever switch leagues (the other was the Milwaukee Brewers in 1998) when they moved from the NL Central to the AL West. That move evened both leagues at 15 teams apiece and incorporated interleague play throughout the season.

4) The Montreal Expos joined the National League in 1969. The franchise moved to the District of Columbia and became the Washington Nationals in 2005. They remained in the National League East Division throughout.

5) As described in the earlier chapter on Juan Nieves, the Milwaukee Brewers franchise has been on the move regularly throughout the years. They started as the Seattle Pilots as part of the newly established AL West in 1969. While remaining in the AL West, the franchise moved to Milwaukee and became the Brewers in 1970. In 1972, the Brewers switched to the AL East and stayed there for the next 22 years. They then moved prior to the 1994 season to the brand-new AL Central when both leagues switched from a two-division format to a three-division structure. In 1998, the Brewers became the first team to ever switch leagues as they joined the National League Central Division

6) The Tampa Bay Devil Rays joined the AL East in 1998. The team changed its name to the Tampa Bay Rays in 2008.

This table demonstrates both ends of the spectrum. The ridiculously short time span of nine days (!) it took Bill Stoneman of the Expos to throw the team's first no-hitter stands out as remarkable. The Los Angeles Angels and Houston Colt .45s second-season no-hitters are not far behind. Both Houston (13) and LA/California/

Anaheim (11) also eclipsed all other expansion teams with the number of no-hitters their teams have thrown over the years.

At the other end of the spectrum are the Padres and the New York Mets. Because they started in 1962, the Mets held the record for the longest time to an expansion team's first no-hitter for decades (until 2012 when Johann Santana threw their first and only one). The Padres eclipsed the Mets' record in 2019.

Along with the Padres and the Mets, there are four other teams that have a single no-hitter to their credit.

Table 23-2. Franchises With Only One Single-pitcher No-hitter

Team	Pitcher	Opponent	Date Score	Franchise Established	No-hitter Accomplished
New York Mets	Johan Santana	St. Louis Cardinals	6/1/2012 NY 8-0	1962	51st Season
Milwaukee Brewers	Juan Nieves	Baltimore Orioles	4/15/1987 Mil 7-0	1969	19th Season
San Diego Padres	Joe Musgrove	Texas Rangers	4/9/2021 SD 3-0	1969	53rd Season
Toronto Blue Jays	Dave Stieb	Cleveland Indians	9/2/1990 Tor 3-0	1977	14th Season
Colorado Rockies	Ubaldo Jimenez	Atlanta Braves	4/17/2010 Col 4-0	1993	18th Season
Tampa Bay Rays	Matt Garza	Detroit Tigers	7/26/2010 TB 5-0	1998	13th Season

METHODOLOGY: Teams in this table have thrown just one no-hitter that has involved a single pitcher. All teams listed are expansion franchises – all the established franchises dating back to 1900 (NL) and 1901 (AL) have thrown at least six no-hitters. No-hitters thrown after the end of the 2021 season aren't included in this analysis. Teams are listed in order of the year they joined the National or American Leagues as a franchise.

LEGEND: Dates are shown as month/day/year (for example, June 12, 2018, is shown as 6/12/2018). "No-hitter Accomplished" identifies which season of a team's existence it threw its first no-hitter. All games listed above were single-pitcher, nine-inning games. None of the games were played as part of a doubleheader.

NOTE: The Milwaukee Brewers got their second franchise no-hitter on September 11, 2021, when Corbin Burnes (8.0 IP) and Josh Hader (1.0 IP) combined to no-hit the Cleveland Indians.

Along with owning the unique accomplishment of this franchise's only no-hitter, Joe Musgrove's effort that day against the Texas Rangers can be considered an exceptional performance. With 10 strikeouts and no walks, it is tied for second for the highest Game Score any Padres pitcher has ever recorded and is tied for first for the highest Padre Game Score in a nine-inning game. The highest all-time San Diego score was achieved as part of a 15-inning effort. Musgrove would have thrown a perfect game, except for hitting Joey Gallo of the Texas Rangers in the leg with two outs in the fourth inning.

Table 23-3. Padres Highest Game Scores

Rank	Pitcher	Date Score	Opponent	GSc	IP, Hits, Runs, ERs, Walks, Strikeouts
1	Clay Kirby	9/24/1971 (1) Hou 2-1 (21 inn)	Houston Astros	109	15.0 IP, 8 Hits, 1 Run, 1 ER, 3 BBs, 15 Ks
2 (tie)	Andy Benes	7/3/1994 SD 7-0	New York Mets	97	9.0 IP, 1 Hit, 0 Runs, 0 ERs, 1 BB, 13 Ks
2 (tie)	Joe Musgrove	4/9/2021 SD 3-0	Texas Rangers	97	9.0 IP, 0 Hits, 0 Runs, 0 ERs, 0 BBs, 10 Ks
4	Clay Kirby	6/7/1972 (2) Pit 1-0 (18 inn)	Pittsburgh Pirates	96	13.0 IP, 8 Hits, 0 Runs, 0 ERs, 3 BBs, 8 Ks
5	Dave Freisleben	8/4/1974 (2) SD 1-0 (14 inn)	Cincinnati Reds	95	13.0 IP, 8 Hits, 0 Runs, 0 ERs, 3 BBs, 7 Ks
6 (tie)	Steve Arlin	7/6/1972 SD 1-0 (14 inn)	New York Mets	94	10.0 IP, 1 Hit, 0 Runs, 0 ERs, 4 BBs, 8 Ks
6 (tie)	Kevin Brown	8/16/1998 (1) SD 4-0	Milwaukee Brewers	94	9.0 IP, 1 Hit, 0 Runs, 0 ERs, 2 BBs, 11 Ks
6 (tie)	Andrew Cashner	4/11/2014 SD 6-0	Detroit Tigers	94	9.0 IP, 1 Hit, 0 Runs, 0 ERs, 2 BBs, 11 Ks
9	Clay Kirby	6/23/1973 (1) SD 2-0	Atlanta Braves	93	9.0 IP, 3 Hits, 0 Runs, 0 ERs, 1 BB, 13 Ks
10 (tie)	Dave Roberts	8/11/1971 SD 1-0 (12 inn)	New York Mets	92	12.0 IP, 7 Hits, 0 Runs, 0 ERs, 3 BBs, 7 Ks

Rank	Pitcher	Date Score	Opponent	GSc	IP, Hits, Runs, ERs, Walks, Strikeouts
10 (tie)	Andy Benes	8/29/1991 SD 1-0	St. Louis Cardinals	92	9.0 IP, 2 Hits, 0 Runs, 0 ERs, 1 BB, 10 Ks
10 (tie)	Kevin Brown	9/29/1998 SD 2-1	Houston Astros	92	8.0 IP, 2 Hits, 0 Runs, 0 ERs, 2 BBs, 16 Ks
10 (tie)	Andrew Cashner	9/16/2013 SD 2-0	Pittsburgh Pirates	92	9.0 IP, 1 Hit, 0 Runs, 0 ERs, 0 BBs, 7 Ks

METHODOLOGY: This table includes the highest Game Scores thrown by a Padres pitcher from 1969-2021. Games are ranked by Game Score (GSc) and consider all franchise regular season and postseason games. Game Score measures a pitcher's performance in any given game started. Introduced by baseball writer/statistician Bill James in the 1980s, Game Score is presented as a figure between 0-100 — except for extreme outliers — and usually falls between 40-70.

LEGEND: Dates are shown as month/day/year (for example, June 12, 2018, is shown as 6/12/2018); IP = innings pitched. BB(s) = base(s) on balls. K(s) = strikeout(s). ER(s) = earned run(s). inn = innings (associated with the length of games that were more or less than nine innings). BB(s) = base(s) on balls; K(s) = strikeout(s). (1) or (2) indicates the game is the first or second game of a doubleheader. The Padres became an original member of the National League West Division in 1969 as an expansion team.

NOTE 1: The highest postseason Game Score thrown by a Padres pitcher was a 92 by Kevin Brown in Game 1 of the 1998 NLDS against Randy Johnson and the 102-win Astros. Brown pitched eight innings of two-hit shutout ball against a Houston team that led the league in runs scored and featured Hall of Famers Craig Biggio and Jeff Bagwell, among other extraordinary hitters. Brown was pulled for a pinch-hitter in the top of the ninth after throwing 119 pitches in a 2-0 game. Closer Trevor Hoffman closed out the game in a tense bottom of the ninth when Houston scored on a double, single and error. The final out was made when Hoffman got Carl Everett to fly out to center field with the tying run on first.

NOTE 2: After Brown's winning effort in the 1998 NLDS opener against Houston, the Padres would win the series three games to one. San Diego would go on to defeat the heavily favored Braves in the NLCS four games to two, before getting swept by the Yankees in the World Series. Brown's 16 strikeouts in the opening playoff game against the Astros is tied for the most strikeouts in a single game by a Padres pitcher. Jake Peavy also achieved 16 strikeouts in a seven-inning effort against the Diamondbacks on April 25, 2007. By the end of the seventh inning, Peavy had struck out 16 and had held Arizona scoreless. He had also thrown 117 pitches and given up two hits and three walks, so his no-hitter was long gone. San Diego was leading 2-0 at the time, but Padre relievers allowed three runs in the eighth and ninth innings and the Diamondbacks won the game 3-2. Peavy also struck out 16 in a seven-inning losing effort against the Braves in 2006. In that game, the San Diego offense came up on the short end of a 3-1 game.

NOTE 3: Clay Kirby's 15-inning effort is by far the highest game score achieved by a Padre pitcher. The only run scored against him was a fourth inning, two-out, solo home run by Houston left fielder Rich Chiles. Kirby's 15.0 innings pitched is the most ever by a San Diego pitcher and his 15 strikeouts is tied for the second-most strikeouts in a single game in San Diego's history.

NOTE 4: Andy Benes allowed his first baserunner on a two-out walk in the third inning of his 1994 one-hitter against the Mets. The one hit for the Mets came on a leadoff double by Rico Brogna in the eighth.

NOTE 5: Steve Arlin's 10-inning effort against the Mets in 1972 deserves mention, too. His first baserunner allowed was on a one-out walk in the second inning. The only hit he gave up was a single to Dave Marshall leading off the fourth inning. Over the course of 10 innings, Arlin managed to hold a dangerous Mets lineup scoreless, as the Padres finally scored in the top of the 14th inning at Shea Stadium to win the game 1-0.

NOTE 6: After walking a batter with two outs in the first inning, Kevin Brown allowed a walk and a single with two outs in the seventh inning in his 1998 game against the Brewers. That was it. Almost 16 years later, Andrew Cashner would record an identical box score line (including a game score of 94) in his one-hitter against the Tigers. Cashner would also allow his first baserunner with two outs in the first. His lone hit given up was a one-out single in the sixth inning.

NOTE 7: In his near-perfect game in 2013, Andrew Cashner only allowed one baserunner when Pittsburgh's Jose Tabata led off the seventh inning with a single through the infield to right field. Two batters later, Tabata was erased on a double play grounder. There were no other baserunners for the Pirates as Cashner faced the minimum 27 batters in his 2-0 win.

Of the games listed above, two Padre pitchers appear three times each (Clay Kirby and Andy Benes) and two appear twice (Kevin Brown and Andrew Cashner). Everyone else represents a single entry. With some extraordinary pitchers who have excelled in San Diego (such as Randy Jones, Gaylord Perry, Kevin Brown, Jake Peavy, and many more), only Brown and Peavy appear on this list. This demonstrates the exceptional talent it takes to achieve a Game Score that ranks in the "Top 10" in the franchise's history.

The Padres jumped ahead early in Musgrave's no-hit game. Wil Myers knocked in the first run when he doubled in Eric Hosmer from first base with no outs in the second inning. After one out was registered, Myers scored from second on a Tommy Pham flyout followed by an error by Texas centerfielder Leody Taveras. It was then 2-0 in favor of San Diego. In the next (third) inning, Trent Grisham scored from third base when Manny Machado tripled with two outs. The Padres led 3-0 after three innings, which would become the final score.

Finishing the year at 60-102, the 2021 season was clearly a disappointment for the Texas Rangers. A big part of their challenge was the team's substandard hitting, as they finished last in the American League in runs scored, on-base percentage, and slugging percentage. Led by All-Star slugger Joey Gallo and designated hitter Nathaniel Lowe, there were bright spots in the Texas lineup that day. Musgrove handled them all expertly. There were only two times Musgrove's no-hitter was threatened during the game. In the eighth inning, Texas catcher Jose Trevino ripped a hard hit, two-out line drive to Myers in right, and pinch-hitter David Dahl scorched a line drive to Jake Cronenworth at second to lead off the ninth. Neither play was exceptionally difficult to make, as the players were positioned well. Only three Ranger batters ever got to a three-ball count, and two of those times the at-bat ended in a swinging strikeout.

Since the advent of regular season interleague play in June 1997, the general rule associated with the usage of the designated hitter was that the DH would be used in American League ballparks, and pitchers would hit for themselves in National League ballparks. During the abbreviated 2020 coronavirus season, the DH was used universally. Starting in 2022, the National League adopted the DH rule; consequently, there's now no differentiation between NL and AL teams as to whether a DH or a pitcher is hitting in the lineup that day.

As a result of different lineup rules being used in National League and American League ballparks from 1997-2019 and 2021, the perception was that the visiting team was at something of a general disadvantage. This was because the visitors had to find someone who would fill in as DH in an AL ballpark, and AL pitchers had to hit for themselves in a NL ballpark (something AL pitchers rarely practiced).

There have been 13 no-hitters in interleague games, including the one Joe Musgrove hurled in 2021. The entire list is in the table below, along with the designation as to whether the team throwing the no-hitter was in an AL or NL ballpark.

Looking at the table below, we find there have been seven no-hitters thrown by American Leaguers (six by National Leaguers) – about as even as possible with an odd number of games. However, all but one of the no-hitters have been thrown in American League ballparks. Only Henderson Alvarez's no-hitter for the Miami Marlins against a depleted, last-game-of-the-season, playoff-bound Detroit team was thrown in a National League ballpark. This would appear to be counterintuitive, since the DH rule would have been used in AL parks, and pitchers would not have had to bat for themselves. Of course, Don Larsen's perfect game was thrown when there was no DH rule.

Table 23-4. Interleague No-hitters

Pitcher (Innings Pitched)	Team	Opponent	Date Score	IP, Walks, Strikeouts (Game Score)
Lucas Giolito (9.0)	Chi W. Sox	Pit Pirates	8/25/2020 Chi 4-0	9.0 IP, 1 BB, 13 Ks (GSc = 99)
David Cone (9.0)	NY Yankees	Mon Expos	7/18/1999 NY 6-0	9.0 IP, 0 BBs, 10 Ks (GSc = 97)
Joe Musgrove (9.0)	SD Padres	Tex Rangers	4/9/2021 SD 3-0	9.0 IP, 0 BBs, 10 Ks (GSc = 97)
Justin Verlander (9.0)	Det Tigers	Mil Brewers	6/12/2007 Det 4-0	9.0 IP, 4 BBs, 12 Ks (GSc = 95)
Corbin Burnes (8.0) Josh Hader (1.0)	Mil Brewers	Cle Indians	9/11/2021 Mil 3-0	Combined totals 9.0 IP, 1 BB, 16 Ks (Burnes GSc = 95, Comb. GSc = 102)
Don Larsen (9.0)	NY Yankees	Bro Dodgers	10/7/1956 NY 2-0	9.0 IP, 0 BBs, 7 Ks (GSc = 94)
Mike Fiers (9.0)	Hou Astros	LA Dodgers	8/21/2015 Hou 3-0	9.0 IP, 3 BBs, 10 Ks (GSc = 94)

Pitcher (Innings Pitched)	Team	Opponent	Date Score	IP, Walks, Strikeouts (Game Score)
Wade Miley (9.0)	Cin Reds	Cle Indians	5/7/2021 Cin 3-0	9.0 IP, 1 BB, 8 Ks (GSc = 94)
Mike Fiers (9.0)	Oak A's	Cin Reds	5/7/2019 Oak 2-0	9.0 IP, 2 BBs, 6 Ks (GSc = 91)
Henderson Alvarez III (9.0)	Mia Marlins	Det Tigers	9/29/2013 Mia 1-0	9.0 IP, 1 BBs, 4 Ks (GSc = 90)
Edwin Jackson (9.0)	Ari D-backs	TB Rays	6/25/2010 Ari 1-0	9.0 IP, 8 BBs, 6 Ks (GSc = 85)
Kevin Millwood (6.0) Charlie Furbush (0.2) Stephen Pryor (0.1) Lucas Luetge (0.1) Brandon League (0.2) T. Wilhelmsen (1.0)	Sea M's	LA Dodgers	6/8/2012 Sea 1-0	Combined totals 9.0 IP, 3 BBs, 9 Ks (Millwood GSc = 77, Combined GSc = 93)
Roy Oswalt (1.0) Pete Munro (2.2) Kirk Saarloos (1.1) Brad Lidge (2.0) Octavio Dotel (1.0) Billy Wagner (1.0)	Hou Astros	NY Yankees	6/11/2003 Hou 8-0	Combined totals 9.0 IP, 3 BBs, 13 Ks (Oswalt GSc = 55, Combined GSc = 97)

METHODOLOGY: This table includes all interleague no-hitters accomplished between 1900-2021. Before 1997, the only interleague games played were during the World Series. Games are listed in descending order based upon the GameScore (GSc) achieved by the starting pitcher. GSc measures a pitcher's performance in any given game started. Introduced by baseball writer/statistician Bill James in the 1980s, GSc is presented as a figure between 0-100 -- except for extreme outliers -- and usually falls between 40-70. GSc is conventionally calculated as the Game Score of the starting pitcher. For games involving multiple pitchers, the Game Score was also calculated for the combined efforts of the pitchers involved – this GSc is shown as "Combined" GSc as if the combined statistics were from a single starting pitcher throwing the entire game.

LEGEND: Dates are shown as month/day/year (for example, June 12, 2018, is shown as 6/12/2018); IP = innings pitched. BB(s) = base(s) on balls. K(s) = strikeout(s). ER(s) = earned run(s). inn = innings (associated with the length of games that were more or less than nine innings). BB(s) = base(s) on balls; K(s) = strikeout(s). *Italicized games are perfect games (Don Larsen and David Cone).*

NOTE 1: All games were nine-inning shutouts with no hits allowed. Consequently, hits, runs, and earned runs were not included in the table because they were zero in all cases.

NOTE 2: While not an official part of interleague play because it didn't happen after regular season interleague games were initiated in 1997, Don Larsen's perfect game is in a special category by itself. Occurring during Game 5 of the 1956 World Series, Don Larsen's gem was the only no-hitter/perfect game between an American League and National League team until David Cone's perfect game in 1999. Cone's perfect game was the first regular season interleague no-hitter and the only interleague regular season perfect game ever thrown.

NOTE 3: The only baserunner allowed in Lucas Giolito's no-hitter was a four-pitch walk to Erik Gonzalez to lead off the fourth inning. He retired the next 18 batters in a row.

NOTE 4: The only baserunner Joe Musgrove allowed was on a two-out pitch to Joey Gallo in the fourth inning that hit him. There were no Ranger hits or walks in this game.

NOTE 5: Corbin Burnes had been dominating for eight innings for the Brewers, racking up 14 strikeouts while only allowing one baserunner on a leadoff walk in the seventh inning. By the end of the eighth inning, he had already thrown 115 pitches and Milwaukee manager Craig Counsell decided to call upon All-Star closer Josh Hader to finish the game. Hader got three straight outs, completing the no-hitter and adding two more strikeouts to the total. As it stood, Burnes had a game score of 95 over eight innings. If Hader's inning of relief is added to Burnes' accomplishments, the combined nine-inning totals would equate to a Game Score of 102.

NOTE 6: Both Cleveland runners during Wade Miley's no-hitter against the Indians reached base in the sixth inning on a two-error play by the Cincinnati second baseman, followed by a walk issued to Cesar Hernandez with two outs.

NOTE 7: Mike Fiers appears twice on this list. Both of his no-hitters were interleague games while pitching at home for different American League teams (Houston in 2015 and Oakland in 2019).

NOTE 8: Kevin Millwood's effort in 2012 with the Mariners ended after six innings due to a groin strain. He had allowed one walk and struck out six by that point in the game. Five Seattle relievers would combine to complete the no-hitter.

Millwood also threw a complete game no-hitter in 2003 against the Giants when he was with the Braves.

NOTE 9: Roy Oswalt was removed from his game after one inning because of a groin pull. He had two strikeouts and no walks by that point. Five Houston relievers combined to finish the game and complete the no-hitter. Both Oswalt's and Millwood's games reflected in this table hold the record for most pitchers to throw a combined no-hitter (six). The next closest to the record set in those two games are five no-hitters that involved four pitchers.

Joe Musgrove is from El Cajon, California, a suburb of San Diego. He went to Grossmont High School in El Cajon and was drafted in the first round of the MLB June 2011 draft by the Toronto Blue Jays. He was in the minors off and on from 2011-2018 in the Toronto, Houston, and Pittsburgh systems, where he compiled a record of 30-13. He broke into the majors with Houston in 2016 and played in Pittsburgh from 2018-2020, compiling a record of 29-38.

Musgrove was traded to the Padres as part of a three-team deal just prior to the 2021 season. Musgrove came into his own as a pitcher in 2021, throwing two shutouts, including his no-hitter, and posting a 3.18 ERA along with his 11-9 record.

Víctor Caratini, Joe Musgrove's batterymate, is a native of Puerto Rico. He was drafted by the Atlanta Braves in the second round of the 2013 MLB June Amateur Draft out of Miami Dade College, Kendall Campus in Florida. He was traded to the Chicago Cubs the following season and debuted with Chicago in 2017. Caratini was sent to the Padres in the same trade that brought Yu Darvish to San Diego in exchange for multiple minor leaguers as the Cubs started their rebuild.

While with the Chicago Cubs, Caratini caught Alec Mills' no-hitter with just a few weeks left in the 2020 season. Combined with Joe Musgrove's no-hitter at the beginning of the 2021 season, this was the second no-hitter he had caught in just a couple of months of baseball. There had not been a no-hitter in MLB since Caratini had caught one with the Cubs, which made Caratini the first catcher in MLB history to catch consecutive no-hitters for two different teams.

Chapter 24

The Remarkable 2022 and 2023 Seasons

As this book was years in the making, I made the early decision to conduct all analysis based on games from the modern era of baseball, generally seen as starting in 1900. I also decided to use 2021 as my upper time limit so that data would be standardized throughout the book and the beginning chapters would be using the same parameters as the last chapters. Because of that decision, events from the 2022 and 2023 seasons weren't included in the book.

Of course, some amazing things happened in 2022 and 2023, including eight more no-hitters. Among the most remarkable pitching performances during these two seasons were a perfect game thrown by the Yankees' Domingo German, a multi-pitcher World Series no-hitter by the Houston Astros, and three separate no-hit attempts broken up with two outs in the ninth inning.

This chapter will discuss the no-hitters thrown during these two seasons, along with analysis of the best games pitched by the Philadelphia Phillies and Detroit Tigers. Pitchers from both these teams threw no-hitters in 2023, and neither team has been analyzed in-depth in previous chapters.

To start, here are the no-hitters thrown in 2022 and 2023 ranked by Game Score.

Table 24-1. No-hitters Thrown in 2022-2023

Rank	Pitcher	Team	Date Score	Opponent	GSc	IP, Hits, Runs, ERs, Walks, Strikeouts
1	Domingo German	NY Yankees	6/28/2023 NY 11-0	Oak Athletics	96	9.0 IP, 0 Hits, 0 Runs, 0 ERs, 0 BBs, 9 Ks

Rank	Pitcher	Team	Date Score	Opponent	GSc	IP, Hits, Runs, ERs, Walks, Strikeouts
2	Framber Valdez	Hou Astros	8/1/2023 Hou 2-0	Cle Guardians	93	9.0 IP, 0 Hits, 0 Runs, 0 ERs, 1 BBs, 7 Ks
3	Cristian Javier +2	Hou Astros	6/25/2022 Hou 3-0	NY Yankees	89	7.0 IP, 0 Hits, 0 Runs, 0 ERs, 1 BB, 13 Ks
4 (tie)	Reid Detmers	LA Angels	5/10/2022 LA 12-0	TB Rays	88	9.0 IP, 0 Hit, 0 Runs, 0 ERs, 1 BBs, 2 Ks
4 (tie)	Michael Lorenzen	Phi Phillies	8/9/2023 Phi 7-0	Was Nationals	88	9.0 IP, 0 Hits, 0 Runs, 0 ERs, 4 BBs, 5 Ks
6	Cristian Javier +3	Hou Astros	11/2/2022 Hou 5-0	Phi Phillies	79	6.0 IP, 0 Hits, 0 Runs, 0 ERs, 2 BBs, 9 Ks
7	Matt Manning +2	Det Tigers	7/8/2023 Det 2-0	Tor Blue Jays	76	6.2 IP, 0 Hits, 0 Runs, 0 ERs, 3 BBs, 5 Ks
8	Tyler Megill +4	NY Mets	4/29/2022 NY 3-0	Phi Phillies	69	5.0 IP, 0 Hits, 0 Runs, 0 ERs, 3 BBs, 5 Ks

METHODOLOGY: This table includes all 2022-2023 regular season and postseason no-hit games. The games are ranked in descending order by Game Score (GSc). GSc measures a starting pitcher's performance in any given game. Introduced by baseball writer/statistician Bill James in the 1980s, Game Score is presented as a figure between 0-100 — except for extreme outliers — and usually falls between 40-70.

LEGEND: Dates are shown as month/day/year (for example, June 12, 2018, is shown as 6/12/2018). The pitcher listed is the starting pitcher and the statistics at the end of the row are his. +2, +3, or +4 indicates how many additional pitchers participated in the no-hitter for multi-pitcher games. IP = innings pitched. One-third of an inning pitched has 0.1 added and two-thirds of an inning pitched has 0.2 added (for example, Matt Manning's 6 2/3 innings pitched is displayed as 6.2); BB(s) = base(s) on balls; K(s) = strikeout(s); and ER(s) = earned run(s). *Italicized game (Domingo German in 2023) was a perfect game.*

NOTE: On May 15, 2022, Hunter Greene and Art Warren of the Cincinnati Reds threw a combined eight innings of no-hit ball in a losing effort against the Pittsburgh Pirates. Greene threw into the eighth inning of a scoreless game but was pulled by manager David Bell after retiring the leadoff hitter followed by two full-count walks. Greene had already thrown 118 pitches when reliever Art Warren entered the game. Warren issued a four-pitch walk to load the bases. Pittsburgh's Ben Gamel grounded into a fielder's choice at second and he beat out the throw to first, allowing Rodolfo Castro to score from third. The Pirates would shut down the Reds in the top of the ninth, as they won the game 1-0 without needing to bat in the bottom of the inning. Because Greene and Warren threw less than nine innings, this game isn't considered a no-hitter.

On June 28, 2023, Domingo German of the New York Yankees accomplished the nearly impossible and threw a perfect game against the (admittedly struggling) Athletics in front of 12,000 fans at the Oakland-Alameda County Coliseum. The last perfect game before his gem was thrown almost 11 years earlier by Felix Hernandez of the Seattle Mariners in 2012. There were more than 2,400 games between the two events.

German was a rather unlikely pitcher to have thrown the latest perfect game, too. Unlike superstars Justin Verlander, Max Scherzer, Jacob DeGrom, and other All-Stars from the past decade, German's career had been a mixed bag since he broke into the majors in 2017 at the age of 24. His best season, by far, was 2019 when he won 18 games and lost only four. After missing the entire Covid-shortened 2020 season, German had struggled to regain his form as he carried an 11-16 record and a 4.29 Earned Run Average from his return until his perfect game. That type of performance won't carry a 30-year-old pitcher too much farther in his career.

Making this even more remarkable, German had done terribly in his recent outings before the game. During his two starts prior to the perfect game, he had given up 15 runs in just over five innings – this, of course, is not good. He had also been suspended for 10 games in May for putting too much of a foreign substance (rosin) on the balls he was throwing. Before he pitched his perfect game, it was probably a safe bet the Yankees would not renew German's one-year contract when it expired at the end of this season.

Yet, on June 28, German pitched magnificently and accomplished something no current Major League pitcher has ever done. Along with that, German is the first Dominican pitcher to throw a perfect game, a feat not achieved by fellow countrymen and Hall of Famers Juan Marichal and Pedro Martinez, along with a host of Dominican All-Stars.

One of the most renowned games thrown in 2022 was Houston's multi-pitcher no-hitter in Game 4 of the World Series. Led by Cristian Javier, the Astros shut down the Phillies to even the series at two games apiece en route to a six-game World Series victory. This effort was only the third postseason no-hitter behind Don Larsen's perfect game in the 1956 World Series versus the Dodgers and Roy Halladay's no-hitter in Game 1 of the 2010 NLDS against the Reds. The Astros' staff threw a remarkable game in a high-pressure situation. While Javier's Game Score was 79 over his six innings of work, the combined 14-strikeout performance of Javier and relievers Brian Abreu, Rafael Montero, and Ryan Pressly would have yielded an extremely impressive Game Score of 98 if their accomplishments had been added together.

Table 24-2. Postseason No-hitters

Rank	Pitcher	Team	Date Score	Opponent	GSc	IP, Hits, Runs, ERs, Walks, Strikeouts
1 (tie)	Don Larsen	NY Yankees	10/8/1956 NY 2-0	Bro Dodgers	94	9.0 IP, 0 Hits, 0 Runs, 0 ERs, 0 BBs, 7 Ks
1 (tie)	Roy Halladay	Phi Phillies	10/6/2010 Phi 4-0	Cin Reds	94	9.0 IP, 0 Hits, 0 Runs, 0 ERs, 1 BB, 8 Ks
3	Cristian Javier +3	Hou Astros	11/2/2022 Hou 5-0	Phi Phillies	79	6.0 IP, 0 Hits, 0 Runs, 0 ERs, 2 BBs, 9 Ks

METHODOLOGY: This table includes all postseason no-hitters ranked by Game Score. Game Score (GSc) measures a pitcher's performance in any given game started. Introduced by baseball writer/statistician Bill James in the 1980s, Game Score is presented as a figure between 0-100 — except for extreme outliers — and usually falls between 40-70.

LEGEND: Dates are shown as month/day/year (for example, June 12, 2018, is shown as 6/12/2018). The pitcher listed is the starting pitcher and the statistics at the end of the row are his. "+3" indicates three additional pitchers participated in the multi-pitcher no-hitter. IP = innings pitched; BB(s) = base(s) on balls; K(s) = strikeout(s); ER(s) = earned run(s). *Italicized game (Don Larsen in 1956) was a perfect game.*

There have been just 20 multi-pitcher no-hitters from 1900-2023, representing about 7% of the 280 no-hitters thrown during that period. Notably, almost all the multi-pitcher games have occurred since 1990. No-hitters involving more than one pitcher were extremely rare before that, as there were only four in the 90 seasons from 1900 through 1989. In each of those cases, there was a clear reason the starting pitcher did not finish the game: the pitcher had been ejected for arguing with the umpire (Babe Ruth), the pitcher was excessively wild in a close game (Steve Barber and Blue Moon Odom), or the manager wanted to rest a pitcher who was scheduled to start a playoff game within a few days (Vida Blue).

In the 2022 and 2023 seasons, by contrast, multi-pitcher no-hitters were far more common. Of the eight no-hitters thrown during those two years, half of them were multi-pitcher games, including the second-ever no-hitter in a World Series contest. In every one of those four games the starting pitcher was pulled in a close contest because of a rising pitch count. The table below lists all the multi-pitcher no-hitters thrown since 1900. The change in philosophy between the early years and today's game is pronounced, as there is now much less emphasis on allowing a pitcher to finish his no-hit effort regardless of how many pitches he has thrown.

Table 24-3. Multi-pitcher No-hitters

No-hit Pitchers	IP, Walks, Strikeouts	GSc (Tot)	Team	Date Score	Opponent
Babe Ruth Ernie Shore	0.0 IP, 1 BB, 0 Ks 9.0 IP, 0 BBs, 2 Ks	49 (88)	Bos Red Sox	6/23/1917 Bos 4-0	Was Senators
Steve Barber Stu Miller	8.2 IP, 10 BBs, 3 Ks 0.1 IP, 0 BBs, 0 Ks	71 (72)	Bal Orioles	4/30/1967 Det 2-1	Det Tigers
Vida Blue Glenn Abbott Paul Lindblad Rollie Fingers	5.0 IP, 2 BBs, 2 Ks 1.0 IP, 0 BBs, 0 Ks 1.0 IP, 0 BBs, 1 K 2.0 IP, 0 BBs, 2 Ks	67 (90)	Oak A's	9/28/1975 Oak 5-0	Cal Angels
Blue Moon Odom Francisco Barrios	5.0 IP, 9 BBs, 3 Ks 4.0 IP, 2 BBs, 2 Ks	59 (79)	Chi W. Sox	7/28/1976 Chi 2-1	Oak Athletics
Mark Langston Mike Witt	7.0 IP, 4 BBs, 3 Ks 2.0 IP, 0 BBs, 2 Ks	76 (88)	Cal Angels	4/11/1990 Cal 1-0	Seattle Mariners
Bob Milacki Mike Flanagan Mark Williamson Gregg Olson	6.0 IP, 3 BBs, 3 Ks 1.0 IP, 1 BB, 0 Ks 1.0 IP, 0 BBs, 0 Ks 1.0 IP, 0 BBs, 2 Ks	72 (88)	Bal Orioles	7/13/1991 Bal 2-0	Oak Athletics
Kent Mercker Mark Wohlers Alejandro Pena	6.0 IP, 2 BBs, 6 Ks 2.0 IP, 0 BBs, 0 Ks 1.0 IP, 0 BBs, 0 Ks	76 (91)	Atl Braves	9/11/1991 Atl 1-0	SD Padres

From Randy Johnson to Dallas Braden

No-hit Pitchers	IP, Walks, Strikeouts	GSc (Tot)	Team	Date Score	Opponent
Fran. Cordova Ricardo Rincon	9.0 IP, 2 BBs, 10 Ks 1.0 IP, 1 BB, 1 K	95 (100)	Pit Pirates	7/12/1997 Pit 3-0 (10)	Hou Astros
Roy Oswalt Peter Munro Kirk Saarloos Brad Lidge Octavio Dotel Billy Wagner	1.0 IP, 0 BBs, 2 Ks 2.2 IP, 3 BBs, 2 Ks 1.1 IP, 0 BBs, 1 K 2.0 IP, 0 BBs, 2 Ks 1.0 IP, 0 BBs, 4 Ks 1.0 IP, 0 BBs, 2 Ks	55 (97)	Hou Astros	6/11/2003 Hou 8-0	NY Yankees
Kevin Millwood Charlie Furbush Stephen Pryor Lucas Luetge Brandon League Tom Wilhelmsen	6.0 IP, 1 BB, 6 Ks 0.2 IP, 0 BBs, 1 K 0.1 IP, 2 BBs, 1 K 0.1 IP, 0 BBs, 0 Ks 0.2 IP, 0 BBs, 1 K 1.0 IP, 0 BBs, 0 Ks	77 (93)	Sea Mariners	6/8/2012 Sea 1-0	LA Dodgers
Cole Hamels Jake Diekman Ken Giles Jonathan Papelbon	6.0 IP, 5 BBs, 7 Ks 1.0 IP, 0 BBs, 2 Ks 1.0 IP, 2 BBs, 3 Ks 1.0 IP, 0 BBs, 0 Ks	74 (94)	Phi Phillies	9/1/2014	Atl Braves
Walker Buehler Tony Cingrani Yimi Garcia Adam Liberatore	6.0 IP, 3 BBs, 8 Ks 1.0 IP, 2 BBs, 1 K 1.0 IP, 0 BBs, 2 Ks 1.0 IP, 0 BBs, 2 Ks	77 (95)	LA Dodgers	5/4/2018 LA 4-0	SD Padres
Taylor Cole Felix Pena	2.0 IP, 0 BBs, 2 Ks 7.0 IP, 1 BB, 6 Ks	58 (94)	LA Angels	7/12/2019 LA 13-0	Seattle Mariners
Aaron Sanchez Will Harris Joe Biagini Chris Devenski	6.0 IP, 2 BBs, 6 Ks 1.0 IP, 1 BB, 0 Ks 1.0 IP, 1 BB, 1 K 1.0 IP, 0 BBs, 1 K	76 (91)	Hou Astros	8/3/2019 Hou 9-0	Seattle Mariners
Zach Davies Ryan Tepera Andrew Chafin Craig Kimbrel	6.0 IP, 5 BBs, 4 Ks 1.0 IP, 1 BB, 0 Ks 1.0 IP, 1 BB, 0 Ks 1.0 IP, 1 BB, 3 Ks	71 (86)	Chi Cubs	6/24/2021 Chi 4-0	LA Dodgers
Corbin Burnes Josh Hader	8.0 IP, 1 BB, 14 Ks 1.0 IP, 0 BBs, 2 Ks	95 (102)	Mil Brewers	9/11/2021 Mil 3-0	Cle Indians
Tylor Megill Drew Smith Joely Rodriguez Seth Lugo Edwin Diaz	5.0 IP, 3 BBs, 5 Ks 1.1 IP, 1 BB, 4 Ks 1.0 IP, 2 BBs, 0 Ks 0.2 IP, 0 BBs, 0 Ks 1.0 IP, 0 BBs, 3 Ks	69 (93)	NY Mets	4/29/2022 NY 3-0	Phi Phillies

No-hit Pitchers	IP, Walks, Strikeouts	GSc (Tot)	Team	Date Score	Opponent
Cristian Javier Hector Neris Ryan Pressly	7.0 IP, 1 BB, 13 Ks 1.0 IP, 2 BBs, 0 Ks 1.0 IP, 0 BBs, 2 Ks	89 (99)	Hou Astros	6/25/2022 Hou 3-0	NY Yankees
Cristian Javier Brian Abreu Rafael Montero Ryan Pressly	6.0 IP, 2 BBs, 9 Ks 1.0 IP, 0 BBs, 3 Ks 1.0 IP, 0 BBs, 1 K 1.0 IP, 1 BB, 1 K	79 (98)	Hou Astros	11/2/2022 Hou 5-0	Phi Phillies
Matt Manning Jason Foley Alex Lange	6.2 IP, 3 BBs, 5 Ks 1.1 IP, 0 BBs, 1 K 1.0 IP, 0 BBs, 1 K	76 (91)	Det Tigers	7/8/2023 Det 2-0	Tor B. Jays

METHODOLOGY: This table lists all 20 multi-pitcher no-hitters from 1900-2023. The games are listed chronologically.

LEGEND: Each row in the table represents a multi-pitcher no-hit game. Each line within the individual rows lists each pitcher's performance. IP = innings pitched. One-third of an inning pitched has 0.1 added and two-thirds of an inning pitched has 0.2 added (for example, 8 2/3 innings pitched is displayed as 8.2); BB(s) = base(s) on balls; K(s) = strikeout(s). Pitchers are listed in their order of appearance during the multi-pitcher game. GSc = Game Score. Game Score measures a pitcher's performance in any given game started. Introduced by baseball writer/statistician Bill James in the 1980s, Game Score is presented as a figure between 0-100 — except for extreme outliers — and usually falls between 40-70. Officially, GSc is only computed for the starting pitcher of the game, and that is what is displayed in the GSc column for each game. For purposes of this analysis, a "combined Game Score" is provided for the total (Tot) pitching performance for all pitchers who contributed to the no-hitter as if the game was thrown by a single pitcher. That combined Game Score (Tot) is portrayed in parentheses underneath the starting pitcher's GSc. The "Team" is the team the pitchers were on when they threw the no-hitter. Dates show when the no-hitter was thrown and are written as month/day/year (for example, June 12, 2018, is shown as 6/12/2018). (10) indicates the game was a 10-inning contest. "Opponent" is the opponent on the day of the no-hitter. "Score" is the final score of the game.

The first post-1900 multi-pitcher no-hitter was thrown in 1917 when starting pitcher Babe Ruth of the Boston Red Sox was thrown out of the game after he slugged home plate umpire Brick Owen. Ruth was angered when Owen called two balls to leadoff hitter Ray Morgan of the Washington Senators, allowing Morgan to reach first base on a walk. Reliever Ernie Shore came in and Morgan was promptly caught stealing. Shore then retired the next 26 batters in a row in what can be described as a perfect game in relief.

The next multi-pitcher no-hitter came 50 years later when Steve Barber of the Baltimore Orioles was pulled with two outs in the top of the ninth inning after he had walked three batters and thrown a wild pitch, resulting in a 1-1 tie. With runners on first and third and Barber having already recorded 10 walks for the game, manager Hank Bauer had enough and called in ace reliever Stu Miller to finish the inning. Unfortunately, Baltimore second baseman Mark Belanger bobbled a throw from the shortstop to force the runner coming from first. This resulted in the runner on third scoring on the error, giving Detroit a 2-1 lead. The Tigers held off the Orioles in the bottom of the inning and won the game.

Vida Blue was scheduled to start Game 2 of the 1975 ALCS against the Red Sox, and the Athletics had already clinched the AL West title as Blue was on tap to start the last game of the regular season. Understandably, Oakland manager Al Dark only allowed Blue to throw five innings before calling in the relievers. Similar to Steve Barber in 1967, Blue Moon Odom was excessively wild in his 1976 no-hitter, giving up nine walks in only five innings of a one-run game before manager Paul Richards pulled him.

Beginning in 1990, the frequency of multi-pitcher no-hitters increased markedly. While there certainly were injuries involved in some games – notably Roy Oswalt's no-hitter in 2003 – the majority of multi-pitcher no-hitters since then were due to pitch count limits. This trend of multi-pitcher games has been accelerated with the advent of relief pitcher starts designed specifically to take out the starter after just an inning or two.

The four multi-pitcher no-hitters in 2022-2023 were all centered around the desire to limit pitch counts for the starters and to maintain pitching effectiveness in close games. The latter reason was especially apparent in the must-win fourth game of the 2022 World Series where Houston was fighting back from a two-games-to-one deficit against Philadelphia. On other occasions, limiting pitch count was important because the starter was recovering from an injury and the team didn't want to push it.

This was the case in Matt Manning's no-hitter with Detroit in July 2023. He had just come off the injured list and manager A.J. Hinch detected Manning was laboring after walking a batter on his 91st pitch. Jason Foley and Alex Lange finished the game and Detroit had its ninth no-hitter in the books – the team's first one ever thrown by more than one pitcher.

It's surprising the Tigers have only thrown nine no-hitters, given the wealth of pitching talent displayed by Detroit over the years. Most recently, Justin Verlander has excelled, as he is listed prominently in Table 24-4 among the top Game Scores for Tiger pitchers since the team was established in 1901.

Table 24-4. Tigers Highest Game Scores

Rank	Pitcher	Date Score	Opponent	GSc	IP, Hits, Runs, ERs, Walks, Strikeouts
1	Ed Summers	7/16/1909 0-0 Tie (18 inn)	Washington Senators	126	18.0 IP, 7 Hits, 0 Runs, 0 ERs, 2 BBs, 10 Ks
2 (tie)	Eric Erickson	5/24/1918 2-2 Tie (16 inn)	Washington Senators	112	16.0 IP, 8 Hits, 2 Runs, 1 ER, 0 BBs, 12 Ks
2 (tie)	Les Mueller	7/21/1945 1-1 Tie (24 inn)	Philadelphia Athletics	112	19.2 IP, 13 Hits, 1 Run, 0 ERs, 5 BBs, 6 Ks
4	Virgil Trucks	9/7/1951 (2) Det 2-1 (14 inn)	Chicago White Sox	103	14.0 IP, 5 Hits, 1 Run, 0 ERs, 4 BBs, 7 Ks
5	Al Aber	8/13/1954 Chi 1-0 (16 inn)	Chicago White Sox	101	15.1 IP, 9 Hits, 1 Run, 1 ER, 3 BBs, 8 Ks
6	Harry Coveleski	5/19/1916 2-2 Tie (16 inn)	New York Yankees	99	16.0 IP, 8 Hits, 2 Runs, 2 ERs, 6 BBs, 7 Ks
7	Ed Killian	7/22/1904 0-0 Tie (13 inn)	Washington Senators	98	13.0 IP, 8 Hits, 0 Runs, 0 ERs, 0 BBs, 7 Ks
8 (tie)	Tommy Bridges	8/11/1942 (1) 0-0 Tie (14 inn)	Cleveland Indians	97	14.0 IP, 9 Hits, 0 Runs, 0 ERs, 5 BBs, 8 Ks
8 (tie)	Jim Bunning	7/20/1958 (1) Det 3-0	Boston Red Sox	97	9.0 IP, 0 Hits, 0 Runs, 0 ERs, 2 BBs, 12 Ks
10 (tie)	George Mullin	5/21/1904 0-0 Tie (11 inn)	Washington Senators	95	11.0 IP, 4 Hits, 0 Runs, 0 ERs, 2 BBs, 8 Ks
10 (tie)	Schoolboy Rowe	9/21/1941 (2) 1-1 Tie (14 inn)	Chicago White Sox	95	14.0 IP, 8 Hits, 1 Run, 1 ER, 3 BBs, 6 Ks
10 (tie)	Justin Verlander	6/12/2007 Det 4-0	Milwaukee Brewers	95	9.0 IP, 0 Hits, 0 Runs, 0 ERs, 4 BBs, 12 Ks

Rank	Pitcher	Date Score	Opponent	GSc	IP, Hits, Runs, ERs, Walks, Strikeouts
10 (tie)	Justin Verlander	5/18/2012 Det 6-0	Pittsburgh Pirates	95	9.0 IP, 1 Hit, 0 Runs, 0 ERs, 2 BBs, 12 Ks

METHODOLOGY: This table includes the highest Game Scores thrown by a Tigers pitcher from 1901-2023. Games are ranked by Game Score (GSc) and consider all franchise regular season and postseason games. Table 24-5 below limits the eligible games to those pitching performances that were 10 innings or less. Game Score (GSc) measures a pitcher's performance in any given game started. Introduced by baseball writer/statistician Bill James in the 1980s, Game Score is presented as a figure between 0-100 — except for extreme outliers — and usually falls between 40-70.

LEGEND: Dates are shown as month/day/year (for example, June 12, 2018, is shown as 6/12/2018). IP = innings pitched. One-third of an inning pitched has 0.1 added and two-thirds of an inning pitched has 0.2 added (for example, 9 1/3 innings pitched is displayed as 9.1); BB(s) = base(s) on balls; K(s) = strikeout(s); ER(s) = earned run(s); inn = innings (associated with the length of extra-inning games); and (1) or (2) = first or second game of a doubleheader. Detroit was one of the original eight teams in the American League when it was established in 1901. The team has been known as the Tigers the entire time, and when the two leagues moved to the two-division structure in 1969, Detroit became part of the American League East Division. In 1998, Detroit moved to the Central Division when the Tampa Bay Devil Rays joined the league as part of the East Division.

NOTE 1: The highest postseason Game Score thrown by a franchise pitcher was an 89 by Justin Verlander in the decisive Game 5 of the 2012 ALDS against the Oakland Athletics. After coming back from a two-games-to-zero deficit to even the best of five series, Oakland hoped to close out the ALDS at home against the Tigers that evening. Detroit chose to send Verlander, the winner of the series opener, to the mound. He responded by throwing a complete game, four-hit shutout against a powerful A's lineup that included Yoenis Cespedes, Josh Reddick, and Coco Crisp. The 6-0 victory advanced the Tigers to the ALCS, where they swept the New York Yankees in four games. Detroit would go on to be swept themselves by the San Francisco Giants.

NOTE 2: Even though multiple Tiger pitchers listed in this table have struck out 12 opposing batters, that's not close to the team record. In 2013, Anibal Sanchez struck out 17 Braves in a 10-0 win. During that game, he allowed five hits and was pulled after eight innings because Detroit had a commanding lead and Sanchez had thrown 121 pitches.

NOTE 3: Ed Summers pitched a remarkable 18-inning shutout in 1909 that ended in a 0-0 tie with Washington that was called due to darkness. His Game Score of 126 is tied for fifth best in Major League history. Les Mueller's 19.2-inning effort in 1945 is the second-most innings ever thrown by a Detroit pitcher in a single game. Tiger hurler Les Uhle threw 20 innings in a 21-inning 6-5 win over the White Sox in 1929. Eric Erickson's 16-inning pitching duel with Washington's Harry Harper resulted in a 2-2 tie called on account of darkness. The game was played in front of President Woodrow Wilson, who came to the ballpark to escape the stresses of being a wartime president during World War I.

Of course, many of the games listed above were lengthy extra-inning efforts, which gave starting pitchers a chance to rack up points for retiring batters and accumulating strikeouts. To compare efforts in typical games, Table 24-5 ranks the highest franchise Game Scores of 10 innings or less from 1901-2023. All nine of the team's no-hitters are included in the table.

Table 24-5. Tigers Highest Game Scores of 10 innings or less

Rank	Pitcher	Date Score	Opponent	GSc	IP, Hits, Runs, ERs, Walks, Strikeouts
1	Jim Bunning	7/20/1958 (1) Det 3-0	Boston Red Sox	97	9.0 IP, 0 Hits, 0 Runs, 0 ERs, 2 BBs, 12 Ks
2 (tie)	Justin Verlander	6/12/2007 Det 4-0	Milwaukee Brewers	95	9.0 IP, 0 Hits, 0 Runs, 0 ERs, 4 BBs, 12 Ks
2 (tie)	Justin Verlander	5/18/2012 Det 6-0	Pittsburgh Pirates	95	9.0 IP, 1 Hit, 0 Runs, 0 ERs, 2 BBs, 12 Ks
4 (tie)	Ed Summers	9/25/1908 (2) Det 1-0 (10 inn)	Philadelphia Athletics	94	10.0 IP, 2 Hits, 0 Runs, 0 ERs, 0 BBs, 6 Ks
4 (tie)	Tommy Bridges	8/20/1941 Det 1-0 (10 inn)	New York Yankees	94	10.0 IP, 2 Hits, 0 Runs, 0 ERs, 3 BBs, 9 Ks
4 (tie)	Virgil Trucks	8/25/1952 Det 1-0	New York Yankees	94	9.0 IP, 0 Hits, 0 Runs, 0 ERs, 1 BB, 8 Ks

FROM RANDY JOHNSON TO DALLAS BRADEN

Rank	Pitcher	Date Score	Opponent	GSc	IP, Hits, Runs, ERs, Walks, Strikeouts
4 (tie)	Jeff Weaver	5/22/2002 Det 2-0	Cleveland Indians	94	9.0 IP, 1 Hit, 0 Runs, 0 ERs, 2 BBs, 11 Ks
4 (tie)	Justin Verlander	6/14/2011 Det 4-0	Cleveland Indians	94	9.0 IP, 2 Hits, 0 Runs, 0 ERs, 1 BB, 12 Ks
4 (tie)	Anibal Sanchez	5/24/2013 Det 6-0	Minnesota Twins	94	9.0 IP, 1 Hit, 0 Runs, 0 ERs, 3 BBs, 12 Ks
4 (tie)	Spencer Turnbull	5/18/2021 Det 5-0	Seattle Mariners	94	9.0 IP, 0 Hits, 0 Runs, 0 ERs, 2 BBs, 9 Ks
11 (tie)	Virgil Trucks	5/15/1952 Det 1-0	Washington Senators	93	9.0 IP, 0 Hits, 0 Runs, 0 ERs, 1 BB, 7 Ks
36 (tie)	Justin Verlander	5/7/2011 Det 9-0	Toronto Blue Jays	90	9.0 IP, 0 Hits, 0 Runs, 0 ERs, 1 BB, 4 Ks
54 (tie)	Jack Morris	4/7/1984 Det 4-0	Chicago White Sox	89	9.0 IP, 0 Hits, 0 Runs, 0 ERs, 6 BBs, 8 Ks
96 (tie)	George Mullin	7/4/1912 (2) Det 7-0	St. Louis Browns	87	9.0 IP, 0 Hits, 0 Runs, 0 ERs, 5 BBs, 5 Ks
1247 (tie)	Matt Manning +2	7/8/2023 Det 2-0	Toronto Blue Jays	76	6.2 IP, 0 Hits, 0 Runs, 0 ERs, 3 BBs, 5 Ks

METHODOLOGY: This table includes the highest Game Scores of 10 innings or less thrown by a Tigers pitcher from 1901-2023. Games are ranked by Game Score (GSc) and consider all franchise regular season and postseason games. For comparison purposes, all nine Detroit no-hitters are included in this table. Game Score (GSc) measures a pitcher's performance in any given game started. Introduced by baseball writer/statistician Bill James in the 1980s, Game Score is presented as a figure between 0-100 — except for extreme outliers — and usually falls between 40-70.

LEGEND: Dates are shown as month/day/year (for example, June 12, 2018, is shown as 6/12/2018). IP = innings pitched. One-third of an inning pitched has 0.1 added and two-thirds of an inning pitched has 0.2 added (for example, 9 1/3 innings pitched is displayed as 9.1); BB(s) = base(s) on balls; K(s) = strikeout(s); ER(s) = earned run(s); inn = innings (associated with the length of extra-inning games); and (1) or (2) = first or second game of a doubleheader. Detroit was one of the original eight teams in the American League when it was established in 1901. The team has been known as the Tigers the entire time, and when the two leagues moved to the two-division structure in 1969, Detroit became part of the American League East Division. In 1998, Detroit moved to the Central Division when the Tampa Bay Devil Rays joined the league as part of the East Division.

NOTE 1: Matt Manning threw the first 6.2 innings of a multi-pitcher no-hitter against the Toronto Blue Jays in 2023. Manager A.J. Hinch relieved Manning with two outs in the top of the seventh after Manning walked Cavan Biggio in a 2-0 game. The next batter, Whit Merrifield, represented the tying run and Manning had already thrown 91 pitches. Jason Foley relieved Manning, retired Merrifield, and then put down the Blue Jays in order in the eighth. Alex Lange threw a 1-2-3 ninth inning for the save and to complete the no-hitter. If the combined efforts of the three pitchers were added together, they would have achieved a Game Score of 91 (9.0 innings, no runs or hits, three walks, and seven strikeouts).

NOTE 2: Virgil Trucks threw two no-hitters in 1952 for the 50-104 Tigers, one of the worst teams in franchise history. Finishing in last place with the fewest runs scored of any American League team, Detroit routinely victimized Trucks by denying him run support. Of the 35 games he started that season, the Tigers scored two or less runs in almost half of them. Trucks' record of 5-19 for the season is a tribute to his ability to persevere, as he threw two no-hitters, a one-hitter, a two-hitter, and a six-hitter for the victories. In Trucks' first no-hitter in May, it was a scoreless tie until teammate Vic Wertz hit a two-out solo home run over the right field wall for the walk off win. Remarkably, when Trucks threw his first no-hitter of 1952, it had been almost 40 years since George Mullin had thrown the first and only no-hitter for Detroit in 1912.

Trucks' second no-hitter that year was also a 1-0 win, this time against Mickey Mantle, Yogi Berra, and the World Champion New York Yankees. Detroit scored its only run in the seventh inning off a one-out double by Walt Dropo followed by a Bud Souchock single down the left field line. In both of his no-hitters, Trucks only allowed a single walk to opposing batters. Trucks had an exceptional 17-season career – mostly with Detroit – accumulating 177 wins in the process. His record would have been even more impressive if not for two years of service in the Navy during World War II from 1944-1945. He managed to return from the war in time for Detroit's final two games of the 1945 season. He was immediately thrown in to start a must-win game and, as a result, the Tigers won the pennant. Trucks went on to start two games in Detroit's seven-game World Series victory over the Chicago Cubs.

NOTE 3: In Justin Verlander's 2011 no-hitter against the Blue Jays, he faced the minimum 27 batters. The one Toronto batter who reached base was J.P. Arencibia, who reached first on a one-out full count walk in the eighth inning. The next batter hit into a double play. In his 2012 one-hitter against the Pirates, Verlander had a no-hitter going with one out in the ninth when Josh Harrison hit a groundball single up the middle. With a record of 183-114 over 2,300 strikeouts with Detroit, Justin Verlander is arguably the best pitcher to ever wear a Tiger uniform, although, cases certainly can be made for Hall of Famers Hal Newhouser, Jim Bunning, and Jack Morris, along with stalwart Mickey Lolich, and turn-of-the century stars like George Mullin and Hooks Dauss. The big difference is that Verlander has excelled for the Houston Astros, also, leading that team to two World Series championships. The other pitchers listed almost exclusively played for the Tigers (with the exception of Jack Morris). If a player's entire career is considered along with the impact he had on a specific team – like what Verlander meant to the Tigers – while he was with them, I believe Verlander wins hands down. Verlander has also thrown three of the top 10 (including two of the top three) Game Scores in this table. No one else is in the Top 10 list more than once.

NOTE 4: Both Jeff Weaver and Anibal Sanchez threw exceptional games that were nearly no-hitters. In Weaver's 2002 one-hitter against Cleveland, he had a no-hitter with two outs in the eighth inning that was broken up by a Chris Magruder double. For Sanchez, his 2013 no-hitter was broken up with one out in the ninth inning when Minnesota's Joe Mauer hit a groundball single up the middle.

On August 9, 2023, Philadelphia pitcher Michael Lorenzen threw a magnificent no-hitter against the Washington Nationals. It was his second start for the team since his trade from Detroit. It was also his first start at home, with his wife, mother, and nine-month-old daughter in the stands. Lorenzen's no-hitter was the 12th no-hitter for Philadelphia since 1900, and the first from a Phillies pitcher since Cole Hamels shut down the Chicago Cubs in 2015. Across the diamond, the Nationals entered the game owning the longest active streak of any franchise without being no-hit. The last no-hitter thrown against them, when they were the Montreal Expos, was David Cone's perfect game with the New York Yankees in 1999.

The Phillies have a long record of outstanding individual pitchers, starting with Robin Roberts, Jim Bunning, Steve Carlton, Roy Halladay, and Cole Hamels. The highest Game Scores for the franchise are listed in Table 24-6, with the highest Game Scores of 10 innings or less compiled in Table 24-7.

Table 24-6. Phillies Highest Game Scores

Rank	Pitcher	Date Score	Opponent	GSc	IP, Hits, Runs, ERs, Walks, Strikeouts
1	Chris Short	10/2/1965 (2) 0-0 Tie (18 inn)	New York Mets	114	15.0 IP, 9 Hits, 0 Runs, 0 ERs, 3 BBs, 18 Ks
2	Ad Brennan	7/19/1913 Phi 3-2 (16 inn)	Cincinnati Reds	103	16.0 IP, 8 Hits, 2 Runs, 1 ER, 0 BBs, 3 Ks
3	Joe Oeschger	9/4/1917 0-0 Tie (14 inn)	Brooklyn Robins	102	14.0 IP, 6 Hits, 0 Runs, 0 ERs, 3 BBs, 5 Ks
4	Tully Sparks	8/24/1905 Chi 2-1 (20 inn)	Chicago Cubs	101-103	20.0 IP, 19 Hits, 2 Runs, 1 or 2 ERs, 1 BB, 6 Ks
5	Lee Meadows	7/17/1919 Phi 1-0 (12 inn)	St. Louis Cardinals	99	12.0 IP, 4 Hits, 0 Runs, 0 ERs, 3 BBs, 8 Ks
6 (tie)	Steve Carlton	4/25/1972 Phi 3-0	San Francisco Giants	98	9.0 IP, 1 Hit, 0 Runs, 0 ERs, 1 BB, 14 Ks
6 (tie)	*Roy Halladay*	*5/29/2010* *Phi 1-0*	*Florida Marlins*	*98*	*9.0 IP, 0 Hits, 0 Runs, 0 ERs, 0 BBs, 11 Ks*
6 (tie)	Cole Hamels	7/25/2015 Phi 5-0	Chicago Cubs	98	9.0 IP, 0 Hits, 0 Runs, 0 ERs, 2 BBs, 13 Ks
9 (tie)	Milt Watson	7/17/1918 Chi 2-1 (21 inn)	Chicago Cubs	97	20.0 IP, 19 Hits, 2 Runs, 2 ERs, 4 BBs, 5 Ks
9 (tie)	Oscar Judd	7/27/1945 Phi 2-0 (11 inn)	New York Giants	97	11.0 IP, 3 Hits, 0 Runs, 0 ERs, 2 BBs, 8 Ks
9 (tie)	*Jim Bunning*	*6/21/1964 (1)* *Phi 6-0*	*New York Mets*	*97*	*9.0 IP, 0 Hits, 0 Runs, 0 ERs, 0 BBs, 10 Ks*
9 (tie)	Vince Velasquez	4/14/2016 Phi 3-0	San Diego Padres	97	9.0 IP, 3 Hits, 0 Runs, 0 ERs, 0 BBs, 16 Ks

METHODOLOGY: This table includes the highest Game Scores thrown by a Phillies pitcher from 1900-2023. Games are ranked by Game Score (GSc) and consider all franchise regular season and postseason games. Table 24-5 below limits the eligible games to those pitching performances that were 10 innings or less.

Game Score (GSc) measures a pitcher's performance in any given game started. Introduced by baseball writer/statistician Bill James in the 1980s, Game Score is presented as a figure between 0-100 -- except for extreme outliers -- and usually falls between 40-70.

LEGEND: Dates are shown as month/day/year (for example, June 12, 2018, is shown as 6/12/2018). IP = innings pitched. One-third of an inning pitched has 0.1 added and two-thirds of an inning pitched has 0.2 added (for example, 9 1/3 innings pitched is displayed as 9.1); BB(s) = base(s) on balls; K(s) = strikeout(s); ER(s) = earned run(s); inn = innings (associated with the length of extra-inning games); and (1) or (2) = first or second game of a doubleheader. The franchise was known as the Philadelphia Quakers when they started in the National League in 1883. They became the Phillies in 1890. *Italicized games (Jim Bunning in 1964 and Roy Halladay in 2010) were perfect games.*

NOTE 1: The highest postseason Game Score thrown by a franchise pitcher was a 94 by Roy Halladay in Game 1 of the 2010 NLDS against the Reds. At the time, this game was the second postseason no-hitter in history, 54 years after Don Larsen's perfect game in the 1956 World Series against the Brooklyn Dodgers. Halladay held a powerful Cincinnati lineup featuring Joey Votto, Scott Rolen, and Jay Bruce hitless over nine innings in the opening game of the division series. Philadelphia would sweep the Reds convincingly, holding Cincinnati to just four runs over the three games. The Phillies would fall to the upstart Giants in the NLCS in six games. The Giants would go on to win their first World Series championship since the team moved to San Francisco in 1958.

NOTE 2: Tully Sparks threw his 20-inning, 19-hit losing effort at a time when baseball didn't differentiate between earned and unearned runs. Because of that, it's officially uncertain as to whether he allowed one unearned run out of the two runs scored against him because shortstop Mickey Doolin made an error at some point during the game. That said, his Game Score can only be either a 103 (if one run was unearned) or 101 (if both runs he allowed were earned). Based on the game story from contemporary newspaper reports, it looks like both runs were earned. Sparks himself threw an amazing game, facing 77 batters and allowing only two runs despite Chicago putting 23 men on base over 20 innings. Sparks is tied with Joe Oeschger for the most innings ever thrown by a Phillies pitcher in a single game. Oeschger threw his 20 innings in a 9-9 tie against the Brooklyn Robins in 1919. Oeschger is also the co-holder of the major league innings pitched record, as he threw 26 innings while a member of the Boston Braves in a 1-1 tie game against Brooklyn in 1920.

NOTE 3: Chris Short achieved the highest Game Score for a Phillies pitcher as he threw 15 innings of shutout ball against the Mets, during which he set a Philadelphia record for most strikeouts in a game with 18. The second game of a no-hitter against the Mets on the last day of the season, the 18-inning game ended in a 0-0 tie and was never played to completion, as it didn't matter in the pennant race that year. The second-most strikeouts in a game was by Art Mahaffey with 17. He accomplished that in only nine innings against the Cubs in a 6-0 win.

Table 24-7. Phillies Highest Game Scores of 10 innings or less

Rank	Pitcher	Date Score	Opponent	GSc	IP, Hits, Runs, ERs, Walks, Strikeouts
1 (tie)	Steve Carlton	4/25/1972 Phi 3-0	SF Giants	98	9.0 IP, 1 Hit, 0 Runs, 0 ERs, 1 BB, 14 Ks
1 (tie)	Roy Halladay	5/29/2010 Phi 1-0	Florida Marlins	98	9.0 IP, 0 Hits, 0 Runs, 0 ERs, 0 BBs, 11 Ks
1 (tie)	Cole Hamels	7/25/2015 Phi 5-0	Chicago Cubs	98	9.0 IP, 0 Hits, 0 Runs, 0 ERs, 2 BBs, 13 Ks
4 (tie)	Jim Bunning	6/21/1964 (1) Phi 6-0	New York Mets	97	9.0 IP, 0 Hits, 0 Runs, 0 ERs, 0 BBs, 10 Ks
4 (tie)	Vince Velasquez	4/14/2016 Phi 3-0	San Diego Padres	97	9.0 IP, 3 Hits, 0 Runs, 0 ERs, 0 BBs, 16 Ks
6 (tie)	Johnny Lush	5/1/1906 Phi 3-0	Brooklyn Superbas	95	9.0 IP, 0 Hits, 0 Runs, 0 ERs, 3 BBs, 11 Ks
6 (tie)	Curt Simmons	5/16/1953 Phi 3-0	Milwaukee Braves	95	9.0 IP, 1 Hit, 0 Runs, 0 ERs, 0 BBs, 10 Ks
6 (tie)	Art Mahaffey	4/23/1961 (2) Phi 6-0	Chicago Cubs	95	9.0 IP, 4 Hits, 0 Runs, 0 ERs, 1 BB, 17 Ks
6 (tie)	Steve Carlton	9/21/1981 Mon 1-0 (17 inn)	Montreal Expos	95	10.0 IP, 3 Hits, 0 Runs, 0 ERs, 3 BBs, 12 Ks
6 (tie)	Terry Mulholland	8/15/1990 Phi 6-0	SF Giants	95	9.0 IP, 0 Hits, 0 Runs, 0 ERs, 0 BBs, 8 Ks
6 (tie)	Curt Schilling	8/21/1996 Phi 6-0	LA Dodgers	95	9.0 IP, 2 Hits, 0 Runs, 0 ERs, 0 BBs, 12 Ks

From Randy Johnson to Dallas Braden

Rank	Pitcher	Date Score	Opponent	GSc	IP, Hits, Runs, ERs, Walks, Strikeouts
12 (tie)	Kevin Millwood	4/27/2003 Phi 1-0	SF Giants	94	9.0 IP, 0 Hits, 0 Runs, 0 ERs, 3 BBs, 10 Ks
12 (tie)	Roy Halladay	10/6/2010 Phi 4-0	Cincinnati Reds	94	9.0 IP, 0 Hits, 0 Runs, 0 ERs, 1 BB, 8 Ks
43 (tie)	Tommy Greene	5/23/1991 Phi 2-0	Montreal Expos	90	9.0 IP, 0 Hits, 0 Runs, 0 ERs, 7 BBs, 10 Ks
59 (tie)	Rick Wise	6/23/1971 Phi 4-0	Cincinnati Reds	89	9.0 IP, 0 Hits, 0 Runs, 0 ERs, 1 BB, 3 Ks
77 (tie)	Michael Lorenzen	8/9/2023 Phi 7-0	Washington Nationals	88	9.0 IP, 0 Hits, 0 Runs, 0 ERs, 4 BBs, 5 Ks
138 (tie)	Chick Fraser	9/18/1903 (2) Phi 10-0	Chicago Cubs	86	9.0 IP, 0 Hits, 0 Runs, 0 ERs, 5 BBs, 4 Ks
---	Cole Hamels +3	9/1/2014 Phi 7-0	Atlanta Braves	74	6.0 IP, 0 Hits, 0 Runs, 0 ERs, 5 BBs, 7 Ks

METHODOLOGY: This table includes the highest Game Scores of 10 innings or less thrown by a Phillies pitcher from 1900-2023. Games are ranked by Game Score (GSc) and consider all franchise regular season and postseason games. For comparison purposes, all twelve post-1900 Philadelphia no-hitters are included in this table. Game Score (GSc) measures a pitcher's performance in any given game started. Introduced by baseball writer/statistician Bill James in the 1980s, Game Score is presented as a figure between 0-100 -- except for extreme outliers -- and usually falls between 40-70.

LEGEND: Dates are shown as month/day/year (for example, June 12, 2018, is shown as 6/12/2018). IP = innings pitched. One-third of an inning pitched has 0.1 added and two-thirds of an inning pitched has 0.2 added (for example, 9 1/3 innings pitched is displayed as 9.1); BB(s) = base(s) on balls; K(s) = strikeout(s); ER(s) = earned run(s); inn = innings (associated with the length of extra-inning games); and (1) or (2) = first or second game of a doubleheader. The franchise was known as the Philadelphia Quakers when they started in the National League in 1883. They became the Phillies in 1890. For comparison purposes, all post-1900 Phillies no-hitters are included in this table. *Italicized games (Jim Bunning in 1964 and Roy Halladay in 2010) were perfect games.*

NOTE: Cole Hamels and three other Philadelphia pitchers threw their combined no-hitter against the Braves in September 2014. Hamels threw six innings, while Jake Diekman, Ken Giles, and Jonathan Papelbon each threw a 1-2-3 inning to close out the no-hitter. Diekman struck out two Braves in the seventh and Giles struck out the side in the eighth. Altogether, the four pitchers struck out 12 batters and walked five (all by Hamels). If their statistics were combined into a single Game Score, they would have earned a 94 GSc, which would have placed them in a tie for 12th best in Phillies history.

The Philadelphia Phillies endured decades of frustration in the early part of the 20th Century, as they advanced to the postseason only twice in a 74-season stretch between 1900 and 1974. Even then, the team won only one World Series game as they were defeated by the Red Sox 4-1 in 1915 and were swept by the Yankees in 1950. The team's lack of success was epitomized by their record-setting pitching futility as the team failed to pitch a no-hitter over a 58-year stretch between Johnny Lush blanking the Brooklyn Superbas in 1906 and Jim Bunning throwing a perfect game against the expansion Mets in 1964. For the record, Table 24-8 below displays the longest no-hitter gaps since 1900. Note that in fifth place, the Cleveland Indians have the longest current streak, having not thrown a no-hitter since Len Barker's perfect game 42 years ago in 1981.

Table 24-8. Longest Time Between No-hitters

Rank	Team	Pitcher	Date	Opponent	Score	Time
1	Phi Phillies	Johnny Lush *Jim Bunning*	5/2/1906 6/20/1964	Bro Superbas *NY Mets*	Phi 6-0 *Phi 6-0*	Over 58 years
2	SD Padres	(first game) Joe Musgrove	4/8/1969 4/8/2021	N/A Tex Rangers	N/A SD 3-0	Exactly 52 years
3	NY Mets	(first game) Johan Santana	4/11/1962 6/1/2012	N/A StL Cardinals	N/A NY 8-0	Over 50 years
4	Pit Pirates	Nick Maddox Cliff Chambers	9/20/1907 5/6/1951	Bro Superbas Bos Braves	Pit 2-1 Pit 3-0	Over 43 years
5	Cle team	*Len Barker* (ongoing)	5/15/1981 TBD	*Tor Blue Jays* TBD	Cle 3-0 TBD	Over 42 years
6	Det Tigers	George Mullin Virgil Trucks	7/4/1912 5/15/1952	StL Browns Was Senators	Det 7-0 Det 1-0	Almost 40 years

FROM RANDY JOHNSON TO DALLAS BRADEN

Rank	Team	Pitcher	Date	Opponent	Score	Time
7	Chi Cubs	Jimmy Lavender Sam Jones	8/31/1915 5/12/1955	NY Giants Pit Pirates	Chi 2-0 Chi 4-0	Over 39 years
8	Chi Cubs	Milt Pappas Carlos Zambrano	9/2/1972 9/14/2008	SD Padres Hou Astros	Chi 8-0 Chi 5-0	Over 36 years
9	StL Browns	Bob Groom Bobo Holloman	5/6/1917 5/6/1953	Chi White Sox Phi Athletics	StL 3-0 StL 6-0	Exactly 36 years
10	Bos Red Sox	Dave Morehead Hideo Nomo	9/16/1965 4/4/2001	Chi White Sox Bal Orioles	Bos 1-0 Bos 3-0	Over 35 years

METHODOLOGY: The table lists the 10 longest time gaps between no-hitters for a franchise. The teams are ranked with the longest gap listed first, the next longest listed second, and so on.

LEGEND: Each row in the table displays the two games which represent the beginning and end of the no-hitter gap. Dates show when the no-hitter was thrown and are written as month/day/year (for example, June 12, 2018, is shown as 6/12/2018). The "Franchise" is the team that achieved the gap. In this table, all franchises listed remained in the same city and had the same name the entire time, with the exception of the Cleveland franchise – they changed from being the Indians to the Guardians after the 2021 season. "Opponent" is the opponent on the day of the no-hitter. The "Score" is the final score of each game. "Time Between" is the number of years between the team's last no-hitter before the streak began and the no-hitter that ended the streak. For the San Diego Padres and New York Mets, the first game listed is the first game each franchise played. For the Cleveland franchise, the team's ongoing streak has lasted for more than 42 years, so there is no end game listed. *Italicized games (Jim Bunning in 1964 and Len Barker in 1981) were perfect games.*

NOTE: In some cases, the team's home location or nickname has changed over the years. The Brooklyn Superbas changed names several times and became the Los Angeles Dodgers (1958); the Boston Braves moved to Milwaukee (1953) and are now in Atlanta (1966); the St. Louis Browns became the Baltimore Orioles (1954); the Washington Senators became the Minnesota Twins (1961); the New York Giants moved to San Francisco (1958), and the Philadelphia Athletics ("A's") moved to Kansas City (1955) and then to Oakland (1968).

In the 122 seasons from 1900-2021, there were 62 no-hit efforts that were broken up in the ninth inning with two outs, equating to roughly one every other year. In 2022 and 2023, there were three more of these close calls thrown by Miles Mikolas (Cardinals), Dylan Cease (White Sox), and Alex Cobb (Giants).

Even more astounding, there were also two games during these two seasons that were no-hitters through a full nine innings before the pitchers involved allowed a hit in extra innings. There have only been 16 potential no-hitters that were broken up in extra innings since 1900 – averaging about one every seven or eight years – so to have two more added in 2022 and 2023 is remarkable.

On April 23, 2022, the Tampa Bay Rays threw a nine-inning no-hit effort against the Red Sox that was broken up in the top of the tenth inning. In what was clearly intended to be a reliever game, J.P. Feyereisen began with two innings of hitless ball. Javy Guerra (0.2 IP), Jeffrey Springs (2.0 IP), Jason Adam (1.1 IP), Ryan Thompson (1.0 IP), and Andrew Kittredge (2.0) threw nine hitless frames in a scoreless game. In the top of the 10th, Tampa Bay's seventh pitcher, Matt Wisler, allowed a leadoff triple to Boston's Bobby Dalbec, which scored the extra-innings runner on second base. The Rays would win the game 3-2 in the bottom of the inning on a walk-off Kevin Kiermaier two-out, two-run home run.

On September 10, 2023, the Milwaukee Brewers threw 10 combined no-hit innings against the New York Yankees. Corbin Burnes threw eight full innings of no-hit ball before being relieved by Devin Williams, who shut down the Yankees in the ninth. Abner Uribe threw a hitless 10th inning as neither team scored a run. In the top of the 11th, the Brewers scored their first run and took a 1-0 lead. The Brewers' no-hitter was broken up in the bottom of the 11th, when Oswaldo Cabrera of New York rapped a double to lead off the inning against reliever Joel Payamps. Cabrera's hit scored the automatic runner on second base and tied the game. The Yankees ultimately won the game 4-3 on a Kyle Higashioka double in the bottom of the 13th inning off Milwaukee's Hoby Milner. This was the longest no-hit performance since Jim Maloney's 10-inning no-hitter in 1965. Pittsburgh's Harvey Haddix had the longest single-game no-hit streak in 1959 when he threw twelve perfect innings against the Milwaukee Braves before allowing a hit and a run in the 13th inning.

The table below shows the most recent no-hitter attempts that were broken up with two outs in the ninth inning.

Table 24-9. Recent No-Hitter Attempts Broken Up with Two Outs in Ninth Inning

Pitcher	Team	Date Score	Opponent	Broken Up By	Game Situation and Result
Alex Cobb	SF Giants	8/29/2023 SF 6-1	Cin Reds	Spencer Steer	SF Leading 6-0 Double to LF
Dylan Cease	Chicago White Sox	9/3/2022 Chi 13-0	Min Twins	Luis Arraez	Chi leading 13-0 Line drive single
Miles Mikolas	St. Louis Cardinals	6/14/2022 (2) StL 9-1	Pit Pirates	Cal Mitchell	StL leading 9-1 Ground rule 2B
Sean Newcomb	Atlanta Braves	7/29/2018 Atl 4-1	LA Dodgers	Chris Taylor	Atl leading 4-0 Groundball single
Matthew Boyd	Detroit Tigers	9/17/2017 Det 12-0	Chicago W. Sox	Tim Anderson	Det leading 12-0 Line drive double
Matt Moore	SF Giants	8/25/2016 SF 4-0	LA Dodgers	Corey Seager	SF leading 4-0 Line drive single
Carlos Carrasco	Cleveland Indians	7/1/2015 Cle 8-1	TB Rays	Joey Butler	Cle leading 8-0 Line drive single
Shelby Miller	Atlanta Braves	5/17/2015 Atl 6-0	Miami Marlins	Justin Bour	Atl leading 6-0 Groundball single
Michael Wacha	St. Louis Cardinals	9/24/2013 StL 2-0	Was Nationals	Ryan Z-man	StL leading 2-0 Groundball single
Yusmeiro Petit	*SF Giants*	*9/6/2013 SF 3-0*	*Arizona D-backs*	*Eric Chavez*	*SF leading 3-0 Line drive single*

METHODOLOGY: This table lists the 10 most recent games where a no-hitter was broken up in the ninth inning with two outs. The games are presented in chronological order with the most recent game listed first.

LEGEND: Dates are shown as month/day/year (for example, June 12, 2018, is shown as 6/12/2018). inn = innings (associated with the length of games that were more than nine innings). (1) or (2) indicates the game is the first or second game of a doubleheader. *Italicized game (Yusmeiro Petit in 2013) was a perfect game until Eric Chavez hit a single in the ninth inning with two outs.*

Another major accomplishment achieved during the 2022-2023 seasons was Houston catcher Martin Maldonado catching his third no-hitter. This placed him in a 14-way tie for third place among all catchers who played between 1900-2023. Of note, two of Maldonado's no-hitters were multi-pitcher affairs. The only other multi-pitcher no-hitter on this list is Carlos Ruiz' 2014 no-hitter for the Phillies. Cole Hamels was the starting pitcher for that game, and it was one of four no-hitters Ruiz caught, placing him tied for first with Jason Varitek.

Table 24-10. Catchers Who Have Caught the Most No-Hitters

Rank	Catcher	No	Pitcher (Team)	Date (Score)
1 (tie)	Jason Varitek	4	Hideo Nomo (Bos Red Sox) Derek Lowe (Bos Red Sox) Clay Bucholz (Bos Red Sox) Jon Lester (Bos Red Sox)	4/4/2001 (Bos 3, Bal 0) 4/27/2002 (Bos 10, TB 0) 9/1/2007 (Bos 10, Bal 0) 5/19/2008 (Bos 7, KC 0)
1 (tie)	Carlos Ruiz	4	*Roy Halladay (Phi Phillies)* Roy Halladay (Phi Phillies) Cole Hamels +3 (Phi Phillies) Cole Hamels (Phi Phillies)	*5/29/2010 (Phi 1, Fla 0)* 10/6/2010 (Phi 4, Cin 0) 9/1/2014 (Phi 1, Atl 0) 7/25/2015 (Phi 5, Chi 0)
3 (tie)	Bill Carrigan	3	Smoky Joe Wood (Bos R. Sox) Rube Foster (Bos Red Sox) Dutch Leonard (Bos Red Sox)	7/29/1911 (Bos 5, StL 0) 6/21/1916 (Bos 2, NY 0) 8/30/1916 (Bos 4, StL 0)
3 (tie)	Ray Schalk	3	Joe Benz (Chi White Sox) Eddie Cicotte (Chi White Sox) *Charlie Robertson (Chi W. Sox)*	5/31/1914 (Chi 6, Cle 1) 4/14/1917 (Chi 11, StL 0) *4/30/1922 (Chi 2, Det 0)*
3 (tie)	Val Picinich	3	Bullet Joe Bush (Phi Athletics) Walter Johnson (Was Senators) Howard Ehmke (Bos Red Sox)	8/26/1916 (Phi 5, Cle 0) 7/1/1920 (Was 1, Bos 0) 9/7/1923 (Bos 4, Phi 0)
3 (tie)	Luke Sewell	3	Wes Ferrell (Cle Indians) Vern Kennedy (Chi W. Sox) Bill Dietrich (Chi White Sox)	4/29/1931 (Cle 9, StL 0) 8/31/1935 (Chi 5, Cle 0) 6/1/1937 (Chi 8, StL 0)
3 (tie)	Jim Hegan	3	Don Black (Cle Indians) Bob Lemon (Cle Indians) Bob Feller (Cle Indians)	7/10/1947 (Cle 3, Phi 0) 6/30/1948 (Cle 2, Det 0) 7/1/1951 (Cle 2, Det 1)
3 (tie)	Roy Campanella	3	Carl Erskine (Bro Dodgers) Carl Erskine (Bro Dodgers) Sal Maglie (Bro Dodgers)	6/19/1952 (Bro 5, Chi 0) 5/12/1956 (Bro 3, NY 0) 9/25/1956 (Bro 5, Phi 0)

Rank	Catcher	No	Pitcher (Team)	Date (Score)
3 (tie)	Yogi Berra	3	Allie Reynolds (NY Yankees) Allie Reynolds (NY Yankees) *Don Larsen (NY Yankees)*	7/12/1951 (NY 1, Cle 0) 9/28/1951 (NY 8, Bos 0) *10/8/1956 (NY 2, Bro 0)*
3 (tie)	Del Crandall	3	Jim Wilson (Mil Braves) Lew Burdette (Mil Braves) Warren Spahn (Mil Braves)	6/12/1954 (Mil 2, Phi 0) 8/18/1960 (Mil 1, Phi 0) 9/16/1960 (Mil 4, Phi 0)
3 (tie)	Jeff Torborg	3	*Sandy Koufax (LA Dodgers)* Bill Singer (LA Dodgers) Nolan Ryan (Cal Angels)	*9/9/1965 (LA 1, Chi 0)* 7/20/1970 (LA 5, Phi 0) 5/15/1973 (Cal 3, KC 0)
3 (tie)	Alan Ashby	3	Ken Forsch (Hou Astros) Nolan Ryan (Hou Astros) Mike Scott (Hou Astros)	4/7/1979 (Hou 6, Atl 0) 9/26/1981 (Hou 5, LA 0) 9/25/1986 (Hou 2, SF 0)
3 (tie)	Charles Johnson	3	Al Leiter (Fla Marlins) Kevin Brown (Fla Marlins) A.J. Burnett (Fla Marlins)	5/11/1996 (Fla 11, Col 0) 6/10/1997 (Fla 9, SF 0) 5/12/2001 (Fla 3, SD 0)
3 (tie)	Buster Posey	3	*Matt Cain (SF Giants)* Tim Lincecum (SF Giants) Chris Heston (SF Giants)	*6/13/2012 (SF 10, Hou 0)* 7/13/2013 (SF 9, SD 0) 6/9/2015 (SF 5, NY 0)
3 (tie)	Wilson Ramos	3	J. Zimmermann (Was Nat'ls) Max Scherzer (Was Nationals) Max Scherzer (Was Nationals)	9/28/2014 (Was 1, Mia 0) 6/20/2015 (Was 6, Pit 0) 10/302015 (Was 2, NY 0)
3 (tie)	Martin Maldonado	3	A. Sanchez +3 (Hou Astros) Cristian Javier +2 (Hou Astros) Framber Valdez (Hou Astros)	8/3/2019 (Hou 9, Sea 0) 6/25/2022 (Hou 3, NY 0) 8/1/2023 (Hou 2, Cle 0)

METHODOLOGY: This table is a rank order listing of the catchers who have caught the most no-hitters from 1900-2023. In the case of a tie, the catchers are listed in chronological order of the game they caught their third no-hitter.

LEGEND: Dates are shown as month/day/year (for example, June 12, 2018, is shown as 6/12/2018). "Nbr" = the number of no-hitters the catcher caught. For multi-pitcher no-hitters, the pitcher listed is the starting pitcher, with a +2 or +3 added to indicate how many additional pitchers participated in the no-hitter. Where the score of the no-hitter is listed, three or two letter abbreviations for the teams are used. Because none of the no-hitters listed in this table were interleague games (with the exception of Don Larsen's perfect game against the Brooklyn Dodgers in the 1956 World Series), a team's abbreviation is aligned with the American or

National League team that threw the no-hitter. For example, "NY" in an American League game is the Yankees, and "NY" in a National League game is the Giants (1900-1957) or Mets (1962-2023). *Perfect games are italicized.*

Without a doubt, the 2022 and 2023 seasons provided a great deal of excitement, especially as it relates to no-hitters. This book, published during the 2024 season, would not be complete without this updated chapter describing only a fraction of these extraordinary accomplishments. Just as surely, future seasons will hold more excitement as baseball evolves, records are broken, and more pitchers etch their names into the books as they throw their own no-hitters.

Chapter 25

Best Games and Best Pitchers

This chapter includes the highest Game Scores from 1900-2021 for each of the teams that are not already incorporated in previous chapters. Specifically, this includes the Braves, Browns and Orioles, Cubs, Indians, Rays, Red Sox, Rockies, and Royals. For comparison purposes, each franchise's no-hitters are included in that team's "Highest Game Scores" table (for expansion teams) or "Highest Game Scores of 10 innings or less" (for original, pre-expansion teams). This chapter also includes the best pitchers of each decade from 1900 to 1949. The 1950s, 1960s, and other decades up through the 2010s are included as part of other chapters.

Table 25-1. Highest Braves Game Scores

Rank	Pitcher (Team)	Date Score	Opponent	GSc	IP, Hits, Runs, ERs, Walks, Strikeouts
1	Joe Oeschger (Bos Braves)	5/1/1920 1-1 Tie (26 inn)	Bro Robins	153	26.0 IP, 9 Hits, 1 Run, 1 ER, 4 BBs, 7 Ks
2	Art Nehf (Bos Braves)	8/1/1918 Pit 2-0 (21 inn)	Pit Pirates	118	21.0 IP, 12 Hits, 2 Runs, 2 ERs, 5 BBs, 8 Ks
3	Vive Lindaman (Bos Doves)	6/4/1908 1-1 Tie (17 inn)	Chi Cubs	116-118	17.0 IP, 5 Hits, 1 Run, ? ERs, 1 BB, 4 Ks
4	Dale Fillingim (Bos Braves)	5/3/1920 Bos 2-1 (19 inn)	Bro Robins	111	19.0 IP, 12 Hits, 1 Run, 0 ERs, 4 BBs, 4 Ks
5	Bill Dinneen (Bos Nationals)	9/21/1901 Chi 1-0 (17 inn)	Chi Orphans	109	16.1 IP, 8 Hits, 1 Run, 1 ER, 1 BB, 7 Ks
6	Jim Turner (Bos Bees)	5/18/1938 Bos 2-1 (14 inn)	Cin Reds	105	14.0 IP, 5 Hits, 1 Run, 1 ER, 1 BB, 8 Ks
7 (tie)	Art Nehf (Bos Braves)	9/22/1917 0-0 Tie (14 inn)	StL Cards	104	14.0 IP, 7 Hits, 0 Runs, 0 ERs, 2 BBs, 8 Ks

Rank	Pitcher (Team)	Date Score	Oppo-nent	GSc	IP, Hits, Runs, ERs, Walks, Strikeouts
7 (tie)	W. Blasingame (Mil Braves)	5/5/1965 Mil 2-1 (14 inn)	Hou Astros	104	14.0 IP, 5 Hits, 1 Run, 1 ER, 6 BBs, 12 Ks
9	Warren Spahn (Bos Braves)	9/6/1948 (1) Bos 2-1 (14 inn)	Bro Dodgers	102	14.0 IP, 5 Hits, 1 Runs, 1 ERs, 4 BBs, 8 Ks
10	Warren Spahn (Bos Braves)	6/14/1952 Chi 3-1 (15 inn)	Chi Cubs	101	15.0 IP, 10 Hits, 3 Runs, 3 ERs, 2 BBs, 18 Ks
11	Warren Spahn (Mil Braves)	9/16/1960 Mil 4-0	Phi Phillies	100	9.0 IP, 0 Hits, 0 Run, 0 ER, 2 BBs, 15 Ks

METHODOLOGY: This table includes the highest Game Scores thrown by a Braves pitcher from 1900-2021. Games are ranked by Game Score (GSc) and consider all franchise regular season and postseason games. This table includes all games that achieved a Game Score of 100 or more. Table 25-2 below limits the eligible games to those pitching performances that were 10 innings or less. Game Score measures a pitcher's performance in any given game started. Introduced by baseball writer/statistician Bill James in the 1980s, Game Score is presented as a figure between 0-100 — except for extreme outliers — and usually falls between 40-70.

LEGEND: Dates are shown as month/day/year (for example, June 12, 2018, is shown as 6/12/2018); GSc = Game Score. IP = innings pitched. BB(s) = base(s) on balls. K(s) = strikeout(s). ER(s) = earned run(s). inn = innings (associated with the length of games that were more or less than nine innings). One-third of an inning pitched has 0.1 added and two-thirds of an inning pitched has 0.2 added (for example, 9 1/3 innings pitched is displayed as 9.1). BB(s) = base(s) on balls; K(s) = strikeout(s). (1) or (2) indicates the game is the first or second game of a doubleheader. The Braves were based in Boston when they started in the National League in 1876. They began as the Boston Reds in 1876 – ironically, the same nickname as the team from Cincinnati – before dropping any nickname and just being known as "Boston" from 1877-1900. The team became the Nationals in 1901 when the American League began with a Boston franchise of their own. They were known as the Doves from 1907-1910, and in 1911, the team again played with no nickname. They became the Braves in 1912 and stayed that way until 1936, when they changed to the Bees. They settled on the Braves for good in 1941 and kept that nickname when they moved to Milwaukee (1953) and Atlanta (1966). The team's home city and name for each of the games in the table is indicated in the (Team) entry underneath the pitcher's name. Opponent names are shown as they were when the games were played. For example, Chicago's National League team was known as the Orphans when Boston's Bill Dinneen threw against them in 1901. Chicago's team became the Cubs in 1903. The Brooklyn team that became the Dodgers was known as the Robins from 1916-31. The team was renamed the Dodgers in 1932 and continued to play in Brooklyn until they moved to Los Angeles in 1958.

NOTE 1: The highest postseason Game Score thrown by a franchise pitcher was an 89 by Kevin Millwood in Game 2 of the 1999 National League Divisional Series against the Astros. The Astros had several great players in the lineup that day, including Hall of Famers Craig Biggio and Jeff Bagwell, along with third baseman Ken Caminiti. The powerful 1999 Atlanta team featured sluggers like Hall of Famer Chipper Jones, Ryan Klesko, and Andruw Jones. Milwood allowed only one home run to Caminiti that day for a critical win that tied the series at one game each with Houston. Atlanta would go on to beat Houston three games to one en route to winning the National League pennant. Atlanta would get swept by the Yankees in the World Series.

NOTE 2: Joe Oeschger's 153 Game Score is the highest in Major League history. At 26 innings, he is tied with his opponent that day (Brooklyn's Leon Cadore) for the most innings ever thrown in a single game. Even though it only took three hours and 50 minutes, this 26-inning marathon is the longest game – in terms of innings played – in Major League history. Oeschger is also the only pitcher to throw two games of 20 innings or more – he pitched 20 innings for the Phillies in a tie game against Brooklyn in 1919. In 1919, while with the Braves, Oeschger was roommates with former Olympic great Jim Thorpe. When Oeschger was asked about Thorpe, he said something to the effect that Thorpe had a hard time hitting the curve, but he was also very fast and beat out a lot of infield grounders.

NOTE 3: The legendary Hall of Famer Warren Spahn, easily the best Braves' pitcher of his era, is featured three times in this table – more than anyone else. Winner of 363 games, named to 17 All-Star teams, and recipient of the Cy Young Award, Spahn was a workhorse. Spahn's no-hitter in 1960 against the Phillies is likely the best game ever pitched by a Brave, as he struck out 15 while achieving a Game Score of 100 in a nine-inning game. Spahn also holds the Braves' record for most strikeouts in a game with 18. He achieved that in his 15-inning effort against the Cubs in 1952. It is highly likely that Warren Spahn would have achieved more than he did, as his career was interrupted because he was drafted into the Army after his first Major League season in 1942. He served with distinction in Europe and was awarded a Purple Heart for his wounds and a Bronze Star for heroism. The most decorated ballplayer who served in World War II, Spahn saw action in the Battle of the Bulge and at the Ludendorff Bridge as a combat engineer and was awarded a battlefield commission. The three games listed in this table are among Spahn's most notable performances, although, his nine-inning no-hitter against the Phillies may be his very best.

NOTE 4: With two games, Art Nehf is the only other player listed more than once on this table. Nehf holds second place for the highest Game Score by a franchise pitcher due to his extraordinary 21-inning, two-run effort against the Pirates in 1920. Nehf lost that game 2-0, as he allowed two runs in the top of the 21st inning after having thrown 20 innings of shutout ball. Nehf's other game was a stellar 14-inning shutout that ended as a 0-0 tie with the Cardinals. Nehf is probably best known for being a star with the two-time World Champion and four-time National League pennant winner New York Giants from 1921-1924.

NOTE 5: In 1965, Wade Blasingame threw his extraordinary 14-inning, one-run performance against the newly christened Houston Astros in front of just 1,391 fans at cavernous County Stadium in Milwaukee. Fans were angry with their beloved Braves as ownership had already announced the team would be moving to Atlanta in 1966, so they stayed away in droves. A promising 21-year-old, Blasingame held Houston to just one run on five hits, as he struck out 12. Hall of Famer Eddie Mathews knocked in the winning run with a walk-off double in the bottom of the 14th. Unfortunately, Blasingame's star would fade due to lack of control after his 16-win rookie season in 1965. He would continue to pitch for another six seasons, mostly in relief.

NOTE 6: In the 1938 game listed above, Jim Turner pitched 14 innings as Boston beat Cincinnati 2-1. His rookie season was in 1937, at age 33. He was a pitching coach with the Yankees from 1949-1959, with Cincinnati from 1961-1965, and back with the Yankees again from 1966-1973. Turner's nickname was "Milkman" because that was his off-season job. When I did my interview with Jim Maloney, I asked him which coach helped him the most in his climb to the big leagues. He said it was Jim Turner.

NOTE 7: For almost 20 years, Bill Dinneen held the record for the best game pitched for the Boston franchise with his 16+ inning one-run effort against Chicago. He was a solid pitcher in a long career with the Nationals (Braves), Browns, Red Sox, and Senators, accumulating a won-loss record of 170-177. He retired in 1909 and immediately became an umpire, a job that lasted for 28 years. With the fourth-best Game Score in the table, Dana Fillingim threw his 19-inning game two days after Oeschger pitched 26 innings against Brooklyn.

NOTE 8: Vive (rhymes with "Ivy") Lindaman threw a remarkable 17 inning game in 1908, allowing only five hits, one walk, and one run en route to a 1-1 tie against Jack Pfiester of the Cubs. It is uncertain whether the game ended because of darkness or weather, but because the statistic of "earned run" wasn't invented yet, his game isn't officially given a Game Score because it cannot be determined whether the run was earned (-4 points) or unearned (-2 points). That said, the only run Lindaman allowed was a home run to Cubs left fielder Del Howard in the top of the seventh inning. This almost certainly means the run would have been considered earned, which would have given Lindaman a Game Score of 116, putting him in third place on this list.

Table 25-2. Highest Braves Game Scores of 10 innings or less

Rank	Pitcher (Team)	Date Score	Opponent	GSc	IP, Hits, Runs, ERs, Walks, Strikeouts
1	Warren Spahn (Mil Braves)	9/16/1960 Mil 4-0	Philadelphia Phillies	100	9.0 IP, 0 Hits, 0 Runs, 0 ERs, 2 BBs, 15 Ks
2	K. Millwood (Atl Braves)	4/14/1998 Atl 6-0	Pittsburgh Pirates	98	9.0 IP, 1 Hit, 0 Runs, 0 ERs, 0 BBs, 13 Ks
3 (tie)	K. Millwood (Atl Braves)	8/28/1999 Atl 3-0 (13 inn)	St. Louis Cardinals	96	10.0 IP, 2 Hits, 0 Runs, 0 ERs, 1 BB, 9 Ks
3 (tie)	Greg Maddux (Atl Braves)	5/2/2001 Atl 1-0	Milwaukee Brewers	96	9.0 IP, 2 Hits, 0 Runs, 0 ERs, 1 BB, 14 Ks
5 (tie)	Warren Spahn (Mil Braves)	8/1/1953 Mil 5-0	Philadelphia Phillies	93	9.0 IP, 1 Hit, 0 Runs, 0 ERs, 0 BBs, 8 Ks
5 (tie)	Kent Mercker (Atl Braves)	4/8/1994 Atl 6-0	Los Angeles Dodgers	93	9.0 IP, 0 Hits, 0 Runs, 0 ERs, 4 BBs, 10 Ks
5 (tie)	John Smoltz (Atl Braves)	9/6/1998 Atl 4-0	New York Mets	93	9.0 IP, 3 Hits, 0 Runs, 0 ERs, 0 BBs, 12 Ks
5 (tie)	M. Foltynewicz (Atl Braves)	6/1/2018 Atl 4-0	Washington Nationals	93	9.0 IP, 2 Hits, 0 Runs, 0 ERs, 1 BB, 11 Ks
9 (tie)	Tom Hughes (Bos Braves)	6/16/1916 Bos 2-0	Pittsburgh Pirates	92	9.0 IP, 0 Hits, 0 Runs, 0 ERs, 2 BBs, 7 Ks

Rank	Pitcher (Team)	Date Score	Opponent	GSc	IP, Hits, Runs, ERs, Walks, Strikeouts
9 (tie)	Juan Pizarro (Mil Braves)	7/3/1959 Mil 6-0	Pittsburgh Pirates	92	9.0 IP, 2 Hits, 0 Runs, 0 ERs, 2 BBs, 11 Ks
9 (tie)	Greg Maddux (Atl Braves)	4/24/1994 Atl 3-0	Pittsburgh Pirates	92	9.0 IP, 3 Hits, 0 Runs, 0 ERs, 0 BBs, 11 Ks
9 (tie)	Greg Maddux (Atl Braves)	8/20/1995 Atl 1-0	St. Louis Cardinals	92	9.0 IP, 2 Hits, 0 Runs, 0 ERs, 0 BBs, 9 Ks
9 (tie)	John Smoltz (Atl Braves)	4/14/1996 Atl 4-0	San Diego Padres	92	8.0 IP, 1 Hit, 0 Runs, 0 ERs, 1 BB, 13 Ks
9 (tie)	Jair Jurrjens (Atl Braves)	7/1/2011 Atl 4-0	Baltimore Orioles	92	9.0 IP, 1 Hit, 0 Runs, 0 ERs, 1 BB, 8 Ks
9 (tie)	Julio Teheran (Atl Braves)	6/9/2016 Atl 6-0	New York Mets	92	9.0 IP, 1 Hit, 0 Runs, 0 ERs, 0 BBs, 7 Ks
16 (tie)	Jim Tobin (Bos Braves)	4/27/1944 Bos 2-0	Brooklyn Dodgers	91	9.0 IP, 0 Hits, 0 Runs, 0 ERs, 2 BBs, 6 Ks
16 (tie)	Jim Wilson (Mil Braves)	6/12/1954 Mil 2-0	Philadelphia Phillies	91	9.0 IP, 0 Hits, 0 Runs, 0 ERs, 2 BBs, 6 Ks
30 (tie)	Lew Burdette (Mil Braves)	8/18/1960 Mil 1-0	Philadelphia Phillies	90	9.0 IP, 0 Hits, 0 Runs, 0 ERs, 0 BB, 3 Ks
30 (tie)	Warren Spahn (Mil Braves)	4/28/1961 Mil 1-0	SF Giants	90	9.0 IP, 0 Hits, 0 Runs, 0 ERs, 2 BB, 5 Ks
44 (tie)	Big Jeff Pfeffer (Bos Doves)	5/8/1907 Bos 6-0	Cincinnati Reds	89	9.0 IP, 0 Hits, 0 Runs, 0 ERs, 1 BB, 3 Ks
60 (tie)	Phil Niekro (Atl Braves)	8/5/1973 Atl 9-0	San Diego Padres	88	9.0 IP, 0 Hits, 0 Runs, 0 ERs, 3 BB, 4 Ks
116 (tie)	Vern Bickford (Bos Braves)	8/11/1950 Bos 7-0	Brooklyn Dodgers	86	9.0 IP, 0 Hits, 1 Run, 0 ERs, 4 BB, 3 Ks
116 (tie)	George Davis (Bos Braves)	9/9/1914 (2) Bos 7-0	Philadelphia Phillies	86	9.0 IP, 0 Hits, 0 Runs, 0 ERs, 5 BBs, 4 Ks
---	Jim Tobin (Bos Braves)	6/22/1944 (2) Bos 7-0 (5 inn)	Philadelphia Phillies	66	5.0 IP, 0 Hits, 0 Runs, 0 ERs, 2 BBs, 1 K

METHODOLOGY: This table includes the highest Game Scores of 10 innings or less thrown by a Braves pitcher from 1900-2021. Games are ranked by Game Score (GSc) and consider all franchise regular season and postseason games. For comparison purposes, all eleven post-1900 Boston no-hitters are included in this table. Table 25-2 below limits the eligible games to those pitching performances that were 10 innings or less. Games are ranked by pitcher Game Score in descending order. Game Score measures a pitcher's performance in any given game started. Introduced by baseball writer/statistician Bill James in the 1980s, Game Score is presented as a figure between 0-100 — except for extreme outliers — and usually falls between 40-70.

LEGEND: Dates are shown as month/day/year (for example, June 12, 2018, is shown as 6/12/2018); IP = innings pitched. BB(s) = base(s) on balls. K(s) = strikeout(s). ER(s) = earned run(s). inn = innings (associated with the length of games that were more or less than nine innings). One-third of an inning pitched has 0.1 added and two-thirds of an inning pitched has 0.2 added (for example, 9 1/3 innings pitched is displayed as 9.1). BB(s) = base(s) on balls; K(s) = strikeout(s). (1) or (2) indicates the game is the first or second game of a doubleheader. The Braves were based in Boston when they started in the National League in 1876. They started as the Boston Reds in 1876 – ironically, the same nickname as the team from Cincinnati – before dropping any nickname and just being known as "Boston" from 1877-1900. The team became the Nationals in 1901 when the American League began with a Boston franchise of their own. They were known as the Doves from 1907-1910, and in 1911, the team again played with no nickname. They became the Braves in 1912 and stayed that way until 1936, when they changed to the Bees. They settled on the Braves for good in 1941 and kept that nickname when they moved to Milwaukee (1953) and Atlanta (1966). The team's home city and name for each of the games in the table is indicated in the "Team" entry underneath the pitcher's name. The Dodgers played in Brooklyn until they moved to Los Angeles in 1958.

NOTE 1: Four Hall of Famers are listed in this table: Warren Spahn (three times), Greg Maddux (three times), John Smoltz (twice), and Phil Niekro (once). Warren Spahn was discussed in the notes associated with the franchise all-time highest Game Scores (no innings limitations). While many of his accomplishments came earlier in his career with the Cubs, Greg Maddux has to be regarded as the best Braves pitcher of his era. The three shutouts of his listed in the Top 10 table speak to his extraordinary control as a pitcher. Maddux struck out 34 batters combined during those three games while walking a single hitter. During his 11 seasons with the Braves from 1993-2003, he struck out 1,828 hitters while walking only 383 for a phenomenal ratio of 4.7 to 1. While Maddux never threw a no-hitter, he was a perennial All-Star and three-time Cy Young Award winner with the Braves. Most importantly, Atlanta won the National League East Division every year he was on the team.

NOTE 2: Kevin Millwood deserves special mention, as he is behind only Warren Spahn for highest Game Score in a game of 10 innings or less. His one-hitter in 1998, a 13-strikeout shutout against Pittsburgh, is the second highest franchise GSc for a nine-inning game. The only hit he allowed was a one-out double to Jermaine Allensworth in the fifth inning. While not throwing a no-hitter for the Braves, Millwood has one to his credit while pitching for the Phillies in 2003. He also was the starting pitcher who threw six innings in a 2012 multi-pitcher no-hitter as a member of the Seattle Mariners.

NOTE 3: John Smoltz was also a key member of the extraordinary Atlanta teams of the 1990s and early 2000s. Racking up 13 strikeouts while allowing no walks, the three hits he allowed in his 1998 shutout against the Mets were scattered singles. No New York runner ever made it past first base. Smoltz also earned his way onto this table by throwing eight innings of 13-strikeout, one-hit ball against the Padres in 1996. He was pulled ahead of the ninth inning, as he had thrown 129 pitches by that point. The only hit he allowed was a one-out double by Hall of Famer Tony Gwynn in the seventh inning.

NOTE 4: Knuckleball Hall of Famer Phil Niekro was a stalwart in the Braves' rotation from 1967-1983, routinely leading the league in innings, as he often reached more than 300. A four-time All-Star with Atlanta, Niekro pitched well into his late-40s. His 1973 no-hitter versus the Padres was not the highest Game Score he ever achieved; however, it can be argued it was the best game he ever pitched. Niekro threw two one-hitters and 17 two-hitters during his career, so he came close to a no-hitter on multiple occasions. His game against San Diego, though, was the only time he went the distance for a no-hitter.

NOTE 5: Lew Burdette's 1960 no-hitter versus Philadelphia was the first of two the Milwaukee Braves threw against the last-place Phillies that season. Warren Spahn would throw the second one against the 95-loss team less than one month later. In Burdette's game, he faced the minimum 27 batters. The only baserunner he allowed was when he hit Tony Gonzalez with one out in the fifth inning. The next batter, Lee Walls, grounded into a double play. Jair Jurrjens' 2011 no-hit attempt versus the Orioles was broken up with one out in the seventh inning when Adam Jones hit a groundball single up the middle. Julio Tehran faced only 28 batters in his

2016 one-hitter against the Mets. A line-drive single by Michael Conforto leading off the third inning was the only time a Met reached base.

NOTE 6: Boston knuckleballer Jim Tobin is also listed in this table twice. The first time is for his excellent 1944 no-hitter against the Dodgers, in which he struck out six and walked only two batters in a 2-0 win. The second time was for a no-hit shutout of the Phillies less than two months later. That game – the second game of a doubleheader – lasted only five innings and was called due to darkness with the Braves leading 7-0. Because the game went the minimum five innings, it was considered official, yet Tobin does not get credit for a no-hitter because he didn't go at least nine full innings.

Table 25-3. Highest Browns and Orioles Game Scores

Rank	Pitcher (Team)	Date Score	Opponent	GSc	IP, Hits, Runs, ERs, Walks, Strikeouts
1	Jerry Walker (Bal Orioles)	9/11/1959 (2) Bal 1-0 (16 inn)	Chi White Sox	111	16.0 IP, 6 Hits, 0 Runs, 0 ERs, 3 BBs, 4 Ks
2	Jack Powell (StL Browns)	8/14/1903 (1) Was 1-0 (15 inn)	Was Senators	110	15.0 IP, 6 Hits, 1 Run, 1 ER, 1 BB, 10 Ks
3	Bob Turley (StL Browns)	9/5/1953 StL 1-0 (12 inn)	Det Tigers	106	12.0 IP, 6 Hits, 1 Run, 1 ER, 4 BBs, 14 Ks
4	G. Baumgardner (StL Browns)	4/20/1912 0-0 Tie (15 inn)	Chi White Sox	101	15.0 IP, 9 Hits, 0 Runs, 0 ER, 8 BB, 10 Ks
5 (tie)	Mike Flanagan (Bal Orioles)	8/15/1979 Bal 2-1 (12 inn)	Chi White Sox	99	12.0 IP, 5 Hits, 1 Run, 1 ER, 1 BB, 12 Ks
5 (tie)	Harry Howell (StL Browns)	4/23/1905 Bal 1-0 (11 inn)	Cle Napoleons	99	11.0 IP, 4 Hits, 0 Runs, 0 ERs, 0 BBs, 10 Ks
5 (tie)	Ernie Koob (StL Browns)	7/14/1916 0-0 Tie (17 inn)	Bos Red Sox	99	17.0 IP, 14 Hits, 0 Runs, 0 ERs, 3 BBs, 3 Ks
5 (tie)	John Means (Bal Orioles)	5/5/2021 Bal 6-0	Sea Mariners	99	9.0 IP, 0 Hits, 0 Runs, 0 ERs, 0 BBs, 12 Ks
9 (tie)	Mike Mussina (Bal Orioles)	8/1/2000 Bal 10-0	Min Twins	98	9.0 IP, 1 Hit, 0 Runs, 0 ERs, 2 BBs, 15 Ks
9 (tie)	Erik Bedard (Bal Orioles)	7/7/2007 Bal 3-0	Tex Rangers	98	9.0 IP, 2 Hits, 0 Runs, 0 ERs, 0 BBs, 15 Ks

METHODOLOGY: This table includes the highest Game Scores thrown by a Browns or Orioles pitcher from 1901-2021. Games are ranked by Game Score (GSc) and consider all franchise regular season and postseason games. Table 25-4 below limits the eligible games to those pitching performances that were 10 innings or less. Game Score (GSc) measures a pitcher's performance in any given game started. Introduced by baseball writer/statistician Bill James in the 1980s, Game Score is presented as a figure between 0-100 — except for extreme outliers — and usually falls between 40-70.

LEGEND: Dates are shown as month/day/year (for example, June 12, 2018, is shown as 6/12/2018); GSc = Game Score. IP = innings pitched. BB(s) = base(s) on balls. K(s) = strikeout(s). ER(s) = earned run(s). inn = innings (associated with the length of games that were more or less than nine innings). One-third of an inning pitched has 0.1 added and two-thirds of an inning pitched has 0.2 added (for example, 9 1/3 innings pitched is displayed as 9.1). BB(s) = base(s) on balls; K(s) = strikeout(s). (1) or (2) indicates the game is the first or second game of a doubleheader. The St. Louis/Baltimore franchise was based in Milwaukee and known as the Brewers when they joined the brand-new American League in 1901. The team moved to St. Louis and took the name Browns the next season (1902). They remained the St. Louis Browns through 1953, then moved to Baltimore and became the Orioles in 1954. The team's home city and name (StL Browns or Bal Orioles) for each of the games in the table is indicated in the (Team) entry underneath the pitcher's name. For comparison purposes, all franchise no-hitters are included in this table.

NOTE 1: The highest postseason Game Score thrown by a franchise pitcher was a 97 by Dave McNally in Game 2 of the 1969 ALCS against a powerful Minnesota lineup that featured Hall of Famers Harmon Killebrew, Tony Oliva, and Rod Carew. McNally threw 11 innings of three-hit, shutout ball en route to a 1-0 win. Pinch-hitter Curt Motton hit a line drive, two-out single in the bottom of the 11th to break a scoreless tie that gave the Orioles a win. This put Baltimore ahead by two games in the series, needing just one win for the ALCS victory. Baltimore would go on to sweep the Twins in three games to win the AL pennant. The underdog New York Mets beat the heavily favored Orioles in five games in the World Series.

NOTE 2: The highest Game Score in the 121-year history of this franchise was 111, achieved in a 16-inning shutout thrown by Baltimore's Jerry Walker against the White Sox in 1959. That season's Chicago team was impressive. Affectionately known as the "Go-Go Sox," Chicago managed to dethrone the reigning four-time American

League Champion New York Yankees to win the pennant. With a combination of exceptional pitching, speed, and timely hitting, the Sox featured a pair of Hall of Famers in their lineup (Nellie Fox and Luis Aparicio), along with perennial All-Star slugger Ted Kluszewski and hot-hitting rookie catcher Johnny Romano. Against this formidable team, 20-year-old Walker shut down Chicago for 178 pitches, allowing only six singles and three walks. The game was scoreless until the bottom of the 16th, when Hall of Famer Brooks Robinson hit a two-out, walk-off single, scoring Al Pilarcik from third. Baltimore won both games of the doubleheader that day – Jerry Walker had started the second game – as the Orioles held the White Sox scoreless on nine hits over 25 innings. For the record, Walker's 16 innings is not the longest pitching performance in franchise history. That distinction belongs to Dixie Davis, who went 19 innings for St. Louis in an 8-6, complete-game win over Washington in August 1921. After a rocky start, Davis threw nine no-hit shutout innings for the victory.

NOTE 3: Jack Powell was the losing pitcher in a 15-inning, 1-0 defeat at the hands of the Senators in 1903. Washington first baseman William Clarke hit a single in the top of the 15th to knock in right fielder Rabbit Robinson from second base for the only run of the game. Powell pitched a magnificent game, allowing just six hits – all but one singles – while striking out 10 and walking only one batter. Jack Powell also has the distinction of being a member of what is typically seen as the worst team to ever play Major League baseball: the late-nineteenth century Cleveland Spiders of the National League. Powell escaped the worst of it, though. He was traded before the 1899 season as Cleveland finished that year at an all-time worst record of 20-134, 84 games out of first place and 35 games behind the 11th place Washington team.

NOTE 4: Rube Waddell's 10-inning, 17-strikeout gem in 1908 against the Senators is arguably one of the best games ever thrown by a franchise pitcher. To begin with, it's the shortest outing of any game in the top five franchise Game Scores. Along with that, his 17 strikeouts are the most ever achieved by a franchise pitcher in a single game. Waddell also has the second most strikeouts (16), accomplished in a game against the Philadelphia Athletics two months before he struck out 17 Senators – he established the American League record both times. Hall of Famer Rube Waddell is primarily known for two reasons: his exceptional pitching and his eccentric behavior. Waddell played for the Browns at the end of his career, and he was still an excellent pitcher. Before that, though, he was part of a dominant pitching duo with fellow Hall of Famer Eddie Plank, playing for the Philadelphia Athletics. Waddell was especially adept at racking up strikeouts, leading the American League for six years straight from 1902-1907. Waddell has also had books written about him for his off-the-field antics, sometimes resulting in him being unceremoniously fired from teams despite his extraordinary talent. Sadly, he died at the age of 37 from tuberculosis.

NOTE 5: 22-year-old Bob Turley's impressive 12-inning win against the Tigers in 1953 came during his only stint with the Browns (except for an unremarkable end-of-season start two years earlier). A late-season call-up, Turley later became a star with the New York Yankees, earning the 1958 Cy Young Award for the World Champions, along with being named as the 1958 World Series MVP in their seven-game win over the Milwaukee Braves.

Table 25-4. Highest Browns and Orioles Game Scores of 10 innings or less

Rank	Pitcher (Team)	Date Score	Opponent	GSc	IP, Hits, Runs, ERs, Walks, Strikeouts
1	John Means (Bal Orioles)	5/5/2021 Bal 6-0	Sea Mariners	99	9.0 IP, 0 Hits, 0 Runs, 0 ERs, 0 BBs, 12 Ks
2 (tie)	Mike Mussina (Bal Orioles)	8/1/2000 Bal 10-0	Min Twins	98	9.0 IP, 1 Hit, 0 Runs, 0 ERs, 2 BBs, 15 Ks
2 (tie)	Erik Bedard (Bal Orioles)	7/7/2007 Bal 3-0	Tex Rangers	98	9.0 IP, 2 Hits, 0 Runs, 0 ERs, 0 BBs, 15 Ks
4 (tie)	Mike Mussina (Bal Orioles)	5/30/1997 Bal 3-0	Cle Indians	95	9.0 IP, 1 Hit, 0 Runs, 0 ERs, 0 BBs, 10 Ks
4 (tie)	Dylan Bundy (Bal Orioles)	8/29/2017 Bal 4-0	Sea Mariners	95	9.0 IP, 1 Hit, 0 Runs, 0 ERs, 2 BBs, 12 Ks
6 (tie)	Milt Pappas (Bal Orioles)	9/2/1964 Bal 2-0	Min Twins	94	9.0 IP, 1 Hit, 0 Runs, 0 ERs, 1 BB, 10 Ks
6 (tie)	Mike Mussina (Bal Orioles)	7/17/1992 Bal 8-0	Tex Rangers	94	9.0 IP, 1 Hit, 0 Runs, 0 ERs, 1 BB, 10 Ks
8 (tie)	Hoyt Wilhelm (Bal Orioles)	9/20/1958 Bal 1-0	NY Yankees	93	9.0 IP, 0 Hits, 0 Runs, 0 ERs, 2 BBs, 8 Ks
8 (tie)	Tom Phoebus (Bal Orioles)	4/27/1968 Bal 6-0	Bos Red Sox	93	9.0 IP, 0 Hits, 0 Runs, 0 ERs, 3 BBs, 9 Ks

From Randy Johnson to Dallas Braden

Rank	Pitcher (Team)	Date Score	Opponent	GSc	IP, Hits, Runs, ERs, Walks, Strikeouts
10 (tie)	Rube Waddell (StL Browns)	9/20/1908 StL 2-1 (10 inn)	Was Senators	92-94	10.0 IP, 5 Hits, 1 Run, ? ERs, 5 BBs, 17 Ks
10 (tie)	Dave McNally (Bal Orioles)	10/1/1965 (1) Bal 2-0	Cle Indians	92	9.0 IP, 2 Hits, 0 Runs, 0 ERs, 1 BB, 10 Ks
10 (tie)	Mike Cuellar (Bal Orioles)	7/26/1975 Bal 4-0	Mil Brewers	92	9.0 IP, 1 Hit 0 Runs, 0 ERs, 3 BBs, 10 Ks
10 (tie)	Wayne Garland (Bal Orioles)	6/21/1976 Bal 2-0	Bos Red Sox	92	9.0 IP, 2 Hits, 0 Runs, 0 ERs, 1 BB, 10 Ks
67 (tie)	Jim Palmer (Bal Orioles)	8/13/1969 Bal 8-0	Oak Athletics	89	9.0 IP, 0 Hits, 0 Runs, 0 ERs, 6 BBs, 8 Ks
91 (tie)	Bob Groom (StL Browns)	5/6/1917 (2) StL 3-0	Chi White Sox	88	9.0 IP, 0 Hits, 0 Runs, 0 ERs, 3 BBs, 4 Ks
207 (tie)	Bobo Holloman (StL Browns)	5/6/1953 StL 6-0	Phi Athletics	85	9.0 IP, 0 Hits, 0 Runs, 0 ERs, 5 BBs, 3 Ks
277 (tie)	Ernie Koob (StL Browns)	5/5/1917 StL 1-0	Chi White Sox	84	9.0 IP, 0 Hits, 0 Runs, 0 ERs, 5 BBs, 2 Ks
---	Earl Hamilton (StL Browns)	8/30/1912 StL 5-1	Det Tigers	81-83	9.0 IP, 0 Hits, 1 Run, ? ERs, 2 BBs, 0 Ks
---	John Whitehead (StL Browns)	8/5/1940 (2) StL 4-0 (6 inn)	Det Tigers	73	6.0 IP, 0 Hits, 0 Runs, 0 ERs, 1 BB, 2 Ks
---	Bob Milacki +3 (Bal Orioles)	7/13/1991 Bal 2-0	Oak Athletics	72	6.0 IP, 0 Hits, 0 Runs, 0 ERs, 3 BBs, 3 Ks
---	Steve Barber +1 (Bal Orioles)	4/30/1967 (1) Det 2-1	Det Tigers	71	8.2 IP, 0 Hits, 2 Runs, 1 ER, 10 BBs, 3 Ks

METHODOLOGY: This table includes the highest Game Scores of 10 innings or less thrown by a Browns or Orioles pitcher from 1901-2021. Games are ranked by Game Score (GSc) and consider all franchise regular season and postseason games. For comparison purposes, all ten of the team's no-hitters are included in this table. Game Score (GSc) measures a pitcher's performance in any given game started. Introduced by baseball writer/statistician Bill James in the 1980s, Game Score is presented as a figure between 0-100 — except for extreme outliers — and usually falls between 40-70.

LEGEND: Dates are shown as month/day/year (for example, June 12, 2018, is shown as 6/12/2018); GSc = Game Score. IP = innings pitched. BB(s) = base(s) on balls. K(s) = strikeout(s). ER(s) = earned run(s). inn = innings (associated with the length of games that were more or less than nine innings). One-third of an inning pitched has 0.1 added and two-thirds of an inning pitched has 0.2 added (for example, 9 1/3 innings pitched is displayed as 9.1). BB(s) = base(s) on balls; K(s) = strikeout(s). (1) or (2) indicates the game is the first or second game of a doubleheader. For multi-pitcher games, the starting pitcher, his statistics, and Game Score are listed, with the "+1" and "+3" indicating the number of additional pitchers who were a part of the no-hitter. The St. Louis/Baltimore franchise was based in Milwaukee and known as the Brewers when they joined the brand-new American League in 1901. The team moved to St. Louis and took the name Browns the next season (1902). They remained the St. Louis Browns through 1953, then moved to Baltimore and became the Orioles in 1954. The team's home city and name (StL Browns or Bal Orioles) for each of the games in the table is indicated in the (Team) entry underneath the pitcher's name.

NOTE 1: John Means threw the highest nine-inning Game Score of any franchise pitcher when he threw a 99 against Seattle in May 2021. His 113-pitch no-hitter was near-perfect, as he faced the minimum 27 batters. The only Mariner to reach base was left fielder Sam Haggerty, who went to first base on a strikeout and a wild pitch. He was caught stealing on the very next pitch. Means had extraordinary control that day, too, as 10 of his 12 strikeouts came on swinging strikes. Erik Bedard is just behind Means in the ranking, as he achieved a 98 Game Score in his 15-strikeout, no-walk performance against the Rangers in 2007. Bedard would also face the minimum 27 batters, as both Texas players who reached base against him were the victims of double-play groundballs from the next hitters.

NOTE 2: Rube Waddell's Game Score of 92-94 in 1908 is unofficial. It's not recognized as a Game Score because runs weren't differentiated as "earned" or "unearned" until 1912. Waddell's game could only have been either 92 (if the one run he allowed was earned) or 94 (if it was unearned). Either way, it merits inclusion in this table.

NOTE 3: The highest nine-inning Game Score from the St. Louis Browns era was a 91, achieved by Jack Kramer against the White Sox on September 16, 1944. A star pitcher on a perennially underperforming St. Louis franchise, Kramer blanked Chicago on one hit while striking out six with no walks. The Browns won the game 9-0 en route to winning the American League pennant that year. 1944 was the only season the Browns would make the postseason in the 53 years before the franchise moved to Baltimore and became the Orioles. For the record, the highest Game Score for the franchise during the one season they played in Milwaukee as the Brewers (1901) was an 85 thrown by Tully Sparks in a 6-1 victory over the Philadelphia Athletics. Sparks would go on to achieve considerable success with the National League's Phillies, winning 95 games for Philadelphia from 1903-1910, and throwing the fourth highest Game Score in the team's history for his 20-inning, 2-1 loss against the Cubs. This was the team's highest team Game Score at the time and is still tied for the most innings thrown by a Phillies pitcher in a single game.

NOTE 4: Hall of Famer Mike Mussina came as close as he could to throwing a no-hitter for the Orioles, as he threw three one-hitters for Baltimore, all of which are included in the top seven games thrown by a franchise pitcher. The only hit he allowed against the Rangers in his 1992 game in Texas was a fifth inning double by Kevin Reimer. Ron Coomer's two-out, seventh inning single was the only hit in Mussina's 2000 one-hitter against the Twins. In his 1997 one-hitter against the Indians, his perfect game was broken up by Sandy Alomar when he hit a single to left field with one out in the ninth inning. That wasn't the closest Mussina came to a no-hitter, though. While pitching for the Yankees in 2001, Mussina was down to his last strike when he lost a no-hitter with two outs in the ninth inning as Boston's Carl Everett hit a line drive single to left field.

NOTE 5: A Hall of Fame relief pitcher, Hoyt Wilhem threw his 1958 no-hitter against the three-time American League Champion New York Yankees who were en route to a fourth consecutive title that season. The fearsome New York lineup featured hitters such as Mickey Mantle, Hank Bauer, Elston Howard, and Bill Skowron. Jim Palmer, the only other Oriole pitcher in the Hall of Fame, threw his no-hitter against Reggie Jackson, Sal Bando, Campy Campaneris and the up-and-coming Oakland Athletics in 1969.

NOTE 6: Milt Pappas gave up the only hit in his 1964 game against the Twins when Zoilo Versalles hit a single to left field with two outs in the eighth inning. Dylan Bundy's 2017 no-hitter was broken up when Kyle Seager bunted for a base hit in the fourth inning. That was the only hit for Seattle during the entire game. Mike Cuellar's no-hit attempt in 1975 was broken up in the bottom of the seventh when Milwaukee first baseman George Scott lined a single to center field leading off the inning. That was the only hit Cuellar allowed.

NOTE 7: The extraordinary duo of Ernie Koob and Bob Groom threw no-hitters on consecutive days against the White Sox in 1917. Making this even more remarkable was that the Browns were terrible that season, finishing in seventh place in the eight-team American League with a record of 57-97. Unbelievably, the Chicago squad that was no-hit two days in a row was the best team in baseball. Led by Eddie Collins and Shoeless Joe Jackson, the White Sox won the American League pennant with a record of 100-54, and they beat the New York Giants four games to two in the 1917 World Series

NOTE 8: Thirty-year-old rookie Bobo Holloman of the Browns threw his no-hitter in his first start as a major league pitcher in 1953. He would start only 10 games in his entire career, as he pitched just 65 innings in his one season in the big leagues. For one brief, shining moment, though, Holloman was a star, as he no-hit the hapless Philadelphia Athletics, who would finish the season just ahead of the last-place Browns in the American League.

NOTE 9: The Orioles have thrown two of the 16 multi-pitcher no-hitters in baseball history. Their first was by Steve Barber (8.2 innings) and Stu Miller (0.1 inning) in a 2-1 loss to the Detroit Tigers in 1967. At the time, it was only the second multi-pitcher no-hitter ever thrown, with the first one involving the Red Sox pitcher (Babe Ruth) being ejected from the game in the first inning. In his game, Barber was removed for excessive wildness, having already walked 10 batters by the time he was pulled. This resulted in the game-tying run being scored and his putting the go-ahead runner on third base with two outs in the top of the ninth. The eventual winning run scored on an error before the final out of the inning was recorded.

NOTE 10: The team's other multi-pitcher no-hitter happened in 1991 when Bob Milacki was removed from the game due to injury. He was hit by a line drive from Oakland's Willie Wilson in the sixth inning. The ball caromed off Milacki's arm and leg and bounced to first baseman Randy Milligan for a force out of the speedy Wilson. Milacki finished the inning, but was replaced by relievers Mike Flanagan, Mark Williamson, and Gregg Olson, each of whom threw an inning of no-hit relief.

NOTE 11: Earl Hamilton threw the Browns' first no-hitter in 1912 as St. Louis defeated the Detroit Tigers 5-1. The one run he allowed was on a play that involved aggressive base running by Ty Cobb and an error by a St. Louis fielder. It's likely that it would have been an unearned run if that statistic had been accounted for in this game. Before the earned-run statistic became official in 1912, records of this game don't include a play-by-play box score, so the one run Detroit scored isn't classified as earned or unearned. Based on newspaper accounts it sounds as if it probably was unearned. If that's the case, Hamilton achieved a Game Score of 83. The only other score he could have is 81 if the run is earned, which is why his GSc in the table is listed as "81-83." He had a relatively low Game Score for a no-hitter because he didn't strike out any Detroit batters. This makes him one of only three no-hit pitchers who didn't strike out an opposing batter – the others are Sad Sam Jones of the New York Yankees in 1923 and Ken Holtzman of the Chicago Cubs in 1969.

NOTE 12: In 1940, Browns' pitcher John Whitehead threw a rain-shortened no-hit effort against the eventual American League champion Detroit Tigers. Only giving up one third inning walk and one runner safe on a shortstop error in the fourth inning, Whitehead held a team that featured three Hall of Famers (Hank Greenberg, Charlie Gehringer, and Earl Averill) scoreless in the second game of a doubleheader that ended in the bottom of the sixth when the skies opened up and rain began to pour. The Tigers had soundly beaten the Browns 9-2 in the opener that day.

Table 25-5. Highest Cubs Game Scores

Rank	Pitcher (Team)	Date Score	Opponent	GSc	IP, Hits, Runs, ERs, Walks, Strikeouts
1	Lefty Tyler (Cubs)	7/17/1918 Chi 2-1 (21 inn)	Phi Phillies	126	21.0 IP, 13 Hits, 1 Run, 0 ERs, 1 BBs, 8 Ks
2	Tom Hughes (Orphans)	9/21/1901 Chi 1-0 (17 inn)	Bos Braves	119	17.0 IP, 8 Hits, 0 Runs, 0 ERs, 5 BBs, 13 Ks
3	Ed Reulbach (Cubs)	8/24/1905 Chi 2-1 (20 inn)	Phi Phillies	115-117	20.0 IP, 13 Hits, 1 Run, ? ERs, 4 BBs, 7 Ks
4	Bob Wicker (Cubs)	6/11/1904 Chi 1-0 (12 Inn)	NY Giants	107	12.0 IP, 2 Hits, 0 Runs, 0 ERs, 1 BB, 10 Ks
5	Jack Pfiester (Cubs)	6/4/1908 1-1 Tie (17 inn)	Bos Doves	106-108	17.0 IP, 9 Hits, 1 Run, ? ERs, 6 BBs, 7 Ks
6	Jack Taylor (no team name)	6/22/1902 Chi 3-2 (19 Inn)	Pit Pirates	106	19.0 IP, 14 Hits, 2 Runs, 2 ERs, 1 BB, 6 Ks
7	Buttons Briggs (Cubs)	9/18/1904 Chi 2-1 (17 inn)	Cin Reds	105-107	17.0 IP, 10 Hits, 1 Run, ? ERs, 3 BBs, 5 Ks
8	Kerry Wood (Cubs)	5/6/1998 Chi 2-0	Hou Astros	105	9.0 IP, 1 Hit, 0 Runs, 0 ERs, 0 BBs, 20 Ks

Rank	Pitcher (Team)	Date Score	Opponent	GSc	IP, Hits, Runs, ERs, Walks, Strikeouts
9	Hippo Vaughn (Cubs)	9/16/1915 Chi 1-0 (12 Inn)	StL Cardinals	101	12.0 IP, 4 Hits, 0 Runs, 0 ERs, 0 BBs, 7 Ks
10 (tie)	Bob Wicker (Cubs)	9/3/1905 Chi 1-0 (11 Inn)	Pit Pirates	99	11.0 IP, 3 Hits, 0 Runs, 0 ERs, 1 BBs, 9 Ks
10 (tie)	G. Alexander (Cubs)	8/2/1919 Phi 2-1 (14 Inn)	Phi Phillies	99	14.0 IP, 9 Hits, 2 Runs, 2 ERs, 2 BBs, 15 Ks
10 (tie)	Guy Bush (Cubs)	5/14/1927 Chi 7-2 (18 Inn)	Bos Braves	99	18.0 IP, 11 Hits, 2 Runs, 2 ERs, 8 BBs, 5 Ks

METHODOLOGY: This table includes the highest Game Scores of 10 innings or less thrown by a Cubs pitcher from 1900-2021. Games are ranked by Game Score (GSc) and consider all franchise regular season and postseason games. Table 25-6 below limits the eligible games to those pitching performances that were 10 innings or less. Games are ranked by pitcher Game Score in descending order. This table includes all franchise regular season and postseason games that achieved a Game Score of 100 or more. Game Score measures a pitcher's performance in any given game started. Introduced by baseball writer/statistician Bill James in the 1980s, Game Score is presented as a figure between 0-100 — except for extreme outliers — and usually falls between 40-70.

LEGEND: Dates are shown as month/day/year (for example, June 12, 2018, is shown as 6/12/2018); IP = innings pitched. BB(s) = base(s) on balls. K(s) = strikeout(s). ER(s) = earned run(s). inn = innings (associated with the length of games that were more or less than nine innings). One-third of an inning pitched has 0.1 added and two-thirds of an inning pitched has 0.2 added (for example, 9 1/3 innings pitched is displayed as 9.1). BB(s) = base(s) on balls; K(s) = strikeout(s). (1) or (2) indicates the game is the first or second game of a doubleheader. The National League's Cubs have been based in Chicago since the team began in 1876. From 1876-1887 they were known as the White Stockings. From 1888-1889 they had no team nickname. Starting in 1890 they were known as the Colts, and they kept that name through 1897. From 1898-1901 they were the Chicago Orphans and again had no team nickname in 1902 and 1903. From 1904-present they have been known as the Chicago Cubs. The team's name for each of the games in the table is indicated in the "Team" entry underneath the pitcher's name.

NOTE 1: The highest postseason Game Score thrown by a franchise pitcher was an 88 by Jake Arrieta in Game 1 of the 2015 NL Wild Card playoff game against the Pirates. Arrieta threw nine innings of five-hit, shutout ball en route to a 4-0 win. The Cubs would go on to win the 2015 NLDS three games to one over St. Louis, then Chicago was swept by the New York Mets in four games in the NLCS. However, the Cubs did win the 2016 World Series the next season.

NOTE 2: Lefty Tyler's 21-inning marathon win in a 1918 game against the Phillies is not just the highest Cubs Game Score ever, it's also tied for fifth place in Major League baseball. At the time, Tyler tied Pittsburgh's Babe Adams and New York's Rube Marquard for the longest National League game ever thrown. Jack Coombs of the Athletics and Boston's Joe Harris had each gone 24 innings in a 1906 duel to set the American League innings pitched record.

NOTE 3: Tom Hughes of the Orphans was having a less than stellar season in 1901, finishing the year with 23 losses for the sixth-place Chicago Orphans. Yet, on September 21, he threw the longest shutout in team history, blanking the Boston Nationals over 17 innings. Hughes allowed only eight hits, as the Orphans scored the game's only run with one out in the bottom of the 17th when second baseman Pete Childs singled in first-baseman Charlie Dexter. Apart from a brief stint the year before, Hughes played with the Orphans only during the 1901 season. He would go on to have a solid career, highlighted by a 20-win season for the Boston Americans in 1903, as he helped propel the team to victory over the Pittsburgh Pirates in the first-ever World Series.

NOTE 4: Three games are included in this table even though they don't have official Game Scores: Ed Reulbach's 20-inning win over the Phillies in 1905, Jack Pfiester's 17-inning victory against the Boston Doves in 1908, and Buttons Briggs' 17-inning tie versus the Reds in 1904. In each case, the pitcher allowed a run against the opposing team and the Cubs committed at least one error during the game. Because earned or unearned runs were not differentiated at that time, and a line-by-line game record isn't available, it's unclear if the runs would have qualified as earned (minus four points on the GSc) or unearned (minus two points). However, since it was only one run allowed in each case, the Game Scores listed are the only two possibilities for the contest. In those three situations, the games qualify for inclusion in this table regardless of the run classification.

Table 25-6. Highest Cubs Game Scores of 10 innings or less

Rank	Pitcher (Team)	Date Score	Opponent	GSc	IP, Hits, Runs, ERs, Walks, Strikeouts
1	Kerry Wood (Cubs)	5/6/1998 Chi 2-0	Hou Astros	105	9.0 IP, 1 Hit, 0 Runs, 0 ERs, 0 BBs, 20 Ks
2	Jake Arrieta (Cubs)	8/30/2015 Chi 2-0	LA Dodgers	98	9.0 IP, 0 Hits, 0 Runs, 0 ERs, 1 BBs, 12 Ks
3 (tie)	Kerry Wood (Cubs)	5/25/2001 Chi 1-0	Mil Brewers	97	9.0 IP, 1 Hit, 0 Runs, 0 ERs, 2 BBs, 14 Ks
3 (tie)	Jake Arrieta (Cubs)	9/16/2014 Chi 7-0	Cin Reds	97	9.0 IP, 1 Hit, 0 Runs, 0 ERs, 1 BB, 13 Ks
5 (tie)	Jack Pfeister (Cubs)	9/25/1906 Chi 1-0 (10 inn)	Bro Dodgers	96	10.0 IP, 1 Hit, 0 Runs, 0 ERs, 2 BBs, 8 Ks
5 (tie)	Lon Warneke (Cubs)	4/17/1934 Chi 6-0	Cin Reds	96	9.0 IP, 1 Hit, 0 Runs, 0 ERs, 2 BBs, 13 Ks
5 (tie)	Frank Castillo (Cubs)	9/25/1995 Chi 7-0	StL Cardinals	96	9.0 IP, 1 Hit, 0 Runs, 0 ERs, 2 BBs, 13 Ks
5 (tie)	C. Zambrano (Cubs)	9/14/2008 Chi 5-0	Hou Astros	96	9.0 IP, 0 Hits, 0 Runs, 0 ERs, 1 BB, 10 Ks
9 (tie)	J. Lavender (Cubs)	8/31/1915 (1) Chi 2-0	NY Giants	94	9.0 IP, 0 Hits, 0 Runs, 0 ERs, 1 BB, 8 Ks
9 (tie)	Hippo Vaughn (Cubs)	5/2/1917 Cin 1-0 (10 inn)	Cin Reds	94	10.0 IP, 2 Hits, 1 Run, 0 ERs, 2 BBs, 10 Ks
9 (tie)	Pat Malone (Cubs)	8/18/1934 Chi 2-0	Phi Phillies	94	9.0 IP, 2 Hits, 0 Runs, 0 ERs, 1 BB, 12 Ks
9 (tie)	Greg Maddux (Cubs)	5/11/1988 Chi 1-0 (10 inn)	Bal Orioles	94	10.0 IP, 3 Hits, 0 Runs, 0 ERs, 0 BBs, 8 Ks
13 (tie)	Don Cardwell (Cubs)	5/15/1960 (2) Chi 4-0	StL Cardinals	93	9.0 IP, 0 Hits, 0 Runs, 0 ERs, 1 BB, 7 Ks
15 (tie)	Milt Pappas (Cubs)	9/2/1972 Chi 8-0	SD Padres	92	9.0 IP, 0 Hits, 0 Runs, 0 ERs, 1 BB, 6 Ks
52 (tie)	Ken Holtzman (Cubs)	6/3/1971 Chi 1-0	Cin Reds	89	9.0 IP, 0 Hits, 0 Runs, 0 ERs, 4 BBs, 6 Ks
52 (tie)	Jake Arrieta (Cubs)	4/21/2016 Chi 16-0	Cin Reds	89	9.0 IP, 0 Hits, 0 Runs, 0 ERs, 4 BBs, 6 Ks
52 (tie)	Alec Mills (Cubs)	9/13/2020 Chi 12-0	Mil Brewers	89	9.0 IP, 0 Hits, 0 Runs, 0 ERs, 3 BBs, 5 Ks
118 (tie)	Burt Hooton (Cubs)	4/16/1972 Chi 4-0	Phi Phillies	87	9.0 IP, 0 Hits, 0 Run, 0 ERs, 7 BBs, 7 Ks

Rank	Pitcher (Team)	Date Score	Opponent	GSc	IP, Hits, Runs, ERs, Walks, Strikeouts
159 (tie)	Sam Jones (Cubs)	5/12/1955 Chi 4-0	Phi Phillies	86	9.0 IP, 0 Hits, 0 Run, 0 ERs, 7 BBs, 6 Ks
285 (tie)	Ken Holtzman (Cubs)	8/19/1969 Chi 3-0	Atl Braves	84	9.0 IP, 0 Hits, 0 Runs, 0 ERs, 3 BBs, 0 Ks
---	Len "King" Cole (Cubs)	7/31/1910 (2) Chi 4-0 (7 inn)	StL Cardinals	74	7.0 IP, 0 Hits, 0 Runs, 0 ERs, 4 BBs, 1 K
---	Zach Davies +3 (Cubs)	6/24/2021 Chi 4-0	LA Dodgers	71	6.0 IP, 0 Hits, 0 Runs, 0 ERs, 5 BBs, 4 Ks

METHODOLOGY: This table includes the highest Game Scores of 10 innings or less thrown by a Cubs pitcher from 1900-2021. Games are ranked by Game Score (GSc) and consider all franchise regular season and postseason games. For comparison purposes, all twelve of the team's no-hitters from 1900-2021 are included in this table. Game Score measures a pitcher's performance in any given game started. Introduced by baseball writer/statistician Bill James in the 1980s, Game Score is presented as a figure between 0-100 — except for extreme outliers — and usually falls between 40-70.

LEGEND: Dates are shown as month/day/year (for example, June 12, 2018, is shown as 6/12/2018); IP = innings pitched. BB(s) = base(s) on balls. K(s) = strikeout(s). ER(s) = earned run(s). inn = innings (associated with the length of games that were more or less than nine innings). One-third of an inning pitched has 0.1 added and two-thirds of an inning pitched has 0.2 added (for example, 9 1/3 innings pitched is displayed as 9.1). BB(s) = base(s) on balls; K(s) = strikeout(s). (1) or (2) indicates the game is the first or second game of a doubleheader. The National League's Cubs have been based in Chicago since it began in 1876. From 1876-1887 they were known as the White Stockings. From 1888-1889 they had no team nickname. Starting in 1890 they were known as the Colts, and they kept that name through 1897. From 1898-1901 they were the Chicago Orphans and again had no team nickname in 1902 and 1903. From 1904-present they have been known as the Chicago Cubs. The team's name for each of the games in the table is indicated in the "Team" entry underneath the pitcher's name. As it happens, all the games in this table took place when the team was known as the Cubs.

NOTE 1: With a Game Score of 105, Kerry Wood has the highest nine-inning GSc in baseball history. Tied for the Major League record of 20 strikeouts in a nine-inning game, his game is also the only nine-inning Game Score above 100 that wasn't a no-hitter. The only two baserunners Wood allowed were a lone single to Houston's Ricky Gutierrez leading off the third inning, and Craig Biggio reaching first on a hit by pitch in the sixth. Making this even more impressive, Wood achieved this record-braking feat against a 102-win Houston team that included Hall of Famers Biggio and Jeff Bagwell, along with sluggers Moises Alou and Derek Bell in the starting lineup.

NOTE 2: Jake Arrieta has two of the top four games on this list – Kerry Wood has the other two. Arrieta and Ken Holtzman are also the only Cub pitchers who have thrown two no-hitters. Arrieta's 2015 no-hitter against a very good Dodger team was a masterpiece. He struck out 12, including the last three batters in the bottom of the ninth, as he only allowed a walk to former MVP Jimmy Rollins in the bottom of the sixth inning. Another runner (Enrique Hernandez) reached base on an error earlier in the game. In his second no-hitter, Arrieta was not quite as overpowering, allowing four walks and striking out six in a 16-0 throttling of the Cincinnati Reds in April 2016. Arrieta's other top Game Score was a 97, achieved against Cincinnati in September 2014. In that game, he struck out 13 Reds while only allowing one hit – a double by Brandon Phillips with one out in the eighth inning. Jake Arrieta was dominating during that 2014-2016 stretch, as he won the Cy Young Award in 2015 and was named to the National League All-Star team in 2016.

NOTE 3: Ken Holtzman threw two no-hitters within two years of each other. His 1969 no-hitter against the Braves was especially notable since he didn't strike out a single batter during the game. There have been just three other no-hitters since 1900 without a strikeout: Pete Dowling of the Cleveland Blues in 1901, Earl Hamilton of the St. Louis Browns in 1912, and Sad Sam Jones of the New York Yankees in 1923. In 1971, Holtzman no-hit Cincinnati's Big Red Machine in a 1-0 win. Holtzman struck out six batters that day, and he scored the game's only run. Holtzman led off the third inning by reaching first on an error by Cincinnati third baseman Tony Perez. He advanced to second on a fielder's choice and scored on a Glenn Beckert single to right field.

NOTE 4: Kerry Wood, Jack Pfeister, Lon Warneke, and Frank Castillo all threw one-hitters that scored high on this table. The lone hit Wood gave up was a single by Milwaukee's Mark Loretta in the seventh inning as he struck out 14 in a 1-0 win. Pfiester's 116-win Cubs team dominated the National League in 1906. In his one-hitter against Brooklyn late in the season, he allowed only a single to catcher

Bill Bergen, as Chicago prevailed 1-0 in 10 innings. Bergen has the distinction of hitting .170 over more than 3,000 at bats during his 11 seasons in the majors. His WAR of -6.9 is the lowest of any catcher in baseball history. Lon Warneke had a no-hitter going until Cincinnati left fielder Adam Comorosky hit a single to center field with one out in the bottom of the ninth. Frank Castillo threw a no-hitter for eight innings until he gave up a two-out triple to St. Louis left fielder Bernard Gilkey in the bottom of the ninth. Gilkey had two strikes on him at the time.

NOTE 5: Sam Jones's 1955 no-hitter was the first no-hitter by a black pitcher. Jones walked the bases loaded with no one out in the ninth inning but then struck out the final three batters to end the game. Don Cardwell's no-hitter was his first start after being traded by the Phillies to the Cubs. Cardwell retired the last 26 batters he faced after a first- inning walk to Cardinal shortstop Alex Grammas. Burt Hooton's no-hitter happened during his fourth career start. Milt Pappas had a perfect game going until he walked San Diego pinch-hitter Larry Stahl with two outs in the ninth inning on a full count. The called ball remains controversial to this day. Carlos Zambrano's 2008 no-hitter against the Astros was played at Miller Park in Milwaukee because of Hurricane Ike, making it the first no-hitter at a neutral site. The only baserunners he allowed was a walk to Michael Bourn in the fourth and a hit-by-pitch to Hunter Pence in the fifth. Alec Mills' no-hitter against Milwaukee was his first complete game and 15th career start. It was the second no-hitter at Miller Park; the first was the one thrown by Zambrano in 2008. Mills' game took place with no fans in attendance due to the COVID-19 pandemic.

NOTE 6: Both Cincinnati pitcher Fred Toney and Cubs pitcher Hippo Vaughn had no-hitters through nine innings in their 1917 game. This was the only game in MLB history where both pitchers had no-hitters through nine innings. Vaughn allowed two hits and an error in the tenth, losing the game 1-0. One of the best pitchers in Cubs history, Hall of Famer Greg Maddux threw a magnificent three-hit shutout against the Padres in 1988 – tied for ninth place on the list above. That season was Maddux's breakout year with Chicago, as he won 18 games and made the National League All-Star team for the first time. He would go on to win the Cy Young Award with the Cubs in 1992 before signing as a free agent with the Braves in 1993.

NOTE 7: King Cole threw a seven-inning no-hitter against the Cardinals during the second game of a doubleheader in 1910. Even though the game was played in St. Louis, by mutual agreement the Cardinals batted first. Along with that, the two teams decided the second game would end promptly at 5:00 PM so they both could catch the same train to New York to play the Brooklyn Superbas and New York Giants the following day. Cole threw seven hitless innings, the Cubs scored four runs, and the game stopped with one out in the bottom of the seventh inning with the Cubs batting. Cole was outstanding for Chicago in 1910, winning 20 games and leading the National League with a 1.80 ERA, just edging teammate and future Hall of Famer Three-Finger Brown. His game against St. Louis counted as a no-hitter until the 1991 ruling that to be recognized as a no-hitter, at least a full nine innings had to be played.

NOTE 8: Zach Davies and three other Cubs pitchers allowed eight Dodgers to reach base during their June 24, 2021, multi-pitcher no-hitter. Davies walked five batters over six innings while relievers Ryan Tepera, Andrew Chafin, and Craig Kimbrel each threw one hitless inning and walked one batter apiece. The Cubs won the game 4-0. If the combined efforts of the four pitchers were added together, they would have compiled a Game Score of 86 that day.

Table 25-7. Highest Indians Game Scores

Rank	Pitcher (Team)	Date Score	Opponent	GSc	IP, Hits, Runs, ERs, Walks, Strikeouts
1	Willis Hudlin (Indians)	8/24/1935 Cle 2-0 (15inn)	Phi Athletics	106	15.0 IP, 8 Hits, 0 Runs, 0 ERs, 1 BB, 6 Ks
2 (tie)	Al Milnar (Indians)	8/11/1942 (1) 0-0 Tie (14 inn)	Det Tigers	104	14.0 IP, 2 Hits, 0 Runs, 0 ERs, 4 BBs, 0 Ks
2 (tie)	Stan Williams (Indians)	8/10/1967 Cle 2-1 (15 inn)	Bal Orioles	104	13.0 IP, 5 Hits, 1 Run, 1 ER, 3 BBs, 14 Ks
4 (tie)	Addie Joss (Naps)	8/26/1904 Cle 1-0 (12 inn)	Was Senators	103	12.0 IP, 4 Hits, 0 Runs, 0 ERs, 2 BBs, 11 Ks
4 (tie)	Stan Coveleski (Indians)	5/24/1918 Cle 3-2 (19 inn)	NY Yankees	103	19.0 IP, 12 Hits, 2 Runs, 2 ERs, 6 BBs, 4 Ks
6 (tie)	Ed Klepfer (Indians)	4/22/1916 tie 1-1 (15 inn)	StL Browns	100	15.0 IP, 10 Hits, 1 Run, 1 ER, 1 BB, 8 Ks
6 (tie)	Sam McDowell (Indians)	9/4/1965 Bal 1-0 (11 inn)	Bal Orioles	100	10.0 IP, 2 Hits, 0 Runs, 0 ERs, 4 BBs, 16 Ks
6 (tie)	Steve Hargan (Indians)	9/13/1966 KC 3-1 (15 inn)	KC Athletics	100	13.0 IP, 5 Hits, 1 Run, 1 ERs, 3 BBs, 10 Ks

Rank	Pitcher (Team)	Date Score	Opponent	GSc	IP, Hits, Runs, ERs, Walks, Strikeouts
6 (tie)	Stan Williams (Indians)	5/18/1968 Cle 1-0 (10 inn)	Bal Orioles	100	10.0 IP, 2 Hits, 0 Runs, 0 ERs, 0 BBs, 12 Ks
10 (tie)	Willis Hudlin (Indians)	7/16/1933 Cle 2-1 (14 inn)	Bos Red Sox	99	14.0 IP, 5 Hits, 1 Run, 0 ERs, 3 BBs, 2 Ks
10 (tie)	Luis Tiant (Indians)	7/03/1968 Cle 1-0 (10 inn)	Min Twins	99	10.0 IP, 6 Hits, 0 Runs, 0 ERs, 0 BBs, 19 Ks
10 (tie)	Addie Joss (Naps)	6/4/1905 Cle 4-2 (16 inn)	Chi W. Sox	97-99	16.0 IP, 9 Hits, 2 Runs, ? ERs, 3 BBs, 4 Ks

METHODOLOGY: This table includes the highest Game thrown by an Indians pitcher from 1901-2021. Games are ranked by Game Score (GSc) and consider all franchise regular season and postseason games. Table 25-8 below limits the eligible games to those pitching performances that were 10 innings or less. Games are ranked by pitcher Game Score in descending order. Game Score measures a pitcher's performance in any given game started. Introduced by baseball writer/statistician Bill James in the 1980s, Game Score is presented as a figure between 0-100 — except for extreme outliers — and usually falls between 40-70.

LEGEND: Dates are shown as month/day/year (for example, June 12, 2018, is shown as 6/12/2018); IP = innings pitched. BB(s) = base(s) on balls. K(s) = strikeout(s). ER(s) = earned run(s). inn = innings (associated with the length of games that were more or less than nine innings). One-third of an inning pitched has 0.1 added and two-thirds of an inning pitched has 0.2 added (for example, 9 1/3 innings pitched is displayed as 9.1). BB(s) = base(s) on balls; K(s) = strikeout(s). (1) or (2) indicates the game is the first or second game of a doubleheader. The team joined the American League in 1901 as the Cleveland Bluebirds, typically shortened to just "Blues." Cleveland would change its nickname to the Bronchos in 1902 for one season. The team was known as the Napoleons (or "Naps") from 1903-1914 because of their star player, Napoleon Lajoie. In 1915, the team became the Indians and stayed that way until they changed to the Guardians before the start of the 2022 season. The team's name for each of the games in the table is indicated in the "Team" entry underneath the pitcher's name.

NOTE 1: Several teams on this list have moved locations and changed names since they joined the American League in 1901. The Athletics started in Philadelphia, then moved to Kansas City in 1955, and further west to Oakland in 1968. The Baltimore Orioles have undergone a couple of name and location changes since they joined the American League in 1901. That season they played in Milwaukee and were known as the Brewers. The team moved to St. Louis in 1902 and became the Browns. In 1954, they moved to Baltimore and were renamed the Orioles. The original Washington Senators moved to Minnesota and became the Twins in 1961.

NOTE 2: The highest postseason Game Score thrown by a franchise pitcher was an 83 by Duster Mails in Game 6 of the 1920 World Series. Mails threw nine innings of three-hit, shutout ball en route to a 1-0 win. Cleveland would go on to beat the Brooklyn Robins in seven games, five games to two. The powerful 1920 Brooklyn team featured Hall of Famers like Zack Wheat, Burleigh Grimes, and Rube Marquard. Cleveland countered with a couple of Hall of Famers of their own: Stan Coveleski and Tris Speaker. Mails only allowed five hits to Brooklyn that day for a critical win that put the Indians ahead by four games to two and within one of winning it all – that season it was a best-of-nine World Series.

NOTE 3: Hall of Famer Addie Joss is included in this table twice. He is first listed for an extraordinary 12-inning, four-hit shutout of the Washington Senators in 1904. His Game Score of 103 was Cleveland's highest until it was surpassed over 30 years later by Willis Hudlin's 15-inning shutout of the Philadelphia Athletics in 1935. Hudlin achieved a score of 106 and is the current Cleveland record-holder. In his game, Hudlin battled Athletics rookie George Turbeville in a scoreless tie until Hall of Famer Earl Averill hit a two-run home run with two out in the bottom of the 15th for a walk-off win. It was Turberville's second career start – he was pulled in the third inning of his first start two weeks earlier. Willis Hudlin is included in this list twice. His second entry was a 14-inning effort where he held the Red Sox to one unearned run on five hits in a 2-1 extra-inning win.

NOTE 4: Stan Coveleski tied Joss's Game Score of 103 in 1918 when he threw 19 innings in a 3-2 win over the Yankees, establishing the record for the most innings ever thrown by a Cleveland starter. Addie Joss threw the second-most innings by a Cleveland pitcher when he hurled 16 of them in a 4-2 win over the White Sox in 1905. Because Naps shortstop Terry Turner committed an error and there was no differentiation between earned and unearned runs until 1908, Joss doesn't have an official Game Score associated with this contest; however, it can only be either 97 or 99, which could potentially tie him for 10th place on this list.

NOTE 5: Al Milnar, who threw a 14-inning, two-hit shutout of the Tigers, deserves special recognition. With an outstanding Game Score of 104, he holds the record for fewest hits allowed (two) in a game of 14 innings or more. He also did this without striking out a single batter. He is one of only five pitchers to ever throw 14 innings or more and not strike out anyone. The record holder for that is Art Nehf, who threw 17 innings of no-strikeout ball for the Giants against the Reds in August 1920. A career starter, Milnar relied heavily on his fielders as a pitcher – he averaged less than two strikeouts a game during his eight years in the majors. Milnar served overseas in an Army unit from 1944-1945 during World War II, but never regained his form when he rejoined the Indians in 1946 and retired soon after the war.

NOTE 6: Luis Tiant pitched a brilliant 10-inning shutout of the Twins in 1968, striking out 19 batters and walking none in the process. His 19 strikeouts are the most ever achieved by a franchise pitcher in a single game, as he broke Hall of Famer Bob Feller's team record of 18 set in 1938. What made Tiant's accomplishment especially impressive was that he achieved this against a Minnesota team that featured Hall of Famers Harmon Killebrew and Tony Oliva and finished the season as the second-best hitting team in the American League. Tiant's Game Score of 99 also ties him for 10th place and is in third place in the 10 inning or less table below.

NOTE 7: The only other Cleveland pitcher besides Addie Joss and Willis Hudlin to appear twice in the table above was Stan Williams. Williams spent most of his career with the Dodgers and was even on the National League All-Star team in 1960, as he finished the 1960 and 1961 seasons among the league's strikeout leaders. He was also a member of the World Series Champion Dodgers in 1959. He was a starter with the Indians only for a short time, compiling a record of 25-29 from 1967-1969. Yet, he managed to throw two of Cleveland's best games in a 121-season span. His first one was a 13-inning performance where he held the reigning champion Orioles to just five hits and one run while he struck out 14 batters. His second entry was a magnificent 10-inning, two-hit shutout win in 1968 – again over Baltimore. Williams struck out 12 batters and walked no one in that game. The first Oriole hit was a single by Brooks Robinson in the fifth inning. Williams provided the winning hit in the walk-off victory when he singled home pinch-runner Dave Nelson from second base with one out in the bottom of the 10th.

Table 25-8. Highest Indians Game Scores of 10 innings or less

Rank	Pitcher (Team)	Date Score	Opponent	GSc	IP, Hits, Runs, ERs, Walks, Strikeouts
1 (tie)	Sam McDowell (Indians)	9/4/1965 Bal 1-0 (11 inn)	Bal Orioles	100	10 IP, 2 Hits, 0 Runs, 0 ERs, 4 BBs, 16 Ks
1 (tie)	Stan Williams (Indians)	5/18/1968 Cle 1-0 (10 inn)	Bal Orioles	100	10 IP, 2 Hits, 0 Runs, 0 ERs, 0 BBs, 12 Ks
3	Luis Tiant (Indians)	7/3/1968 Cle 1-0 (10 inn)	Min Twins	99	10 IP, 6 Hits, 0 Runs, 0 ERs, 0 BBs, 19 Ks
4 (tie)	Dennis Eckersley (Indians)	5/30/1977 Cle 1-0	Cal Angels	98	9.0 IP, 0 Hits, 0 Runs, 0 ERs, 1 BB, 12 Ks
4 (tie)	*Len Barker (Indians)*	*5/15/1981 Cle 3-0*	*Tor Blue Jays*	98	*9.0 IP, 0 Hits, 0 Runs, 0 ERs, 0 BBs, 11 Ks*
4 (tie)	Corey Kluber (Indians)	5/13/2015 Cle 2-0	StL Cardinals	98	8.0 IP, 1 Hit, 0 Runs, 0 ERs, 0 BBs, 18 Ks
4 (tie)	Carlos Carrasco (Indians)	9/25/2015 Cle 6-0	KC Royals	98	9.0 IP, 1 Hit, 0 Runs, 0 ERs, 2 BBs, 15 Ks
8	Bartolo Colon (Indians)	9/18/2000 W 2-0	NY Yankees	97	9.0 IP, 1 Hit, 0 Runs, 0 ERs, 1 BB, 13 Ks
9 (tie)	Bob Feller (Indians)	7/12/1940 W 1-0	Phi Athletics	96	9.0 IP, 1 Hit, 0 Runs, 0 ERs, 2 BB, 13 Ks
9 (tie)	Josh Tomlin (Indians)	6/28/2014 W 5-0	Sea Mariners	96	9.0 IP, 1 Hit, 0 Runs, 0 ERs, 0 BBs, 11 Ks
19 (tie)	Bob Feller (Indians)	4/30/1946 W 1-0	NY Yankees	93	9.0 IP, 0 Hits, 0 Runs, 0 ERs, 5 BBs, 11 Ks
19 (tie)	Sonny Siebert (Indians)	6/10/1966 W 2-0	Was Senators	93	9.0 IP, 0 Hits, 0 Runs, 0 ERs, 1 BB, 7 Ks
23 (tie)	Wes Ferrell (Indians)	4/29/1931 W 9-0	StL Browns	92	9.0 IP, 0 Hits, 0 Runs, 0 ERs, 3 BBs, 8 Ks
31 (tie)	Ray Caldwell (Indians)	9/10/1919 (1) W 3-0	NY Yankees	91	9.0 IP, 0 Hits, 0 Runs, 0 ERs, 1 BB, 5 Ks
31 (tie)	Dick Bosman (Indians)	7/19/1974 W 4-0	Oak Athletics	91	9.0 IP, 0 Hits, 0 Runs, 0 ERs, 0 BBs, 4 Ks
44 (tie)	*Addie Joss (Naps)*	*10/2/1908 W 1-0*	*Chi White Sox*	90	*9.0 IP, 0 Hits, 0 Runs, 0 ERs, 0 BBs, 3 Ks*

Rank	Pitcher (Team)	Date Score	Opponent	GSc	IP, Hits, Runs, ERs, Walks, Strikeouts
44 (tie)	Bob Feller (Indians)	4/16/1940 W 1-0	Chi White Sox	90	9.0 IP, 0 Hits, 0 Runs, 0 ERs, 5 BBs, 8 Ks
94 (tie)	Bob Lemon (Indians)	6/30/1948 W 2-0	Det Tigers	88	9.0 IP, 0 Hits, 1 Run, 0 ERs, 3 BBs, 4 Ks
130 (tie)	Addie Joss (Naps)	4/20/1910 W 1-0	Chi White Sox	87	9.0 IP, 0 Hits, 0 Runs, 0 ERs, 2 BBs, 2 Ks
130 (tie)	Bob Feller (Indians)	7/1/1951 (1) W 1-0	Chi White Sox	87	9.0 IP, 0 Hits, 1 Run, 0 ERs, 3 BBs, 5 Ks
180 (tie)	Don Black (Indians)	7/10/1947 (1) W 3-0	Phi Athletics	86	9.0 IP, 0 Hits, 0 Runs, 0 ERs, 6 BBs, 5 Ks
---	Bob Rhoads (Naps)	9/18/1908 W 2-1	Bos Red Sox	83-85	9.0 IP, 0 Hits, 1 Run, ? ERs, 2 BBs, 2 Ks
---	Pete Dowling (Blues)	6/30/1901 W 7-0	Mil Brewers	83	9.0 IP, 0 Hits, 0 Runs, 0 ERs, 4 BBs, 0 Ks

METHODOLOGY: This table includes the highest Game Scores of 10 innings or less thrown by an Indians pitcher from 1901-2021. Games are ranked by Game Score (GSc) and consider all franchise regular season and postseason games. For comparison purposes, all 14 of the team's no-hitters are included in this table. Game Score measures a pitcher's performance in any given game started. Introduced by baseball writer/statistician Bill James in the 1980s, Game Score is presented as a figure between 0-100 — except for extreme outliers — and usually falls between 40-70.

LEGEND: Dates are shown as month/day/year (for example, June 12, 2018, is shown as 6/12/2018); IP = innings pitched. BB(s) = base(s) on balls. K(s) = strikeout(s). ER(s) = earned run(s). inn = innings (associated with the length of games that were more or less than nine innings). One-third of an inning pitched has 0.1 added and two-thirds of an inning pitched has 0.2 added (for example, 9 1/3 innings pitched is displayed as 9.1). BB(s) = base(s) on balls; K(s) = strikeout(s). (1) or (2) indicates the game is the first or second game of a doubleheader. The team joined the American League in 1901 as the Cleveland Bluebirds, typically shortened to just "Blues." Cleveland would change its nickname to the Bronchos in 1902 for one season. The team was known as the Napoleons (or "Naps") from

1903-1914 because of their star player, Napoleon Lajoie. In 1915, the team became the Indians and stayed that way until they changed to the Guardians before the start of the 2022 season. The team's name for each of the games in the table is indicated in the "Team" entry underneath the pitcher's name. *Italicized games (Addie Joss in 1908 and Len Barker in 1981) were perfect games.*

NOTE 1: Many of the teams in this table moved or changed names over the years. The Baltimore Orioles have undergone a couple of name and location changes since they joined the American League in 1901. That season – the same year they were no-hit by Pete Dowling – they played in Milwaukee and were known as the Brewers. The team moved to St. Louis in 1902 and became the Browns. In 1954, they moved to Baltimore and were renamed the Orioles. There was a different Baltimore Orioles franchise in the brand-new American League from 1901-1902. In 1903, that Baltimore franchise ended, and a new franchise was awarded to New York and played as the Highlanders until 1912. The team changed its name to the Yankees in 1913 and has been known as the New York Yankees since then. There was also another Baltimore Orioles franchise that played in the American Association and National League from 1882-1899. After 1899, the National League contracted from 12 teams to eight, and the Orioles were one of the teams that was removed prior to the 1900 season. The Athletics started in Philadelphia, then moved to Kansas City in 1955, and further west to Oakland in 1968. The original Washington Senators moved to Minnesota and became the Twins in 1961.

NOTE 2: In September 1965, "Sudden Sam" McDowell threw 10 innings of shutout ball, allowing only four walks and two singles against the up-and-coming Orioles. He also struck out 16 batters in a lineup that featured hard-hitting Brooks Robinson and Curt Blefary as mainstays that season. Breaking in with Cleveland just six days before his 19th birthday in 1961, McDowell and his fastball was an instant sensation. As a six-time All-Star with Cleveland, he led the American League with a 2.18 ERA and 325 strikeouts in 1965. McDowell was replaced by reliever Bobby Tiefenauer in the bottom of the 11th that day. Tiefenauer allowed two hits and the Orioles won on a walkoff single by Hall of Famer Luis Aparicio.

NOTE 3: Before Hall of Famer Dennis Eckersley became an iconic closer for the Oakland Athletics, he was an All-Star starting pitcher for the Indians, Red Sox, and Cubs. As a 22-year-old, he no-hit the Angels in May 1977, allowing only one walk to California first baseman Tony Solaita with two outs in the first inning. The only other Angel hitter to reach base was right fielder Bobby Bonds, who went to first on a strikeout and wild pitch leading off in the eighth inning. The Indians won 1-0 on a Jim Norris squeeze bunt that scored Duane Kuiper from third base with one out in the bottom of the first inning. Eckersley had pitched seven hitless innings to finish his previous start, then took a no-hit bid into the sixth inning in his next start after the no-hitter. His 21 consecutive hitless innings was the longest streak since Cy Young's 25 and one-third hitless innings in 1904.

NOTE 4: Len Barker's perfect game in 1981 against the Blue Jays is one of two thrown by the Cleveland franchise – Hall of Famer Addie Joss threw a perfect game for the Naps against the White Sox in 1908. Barker's game was a masterpiece, and he got better as the game went along. His first strikeout was future All-Star Lloyd Moseby with one out in the fourth inning. After that, he struck out 10 of the next 16 Blue Jays he faced, including Lloyd Moseby (again), and hard-hitters George Bell and Willie Upshaw two times apiece. Barker's perfect game is the most recent Cleveland no-hitter,, as the team now holds the current active record for the longest streak without a no-hitter (40+ years).

NOTE 5: There are four Cleveland pitchers who have thrown no-hitters who are also members of the Hall of Fame: Bob Feller, Addie Joss Bob Lemon,, and Dennis Eckersley. Feller and Joss both threw more than one. Feller threw three, with his 1940 no-hitter occuring on Opening Day against the White Sox. His other two happened in 1946 and 1951, after he served in the Navy for nearly four years during World War II. Feller enlisted two days after Pearl Harbor and volunteered for combat duty. He served as a gun captain on the battleship *USS Alabama*, including during the pitched Battle of the Philippine Sea. With 266 wins, a winning percentage of .621, and the baseball leader in strikeouts for seven consecutive seasons, Feller was one of the greatest pitchers of his era and a near-unanimous selection for the Hall of Fame.. One wonders what those relatively few Hall of Fame voters could possibly be thinking when they passed Feller over for selection in 1962, when he first became eligible. Feller is in this table four times, as he threw a one-hitter against the Athletics in 1940 – the highest Game Score (96) he ever achieved and just three months after his first no-hitter. The only hit he gave up was a single to Philadelphia's Dick Siebert leading off the eighth inning.

NOTE 6: Spending his entire career with Cleveland, Addie Joss is a special case. Over a spectacular nine-year pitching career, Joss established a record for lowest "WHIP" (walks plus hits divided by innings pitched) of 0.968 – less than one hit or walk combined per inning. In addition to a magnificent perfect game against the White Sox – where Joss outdueled Hall of Famer and 40-game winner Ed Walsh for a 1-0 win – he threw another no-hitter two years later against this same Chicago team. Joss was truly in the prime of his career. Tragically, Joss contracted tuberculous meningitis early in 1911 and died two days after his 31st birthday in April of that year.

NOTE 7: Carlos Carrasco's near-no-hitter against the World Champion Royals in 2015 was broken up by an Alex Rios line drive single to center field with one out in the seventh inning. Corey Kluber's eight-inning, 18-strikeout near-no-hitter was broken up in the seventh inning when Jhonny Peralta of the Cardinals hit a grounder up the middle with two outs. Kluber was removed after eight innings because he had already thrown 113 pitches and the Indians were ahead 2-0. That day, Kluber set a Major League record for the most strikeouts (18) and Game Score (98) achieved by a pitcher who threw eight innings or less in a game. Bartolo Colon had a no-hitter going in 2000 against the New Yourk Yankees until Luis Polonia hit a line drive single to center field with one out in the eighth inning. The only baserunner Josh Tomlin allowed in his one-hit victory over the Mariners in 2014 was a one-strike line drive single by Kyle Seager leading off the fifth inning.

NOTE 8: Cleveland's Don Black, author of a 1947 no-hitter for the Indians, is remarkable for a variety of reasons. With a career Jaffe Wins Above Replacement Score (JAWS) of negative 1.9 (meaning he had a career value of 1.9 points below replacement level) he has the distinction of having the lowest JAWS of any pitcher to ever throw a no-hitter. On the surface, it might appear that his would have been the most unlikely no-hitter ever thrown, but that would be misleading. After dealing with control issues early in his career – brought on largely by his struggle with alcoholism -- Black had a bright future with the Indians in 1947. He was a key member of a starting staff that included Hall of Famers Bob Feller and Bob Lemon. That season Black threw his no-hitter against a solid Philadelphia team, shutting them down 3-0. A year later, Black suffered a life-threatening brain hemorrhage during a game. He recovered from the burst vessel, but never played baseball at the major league level again.

NOTE 9: Pete Dowling's 1901 no-hitter is not officially recognized by Major League Baseball because there is some discrepancy over whether there was a hit in this game. Baseball-Reference and Retrosheet, two authoritative baseball resources, both credit Dowling with giving up no hits. Newspaper accounts, however, state that Milwaukee's Wid Conroy reached on an infield single in the seventh inning. Conroy's career statistics, though, do not credit him with a hit in this game.

NOTE 10: Bob "Dusty" Rhoads does not have an official Game Score for his 1908 no-hitter. At the time, runs allowed weren't differentiated between "earned" runs and "unearned" runs. Since Rhoads allowed two walks and a hit batsman, and his Cleveland Naps teammates (second baseman Nap Lajoie and third baseman Bill Bradley) committed errors, it can't be determined with certainty whether the run allowed was earned or unearned. There were also four sacrifice hits, but no RBIs recorded for Boston hitters. Descriptions of the game are incomplete at best. It is very likely the run was unearned since the lack of an RBI indicates an error was probably involved in the run scoring. If the run was an earned run, that's minus four points for Rhoads' Game Score. An unearned run subtracts two points. Therefore, his Game Score is either 83 or 85, with the likelihood of it being an 85. Either way, Rhoads qualifies for inclusion in this table.

Table 25-9. Highest Rays Game Scores

Rank	Pitcher (Team)	Date Score	Opponent	GSc	IP, Hits, Runs, ERs, Walks, Strikeouts
1	Chris Archer (Rays)	8/20/2015 TB 1-0	Houston Astros	95	9.0 IP, 1 Hit, 0 Runs, 0 ERs, 1 BB, 11 Ks
2	James Shields (Rays)	10/2/2012 Bal 1-0	Baltimore Orioles	94	9.0 IP, 2 Hits, 1 Run, 1 ER, 0 BBs, 15 Ks
3 (tie)	Ryan Rupe (Devil Rays)	5/23/1999 Ana 4-0 (10 inn)	Anaheim Angels	93	9.0 IP, 1 Hit, 0 Runs, 0 ERs, 0 BBs, 8 Ks
3 (tie)	James Shields (Rays)	5/9/2008 TB 2-0	LA Angels of Anaheim	93	9.0 IP, 1 Hit, 0 Runs, 0 ERs, 0 BBs, 8 Ks
3 (tie)	James Shields (Rays)	5/22/2011 TB 4-0	Florida Marlins	93	9.0 IP, 3 Hits, 0 Runs, 0 ERs, 1 BB, 13 Ks
6 (tie)	Matt Garza (Rays)	7/26/2010 TB 5-0	Detroit Tigers	92	9.0 IP, 0 Hits, 0 Runs, 0 ERs, 1 BB, 6 Ks
6 (tie)	James Shields (Rays)	7/31/2012 TB 8-0	Oakland Athletics	92	9.0 IP, 3 Hits, 0 Runs, 0 ERs, 0 BBs, 11 Ks
8 (tie)	Scott Kazmir (Devil Rays)	7/3/2006 TB 3-0	Boston Red Sox	91	9.0 IP, 2 Hits, 0 Runs, 0 ERs, 2 BBs, 10 Ks

Rank	Pitcher (Team)	Date Score	Opponent	GSc	IP, Hits, Runs, ERs, Walks, Strikeouts
8 (tie)	Jeff Niemann (Rays)	6/3/2009 TB 9-0	Kansas City Royals	91	9.0 IP 2 Hits, 0 Runs, 0 ERs, 1 BB, 9 Ks
8 (tie)	James Shields (Rays)	9/9/2012 TB 6-0	Texas Rangers	91	9.0 IP, 2 Hits, 0 Runs, 0 ERs, 0 BBs, 8 Ks
---	Colin McHugh +4 (Rays)	7/7/2021 (2) TB 4-0 (7 inn)	Cleveland Indians	59	2.0 IP, 0 Hits, 0 Runs, 0 ERs, 0 BBs, 3 Ks

METHODOLOGY: This table includes the highest Game Scores thrown by a Rays pitcher from 1998-2021. Games are ranked by Game Score (GSc) and consider all franchise regular season and postseason games. Game Score measures a pitcher's performance in any given game started. Introduced by baseball writer/statistician Bill James in the 1980s, Game Score is presented as a figure between 0-100 — except for extreme outliers — and usually falls between 40-70.

LEGEND: Dates are shown as month/day/year (for example, June 12, 2018, is shown as 6/12/2018); IP = innings pitched. BB(s) = base(s) on balls. K(s) = strikeout(s). ER(s) = earned run(s). inn = innings (associated with the length of games that were more or less than nine innings). One-third of an inning pitched has 0.1 added and two-thirds of an inning pitched has 0.2 added (for example, 9 1/3 innings pitched is displayed as 9.1). BB(s) = base(s) on balls; K(s) = strikeout(s). (1) or (2) indicates the game is the first or second game of a doubleheader. The team joined the American League as the expansion Tampa Bay Devil Rays in 1998, the same year the Arizona Diamondbacks were established in the National League. The Devil Rays shortened the team name to the Rays in 2008. The team's name for each of the games in the table – "Devil Rays" or "Rays" – is indicated in the "Team" entry underneath the pitcher's name.

NOTE 1: The highest postseason Game Score thrown by a Tampa Bay pitcher was a 77 by Matt Moore in the opening game of the 2011 AL Division Series against the 96-win Texas Rangers. Moore threw seven innings of two-hit, shutout ball against a loaded Texas lineup that featured Josh Hamilton, Adrian Beltre, Michael Young, and Nelson Cruz. Moore allowed only five baserunners on two Josh Hamilton hits, two walks, and a hit batsman. The Rays took charge of the game early, with three runs in the second inning, three more in the third, and two more in the fifth. Moore was pulled after he finished the seventh inning with Tampa Bay ahead 8-0.

He had thrown 98 pitches and manager Joe Maddon didn't want to extend him at the beginning of what might have been a five-game series. The Rays would win the game, but unfortunately for Tampa Bay, they would lose the next three very close contests to the Rangers by a total of four runs. Moore would pitch again in the decisive fourth game, allowing one run over three innings of relief in a 4-3 Texas win. The Rangers would go on to beat the Tigers in the AL Championship Series before losing to the St. Louis Cardinals in an exciting seven-game World Series.

NOTE 2: The highest Game Score by a Tampa Bay pitcher was a 98 by Chris Archer in a 2015 game against the Houston Astros. Archer allowed only one hit – a fifth inning groundball single to left fielder Colby Rasmus – over nine innings of shutout ball in a 1-0 Tampa Bay win. He also allowed a leadoff walk to Jose Altuve in the first inning. Archer struck out 11 in a dominant win over a very good Houston team. A solid pitcher for the Rays, Archer won 55 games with Tampa Bay, and was selected for the American League All-Star team in 2015 and 2017.

NOTE 3: Tampa Bay ace James Shields dominates this list, appearing five times in the best ten games thrown by a Rays pitcher. His two-hitter against the Orioles in 2012 was his highest Game Score at 94, even though he lost the game 1-0 due to a Chris Davis home run in the fourth inning. Shields set the record for most strikeouts in a game for a Tampa Bay pitcher when he struck out 15 Baltimore batters – the record was tied in 2015 by Chris Archer. Shields came very close to throwing a perfect game against the Angels in 2008, as he only allowed one baserunner: Los Angeles third baseman Brandon Wood hit a single up the middle in the third inning. That game was scoreless until it was decided in the bottom of the ninth inning on a walkoff Evan Longoria two-run home run. An All-Star and Cy Young contender in 2011, Shields is recognized as one of the best pitchers in Tampa Bay history, as he holds the team record for most games won (87). Traded to the Kansas City Royals in 2012, Shields would have continued success with the Royals, Padres, and White Sox.

NOTE 4: Matt Garza's near-perfect game against the Tigers in 2010 is the only no-hitter in franchise history. Garza walked Tiger right fielder Brennan Boesch on a full count with one out in the second inning. The next batter hit into a double play, and that was it. Garza would face the minimum 27 batters in his no-hit win. The opposing pitcher, Max Scherzer, would pitch no-hit ball for five and two-thirds innings before giving up a grand slam to Tampa Bay designated hitter Matt Joyce. The Rays would win the game by the score of 5-0. Garza's best year with Tampa Bay was 2010, as he compiled 15 wins and helped the team make it into the postseason for the second time in three years.

NOTE 5: Ryan Rupe also came close to pitching a no-hitter in 1999 against the Angels, as he allowed just one single and set the team record for highest Game Score at 93. Anaheim's lone hit was registered by Darin Erstad leading off the seventh inning. Unfortunately for the Devil Rays, the team didn't score by the end of nine innings. Rupe was pulled and reliever Roberto Hernandez was called upon to pitch the top of the ninth inning. The Angels scored four runs and won the game 4-0. Rupe's Tampa Bay Game Score record was subsequently tied by James Shield in 2008 and 2011, and then broken by Shields in 2012 with a 94 game. Chris Archer holds the current record of 95 with his 2015 one-hitter.

NOTE 6: The Tampa Bay Rays threw a multi-pitcher, seven-inning no-hitter in July 2021. Colin McHugh threw the first two innings, and Josh Fleming (2.2 IP), Diego Castillo (0.1 IP), Matt Wisler (1.0 IP), and Pete Fairbanks (1.0 IP) closed out the 4-0 victory over Cleveland. The game lasted only seven innings because it was the second game of a doubleheader. At that time, doubleheaders consisted of two games of seven innings each. Since the game didn't last nine innings, it isn't officially counted as a no-hitter.

Table 25-10. Highest Red Sox Game Scores

Rank	Pitcher (Team)	Date Score	Opponent	GSc	IP, Hits, Runs, ERs, Walks, Strikeouts
1	Joe Harris (Americans)	9/1/1906 Phi 4-1 (24 inn)	Phi Athletics	126-134	24.0 IP, 16 Hits, 4 Runs, ? ERs, 2 BBs, 14 Ks
2	Cy Young (Americans)	7/4/1905 (2) Phi 4-2 (20 inn)	Phi Athletics	111-119	20.0 IP, 12 Hits, 4 Runs, ? ERs, 0 BBs, 9 Ks
3	Cy Young (Americans)	5/11/1904 Bos 1-0 (15 inn)	Det Tigers	108	15.0 IP, 5 Hits, 0 Runs, 0 ERs, 4 BBs, 5 Ks
4	Cy Young (Americans)	9/9/1907 0-0 Tie (13 inn)	Phi Athletics	104	13.0 IP, 6 Hits, 0 Runs, 0 ERs, 0 BBs, 9 Ks
5 (tie)	Ernie Shore (Red Sox)	9/12/1917 1-1 Tie (16 inn)	Was Senators	103	16.0 IP, 6 Hits, 1 Run, 1 ER, 5 BBs, 2 Ks
5 (tie)	M. McDermott (Red Sox)	7/13/1951 Chi 5-4 (19 inn)	Chi White Sox	103	17.0 IP, 8 Hits, 2 Runs, 2 ERs, 9 BBs, 9 Ks

Rank	Pitcher (Team)	Date Score	Opponent	GSc	IP, Hits, Runs, ERs, Walks, Strikeouts
7	Hideo Nomo (Red Sox)	5/25/2001 Bos 4-0	Tor Blue Jays	99	9.0 IP, 1 Hit, 0 Runs, 0 ERs, 0 BBs, 14 Ks
8 (tie)	Cy Young (Americans)	9/10/1904 Phi 1-0 (13 inn)	Phi Athletics	98	12.2 IP, 7 Hits, 1 Run, 1 ER, 0 BBs, 12 Ks
8 (tie)	Ray Collins (Red Sox)	7/3/1913 Was 1-0 (15 inn)	Was Senators	98	15.0 IP, 9 Hits, 1 Run, 1 ER, 2 BBs, 5 Ks
8 (tie)	Carl Mays (Red Sox)	7/14/1916 0-0 Tie (17 inn)	StL Browns	98	15.0 IP, 9 Hits, 0 Runs, 0 ERs, 8 BBs, 7 Ks
8 (tie)	Ed Durham (Red Sox)	9/12/1931 Bos 1-0 (13 inn)	Det Tigers	98	13.0 IP, 5 Hits, 0 Runs, 0 ERs, 0 BBs, 1 K
8 (tie)	M. McDermott (Red Sox)	7/28/1951 Bos 8-4 (16 inn)	Cle Indians	98	16.0 IP, 11 Hits, 4 Runs, 4 ER, 1 BBs, 15 Ks
8 (tie)	Pedro Martinez (Red Sox)	9/10/1999 Bos 3-1	NY Yankees	98	9.0 IP, 1 Hit, 1 Run, 1 ER, 0 BBs, 17 Ks
8 (tie)	Pedro Martinez (Red Sox)	5/12/2000 Bos 9-0	Bal Orioles	98	9.0 IP, 2 Hits, 0 Runs, 0 ERs, 0 BBs, 15 Ks
8 (tie)	Pedro Martinez (Red Sox)	8/29/2000 Bos 8-0	TB Devil Rays	98	9.0 IP, 1 Hit, 0 Runs, 0 ERs, 0 BBs, 13 Ks

METHODOLOGY: This table includes the highest Game Scores thrown by a Red Sox pitcher from 1901-2021. Games are ranked by Game Score (GSc) and consider all franchise regular season and postseason games. Table 25-11 below limits the eligible games to those pitching performances that were 10 innings or less. Game Score (GSc) measures a pitcher's performance in any given game started. Introduced by baseball writer/statistician Bill James in the 1980s, Game Score is presented as a figure between 0-100 — except for extreme outliers — and usually falls between 40-70.

LEGEND: Dates are shown as month/day/year (for example, June 12, 2018, is shown as 6/12/2018); IP = innings pitched. BB(s) = base(s) on balls. K(s) = strikeout(s). ER(s) = earned run(s). inn = innings (associated with the length of games that were more or less than nine innings). One-third of an inning pitched has 0.1 added and two-thirds of an inning pitched has 0.2 added (for example, 9 1/3 innings pitched is displayed as 9.1). BB(s) = base(s) on balls; K(s) = strikeout(s).

(1) or (2) indicates the game is the first or second game of a doubleheader. The Red Sox have been based in Boston since they started in the American League in 1901. From 1901 through 1907 they were known as the Boston Americans. They have been known as the Red Sox since 1908. The team's name (Americans or Red Sox) for each of the games in the table is indicated in the "Team" entry underneath the pitcher's name.

NOTE 1: The highest postseason Game Score thrown by a Red Sox pitcher was a 97 by Babe Ruth in Game 2 of the 1916 World Series against the Brooklyn Robins (forerunners of the Dodgers). Ruth threw 14 innings of one-run ball en route to a 2-1 win. Ruth allowed only six hits and three walks during a critical win that put the Red Sox ahead of Brooklyn two games to none in the best-of-seven series. Boston would go on to beat the Robins in the World Series four games to one. Brooklyn had the best hitting team in the National League, with a potent lineup that included Hall of Famers Zack Wheat and Casey Stengel.

NOTE 2: The highest Game Score ever recorded by a Boston pitcher is an unofficial tally from a 24-inning game against the Athletics in 1906. Joe Harris threw all 24 innings for the Americans and allowed four runs – one in the third inning and three more in the top of the 24th. Boston catcher Bill Carrigan committed two errors in that game. Because there was no differentiation between earned runs and unearned runs at the time, a Game Score hasn't been officially calculated. That said, newspaper writeups indicate that neither of those errors played a role in Philadelphia runs being scored. Consequently, if they were all earned runs, Harris earned a Game Score of 126, with the highest score he could have achieved being 134 (if all the runs were unearned). Along with throwing the longest game in Boston history, his Game Score of 126 puts Harris at the top of Boston's list. Despite the loss, Harris set a record for throwing 20 consecutive scoreless innings that day. At the time, this was also the longest game in American League history.

NOTE 3: Legendary Hall of Famer Cy Young, namesake for baseball's highest award for pitching excellence, is featured prominently in this table. With four games among the highest team scores, including three of the top four Game Scores in Boston history, he leads the list of most mentions. His 20-inning effort against Philadelphia in 1905 has an unofficial Game Score of between 111 and 119, as there was no distinction between earned and unearned runs then. Because Boston committed six errors during the game, it's entirely likely some of the runs were unearned, but there's no easy way to determine an exact number. Regardless, the range of 111-119 puts this game squarely in second place on the list. Young's 13- and 15-inning shutouts are also among the most impressive games ever thrown by a Boston pitcher.

Table 25-11. Highest Red Sox Game Scores of 10 innings or less

Rank	Pitcher (Team)	Date Score	Opponent	GSc	IP, Hits, Runs, ERs, Walks, Strikeouts
1	Hideo Nomo (Red Sox)	5/25/2001 Bos 4-0	Tor Blue Jays	99	9.0 IP, 1 Hit, 0 Runs, 0 ERs, 0 BBs, 14 Ks
2 (tie)	Pedro Martinez (Red Sox)	9/10/1999 Bos 3-1	NY Yankees	98	9.0 IP, 1 Hit, 1 Run, 1 ER, 0 BBs, 17 Ks
2 (tie)	Pedro Martinez (Red Sox)	5/12/2000 Bos 9-0	Bal Orioles	98	9.0 IP, 2 Hits, 0 Runs, 0 ERs, 0 BBs, 15 Ks
2 (tie)	Pedro Martinez (Red Sox)	8/29/2000 Bos 8-0	TB Devil Rays	98	9.0 IP, 1 Hit, 0 Runs, 0 ERs, 0 BBs, 13 Ks
5 (tie)	Smoky Joe Wood (Red Sox)	7/29/1911 (1) Bos 5-0	StL Browns	97	9.0 IP, 0 Hits, 0 Runs, 0 ERs, 2 BBs, 12 Ks
5 (tie)	Roger Clemens (Red Sox)	4/29/1986 Bos 3-1	Sea Mariners	97	9.0 IP, 3 Hits, 1 Run, 1 ER, 0 BBs, 20 Ks
5 (tie)	Roger Clemens (Red Sox)	9/18/1996 Bos 4-0	Det Tigers	97	9.0 IP, 5 Hits, 0 Runs, 0 ERs, 0 BBs, 20 Ks
8	Roger Clemens (Red Sox)	5/9/1988 Bos 2-0	KC Royals	96	9.0 IP, 3 Hits, 0 Runs, 0 ERs, 1 BB, 16 Ks
9 (tie)	*Cy Young (Americans)*	5/5/1904 Bos 3-0	Phi Athletics	95	*9.0 IP, 0 Hits, 0 Runs, 0 ERs, 0 BBs, 8 Ks*
9 (tie)	Cy Young (Americans)	9/23/1905 (2) Bos 5-0	StL Browns	95	9.0 IP, 2 Hits, 0 Runs, 0 ERs, 0 BBs, 12 Ks
9 (tie)	Ray Culp (Red Sox)	9/21/1968 Bos 2-0	NY Yankees	95	9.0 IP, 1 Hit, 0 Runs, 0 ERs, 1 BB, 11 Ks
9 (tie)	Roger Moret (Red Sox)	8/21/1974 Bos 4-0	Chi White Sox	95	9.0 IP, 1 Hit, 0 Runs, 0 ERs, 2 BBs, 12 Ks
9 (tie)	Roger Clemens (Red Sox)	10/4/1987 Bos 4-0	Mil Brewers	95	9.0 IP, 2 Hits, 0 Runs, 0 ERs, 0 BBs, 12 Ks
9 (tie)	Hideo Nomo (Red Sox)	4/4/2001 Bos 3-0	Bal Orioles	95	9.0 IP, 0 Hits, 0 Runs, 0 ERs, 3 BBs, 11 Ks

Rank	Pitcher (Team)	Date Score	Opponent	GSc	IP, Hits, Runs, ERs, Walks, Strikeouts
15 (tie)	Dave Morehead (Red Sox)	9/16/1965 BOS 2-0	Cle Indians	94	9.0 IP, 0 Hits, 0 Runs, 0 ERs, 1 BB, 8 Ks
15 (tie)	Jon Lester (Red Sox)	5/19/2008 KCR 7-0	KC Royals	94	9.0 IP, 0 Hits, 0 Runs, 0 ERs, 2 BBs, 9 Ks
19 (tie)	B. Monbouquette (Red Sox)	8/1/1962 Bos 1-0	Chi White Sox	93	9.0 IP, 0 Hits, 0 Runs, 0 ERs, 1 BB, 7 Ks
19 (tie)	Clay Buchholz (Red Sox)	9/1/2007 Bos 10-0	Bal Orioles	93	9.0 IP, 0 Hits, 0 Runs, 0 ERs, 3 BBs, 9 Ks
26 (tie)	Derek Lowe (Red Sox)	4/27/2002 Bos 10-0	TB Devil Rays	92	9.0 IP, 0 Hits, 0 Runs, 0 ERs, 1 BB, 6 Ks
33 (tie)	Bill Dinneen (Americans)	9/27/1905 (1) Bos 2-0	Chi White Sox	91	9.0 IP, 0 Hits, 0 Runs, 0 ERs, 2 BBs, 6 Ks
46 (tie)	Jesse Tannehill (Americans)	8/17/1904 Bos 6-0	Chi White Sox	90	9.0 IP, 0 Hits, 0 Runs, 0 ERs, 1 BB, 4 Ks
46 (tie)	Dutch Leonard (Red Sox)	6/3/1918 Bos 5-0	Bal Orioles	90	9.0 IP, 0 Hits, 0 Runs, 0 ERs, 1 BB, 4 Ks
65 (tie)	Mel Parnell (Red Sox)	7/14/1956 Bos 4-0	Chi White Sox	89	9.0 IP, 0 Hits, 0 Runs, 0 ERs, 2 BBs, 4 Ks
92 (tie)	Cy Young (Red Sox)	6/30/1908 Bos 8-0	NY Highlanders	88	9.0 IP, 0 Hits, 0 Runs, 0 ERs, 1 BB, 2 Ks
92 (tie)	Dutch Leonard (Red Sox)	8/30/1916 Bos 4-0	StL Browns	88	9.0 IP, 0 Hits, 0 Runs, 0 ERs, 2 BBs, 3 Ks
92 (tie)	Babe Ruth +1 (Red Sox)	6/23/1917 Bos 4-0	Was Senators	88	9.0 IP, 0 Hits, 0 Runs, 0 ERs, 1 BB, 2 Ks
92 (tie)	Earl Wilson (Red Sox)	6/26/1962 Bos 2-0	LA Angels	88	9.0 IP, 0 Hits, 0 Runs, 0 ERs, 4 BBs, 5 Ks
125 (tie)	Rube Foster (Red Sox)	6/21/1916 Bos 2-0	NY Yankees	87	9.0 IP, 0 Hits, 0 Runs, 0 ERs, 3 BBs, 3 Ks
125 (tie)	Howard Ehmke (Red Sox)	9/7/1923 Bos 4-0	Phi Athletics	87	9.0 IP, 0 Hits, 0 Runs, 0 ERs, 1 BB, 1 K
---	Matt Young (Red Sox)	4/12/1992 (1) Cle 2-1	Cle Indians	73	8.0 IP, 0 Hits, 2 Runs, 2 ERs, 7 BBs, 6 Ks
---	Devern Hansack (Red Sox)	10/1/2006 Bos 9-0 (5 inn)	Bal Orioles	72	5.0 IP, 0 Hits, 0 Runs, 0 ERs, 1 BB, 6 Ks

METHODOLOGY: This table includes the highest Game Scores of 10 innings or less thrown by a Red Sox pitcher from 1901-2021. Games are ranked by Game Score (GSc) and consider all franchise regular season and postseason games. For comparison purposes, all 18 of the team's no-hitters are included in this table. Game Score measures a pitcher's performance in any given game started. Introduced by baseball writer/statistician Bill James in the 1980s, Game Score is presented as a figure between 0-100 — except for extreme outliers — and usually falls between 40-70. For comparison purposes, all 17 franchise no-hitters from 1901-2021 are included in this table.

LEGEND: Dates are shown as month/day/year (for example, June 12, 2018, is shown as 6/12/2018); IP = innings pitched. BB(s) = base(s) on balls. K(s) = strikeout(s). ER(s) = earned run(s). inn = innings (associated with the length of games that were more or less than nine innings). One-third of an inning pitched has 0.1 added and two-thirds of an inning pitched has 0.2 added (for example, 9 1/3 innings pitched is displayed as 9.1). BB(s) = base(s) on balls; K(s) = strikeout(s). (1) or (2) indicates the game is the first or second game of a doubleheader. The Red Sox have been based in Boston since they started in the American League in 1901. From 1901 through 1907 they were known as the Boston Americans. They have been known as the Red Sox since 1908. The team's name (Americans or Red Sox) for each of the games in the table is indicated in the "Team" entry underneath the pitcher's name. *Italicized game (Cy Young in 1904) was a perfect game, and the first of two no-hitters he threw for Boston. He also had a no-hitter in 1897 for the Cleveland Spiders of the National League.*

NOTE 1: Hideo Nomo's one-hitter against the Blue Jays in May 2001 is the highest nine-inning Game Score ever achieved by a Boston pitcher (99). With 14 strikeouts, Nomo nearly threw a perfect game, as he allowed only a double to Toronto's Shannon Stewart leading off the fourth inning. On Boston's second game of the season that same year, Nomo threw his no-hitter against the Orioles. It was Nomo's second career no-hitter and his first game as a member of the Red Sox.

NOTE 2: Hall of Famer Pedro Martinez threw the three games that are tied for second place on this list. The games were all thrown within the space of one year during the 1999 and 2000 seasons. In his 15-strikeout two-hitter in 2000, the only Oriole batters who reached base were on two singles in the fifth inning. The one Yankee hit in Martinez's one-hitter in 1999 was a solo home run by designated hitter Chili Davis. During that game, Martinez struck out 17 of the 28 Yankee batters he faced. New York was in the second of three consecutive seasons where the team won the World Series. In his 2000 one-hitter against the Devil Rays, his no-hitter was broken up by a leadoff single by John Flaherty leading off the ninth inning.

NOTE 3: Roger Clemens also features prominently on this list, appearing in the Top 14 franchise Game Scores four times, more than any other Boston pitcher. Clemens's dominant pitching performances typically featured high strikeout totals, with him achieving 20 strikeouts on two occasions. Along with Kerry Wood and Max Scherzer, Clemens holds the record for the most batters struck out in a single game.

NOTE 4: In Cy Young's 1908 no-hitter against the Highlanders, he allowed a walk to New York second baseman Harry Niles leading off the bottom of the first inning. After that, Young retired the next 27 batters in a row. Young's other no-hitter for Boston was the American League's first perfect game, a 1904 effort against the Philadelphia Athletics. Besides Cy Young, Dutch Leonard is the only other Boston pitcher who has thrown more than one no-hitter. In his second no-hitter – in a 1918 game against Detroit – Leonard nearly pitched a perfect game, allowing only one walk to Tiger left fielder Bobby Veach.

NOTE 5: Bill Monbouquette, Derek Lowe, Jesse Tannehill, and Howard Ehmke all threw no-hitters that were nearly perfect games. Each of them walked only one batter in addition to shutting down the opposing teams with no hits. While it's not known when Tannehill walked George Davis of the White Sox, all the walks in the other games occurred in the fifth inning or earlier. Clay Buchholz's no-hitter in 2007 was his second career game. Jon Lester's 2008 no-hitter was also catcher Jason Varitek's fourth career no-hitter, setting the record for most no-hitters caught.

NOTE 6: Babe Ruth (0.0 innings) and Ernie Shore (9.0 innings) threw baseball's first multi-pitcher no-hitter in 1917. Babe Ruth started the game but was ejected after slugging (!) home plate umpire Brick Owens when Ruth became angry at Owens calling a couple of pitches as balls, resulting in a walk for Washington's leadoff hitter Ray Morgan. Ernie Shore entered as the Red Sox relief pitcher, and Morgan was promptly thrown out attempting to steal second base. Shore retired the next 26 batters to log the no-hitter, with the only Senator baserunner being Morgan leading off the first inning. The Washington lineup that day included Hall of Famer Sam Rice and rookie star Joe Judge.

NOTE 7: While not officially counted as a no-hitter because the game was stopped at less than nine innings, Boston's rookie pitcher Devern Hansack threw five innings of no-hit ball on the last day of the 2006 regular season. A September call-up, it was the second start of Hansack's career. Both the Red Sox and Orioles were out of contention as they played out the string that day. The game was halted at the end of five innings because of rain with Boston leading 9-0. After a 45-minute delay, the game was ended and declared official. Hansack would only pitch in seven more games over the next two seasons, completing his major league career with a 2-2 won-loss record and a total of 24.1 innings pitched. That October day in Boston, though, he was near perfect for five innings.

NOTE 8: On April 12, 1992, Boston's Matt Young threw a complete game no-hitter against Cleveland. Unfortunately for him and the Red Sox, the Indians scored two runs while Boston was held to a single run, resulting in a 2-1 Cleveland win. Both Indian runs were earned, as Cleveland leadoff hitter Kenny Lofton walked on four pitches in the first inning and stole second and third. He then scored on a fielder's choice. Cleveland's second run came on two walks to lead off the third inning, followed by two consecutive fielder's choices. The result was two earned runs scored without benefit of a hit. Young was wild that day, walking seven hitters over his eight innings. He didn't get to pitch the ninth inning because Cleveland was the home team and didn't bat in the bottom of the inning because the Indians had already won. Because Young didn't pitch nine innings, his accomplishment didn't count as a no-hitter. When it happened, it was only the third time a pitcher had thrown an eight-inning complete game no-hitter but had lost the game.

Table 25-12. Highest Rockies Game Scores

Rank	Pitcher	Date Score	Opponent	GSc	IP, Hits, Runs, ERs, Walks, Strikeouts
1	Jon Gray	9/17/2016 Col 8-0	San Diego Padres	95	9.0 IP, 4 Hits, 0 Runs, 0 ERs, 0 BBs, 16 Ks
2	German Marquez	4/14/2019 Col 4-0	San Francisco Giants	94	9.0 IP, 1 Hit, 0 Runs, 0 ERs, 0 BBs, 9 Ks
3 (tie)	Darryl Kyle	9/20/1998 Col 1-0 (11 inn)	San Diego Padres	91	10.0 IP, 3 Hits, 0 Runs, 0 ERs, 2 BBs, 7 Ks
3 (tie)	Jeff Francis	7/24/2006 Col 7-0	St. Louis Cardinals	91	9.0 IP, 2 Hits, 0 Runs, 0 ERs, 0 BBs, 8 Ks
5	Chad Bettis	9/5/2016 Col 6-0	San Francisco Giants	90	9.0 IP, 2 Hits, 0 Runs, 0 ERs, 0 BBs, 7 Ks

Rank	Pitcher	Date Score	Opponent	GSc	IP, Hits, Runs, ERs, Walks, Strikeouts
6 (tie)	Pedro Astacio	8/10/1999 Mil 2-1 (10 inn)	Milwaukee Brewers	89	9.0 IP, 2 Hits, 1 Run, 0 ERs, 1 BB, 9 Ks
6 (tie)	German Marquez	6/29/2021 Col 8-0	Pittsburgh Pirates	89	9.0 IP, 1 Hit, 0 Runs, 0 ERs, 1 BB, 5 Ks
8	Ubaldo Jimenez	4/17/2010 Col 4-0	Atlanta Braves	88	9.0 IP, 0 Hits, 0 Runs, 0 ERs, 6 BBs, 7 Ks
9 (tie)	Jason Jennings	5/29/2006 Col 5-0	San Diego Padres	87	9.0 IP, 2 Hits, 0 Runs, 0 ERs, 3 BBs, 7 Ks
9 (tie)	Kyle Freeland	7/9/2017 Col 10-0	Chicago White Sox	87	8.1 IP 1 Hit, 0 Runs, 0 ERs, 3 BBs, 9 Ks

METHODOLOGY: This table includes the highest Game Scores thrown by a Rockies pitcher from 1993-2021. Games are ranked by Game Score (GSc) and consider all franchise regular season and postseason games. Game Score measures a pitcher's performance in any given game started. Introduced by baseball writer/statistician Bill James in the 1980s, Game Score is presented as a figure between 0-100 — except for extreme outliers — and usually falls between 40-70.

LEGEND: Dates are shown as month/day/year (for example, June 12, 2018, is shown as 6/12/2018); IP = innings pitched. BB(s) = base(s) on balls. K(s) = strikeout(s). ER(s) = earned run(s). inn = innings (associated with the length of games that were more or less than nine innings). One-third of an inning pitched has 0.1 added and two-thirds of an inning pitched has 0.2 added (for example, 9 1/3 innings pitched is displayed as 9.1). BB(s) = base(s) on balls; K(s) = strikeout(s). (1) or (2) indicates the game is the first or second game of a doubleheader. The Rockies joined the National League as an expansion team with the Florida (now Miami) Marlins in 1993. Colorado has been in the West Division since it began.

NOTE 1: The highest postseason Game Score thrown by a Rockies pitcher was a 71 by staff ace Kyle Freeland in the 2018 Wild Card game against the Chicago Cubs. At that time, the Wild Card series was a one-game playoff between the two best non-division winning teams in each league. Because the stakes were so high, the primary incentive was to do everything necessary to win this game and advance to the next round. Freeland pitched very well against a very tough Cubs team. He threw six and two-thirds innings of shutout ball, allowing only four hits and one walk against a lineup that featured stars Ben Zobrist, Kris Bryant, Anthony Rizzo, and Javier Baez. Freeland was pulled in the seventh inning by manager Bud Black with the bases loaded and two outs in a game where Colorado was leading 1-0. Reliever Adam Ottavino managed to get slugger Jason Heyward to strike out swinging to end the inning. The Cubs would tie the game in the eighth inning, but the Rockies would win by the score of 2-1 in the 13th inning on a single by Tony Wolters, scoring Trevor Story from third base. The Rockies advanced to the Division Series against the NL Central Division champion Brewers, but Milwaukee swept Colorado in three games. Overall, the Rockies have qualified for the postseason five times, each time as a Wild Card winner. The team made it to the World Series in 2007, though they got swept by the Red Sox in four games.

NOTE 2: With a Game Score of 95, 24-year-old rookie Jon Gray's shutout of the San Diego Padres in 2016 qualifies as the highest Game Score ever achieved by a Colorado pitcher. What makes this especially impressive was that he accomplished it at Coors Field, a park renowned for being friendly to hitters. Striking out 16 Padres – the most strikeouts ever achieved by a Rockies pitcher in a single game – while walking no one, was also extraordinary. The game was never in doubt, as the Rockies jumped to an early four-run lead in the first inning and were leading 8-0 by the end of the fifth. The victory was Gray's 10th of the season, a mark he would achieve or surpass for the next four seasons with Colorado.

NOTE 3: With nine strikeouts, German Marquez nearly threw a no-hitter against the Giants at Oracle Park in 2019. San Francisco's only hit came with one out in the eighth when third baseman Evan Longoria hit a one-out groundball through the left side of the infield for a single. Longoria was one of only two Giants to reach base, with the other one being a hit batsman in the sixth inning. Marquez also threw a one-hitter in 2021 against the Pirates that may have been even more heartbreaking. That game was played at Coors Field and was broken up in the ninth inning when number eight hitter Ka'ai Tom hit a line drive single to right field leading off the inning. Tom was a 27-year-old rookie who had a total of 108 at bats through the 2021 season. With a career batting average of .138, Tom's single was one of just 15 hits in his career.

NOTE 4: Ubaldo Jimenez's 2010 no-hitter – the only one in Colorado history – came against an excellent Atlanta team that gathered 91 wins throughout the season and earned a postseason berth. The Braves' lineup featured strong hitters like Chipper Jones, Brian McCann, Marting Prado, and rookie Jason Heyward.

Jimenez was already well established in the Colorado rotation, earning the Opening Day start in his third season with the Rockies. The Rockies were a good team, too, having earned a postseason berth in two of the previous three seasons, including the year before. Even though Jimenez was a bit wild at first, he settled down and seemed to get stronger as the game progressed. To date, his effort remains the only no-hitter in Rockies' history.

NOTE 5: Darryl Kile earned a spot on this list by throwing 10 innings of shutout ball against the eventual National League Champion San Diego Padres featuring Tony Gwynn, Greg Vaughn, Steve Finley, and Wally Joyner in their lineup. Any attempt at a no-hitter was ended early, as San Diego leadoff hitter Quilvio Veras doubled to lead off the bottom of the first inning. Larry Walker pinch hit for Kile in the top of the 11th and doubled off relief ace Randy Myers. Walker scored on a single by Darryl Hamilton and the Rockies won by a 1-0 score. With his 10-inning game, Kile holds the record for the most innings ever thrown by a Colorado pitcher. No one else has more than nine.

NOTE 6: Kyle Freeland's no-hit attempt was broken up with one out in the ninth inning against the White Sox in 2017. Chicago left fielder Melky Cabrera hit a line drive single on a 2-2 pitch in a 10-0 game at Coors Field for his team's first hit. Freeland had already thrown 126 pitches, so he was pulled for a reliever to finish the game.

Table 25-13. Highest Royals Game Scores

Rank	Pitcher (Team)	Date Score	Opponent	GSc	IP, Hits, Runs, ERs, Walks, Strikeouts
1	Dick Drago	5/24/1972 Min 1-0 (12 inn)	Minnesota Twins	98	12.0 IP, 6 Hits, 1 Run, 1 ER, 1 BB, 13 Ks
2	Danny Duffy	8/1/2016 KC 3-0	Tampa Bay Rays	95	8.0 IP, 1 Hit, 0 Runs, 0 ERs, 1 BB, 16 Ks
3 (tie)	Roger Nelson	8/23/1972 KC 3-0	Boston Red Sox	93	9.0 IP, 1 Hit, 0 Runs, 0 ERs, 1 BB, 9 Ks
3 (tie)	Kevin Appier	9/15/1995 KC 5-0	California Angels	93	9.0 IP, 3 Hits, 0 Runs, 0 ERs, 1 BB, 13 Ks
5 (tie)	Jim Colborn	5/14/1977 KC 6-0	Texas Rangers	92	9.0 IP, 0 Hits, 0 Runs, 0 ERs, 1 BB, 6 Ks

Rank	Pitcher (Team)	Date Score	Opponent	GSc	IP, Hits, Runs, ERs, Walks, Strikeouts
5 (tie)	Bret Saberhagen	5/9/1987 KC 4-0	Cleveland Indians	92	9.0 IP, 2 Hits, 0 Runs, 0 ERs, 0 BBs, 9 Ks
7 (tie)	Paul Splittorff	9/2/1977 (2) KC 3-0	Milwaukee Brewers	91	9.0 IP, 1 Hit, 0 Runs, 0 ERs, 3 BBs, 9 Ks
7 (tie)	Mark Gubicza	6/11/1988 KC 7-0	California Angels	91	9.0 IP 2 Hits, 0 Runs, 0 ERs, 1 BB, 9 Ks
7 (tie)	Mark Gubicza	9/16/1988 KC 3-0	Oakland Athletics	91	9.0 IP, 2 Hits, 0 Runs, 0 ERs, 0 BBs, 8 Ks
7 (tie)	Kevin Appier	7/23/1992 Cle 1-0 (14 inn)	Cleveland Indians	91	10.0 IP, 2 Hits, 0 Runs, 0 ERs, 1 BB, 4 Ks
7 (tie)	Kevin Appier	7/27/1993 Tex 1-0	Texas Rangers	91	9.0 IP, 1 Hit, 1 Run, 1 ER, 1 BB, 11 Ks
12 (tie)	Bret Saberhagen	8/26/1991 KC 7-0	Chicago White Sox	90	9.0 IP, 0 Hits, 0 Runs, 0 ERs, 2 BBs, 5 Ks
18 (tie)	Steve Busby	6/19/1974 KC 2-0	Milwaukee Brewers	89	9.0 IP, 0 Hits, 0 Runs, 0 ERs, 1 BB, 3 Ks
78 (tie)	Steve Busby	4/27/1973 KC 3-0	Detroit Tigers	85	9.0 IP, 0 Hits, 0 Run, 0 ERs, 6 BBs, 4 Ks

METHODOLOGY: This table includes the highest Game Scores thrown by a Royals pitcher from 1969-2021. Games are ranked by Game Score (GSc) and consider all franchise regular season and postseason games. For comparison purposes, all four of the team's no-hitters are included in this table. Game Score measures a pitcher's performance in any given game started. Introduced by baseball writer/statistician Bill James in the 1980s, Game Score is presented as a figure between 0-100 — except for extreme outliers — and usually falls between 40-70.

LEGEND: Dates are shown as month/day/year (for example, June 12, 2018, is shown as 6/12/2018); IP = innings pitched. BB(s) = base(s) on balls. K(s) = strikeout(s). ER(s) = earned run(s). inn = innings (associated with the length of games that were more or less than nine innings). One-third of an inning pitched has 0.1 added and two-thirds of an inning pitched has 0.2 added (for example, 9 1/3 innings pitched is displayed as 9.1). BB(s) = base(s) on balls; K(s) = strikeout(s). (1) or (2) indicates the game is the first or second game of a doubleheader. The

Royals joined the American League as an expansion team with the Seattle Pilots in 1969. The San Diego Padres and the Montreal Expos joined the National League the same year. The Pilots moved to Milwaukee and became the Brewers in 1970. The Expos moved to Washington and became the Nationals in 2005. The Royals began in the American League West Division in 1969 and moved to the Central Division when it was established in 1994.

NOTE 1: The highest postseason Game Score thrown by a Royals pitcher was an 80 by Johnny Cueto in the second game of the 2015 World Series against the New York Mets. Kansas City won a marathon 14-inning game by the score of 5-4 in the World Series opener that involved seven pitchers from the team's staff. To build on their momentum, the Royals needed a strong performance from Johnny Cueto in Game 2 – and that's exactly what they got. Cueto pitched a complete-game win, allowing only two hits and three walks en route to a decisive 7-1 victory. First baseman Lucas Duda was the only Met who got a hit, and he collected two singles. One of those scored catcher Daniel Murphy from third base to break a 0-0 tie in the top of the fourth inning. The Royals took the lead in the fifth inning with a four-run rally that featured five singles and a walk against Mets starter Jacob DeGrom. Kansas City put the game away in the eighth inning with another three runs. Building on their solid two-games-to-none lead, the Royals convincingly won the World Series four games to one for their first championship since 1985.

NOTE 2: Dick Drago recorded the highest Game Score (98) by a Royals pitcher when he threw a 12-inning six-hitter against the Twins, a team that featured Hall of Famers Rod Carew and Harmon Killebrew in the middle of their lineup. His effort was ultimately fruitless, as the Royals lost 1-0 when Minnesota scored the game's only run in the top of the 12th when Carew singled in shortstop Danny Thompson from second base. The Royals were unable to score against Hall of Famer Jim Kaat and closer Wayne Granger, as Kansas City was held to just five hits. The Royals – only three years removed from their first season as an expansion team – were a good-hitting team in 1972. Featuring stars like John Mayberry, Lou Piniella, and Amos Otis, Kansas City led the 12-team American League in batting average and OPS that season. Drago's 12-inning effort is tied for the second-longest number of innings pitched in a single game by a Royals pitcher. Larry Gura threw 13 innings in a loss to the Oakland Athletics in 1980.

NOTE 3: Danny Duffy holds the record for the highest Royals Game Score in a non-extra-inning game with his eight-inning effort against the Rays in 2016.

With the Royals leading 3-0, Duffy had a no-hitter going into the bottom of the eighth inning. Tampa Bay left fielder Desmond Jennings led off that inning with a double to left field. Jennings was stranded at second base, as Duffy finished the inning by striking out the final two batters for his 15th and 16th strikeouts of the game. Duffy was removed from the game prior to the ninth inning, as he had already thrown 110 pitches, and relief ace Kelvin Herrera threw a 1-2-3 ninth inning for the save. Duffy's 16 strikeouts are the most ever by a Royals pitcher in a single game.

NOTE 4: With 169 career wins over a 16-year career, Kevin Appier is listed three times on this table – more than any other pitcher. His listed efforts include a three-hit shutout in 1995, a 10-inning two-hit effort in 1992, and a 1993 one-hitter against the Rangers where the lone hit was a Rafael Palmeiro home run in the seventh inning. The 1992 and 1993 games were both losses, as the Royals failed to score in either game. Appier was a stalwart member of the Kansas City rotation and was selected for the American League All-Star team in 1995.

NOTE 4: Steve Busby threw the first and second no-hitters in the team's history. As a 23-year-old rookie in 1973, he threw his first no-hitter against a powerful Tiger lineup that featured Bill Freehan, Norm Cash, Dick McAuliffe, and Jim Northrup. His second no-hitter in 1974 against the Milwaukee Brewers might be even more impressive, as he allowed just one baserunner, a second inning walk to Milwaukee first baseman George Scott. Busby was selected for the All-Star team in both 1974 and 1975, but his career was cut short in early 1976 by a rotator-cuff injury at the age of 26. Busby had surgery and played for portions of three seasons after that, but he was never the dominant pitcher he had been before.

NOTE 5: Roger Nelson only allowed two baserunners – a two-out single by left fielder Ben Oglivie in the eighth and a walk to pitcher Sonny Siebert in the third – in his one-hit shutout against the Red Sox in 1972. One of the original Royals in 1969, the 1972 season was Nelson's best with Kansas City, culminating with him coming within four outs of throwing the first no-hitter in the team's history. With a record of 11-6, Nelson was one of the American League pitching leaders with a 2.08 ERA. Throwing a no-hitter in 1977, Jim Colborn's effort against the 94-win Rangers ranks as one of the best games in Royals history. Only two batters made it to first base: Toby Harrah was hit by a pitch in the fourth inning and Jim Sunberg drew a walk in the fifth. Colborn's 18-win season in 1977 was the only full year he spent with Kansas City.

NOTE 6: A Cy Young Award winner in 1985 and 1989 with the Royals, Bret Saberhagen is arguably the best pitcher in Royals history. His 1991 no-hitter against the White Sox is perhaps his best game in Kansas City, as he allowed just three baserunners on two walks and an error. Saberhagen won 110 games for the Royals, and another 57 for the Mets, Rockies, and Red Sox.

NOTE 7: The most wins for a Royals pitcher is 166 by Paul Splittorff from 1970-1984. Splittorff spent his entire career with Kansas City and his best game was a 1977 one-hitter against the Brewers. Milwaukee's only hit was a single by pinch-hitter Charlie Moore with two outs in the eighth inning. Two-time All-Star Mark Gubicza threw two outstanding two-hitters against California and Oakland within a few months of each other in 1988. Led by Mark McGwire and Jose Canseco (the "Bash Brothers"), the 1988 Oakland team dominated the American League that season, as they swept the Red Sox in the ALCS before being upended by the Dodgers in the World Series.

Table 25-14. Best Pitchers of the 1900s (1900-1909)

Rank	Pitcher (Team(s))	Seasons Pitched	Innings Pitched	WAR (per 200 IP)	Wins (per Season)
1	Cy Young (Cardinals, Americans, Red Sox, Naps)	1900-1909	3,344.0	75.4 (4.51)	231 (23.1)
2	Christy Mathewson (Giants)	1900-1909	2,974.2	70.5 (4.74)	236 (23.6)
3	Rube Waddell (Pirates, Orphans, Athletics, Browns)	1900-1909	2,835.1	59.0 (4.16)	183 (18.3)
4	Eddie Plank (Athletics)	1901-1909	2,666.0	56.3 (4.22)	186 (20.7)
5	Joe McGinnity (Superbas, Orioles, Giants)	1900-1908	3,075.0	52.8 (3.43)	218 (24.2)
6	Vic Willis (Nationals, Pirates)	1900-1909	3,130.1	51.4 (3.28)	188 (18.8)
7	Addie Joss (Blues, Naps)	1902-1909	2,219.2	45.3 (4.08)	155 (19.4)
8	Jack Chesbro (Pirates, Highlanders, Red Sox)	1900-1909	2,747.2	42.2 (3.07)	192 (19.2)

Rank	Pitcher (Team(s))	Seasons Pitched	Innings Pitched	WAR (per 200 IP)	Wins (per Season)
9	Mordecai "Three-Finger" Brown (Cardinals, Cubs)	1903-1909	1,827.2	41.1 (4.50)	144 (20.6)
10	Bill Donovan (Superbas, Tigers)	1900-1909	2,426.0	39.0 (3.16)	154 (15.4)
11	Frank "Noodles" Hahn (Reds, Highlanders)	1900-1906	1,720.1	37.6 (4.37)	107 (15.3)
12	Doc White (Phillies, White Sox)	1901-1909	2,315.0	36.7 (3.17)	154 (17.1)

METHODOLOGY: Pitchers are ranked in order of Wins Above Replacement (WAR) achieved from 1900-1909. WAR measures a player's value in all facets of the game by deciphering how many more wins he's worth than a replacement-level player at his same position. Another measure of merit I wanted to include was the number of wins each pitcher accumulated as well. Because a number of pitchers were only present for a portion of the decade, I included two rate measures (WAR per 200 innings pitched and wins per season).

LEGEND: Team(s) = the team(s) a player played for during the 1900s. If a pitcher played for more than one team, teams are listed in chronological order. IP = innings pitched. One-third of an inning is designated as ".1" and two-thirds of an inning is designated as ".2".

NOTE 1: Many of the teams listed in the table moved or changed names over the years. The Cleveland Guardians were named the Cleveland Napoleons (or "Naps") from 1903-1914. When Addie Joss pitched for Cleveland in 1902, the team was known as the Blues. The Chicago Cubs were named the Chicago Orphans from 1898-1901. The Athletics played in Philadelphia from 1901-1954. The modern Baltimore Orioles played in St. Louis and were known as the Browns from 1902-1953. The Giants played in New York from 1885-1957. The Dodgers played in Brooklyn and were known as the Superbas from 1899-1910. The Baltimore Orioles who Joe McGinnity played for existed in the brand new American League from 1901-1902. After the 1902 season, the team was replaced by the New York Highlanders who became the Yankees in 1913. The Braves played in Boston and were known as the Nationals from 1901-1906.

NOTE 2: This is an extraordinary group of talented players. While Cy Young and Christy Mathewson might be the two most renowned pitchers on this list, the seven pitchers who immediately followed them are also in the Hall of Fame: Rube Waddell, Eddie Plank, Joe McGinnity, Vic Willis, Addie Joss, Jack Chesbro, and Three-Finger Brown.

Table 25-15. Best Pitchers of the 1910s

Rank	Pitcher (Team(s))	Seasons Pitched	Innings Pitched	WAR (per 200 IP)	Wins (per Season)
1	Walter Johnson (Senators)	1910-1919	3,427.2	110.3 (6.44)	265 (26.5)
2	Grover Alexander (Phillies, Cubs)	1911-1919	2,753.0	69.1 (5.02)	208 (23.1)
3	Eddie Cicotte (Red Sox, White Sox)	1910-1919	2,535.0	48.7 (3.84)	162 (16.2)
4	Hippo Vaughn (Highlanders, Senators, Cubs)	1910-1919	2,317.1	43.5 (3.75)	156 (15.6)
5	Slim Sallee (Cardinals, Giants, Reds)	1910-1919	2,244.2	35.4 (3.13)	149 (14.9)
6	Ed Walsh (White Sox, Braves)	1910-1917	1,322.0	35.1 (5.31)	85 (10.6)
7	Babe Adams (Pirates)	1910-1916 1918-1919	1,908.2	33.2 (3.48)	119 (13.2)
8	Russ Ford (Highlanders, Yankees, Buffeds)	1910-1915	1,484.1	33.1 (4.46)	100 (16.7)
9	Eddie Plank (Athletics, Terriers, Browns)	1910-1917	1,829.2	31.4 (3.43)	140 (17.5)
10	Dutch Leonard (Red Sox, Tigers)	1913-1919	1,578.2	30.8 (3.90)	104 (14.9)
11	Nap Rucker (Superbas, Dodgers, Robins)	1910-1916	1,457.1	30.5 (4.19)	89 (12.7)
12	Christy Mathewson (Giants, Reds)	1910-1916	1,814.0	30.0 (3.31)	137 (19.6)

METHODOLOGY: Pitchers are ranked in order of Wins Above Replacement (WAR) achieved from 1910-1919. WAR measures a player's value in all facets of the game by deciphering how many more wins he's worth than a replacement-level player at his same position. Another measure of merit I wanted to include was the number of wins each pitcher accumulated as well. Because a number of pitchers were only present for a portion of the decade, I included two rate measures (WAR per 200 innings pitched and wins per season).

LEGEND: Team(s) = the team(s) a player played for during the 1910s. If a pitcher played for more than one team, teams are listed in chronological order. IP = innings pitched. One-third of an inning is designated as ".1" and two-thirds of an inning is designated as ".2".

NOTE 1: Many of the teams listed in the table moved or changed names over the years. The Washington Senators were officially known as the Nationals from 1905-1955 but were commonly known as the Senators throughout that time. The team moved to Minnesota and became the Twins in 1961. The Athletics played in Philadelphia from 1901-1954. The modern Baltimore Orioles played in St. Louis and were known as the Browns from 1902-1953. The Giants played in New York from 1885-1957. The Dodgers played in Brooklyn and were known as the Superbas from 1899-1910, the Dodgers from 1911-1915, and the Robins from 1916-1931. The New York Highlanders joined the American League in 1903 as a replacement team for the old Baltimore Orioles. The Highlanders became the Yankees in 1913. The Braves played in Boston until they moved to Milwaukee in 1953 and then on to Atlanta in 1966. Russ Ford played for the Buffalo Buffeds, and Eddie Plank played for the St. Louis Terriers of the Federal League. The Federal League was a Major League that existed for two years from 1914-1915.

NOTE 2: Walter Johnson dominated pitching during this decade with 265 wins, 2,219 strikeouts, and an ERA of 1.59, resulting in an astounding WAR of 110.3. He, along with Grover Cleveland, Ed Walsh, Eddie Plank, and Christy Mathewson from this list, are members of the Hall of Fame. Mathewson was also one of the top pitchers from 1900-1909, finishing right behind Cy Young in WAR for that decade.

Table 25-16. Best Pitchers of the 1920s

Rank	Pitcher (Team(s))	Seasons Pitched	Innings Pitched	WAR (per 200 IP)	Wins (per Season)
1	Dazzy Vance (Robins)	1922-1929	2,053.2	50.3 (4.90)	147 (18.4)
2	Grover Alexander (Cubs, Cardinals)	1920-1929	2,415.1	48.0 (3.98)	165 (16.5)
3	Red Faber (White Sox)	1920-1929	2,364.0	46.4 (3.93)	149 (14.9)
4	Eddie Rommel (Athletics)	1920-1929	2,243.1	45.6 (4.07)	154 (15.4)
5	Urban Shocker (Browns, Yankees)	1920-1928	2,148.2	45.4 (4.23)	156 (17.3)
6	Herb Pennock (Red Sox, Yankees)	1920-1929	2,313.0	40.7 (3.52)	163 (16.3)
7	Eppa Rixey (Phillies, Reds)	1920-1929	2,678.1	40.3 (3.01)	166 (16.6)
8	Stan Coveleski (Indians, Senators, Yankees)	1920-1928	1,933.2	39.3 (4.06)	133 (14.8)
9	Burleigh Grimes (Robins, Giants, Pirates)	1920-1929	2,797.2	38.6 (2.76)	190 (19.0)
10	Jack Quinn (Yankees, Red Sox, Athletics)	1920-1929	2,042.0	38.3 (3.75)	131 (13.1)
11	Bullet Rogan (Monarchs)	1920-1929	1,492.2	38.1 (5.10)	120 (12.0)
11	Dolf Luque (Reds)	1920-1929	2,479.2	37.9 (3.06)	138 (13.8)

METHODOLOGY: Pitchers are ranked in order of Wins Above Replacement (WAR) achieved from 1920-1929. WAR measures a player's value in all facets of the game by deciphering how many more wins he's worth than a replacement-level player at his same position. Another measure of merit I wanted to include was the number of wins each pitcher accumulated as well. Because a number of pitchers were only present for a portion of the decade, I included two rate measures (WAR per 200 innings pitched and wins per season).

LEGEND: Team(s) = the team(s) a player played for during the 1920s. If a pitcher played for more than one team, teams are listed in chronological order. IP = innings pitched. One-third of an inning is designated as ".1" and two-thirds of an inning is designated as ".2".

NOTE 1: Many of the teams listed in the table moved or changed names over the years. The Dodgers played in Brooklyn and were known as the Robins from 1916-1931. The Washington Senators were officially known as the Nationals from 1905-1955 but were commonly known as the Senators throughout that time. The team moved to Minnesota and became the Twins in 1961. The Athletics played in Philadelphia from 1901-1954. The modern Baltimore Orioles played in St. Louis and were known as the Browns from 1902-1953. The Giants played in New York from 1885-1957. Bullet Rogan played for the Kansas City Monarchs of the Negro National League. He joined the team in its first year as a 26-year-old rookie and was the team's ace from 1921-1928. The Negro League teams typically played between 80-88 games per season. For Rogan to have accumulated 38 WAR pitching in so many fewer games is exceptional. Bullet Rogan was selected for the Hall of Fame by the Veterans Committee in 1998.

NOTE 2: The pitchers on this list were the cream of the crop in the 1920s. Eight of them are Hall of Famers: Dazzy Vance, Grover Cleveland, Red Faber, Herb Pennock, Eppa Rixey, Stan Coveleski, Burleigh Grimes, and of course, Bullet Rogan. Dazzy Vance was even selected as the National League MVP in 1924. There was no separate Cy Young Award recognition at the time.

Table 25-17. Best Pitchers of the 1930s

Rank	Pitcher (Team(s))	Seasons Pitched	Innings Pitched	WAR (per 200 IP)	Wins (per Season)
1	Lefty Grove (Athletics, Red Sox)	1930-1939	2,399.0	80.7 (6.73)	199 (19.9)
2	Carl Hubbell (Giants)	1930-1939	2,596.2	56.2 (4.33)	188 (18.8)
3	Mel Harder (Indians)	1930-1939	2,326.0	45.5 (3.91)	158 (15.8)
4	Dizzy Dean (Cardinals, Cubs)	1930 1932-1939	1,908.1	44.2 (4.63)	147 (16.3)
5	Lefty Gomez (Yankees)	1930-1939	2,234.2	43.6 (3.90)	165 (16.5)

Rank	Pitcher (Team(s))	Seasons Pitched	Innings Pitched	WAR (per 200 IP)	Wins (per Season)
6	Wes Ferrell (Indians, Red Sox, Senators, Yankees)	1930-1939	2,345.1	42.7 (3.64)	170 (17.0)
7	Red Ruffing (Yankees)	1930-1939	2,439.0	38.1 (3.12)	175 (17.5)
8	Larry French (Pirates, Cubs)	1930-1939	2,481.2	35.9 (2.89)	156 (15.6)
9	Tommy Bridges (Tigers)	1930-1939	2,083.0	35.5 (3.41)	150 (15.0)
10	Ted Lyons (White Sox)	1930-1939	1,972.0	32.1 (3.26)	117 (11.7)
11	Lon Warneke (Cubs, Cardinals)	1930-1939	2,021.0	31.5 (3.12)	144 (14.4)
12	Bump Hadley (Senators, White Sox, Browns, Yankees)	1930-1939	2,121.2	28.8 (2.71)	121 (12.1)

METHODOLOGY: Pitchers are ranked in order of Wins Above Replacement (WAR) achieved from 1930-1939. WAR measures a player's value in all facets of the game by deciphering how many more wins he's worth than a replacement-level player at his same position. Another measure of merit I wanted to include was the number of wins each pitcher accumulated as well. Because a number of pitchers were only present for a portion of the decade, I included two rate measures (WAR per 200 innings pitched and wins per season).

LEGEND: Team(s) = the team(s) a player played for during the 1930s. If a pitcher played for more than one team, teams are listed in chronological order. IP = innings pitched. One-third of an inning is designated as ".1" and two-thirds of an inning is designated as ".2".

NOTE 1: Some of the teams listed in the table moved or changed names over the years. The Washington Senators were officially known as the Nationals from 1905-1955 but were more commonly known as the Senators throughout that time. The team moved to Minnesota and became the Twins in 1961. The Athletics played in Philadelphia from 1901-1954. The modern Baltimore Orioles played in St. Louis and were known as the Browns from 1902-1953. The Giants played in New York from 1885-1957.

NOTE 2: This is an impressive list of pitchers. Lefty Grove and Dizzy Dean were named MVPs, and Carl Hubbell was an MVP twice. Grove, Hubbell, Dean, Lefty Gomez, Red Ruffing, and Ted Lyons are members of the Hall of Fame. The All-Star game was created in 1933 and this group has been very well represented during their careers: Hubbell (nine times), Gomez (seven), Grove (six), Ruffing (six), Bridges (six), Warneke (five), Dean (four), Harder (four), Ferrell (twice), Lyons (once), and French (once).

Table 25-18. Best Pitchers of the 1940s

Rank	Pitcher (Team(s))	Seasons Pitched	Innings Pitched	WAR (per 200 IP)	Wins (per Season)
1	Hal Newhouser (Tigers)	1940-1949	2,453.1	54.2 (4.42)	170 (17.0)
2	Bob Feller (Indians)	1940-1941 1945-1949	1,897.0	38.3 (4.04)	137 (19.6)
3	Dizzy Trout (Tigers)	1940-1949	2,026.1	36.7 (3.62)	129 (12.9)
4	Harry Brecheen (Cardinals)	1940 1943-1949	1,388.0	32.3 (4.65)	105 (13.1)
5	Dutch Leonard (Senators, Phillies, Cubs)	1940-1949	2,047.1	31.9 (3.12)	122 (12.2)
6	Bucky Walters (Reds)	1940-1948	1,868.1	28.6 (3.06)	122 (13.6)
7	Mort Cooper (Cardinals, Braves, Giants, Cubs)	1940-1947 1949	1,606.1	28.4 (3.54)	114 (12.7)
8	Claude Passeau (Cubs)	1940-1947	1,693.2	28.0 (3.31)	111 (13.9)
9	Tex Hughson (Red Sox)	1941-1944 1946-1949	1,375.2	26.1 (3.79)	96 (12.0)
10	Nels Potter (Athletics, Red Sox, Browns, Braves)	1940-1941 1943-1949	1,377.1	25.3 (3.67)	82 (9.1)
11	Rip Sewell (Pirates)	1940-1949	1,894.0	25.1 (2.65)	133 (13.3)
12	Tiny Bonham (Yankees, Pirates)	1940-1949	1,551.0	24.2 (3.12)	103 (10.3)

METHODOLOGY: Pitchers are ranked in order of Wins Above Replacement (WAR) achieved from 1940-1949. WAR measures a player's value in all facets of the game by deciphering how many more wins he's worth than a replacement-level player at his same position. Another measure of merit I wanted to include was the number of wins each pitcher accumulated as well. Because a number of pitchers were only present for a portion of the decade, I included two rate measures (WAR per 200 innings pitched and wins per season).

LEGEND: Team(s) = the team(s) a player played for during the 1940s. If a pitcher played for more than one team, teams are listed in chronological order. IP = innings pitched. One-third of an inning is designated as ".1" and two-thirds of an inning is designated as ".2"

NOTE 1: Some of the teams listed in the table moved or changed names over the years. The Washington Senators were officially known as the Nationals from 1905-1955 but were more commonly known as the Senators throughout that time. The team moved to Minnesota and became the Twins in 1961. The Athletics played in Philadelphia from 1901-1954. The modern Baltimore Orioles played in St. Louis and were known as the Browns from 1902-1953. The Giants played in New York from 1885-1957. The Braves played in Boston until they moved to Milwaukee in 1953 and then on to Atlanta in 1966.

NOTE 2: Unlike the other "best pitcher" decades listed in this book, the 1940s featured multiple pitchers who had noticeable gaps in their playing time. Harry Brecheen and Nels Potter were sent to the minors early in their careers to work on their pitching, while Mort Cooper was at the end of his career and played a season in the minors before one last year in the majors. Two players, though, left baseball to serve their country in World War II. Bob Feller joined the Navy two days after Pearl Harbor and served as a gun captain on the battleship *USS Alabama*, participating in combat in the Pacific Theater. Tex Hughson also served in the Pacific. He was part of the Army Air Force, although not in a combat role. Both Feller and Hughson were in the prime of their careers when they volunteered to join the military to fight and win World War II.

NOTE 3: Because of the drain of considerable baseball talent serving in the military during World War II, the 1942-1945 seasons were notable in that the level of play was significantly diminished as replacement talent was used instead of many top players who were off fighting the war. This is perhaps part of the reason there are "just" two Hall of Famers who are included in the list above: Hal Newhouser and Bob Feller. In Feller's case, he made the HOF despite leaving baseball from 1942 through late 1945. Three of the pitchers on the list were named MVP of their leagues: Hal Newhouser (twice), Bucky Walters, and Mort Cooper. Eleven pitchers were named as All-Stars during their careers: Bob Feller (eight times), Hal Newhouser (seven), Bucky Walters (six), Dutch Leonard (five), Claude Passeau (five), Mort Cooper (four), Rip Sewell (four), Tex Hughson (three), Dizzy Trout (two), Harry Brecheen (two), and Tiny Bonham (two).

Conclusion

As this concludes Volume II, I am left with the feeling there is so much more that could be told about this story. Even after writing 25 chapters and more than 200,000 words, I know I could easily – well, maybe not "easily" – add another 10 volumes and the story still wouldn't be fully told.

This is one of the beautiful things about baseball. Baseball is about stars — and it's also about journeymen who make brief appearances in the big leagues and shine during their moment in the spotlight. There are soaring successes and heartbreaking failures. The stories are intricate and they're beautiful, and we don't have to be avid fans to appreciate that. We just have to appreciate the human experiences that are at the core of these stories. That's part of what I hoped to communicate throughout these two volumes.

One of the questions I hoped to explore throughout my two books, and in this volume in particular, is "what is the most unlikely no-hitter ever thrown?" In many ways, this question strikes at the heart of why we watch baseball games. Of course, we cheer for our favorite team, and we also enjoy watching the best players in the world display their skills. Yet, one of the most appealing aspects of going to a game, no matter who is playing, is the feeling that anything can happen. An excellent example of this is that eager feeling we have as the game begins and we wonder if "this might be the day we see a no-hitter."

After reading these two volumes, I expect that everyone has their own favorite choice for the most unlikely no-hitter. The five candidates highlighted in the introduction may have the strongest cases, but there are dozens more who could credibly be chosen as the winner. And that's part of the beauty of this and so many other baseball arguments. Frequently, there's no definitive, "right" answer. We can all be right, and still revel in the joy we feel in making the argument for our own point of view.

Was it struggling Athletics rookie Mike Warren no-hitting the 1983 division champion White Sox? The tandem of Ernie Koob and Bob Groom keeping the powerful 1917 White Sox hitless – a team destined to be World Champions – on consecutive days? Bullet Joe Bush of the 1916 Philadelphia Athletics, playing for what would turn out to be the worst team in the Twentieth Century, no-hitting an infinitely more capable Cleveland team? Cleveland's Don Black, with literally the worst career value of any no-hit pitcher ever, throwing a no-hitter against the Athletics in 1947? Career reliever Jose Jimenez no-hitting the powerful 1999 Arizona Diamondbacks and Randy Johnson? All these events could certainly qualify for being the most unlikely no-hitter.

Arguably, taken as a combined pair of occurrences, the Koob/Groom no-hitters have to be the most unlikely couple of no-hit events. The White Sox were a 100-win team and the Browns finished in seventh place, 43 games behind Chicago. Yet, Koob and Groom both were solid pitchers, so individually their games were not entirely unexpected.

The same is true for Bullet Joe Bush. He pitched for a team that set a record for futility, yet he was a premier pitcher. With 196 career wins, he racked up 15 victories for the Athletics in 1916, amounting to over 40 percent of his team's wins that year. His win was unlikely because he played for the Athletics, not because his talent was insufficient.

While it's true that Don Black struggled at the beginning of his short career, he was on the upswing in 1947, as he was one of four starters on a talented Cleveland staff that included Hall of Famers Bob Feller and Bob Lemon. While his no-hitter was unexpected, as all no-hitters are, it's very likely he would have accomplished far more in baseball if he hadn't suffered from a stroke caused by a brain aneurysm during a game the following season. As a result, it's fair to say he almost certainly would have not been the holder of the "least accomplished" title if he hadn't had a promising career cut short by that stroke.

Which brings us to Mike Warren and Jose Jimenez. These might be the two top contenders for the "unlikeliest" no-hitter. Warren's career value was significantly lower than Jimenez's, and he didn't play nearly as long. Warren also threw his no-hitter against an outstanding Chicago team that was on its way to dominating the American League West Division in 1983. Jimenez, on the other hand, was not a very good starter, to say the least, and he no-hit an extraordinary Arizona team while facing the legendary Randy Johnson.

And I'm going to leave it at that. I have my own opinion about which one is the unlikeliest. Which one would you choose out of these five? Or is there another game you'd put at the top of the list? Tell me about it!

I hope these two volumes are only the beginning of our conversation. Feel free to reach out to me at kevinhurd@sbcglobal.net and share your thoughts about this discussion and my book. I look forward to hearing from you.

Play ball!

Appendix II

Career Ranking of All No-hit Catchers

Table A-2. No-hit Catcher Career JAWS Ranking (1900-2021)

Rank	Catcher	JAWS	Team	No-hitter Date	Pitcher
1	Johnny Bench	61.2	Cincinnati Reds	4/30/1969	Jim Maloney
2	Gary Carter	59.3	Montreal Expos	5/10/1981	Charlie Lea
3	Ivan Rodriguez	54.2	Texas Rangers Detroit Tigers	7/28/1994 6/12/2007	Kenny Rogers Justin Verlander
4	Mike Piazza	51.3	Los Angeles Dodgers Los Angeles Dodgers	7/14/1995 9/17/1996	Ramon Martinez Hideo Nomo
5	Yogi Berra	48.7	New York Yankees New York Yankees *New York Yankees*	7/12/1951 9/28/1951 *10/8/1956*	Allie Reynolds Allie Reynolds *Don Larsen*
6	Ted Simmons	42.6	St. Louis Cardinals St. Louis Cardinals	8/14/1971 4/16/1978	Bob Gibson Bob Forsch
7	Gene Tenace	40.9	Oakland Athletics	9/21/1970	Vida Blue
8	Buster Posey	40.7	*San Francisco Giants* *San Francisco Giants* *San Francisco Giants*	*6/13/2012* *7/13/2013* *6/9/2015*	*Matt Cain* *Tim Lincecum* *Chris Heston*

Rank	Catcher	JAWS	Team	No-hitter Date	Pitcher
9	Roy Campanella	38.5	Brooklyn Dodgers Brooklyn Dodgers Brooklyn Dodgers	6/19/1952 5/12/1956 9/25/1956	Carl Erskine Carl Erskine Sal Maglie
10	Wally Schang	37.9	Boston Red Sox	6/3/1918	Dutch Leonard
11	Jorge Posada	37.6	*New York Yankees*	*5/17/1998*	*David Wells*
12	Roger Bresnahan	36.3	New York Giants	7/4/1908	Hooks Wiltse
13	Jason Kendall	36.0	Pittsburgh Pirates	7/12/1997	Two pitchers
14	Darrell Porter	35.0	Kansas City Royals St. Louis Cardinals	5/14/1977 9/26/1983	Jim Colborn Bob Forsch
15	Jim Sundberg	34.6	Texas Rangers	9/22/1977	Bert Blyleven
16	Lance Parrish	34.0	Detroit Tigers California Angels	4/7/1984 4/11/1990	Jack Morris Two pitchers
17	Ernie Lombardi	30.9	Cincinnati Reds Cincinnati Reds	6/11/1938 6/15/1938	J. Vander Meer J. Vander Meer
18	Ray Schalk	29.4	Chicago White Sox Chicago White Sox *Chicago White Sox*	5/31/1914 4/14/1917 *4/30/1922*	Joe Benz Eddie Cicotte *C. Robertson*
19	Javy Lopez	27.3	Atlanta Braves	4/8/1994	Kent Mercker
20	Manny Sanguillen	27.0	Pittsburgh Pirates	9/20/1969	Bob Moose
21	Duke Farrell	26.4	Boston Red Sox	8/17/1904	Jesse Tannehill
22 (tie)	Del Crandall	26.1	Milwaukee Braves Milwaukee Braves Milwaukee Braves	6/12/1954 8/18/1960 9/16/1960	Jim Wilson Lew Burdette Warren Spahn
22 (tie)	Sherm Lollar	26.1	Chicago White Sox	8/20/1957	Bob Keegan

Rank	Catcher	JAWS	Team	No-hitter Date	Pitcher
24	Ed Bailey	25.1	San Francisco Giants	6/15/1963	Juan Marichal
25	Walker Cooper	25.0	St. Louis Cardinals Boston Braves	8/30/1941 8/11/1950	Lon Warneke Vern Bickford
26 (tie)	Chief Zimmer	24.8	Philadelphia Phillies	9/18/1903	Chick Fraser
26 (tie)	Tim McCarver	24.8	Philadelphia Phillies Montreal Expos	6/23/1971 10/2/1972	Rick Wise Bill Stoneman
26 (tie)	Terry Steinbach	24.8	Oakland Athletics Minnesota Twins	6/29/1990 9/11/1999	Dave Stewart Eric Milton
29	Butch Wynegar	24.6	New York Yankees	7/4/1983	Dave Righetti
30 (tie)	Chief Meyers	23.9	New York Giants	4/15/1915	Rube Marquard
30 (tie)	Bob Boone	23.9	California Angels	9/30/1984	Mike Witt
30 (tie)	Mike Scioscia	23.9	Los Angeles Dodgers Los Angeles Dodgers	6/29/1990 8/17/1992	F. Valenzuela Kevin Gross
33	Steve O'Neill	23.4	Cleveland Indians	9/10/1919	Ray Caldwell
34	Darren Daulton	23.3	Philadelphia Phillies	8/15/1990	Terry Mulholland
35	J.T. Realmuto*	23.2	Miami Marlins	6/3/2017	Edinson Volquez
36	Chris Hoiles	22.9	Baltimore Orioles	7/13/1991	Four pitchers
37	Carlos Ruiz	21.8	*Philadelphia Phillies* Philadelphia Phillies Philadelphia Phillies Philadelphia Phillies	*5/29/2010* 10/6/2010 9/1/2014 7/25/2015	*Roy Halladay* Roy Halladay Four pitchers Cole Hamels
38 (tie)	Charles Johnson	21.5	Florida Marlins Florida Marlins Florida Marlins	5/11/1996 6/10/1997 5/12/2001	Al Leiter Kevin Brown A.J. Burnett

Rank	Catcher	JAWS	Team	No-hitter Date	Pitcher
38 (tie)	Jason Varitek	21.5	Boston Red Sox Boston Red Sox Boston Red Sox Boston Red Sox	4/4/2001 4/27/2002 9/1/2007 5/19/2008	Hideo Nomo Derek Lowe Clay Buchholz Jon Lester
40 (tie)	John Roseboro	20.9	Los Angeles Dodgers Los Angeles Dodgers	6/30/1962 5/11/1963	Sandy Koufax Sandy Koufax
40 (tie)	A.J. Pierzynski	20.9	Chicago White Sox *Chicago White Sox*	4/18/2007 *4/21/2012*	Mark Buehrle *Philip Humber*
42	Hank Gowdy	20.8	Boston Braves	9/9/1914	George Davis
43 (tie)	Bob O'Farrell	20.2	New York Giants	5/8/1929	Carl Hubbell
43 (tie)	Mike Stanley	20.2	Texas Rangers	5/1/1991	Nolan Ryan
45	Ed McFarland	19.0	Chicago White Sox Chicago White Sox	9/20/1902 9/6/1905	Jimmy Callahan Frank Smith
46	Earl Battey	18.7	Minnesota Twins	8/26/1962	Jack Kralick
47	Hank Severeid	18.4	St. Louis Browns St. Louis Browns	5/5/1917 5/6/1917	Ernie Koob Bob Groom
48	Jonathan Lucroy	18.3	Oakland Athletics	4/21/2018	Sean Manaea
49	Yasmani Grandal*	18.2	Los Angeles Dodgers	5/4/2018	Four pitchers
50 (tie)	Heinie Peitz	16.9	Cincinnati Reds	7/12/1900	Noodles Hahn
50 (tie)	Willson Contreras*	16.9	Chicago Cubs	6/24/2021	Four pitchers
52	Steve Yeager	16.3	Los Angeles Dodgers	6/27/1980	Jerry Reuss
53	Alex Avila	16.1	Detroit Tigers	5/7/2011	Justin Verlander
54	Brad Ausmus	15.8	Houston Astros	6/11/2003	Six pitchers

Rank	Catcher	JAWS	Team	No-hitter Date	Pitcher
55	Miguel Montero	15.4	Arizona D-backs Chicago Cubs	6/25/2010 8/30/2015	Edwin Jackson Jake Arrieta
56	Jim Pagliaroni	15.2	Boston Red Sox *Oakland Athletics*	8/1/1962 *5/8/1968*	B. Monbouquette *Catfish Hunter*
57	Chris Iannetta	15.1	Los Angeles Angels	5/2/2012	Jered Weaver
58 (tie)	Johnny Edwards	14.9	Cincinnati Reds St. Louis Cardinals	8/19/1965 9/18/1968	Jim Maloney Ray Washburn
58 (tie)	Mike Lieberthal	14.9	Philadelphia Phillies	4/27/2003	Kevin Millwood
58 (tie)	Wilson Ramos	14.9	Washington Nationals Washington Nationals Washington Nationals	9/28/2014 6/20/2015 10/3/2015	J. Zimmerman Max Scherzer Max Scherzer
61 (tie)	Lou Criger	14.8	*Boston Americans* Boston Americans	*5/5/1904* 6/30/1908	*Cy Young* Cy Young
61 (tie)	George Gibson	14.8	Pittsburgh Pirates	9/20/1907	Nick Maddox
63	Jerry Grote	14.6	Houston Astros	4/23/1964	Ken Johnson
64 (tie)	Art Wilson	14.5	New York Giants Chicago Whales (FL)	9/6/1912 5/15/1915	Jeff Tesreau Claude Hendrix
64 (tie)	Buddy Rosar	14.5	Philadelphia Athletics Philadelphia Athletics	9/9/1945 9/3/1947	Dick Fowler Bill McCahan
66	Ron Hassey	14.2	*Cleveland Indians* *Montreal Expos*	*5/15/1981* *7/28/1991*	*Len Barker* *Dennis Martinez*
67	Gus Triandos	14.1	Baltimore Orioles Philadelphia Phillies	9/20/1958 6/21/1964	Hoyt Wilhelm Jim Bunning
68 (tie)	Ray Fosse	13.9	Cleveland Indians	5/30/1977	Dennis Eckersley
68 (tie)	Ron Karkovice	13.9	Chicago White Sox Chicago White Sox	9/19/1986 8/11/1991	Joe Cowley Wilson Alvarez
70	Phil Masi	13.8	Boston Braves	4/27/1944	Jim Tobin

Rank	Catcher	JAWS	Team	No-hitter Date	Pitcher
71	Ray Mueller	13.7	Cincinnati Reds	5/15/1944	Clyde Shoun
72	Ellie Rodriguez	13.5	California Angels	6/1/1975	Nolan Ryan
73	Jack Warner	13.4	New York Giants	7/15/1901	Christy Mathewson
74	Bill Carrigan	13.2	Boston Red Sox Boston Red Sox Boston Red Sox	7/29/1911 6/21/1916 8/30/1916	Smoky Joe Wood Rube Foster Dutch Leonard
75 (tie)	Jason Castro*	13.0	Houston Astros	8/21/2015	Mike Fiers
75 (tie)	Robinson Chirinos*	13.0	Houston Astros	9/1/2019	Justin Verlander
77	Mike Heath	12.9	Oakland Athletics	9/29/1983	Mike Warren
78	Dick Dietz	12.8	San Francisco Giants	9/17/1968	Gaylord Perry
79	Randy Hundley	12.5	Chicago Cubs Chicago Cubs	4/16/1972 9/2/1972	Burt Hooton Milt Pappas
80	Frankie Hayes	12.2	Cleveland Indians	4/30/1946	Bob Feller
81 (tie)	Ted Easterly	12.0	Kansas City Packers (Federal League)	8/16/1915	Alex Main
81 (tie)	Les Nunamaker	12.0	New York Yankees	4/24/1917	George Mogridge
83	Earl Smith	11.4	New York Giants	5/7/1922	Jesse Barnes
84	John Jaso	11.1	Seattle Mariners	8/15/2012	Felix Hernandez
85 (tie)	Jim Essian	11.0	Chicago White Sox	7/28/1976	Two pitchers
85 (tie)	Mike Zunino*	11.0	Seattle Mariners	5/8/2018	James Paxton

Rank	Catcher	JAWS	Team	No-hitter Date	Pitcher
87	Alan Ashby	10.6	Houston Astros Houston Astros Houston Astros	4/7/1979 9/26/1981 9/25/1986	Ken Forsch Nolan Ryan Mike Scott
88	Matt Nokes	10.2	New York Yankees	9/4/1993	Jim Abbott
89 (tie)	Jimmy Archer	10.1	Chicago Cubs	8/31/1915	Jimmy Lavender
89 (tie)	Dave Valle	10.1	Seattle Mariners	4/22/1993	Chris Bosio
91	Clyde McCullough	9.9	Chicago Cubs	5/12/1955	Sam Jones
92	David Ross	9.8	Chicago Cubs	4/21/2016	Jake Arrieta
93	Mike Gonzalez	9.6	St. Louis Cardinals	7/17/1924	Jesse Haines
94	Jay Clarke	9.5	Cleveland Indians Cleveland Indians	10/2/1908 4/20/1910	Addie Joss Addie Joss
95 (tie)	Joe Azcue	9.4	Cleveland Indians California Angels	6/10/1966 7/3/1970	Sonny Siebert Clyde Wright
95 (tie)	Ryan Hanigan	9.4	Cincinnati Reds Cincinnati Reds	9/28/2012 7/2/2013	Homer Bailey Homer Bailey
95 (tie)	A.J. Ellis	9.4	Los Angeles Dodgers	6/18/2014	Clayton Kershaw
98	Frank Bowerman	9.3	New York Giants	6/13/1905	Christy Mathewson
99	Bill Rariden	9.0	Cincinnati Reds	5/11/1919	Hod Eller
100	Billy Sullivan	8.6	Chicago White Sox	9/20/1908	Frank Smith
101 (tie)	Darrin Fletcher	8.4	Philadelphia Phillies	5/23/1991	Tommy Greene
101 (tie)	Kelly Shoppach	8.4	Tampa Bay Rays	7/26/2010	Matt Garza

Rank	Catcher	JAWS	Team	No-hitter Date	Pitcher
103 (tie)	Ira Thomas	8.2	Philadelphia Athletics	5/12/1910	Charles Bender
103 (tie)	Miguel Olivo	8.2	Florida Marlins Colorado Rockies	9/6/2006 4/17/2010	Anibal Sanchez Ubaldo Jimenez
105	Harry Bemis	8.0	Cleveland Indians	9/18/1908	Bob Rhoads
106	Elrod Hendricks	7.9	Baltimore Orioles	8/13/1969	Jim Palmer
107	James McCann*	7.4	Chicago White Sox	8/25/2020	Lucas Giolito
108 (tie)	Martin Maldonado*	7.2	Houston Astros	8/3/2019	Four pitchers
108 (tie)	Tucker Barnhart*	7.2	Chicago White Sox	5/7/2021	Wade Miley
110	Red Dooin	7.0	Philadelphia Phillies	5/1/1906	Johnny Lush
111	Omar Narvaez*	6.9	Milwaukee Brewers	9/11/2021	Two pitchers
112	Fran Healy	6.5	Kansas City Royals Kansas City Royals	4/27/1973 6/19/1974	Steve Busby Steve Busby
113	Ed Herrmann	6.4	Houston Astros	7/9/1976	Larry Dierker
114	Joe Girardi	6.3	New York Yankees *New York Yankees*	5/14/1996 7/18/1999	Dwight Gooden *David Cone*
115	Luke Sewell	6.2	Cleveland Indians Chicago White Sox Chicago White Sox	4/29/1931 8/31/1935 6/1/1937	Wes Ferrell Vern Kennedy Bill Dietrich
116	Rollie Helmsley	5.9	Cleveland Indians	4/16/1940	Bob Feller
117 (tie)	Jerry May	5.7	Pittsburgh Pirates	6/12/1970	Dock Ellis
117 (tie)	Jeff Reed	5.7	Cincinnati Reds	*9/16/1988*	*Tom Browning*

Rank	Catcher	JAWS	Team	No-hitter Date	Pitcher
119 (tie)	Jim Hegan	5.4	Cleveland Indians	7/10/1947 6/30/1948	Don Black Bob Lemon
119 (tie)	Del Rice	5.4	Chicago Cubs	5/15/1960	Don Cardwell
121	Red Wilson	5.2	Detroit Tigers	7/20/1958	Jim Bunning
122	Bruce Edwards	4.9	Brooklyn Dodgers	9/9/1948	Rex Barney
123	Pat Borders	4.8	Toronto Blue Jays	9/2/1990	Dave Stieb
124	Oscar Stanage	4.7	Detroit Tigers	7/4/1912	George Mullin
125	Dave Rader	4.4	San Francisco Giants	8/24/1975	Ed Halicki
126	Buck Rodgers	4.3	Los Angeles Angels	5/5/1962	Bo Belinsky
127	John Ellis	4.2	Cleveland Indians	7/19/1974	Dick Bosman
128 (tie)	Brent Mayne	4.1	Kansas City Royals	8/26/1991	Brett Saberhagen
128 (tie)	Scott Servais	4.1	Houston Astros	9/8/1993	Darryl Kile
130 (tie)	Val Picinich	3.9	Philadelphia Athletics Washington Senators Boston Red Sox	8/26/1916 7/1/1920 9/7/1923	Bullet Joe Bush Walter Johnson Howard Ehmke
130 (tie)	Duffy Dyer	3.9	Pittsburgh Pirates	8/9/1976	John Candelaria
132	Sammy White	3.6	Boston Red Sox	7/14/1956	Mel Parnell
133	Ramon Castro	3.3	*Chicago White Sox*	*7/23/2009*	*Mark Buehrle*
134	Bill DeLancey	3.4	St. Louis Cardinals	9/21/1934	Paul Dean

Rank	Catcher	JAWS	Team	No-hitter Date	Pitcher
135 (tie)	Ray Lamanno	3.0	Cincinnati Reds	6/18/1947	Ewell Blackwell
135 (tie)	Les Moss	3.0	St. Louis Browns	5/6/1953	Bobo Holloman
135 (tie)	Pedro Severino*	3.0	Baltimore Orioles	5/5/2021	John Means
138 (tie)	John Bateman	2.8	Houston Astros Montreal Expos	5/17/1963 4/17/1969	Don Nottebart Bill Stoneman
138 (tie)	Paul Casanova	2.8	Atlanta Braves	8/5/1973	Phil Niekro
138 (tie)	Bill Schroeder	2.8	Milwaukee Brewers	4/15/1987	Juan Nieves
141	Josh Phegley	2.4	Oakland Athletics	5/7/2019	Mike Fiers
142	Ed Fitz Gerald	2.3	Pittsburgh Pirates	5/6/1951	Cliff Chambers
143 (tie)	Charlie Lau	2.2	Milwaukee Braves	4/28/1961	Warren Spahn
143 (tie)	Greg Olson	2.2	Atlanta Braves	9/11/1991	Three pitchers
145	Matt Batts	2.1	Detroit Tigers	8/25/1952	Virgil Trucks
146	Grover Hartley	1.9	St. Louis Terriers (Federal League)	9/7/1915	Dave Davenport
147	Daulton Varsho*	1.8	Arizona Diamondbacks	8/14/2021	Tyler Gilbert
148	Alberto Castillo	1.7	St. Louis Cardinals	6/25/1999	Jose Jimenez
149	Hank DeBerry	1.5	Brooklyn Dodgers	9/13/1925	Dazzy Vance
150 (tie)	Bruno Block	1.4	Chicago White Sox	8/27/1911	Ed Walsh
150 (tie)	Victor Caratini*	1.4	Chicago Cubs San Diego Padres	9/13/2020 4/9/2021	Alec Mills Joe Musgrove

Rank	Catcher	JAWS	Team	No-hitter Date	Pitcher
152	Joe Ginsberg	1.3	Detroit Tigers	5/15/1952	Virgil Trucks
153 (tie)	Yip Owens	1.2	Brooklyn Tip-Tops (Federal League)	9/19/1914	Ed Lafitte
153 (tie)	Eric Haase*	1.2	Detroit Tigers	5/18/2021	Spencer Turnbull
155	Claude Berry	1.0	Pittsburgh Rebels (Federal League)	4/24/1915	Frank Allen
156 (tie)	Walt Alexander	0.9	St. Louis Browns	8/30/1912	Earl Hamilton
156 (tie)	Dustin Garneau*	0.9	Los Angeles Angels	7/12/2019	Two pitchers
158	Bobby Wilson	0.8	Los Angeles Angels	7/27/2011	Ervin Santana
159 (tie)	Bob Tillman	0.6	Boston Red Sox Boston Red Sox	6/26/1962 9/16/1965	Earl Wilson Dave Morehead
159 (tie)	Gary Alexander	0.6	San Francisco Giants	9/29/1976	John Montefusco
159 (tie)	Robby Hammock	0.6	Arizona Diamondbacks	5/18/2004	Randy Johnson
159 (tie)	Kyle Higashioka*	0.6	New York Yankees	5/19/2021	Corey Kluber
163 (tie)	Jeff Torborg	0.4	Los Angeles Dodgers Los Angeles Dodgers California Angels	9/9/1965 7/20/1970 5/15/1973	Sandy Koufax Bill Singer Nolan Ryan
163 (tie)	Pat Corrales	0.4	Cincinnati Reds	7/29/1968	George Culver
165 (tie)	Sam Brown	0.2	Boston Braves	5/8/1907	Jeff Pfeffer
165 (tie)	Landon Powell	0.2	*Oakland Athletics*	*5/9/2010*	*Dallas Braden*
167	Hector Sanchez	0.0	San Francisco Giants	6/25/2014	Tim Lincecum

Rank	Catcher	JAWS	Team	No-hitter Date	Pitcher
168 (tie)	Harry Barton	-0.1	Philadelphia Athletics	7/22/1905	Weldon Henley
168 (tie)	Herman Franks	-0.1	Brooklyn Dodgers	4/30/1940	Tex Carleton
170 (tie)	Ferrell Anderson	-0.2	Brooklyn Dodgers	4/23/1946	Ed Head
171 (tie)	Scott Bradley	-0.2	Seattle Mariners	6/2/1990	Randy Johnson
172 (tie)	Charles Armbruster	-0.5	Boston Red Sox	9/27/1905	Bill Dinneen
172 (tie)	Jesus Sucre	-0.5	Seattle Mariners	8/12/2015	Hisashi Iwakuma
174 (tie)	Danny Breeden	-0.7	Chicago Cubs	6/3/1971	Ken Holtzman
174 (tie)	Dick Billings	-0.7	Texas Rangers	7/30/1973	Jim Bibby
174 (tie)	Eli Whiteside	-0.7	San Francisco Giants	7/10/2009	Jonathan Sanchez
176 (tie)	Doug Camili	-0.8	Los Angeles Dodgers	6/4/1964	Sandy Koufax
176 (tie)	Josh Thole	-0.8	New York Mets	6/1/2012	Johan Santana
179	Don Bryant	-0.9	Houston Astros	5/1/1969	Don Wilson
180	Fred Hoffman	-1.1	New York Yankees	9/4/1923	Sam Jones
181 (tie)	Lew Ritter	-1.2	Brooklyn Dodgers	7/20/1906	Mal Eason
181 (tie)	Joe Glenn	-1.2	New York Yankees	8/27/1938	Monte Pearson
183	Zack Collins*	-1.5	Chicago White Sox	4/14/2021	Carlos Rodon
184	Johnny Grabowski	-1.6	Chicago White Sox	8/21/1926	Ted Lyons

Rank	Catcher	JAWS	Team	No-hitter Date	Pitcher
185 (tie)	Dave Adlesh	-1.8	Houston Astros	6/18/1967	Don Wilson
185 (tie)	J.C. Martin	-1.8	Chicago White Sox	9/10/1967	Joe Horlen
187 (tie)	Jerry Zimmerman	-1.9	Minnesota Twins	8/25/1967	Dean Chance
187 (tie)	Art Kusnyer	-1.9	California Angels	7/15/1973	Nolan Ryan
187 (tie)	Matt Walbeck	-1.9	Minnesota Twins	4/27/1994	Scott Erickson
190	Roy Spencer	-2.0	Washington Senators	8/8/1931	Bobby Burke
191 (tie)	John Russell	-2.2	Texas Rangers	6/11/1990	Nolan Ryan
191 (tie)	Drew Butera	-2.2	Minnesota Twins Los Angeles Dodgers	5/3/2011 5/25/2014	Francisco Liriano Josh Beckett
193	Don Werner	-2.3	Cincinnati Reds	6/16/1978	Tom Seaver
194	Emil Huhn	-2.4	Cincinnati Reds	5/2/1917	Fred Toney
195	Koyie Hill	-2.6	Miami Marlins	9/29/2013	Henderson Alvarez III
196	Tom Egan	-2.9	California Angels	9/28/1974	Nolan Ryan
197	Bill Bergen	-4.6	Brooklyn Superbas	9/5/1908	Nap Rucker

METHODOLOGY: All catchers who have caught a no-hitter from 1900-2021 are included in this table. Catchers are ranked by their career Jaffe Wins Above Replacement Score (JAWS). JAWS is a sabermetric baseball statistic developed to evaluate the strength of a player's career and merit for induction into the Baseball Hall of Fame. It is created by averaging a player's career Wins Above Replacement (WAR) with their 7-year peak WAR (WAR7). WAR measures a player's value in all facets of the game by deciphering how many more wins he's worth than a replacement-level player at his same position. In the event of a tie, the player who caught the earlier no-hitter is listed first.

LEGEND: An asterisk (*) next to a player's name indicates the player is still active beyond 2021. Their career JAWS will be affected and they may even catch another no-hitter. *Italicized no-hitters are perfect games.* Pitcher names or other terms are occasionally abbreviated to conserve space:

B. Monbouquette = Bill Monbouquette (of the Boston Red Sox)
C. Robertson = Charlie Robertson (of the Chicago White Sox)
D-backs = Diamondbacks (nickname of the Arizona team)
FL = Federal League (a major league that operated from 1914-1915)
J. Vander Meer = Johnny Vander Meer (of the Cincinnati Reds)
J. Zimmermann = Jordan Zimmermann (of the Washington Nationals)

NOTE: Chief Zimmer caught another no-hitter on 9/18/1897, Heinie Peitz caught another no-hitter on 4/22/1898, and Ed McFarland caught another no-hitter on 7/8/1898. These aren't included in this table because they occurred prior to 1900.

About the Author

Kevin Hurd grew up in the town of Los Altos, California, a suburb of San Francisco in an area now known as "Silicon Valley." Kevin is a 1975 graduate of Homestead High School in Cupertino. He attended nearby De Anza Community College from 1975-1977 and then transferred to California Polytechnic State University in San Luis Obispo, where he graduated in 1979 with a bachelor's degree in business administration. While working full-time as an Air Force Reserve officer, he earned his master's in business administration degree with a specialization in aviation from Embry-Riddle Aeronautical University in 2000.

Kevin has been an avid San Francisco Giants fan since 1965, and he estimates he attended around 20 games from 1965-1982. While he enjoyed every one of them, two games stood out in his memory. As a nine-year-old fan in 1966, he saw legendary Giant Willie McCovey hit three home runs – including a walk-off blast in the bottom of the 10th inning – in a 6-4 win versus the New York Mets. His other favorite game was witnessing Ed Halicki's 1975 no-hitter at Candlestick Park.

That game, in part, inspired him later in life to research and write about no-hitters. Halicki's unforgettable no-hitter is featured in Chapter 5 of Volume I. Included in that chapter is Kevin's interview with Halicki himself. Understandably, the Giants seasons he has enjoyed the most have been the Word Series championship years of 2010, 2012, and 2014.

Sports have always been a big part of Kevin's life. He was a standout defensive middle guard on the Homestead High School football team, achieving Honorable Mention All-League status in the highly competitive Santa Clara Valley Athletic League. He also excelled at track and field as a high school discus thrower, being voted the Most Valuable Player on his team during his junior year. Additionally, Kevin was an accomplished javelin thrower in college. During his sophomore year at De Anza, he finished in fifth place in the Northern California Junior College Track and Field Finals.

Apart from his athletic success and his lifelong interest in baseball, Kevin crafted a very successful and personally rewarding 30-year Air Force career. After graduating from Officer Training School at Lackland Air Force Base, Texas, in 1984, he attended Undergraduate Navigator Training, followed by Advanced Navigator Training in the KC-135, where he was the top graduate in his class. Throughout his career, Kevin served with distinction as a KC-135 (air refueling tanker) and RC-135 (strategic reconnaissance aircraft) navigator and staff officer, retiring at the rank of lieutenant colonel in 2014.

During his Air Force career, Kevin was called upon to fly combat and combat support missions while deployed to Saudi Arabia during the 1991 Gulf War and to the Mediterranean in support of the 1999 Kosovo War. Kevin was awarded numerous medals during his career, including the Air Force Meritorious Service Medal for meritorious service to the United States, and the Air Medal on eight separate occasions for acts of heroism or meritorious achievement while participating in aerial flight. While he admits his wartime service was demanding, the mission he recalls as being the most stressful was while he and his crew were en route to Italy as they deployed in support of Kosovo operations. His aircraft stalled over the North Atlantic Ocean and rapidly fell 23,000 feet before the crew recovered control. This necessitated an emergency return and landing at a Canadian air base and a subsequent ground evacuation for the crew and all 50 passengers onboard. Kevin received an Aerial Achievement Medal for his actions that day.

Kevin had a post-Air Force stint working six years in security operations at the Western Currency Facility in Fort Worth, Texas, before deciding to devote his time and energy to writing. More specifically, he was inspired to write about baseball, a topic he has been passionate about his entire life. "From Randy Johnson to Dallas Braden" is Kevin's first book of what he hopes will be many more.

Kevin lives near Fort Worth with his lovely wife Doris. They have been married for 34 years and have two wonderful adult daughters, Christine and Catherine.

www.ingramcontent.com/pod-product-compliance
Lightning Source LLC
LaVergne TN
LVHW091532070526
838199LV00001B/31